Before we begin, I would like to thank everyone that made this book possible. Peter Jones made available the resources and professional advice that turned my idea into a reality. His insight and generosity are unparalleled. Tracy Rudhe, someone close to me since the beginning of this journey, has been a great sounding board. I'm appreciative of her friendship and for loaning me some of her talent to get the words on the pages. Seth Gouker, who designed the book cover, is an exceptional artist and I am so grateful for his ideas and assistance. Finally, I could not get these crazy shots without the coordination and drive of my local crew... and without the love and encouragement from all of the homies who bought pics and books to back me on this ride. Without you, this dream would be just that...a dream...so I am really thankful for you all. Your support does not go unrecognized, and I just hope my work makes you as proud as I am to represent you!

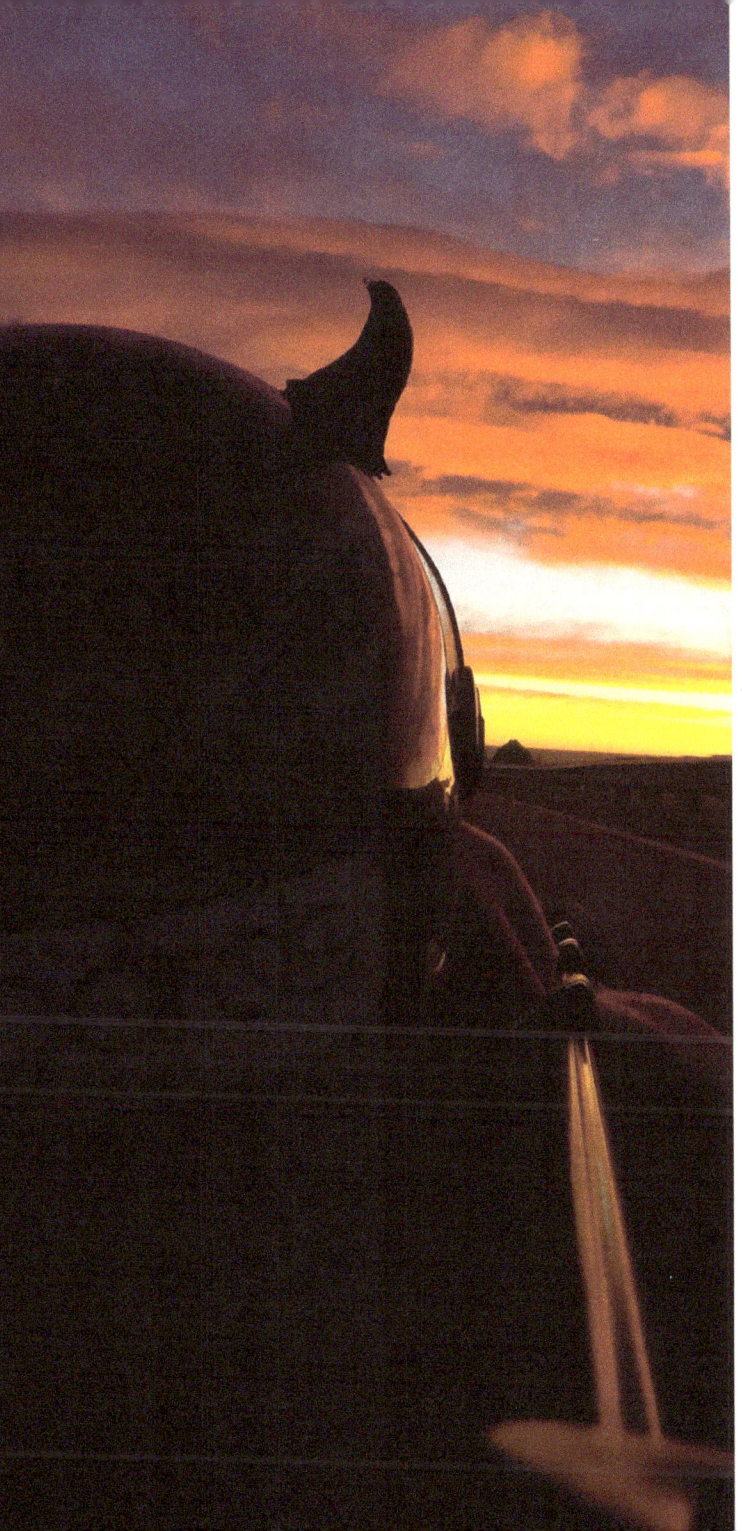

Table of Contents

Chapter	Pages
#Dawnpatrol	4-25
#Sk8face	26-43
#Localsonly	44-79
#Gloryhole	80-92
#Laydown (It's faster!)	93-112
#Heyladies	113-131
#Californication	132-149
#Maryhillandchill	150-181
#Sweetpotato	182-189
#Instabagers	190-219

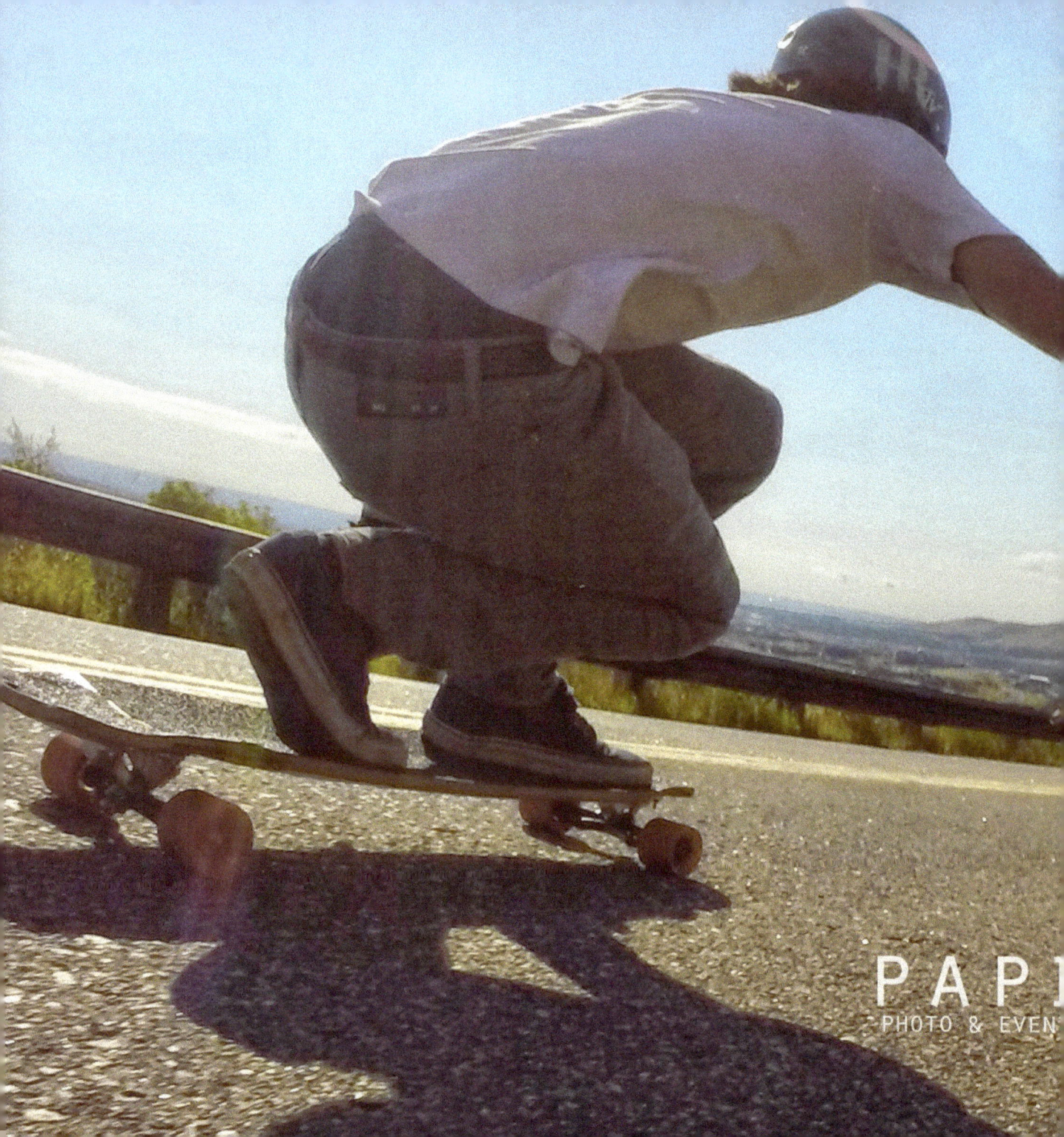

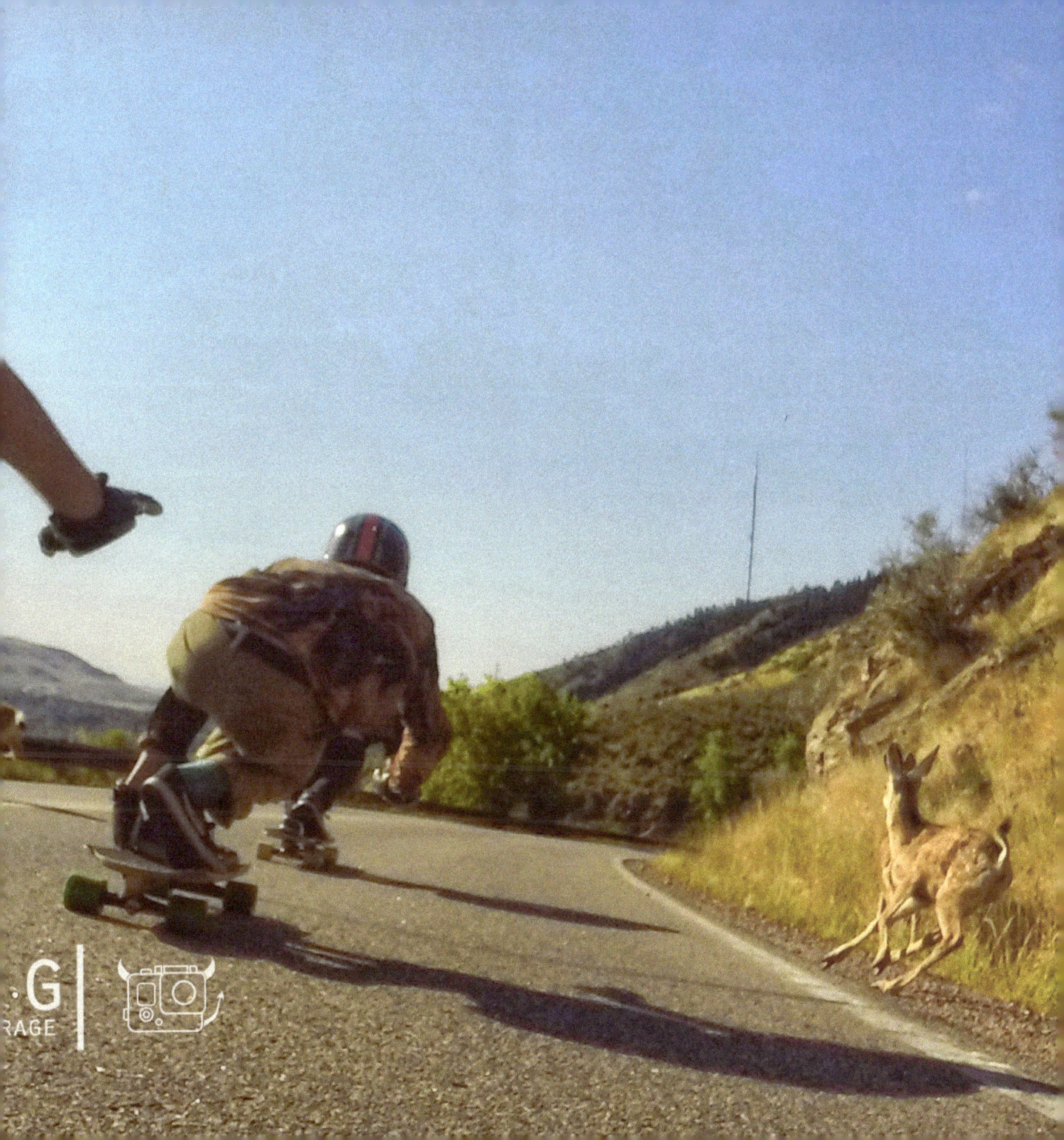

#Dawnpatrol

It's a spiritual experience...

The sun paints the sky, casting shadows that stretch reality, while gravity tickles your adrenaline glands as you soar down the mountain.

(Be careful...it's easy to get addicted! AND ticketed!)

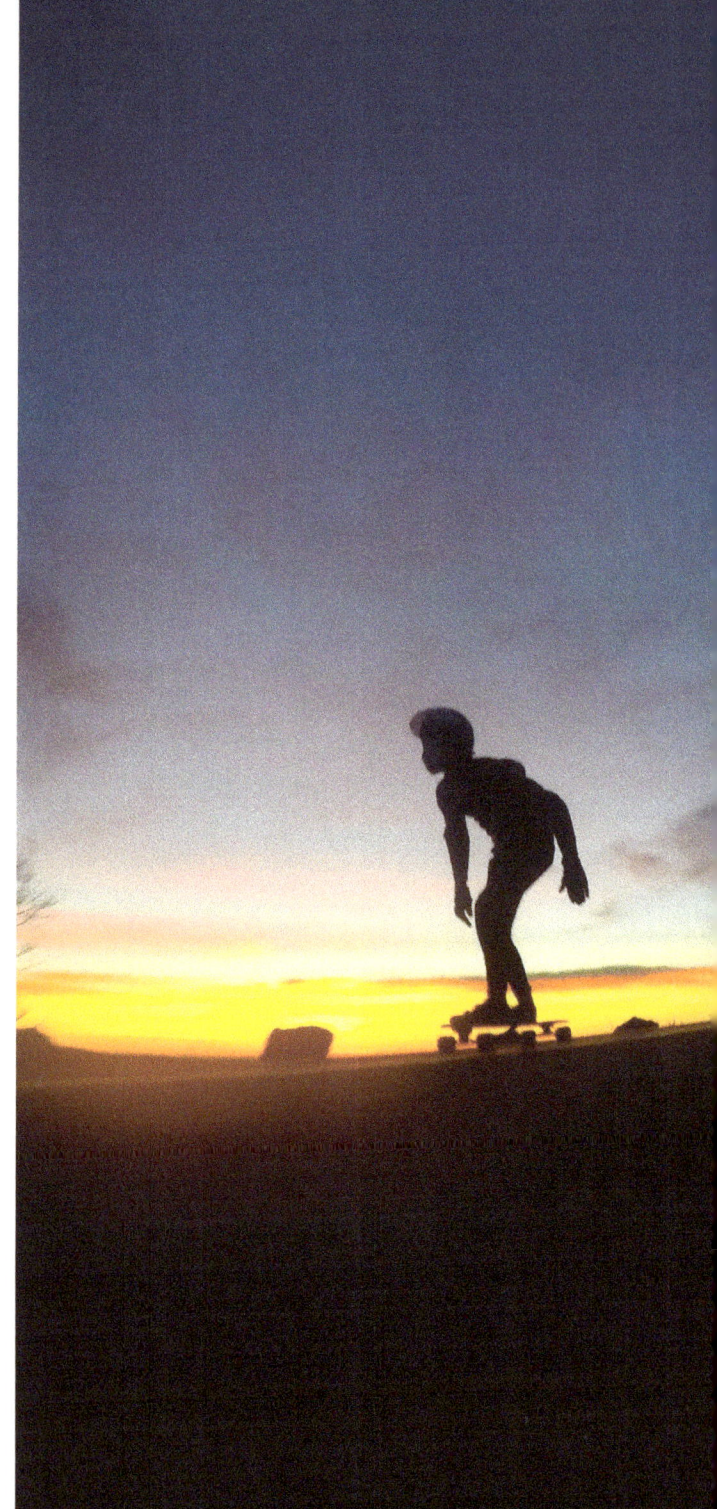

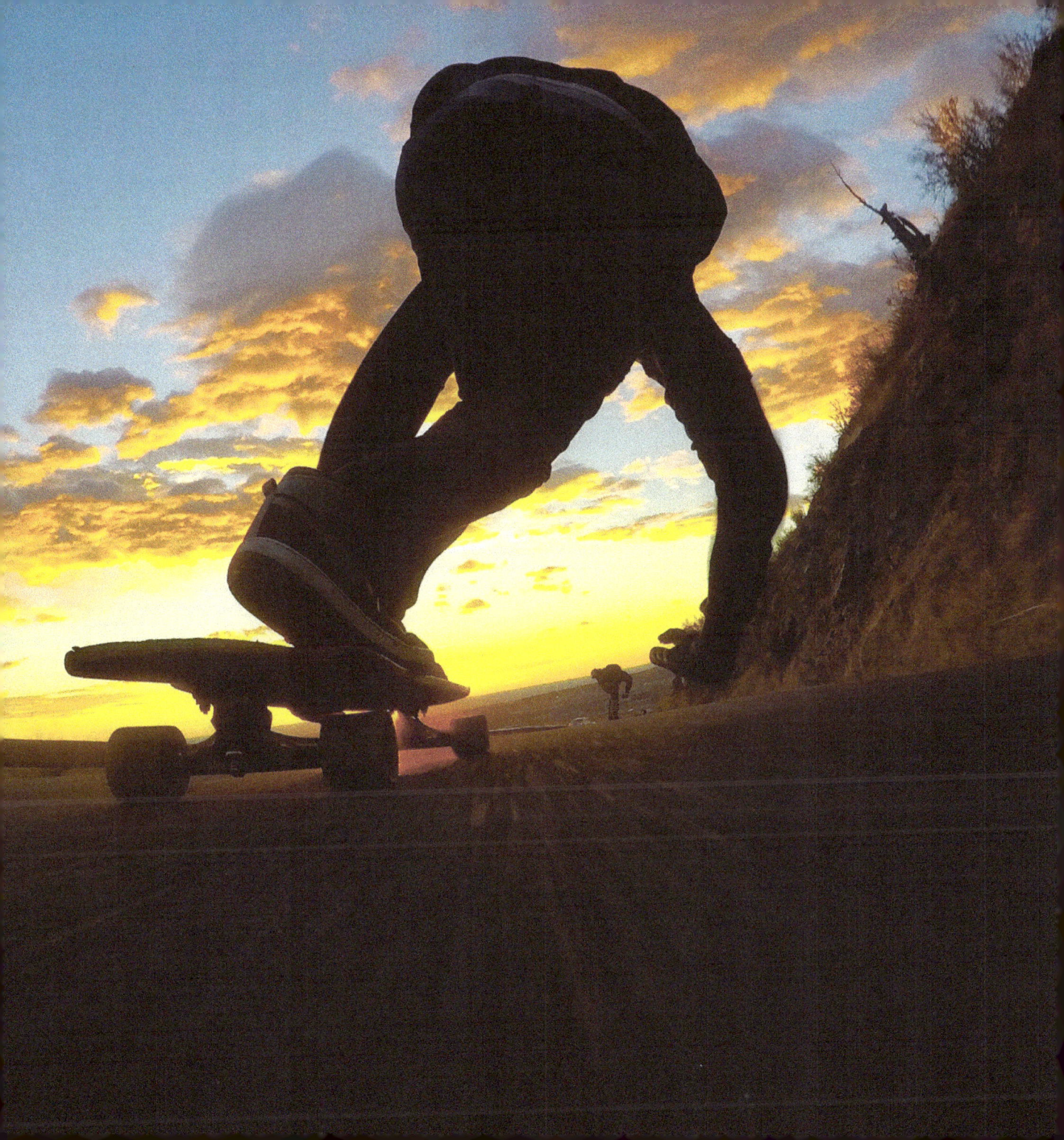

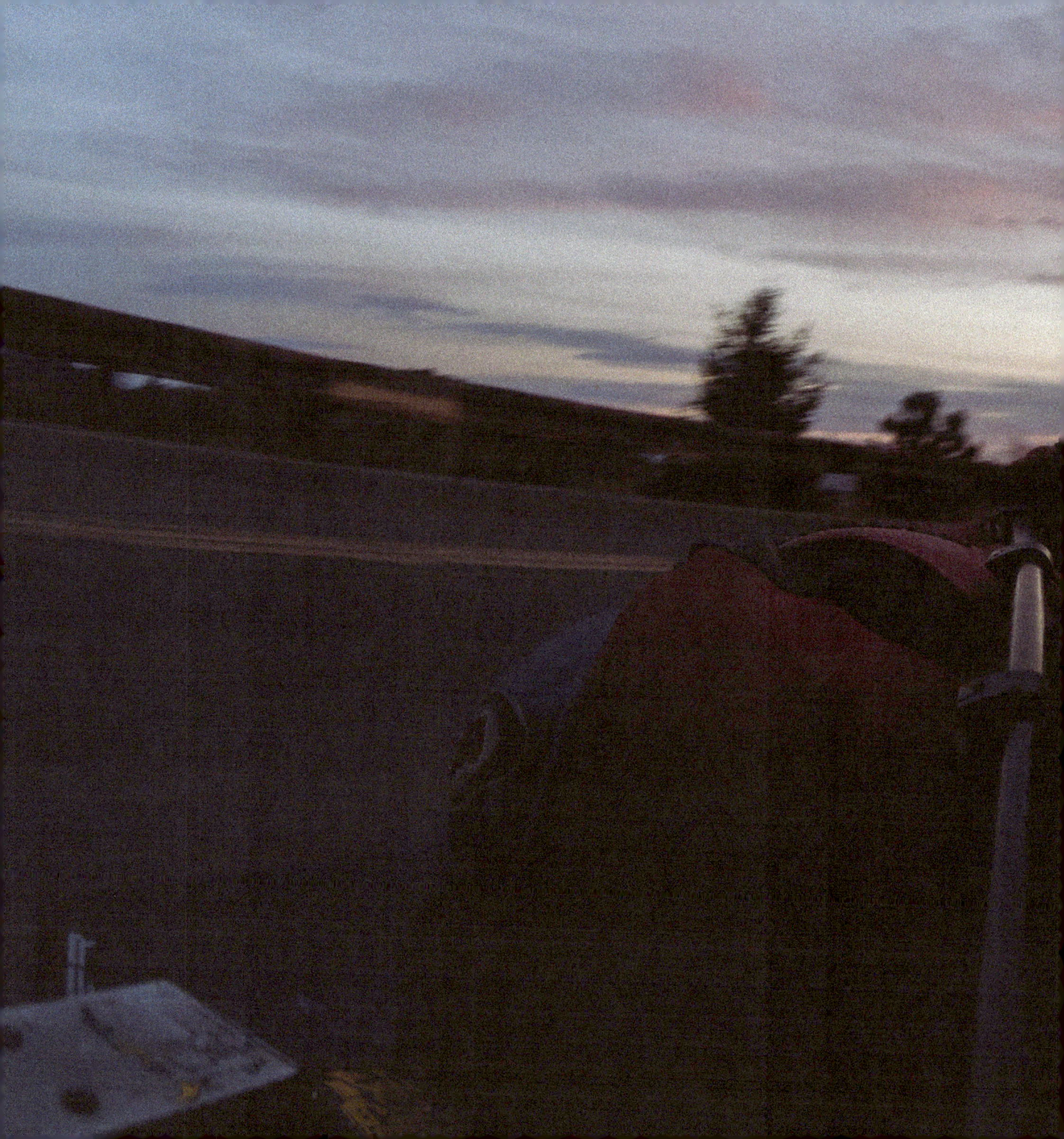

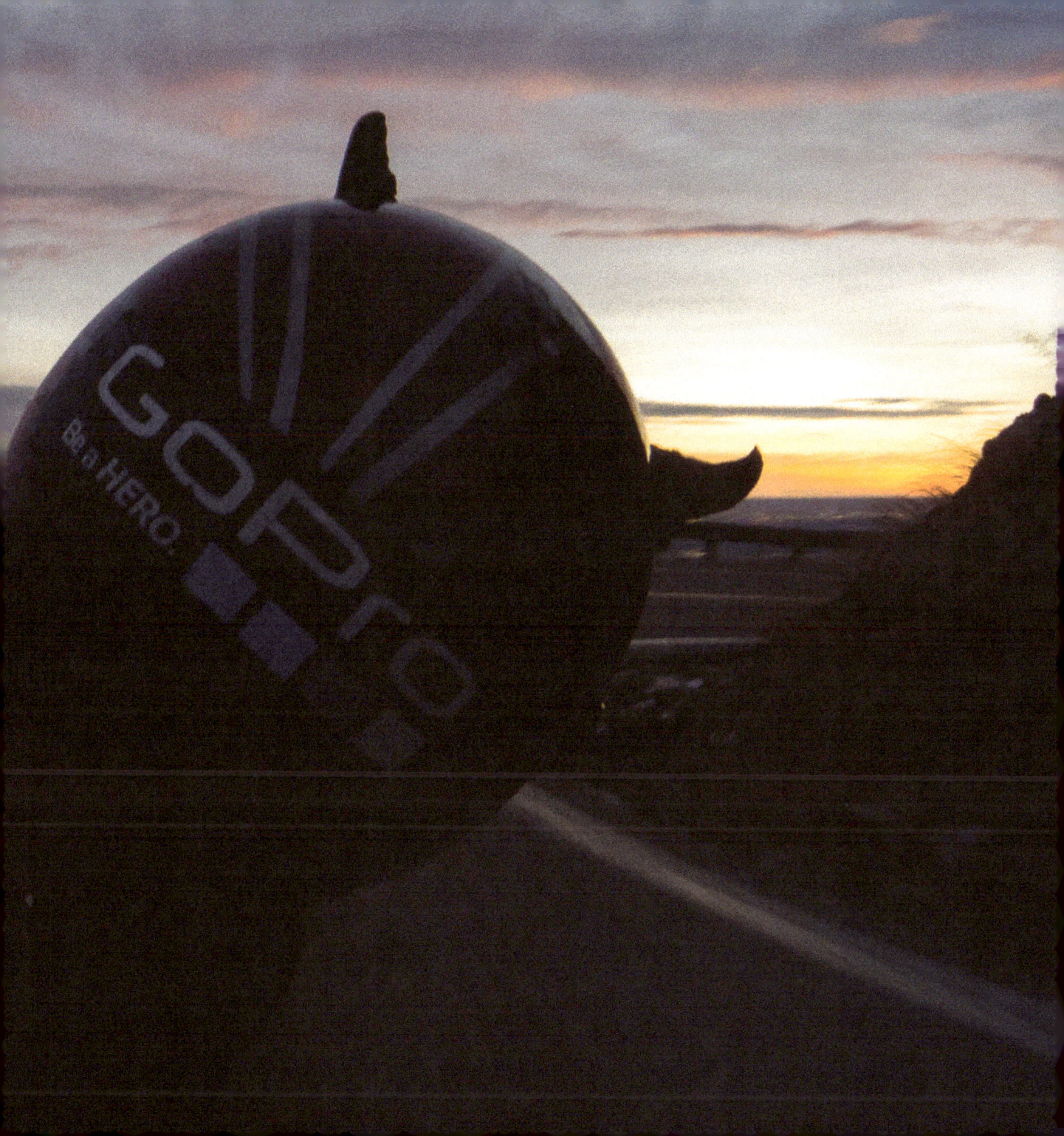

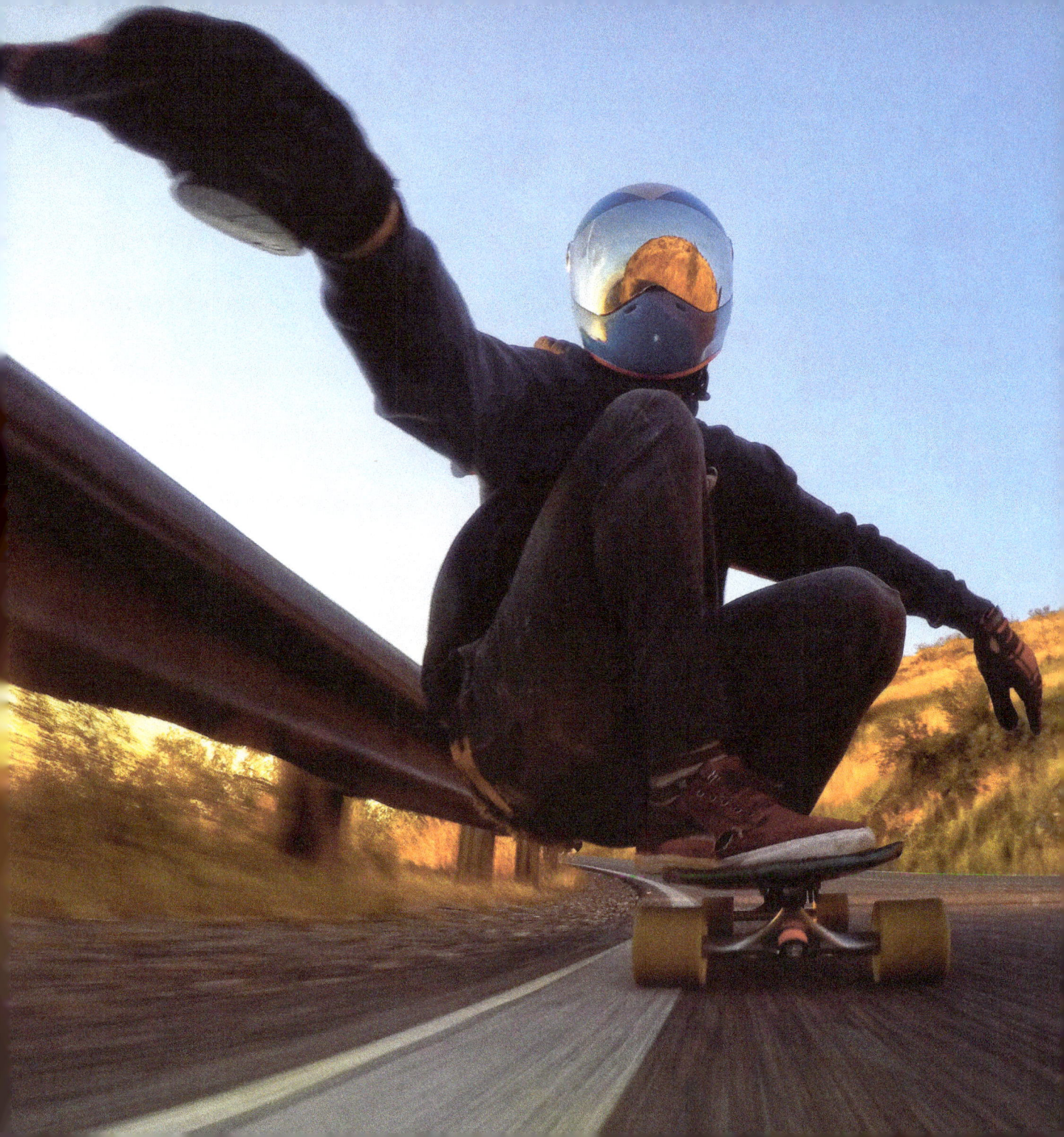

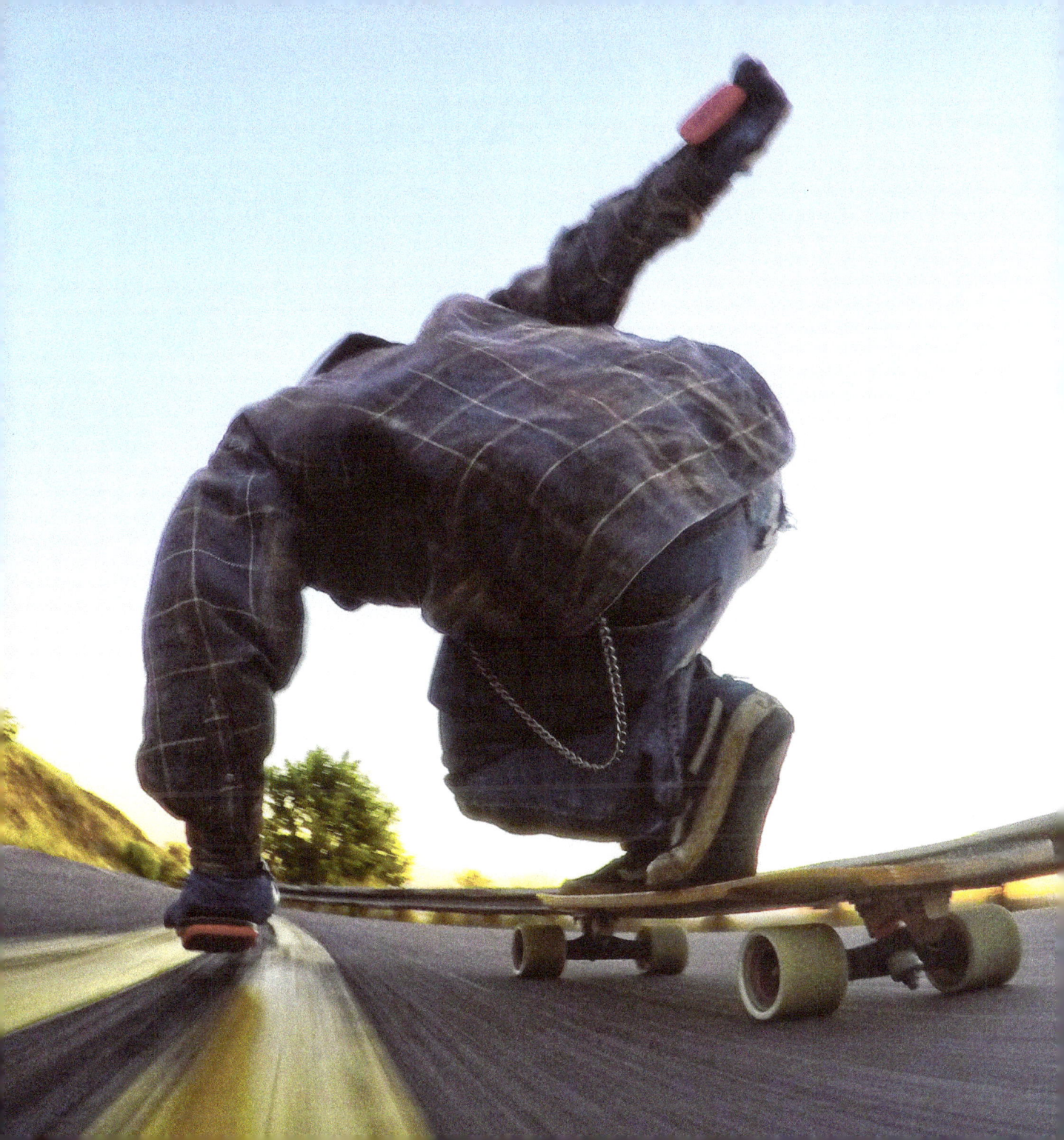

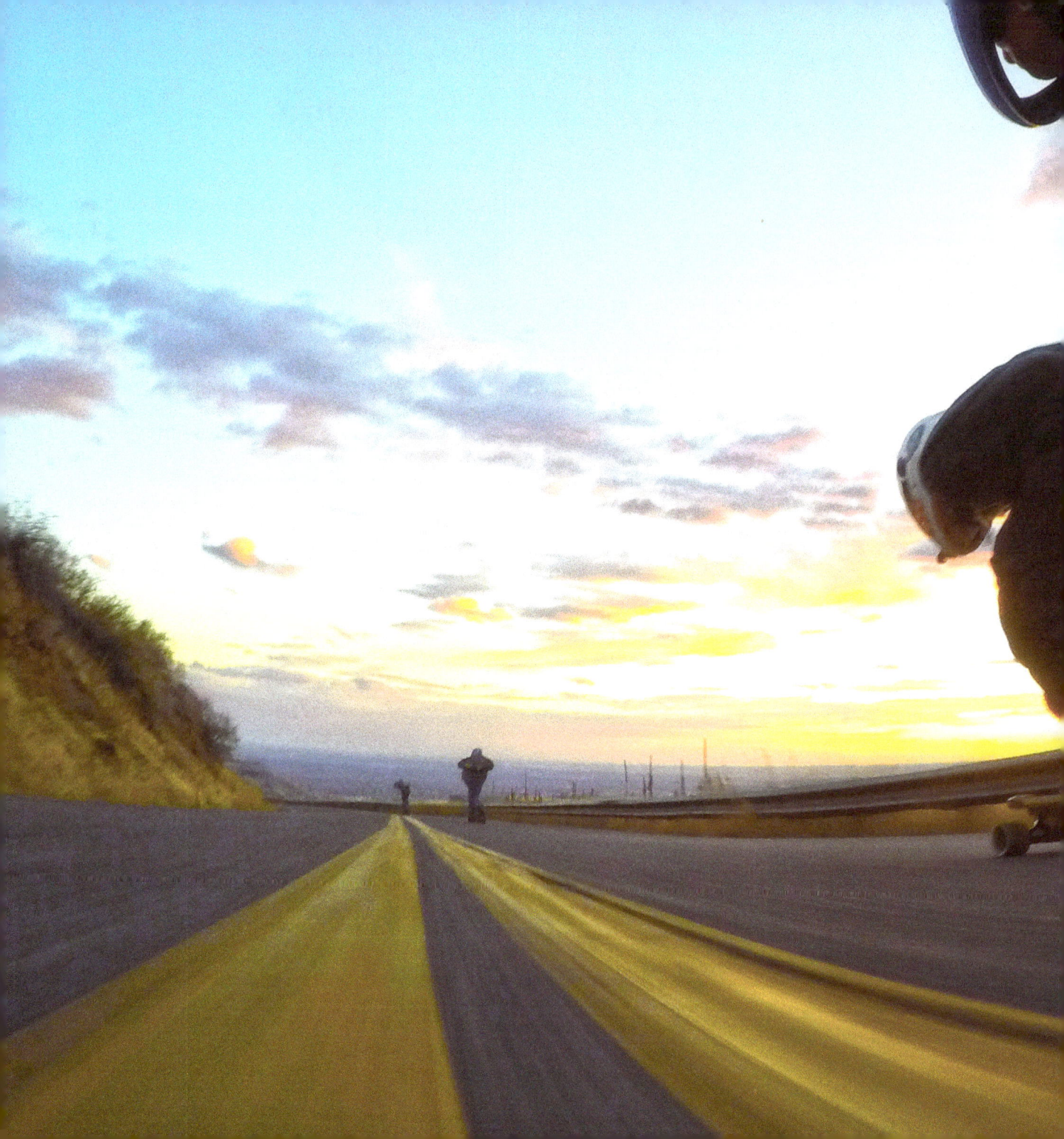

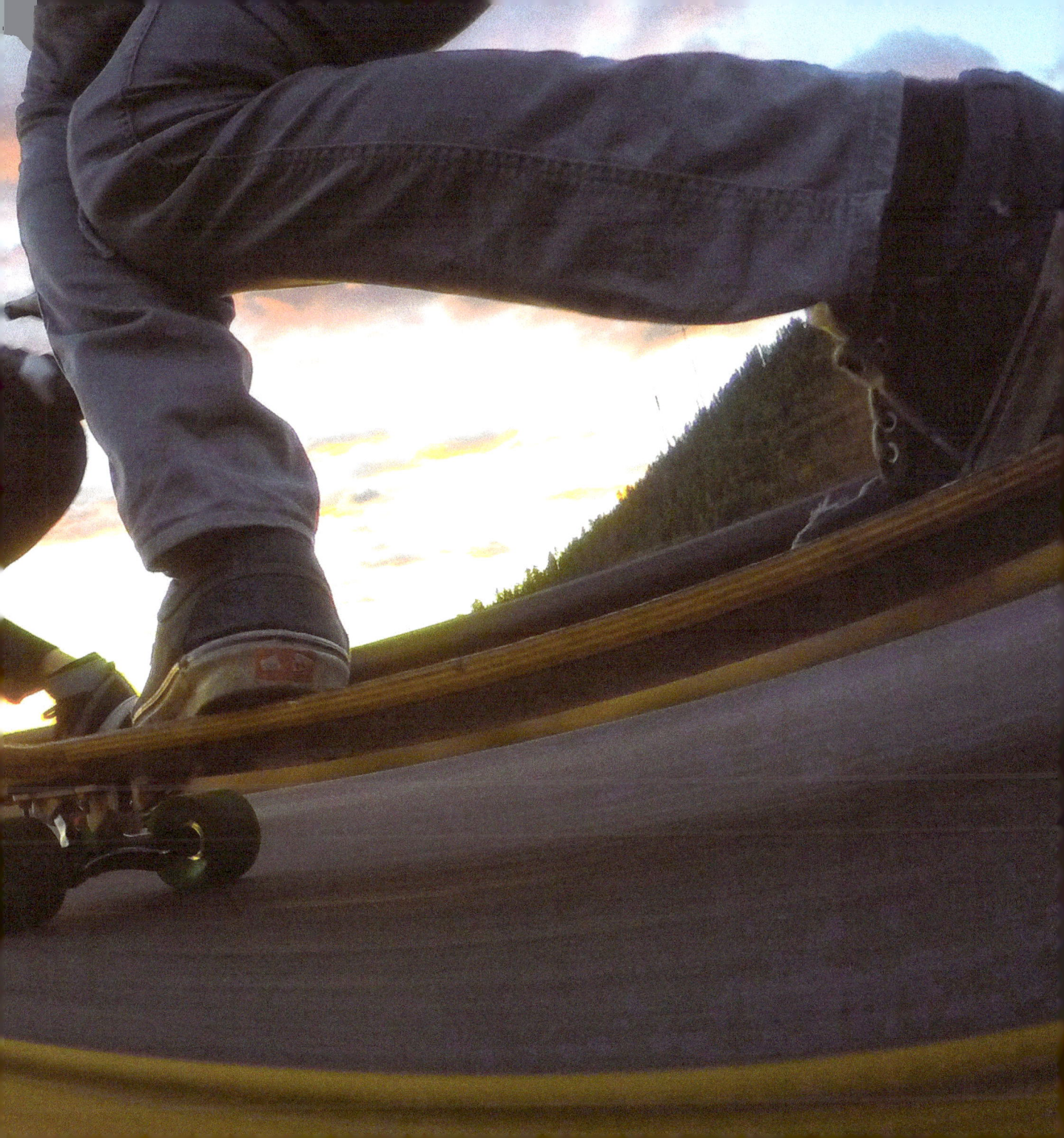

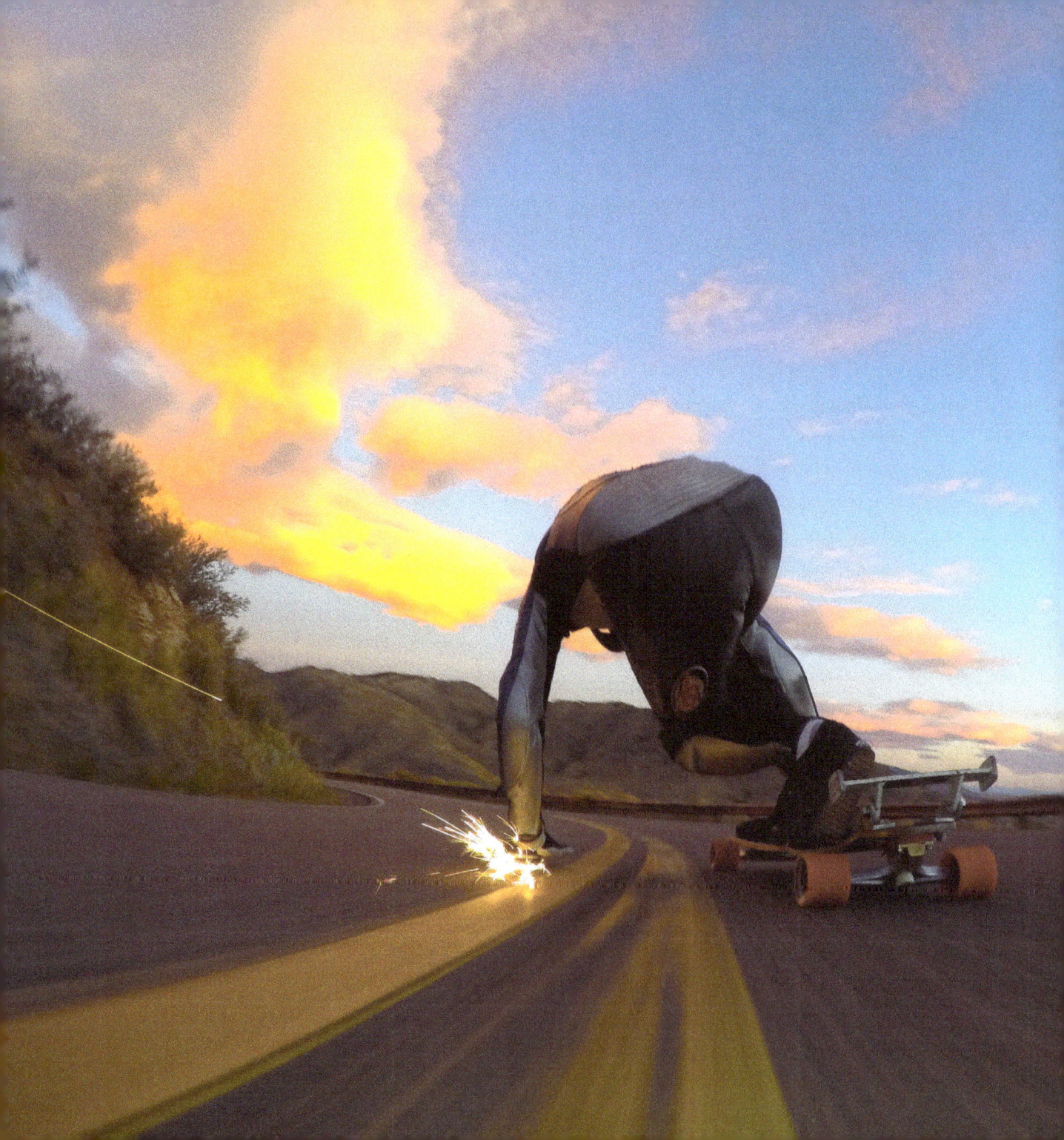

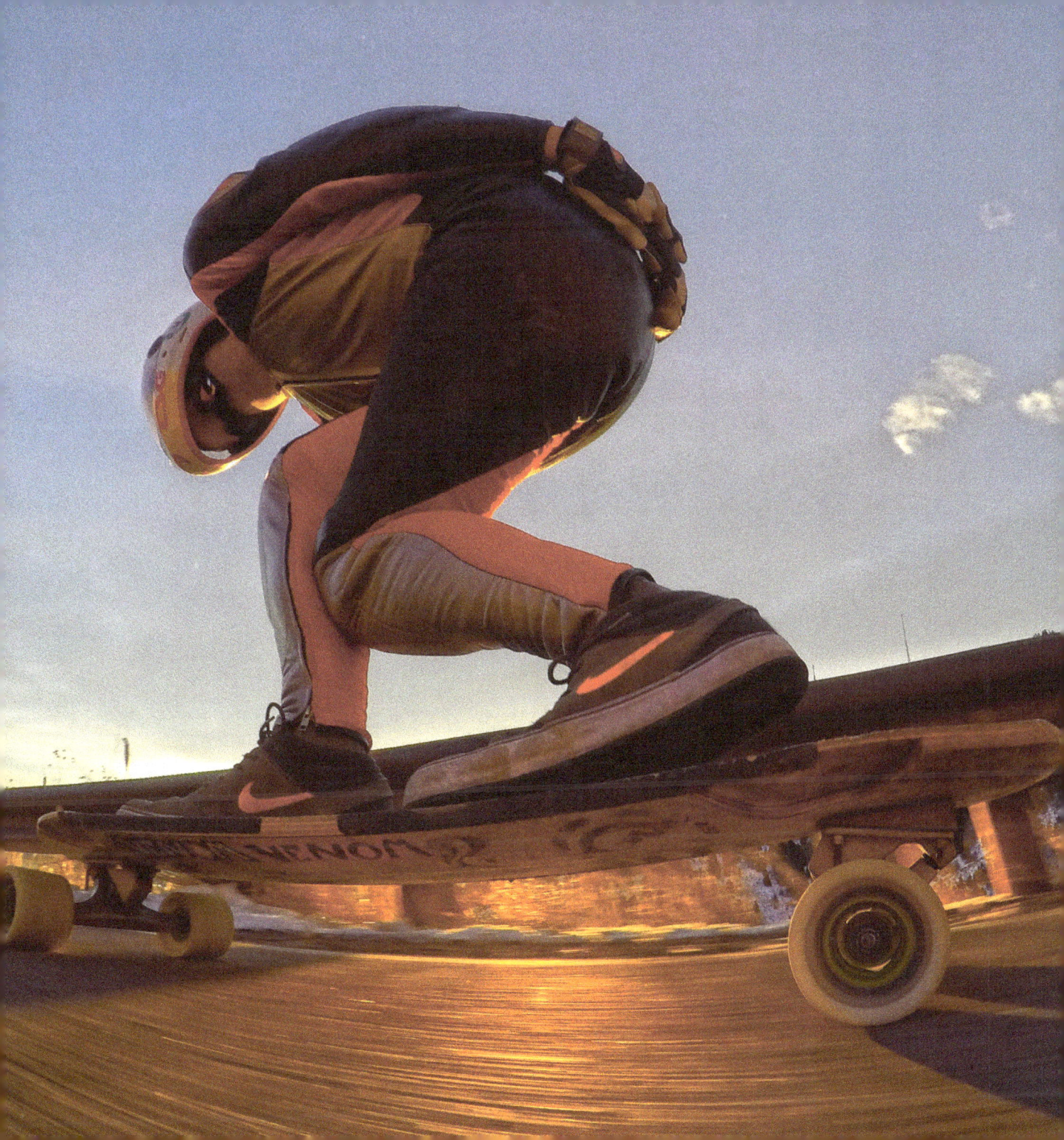

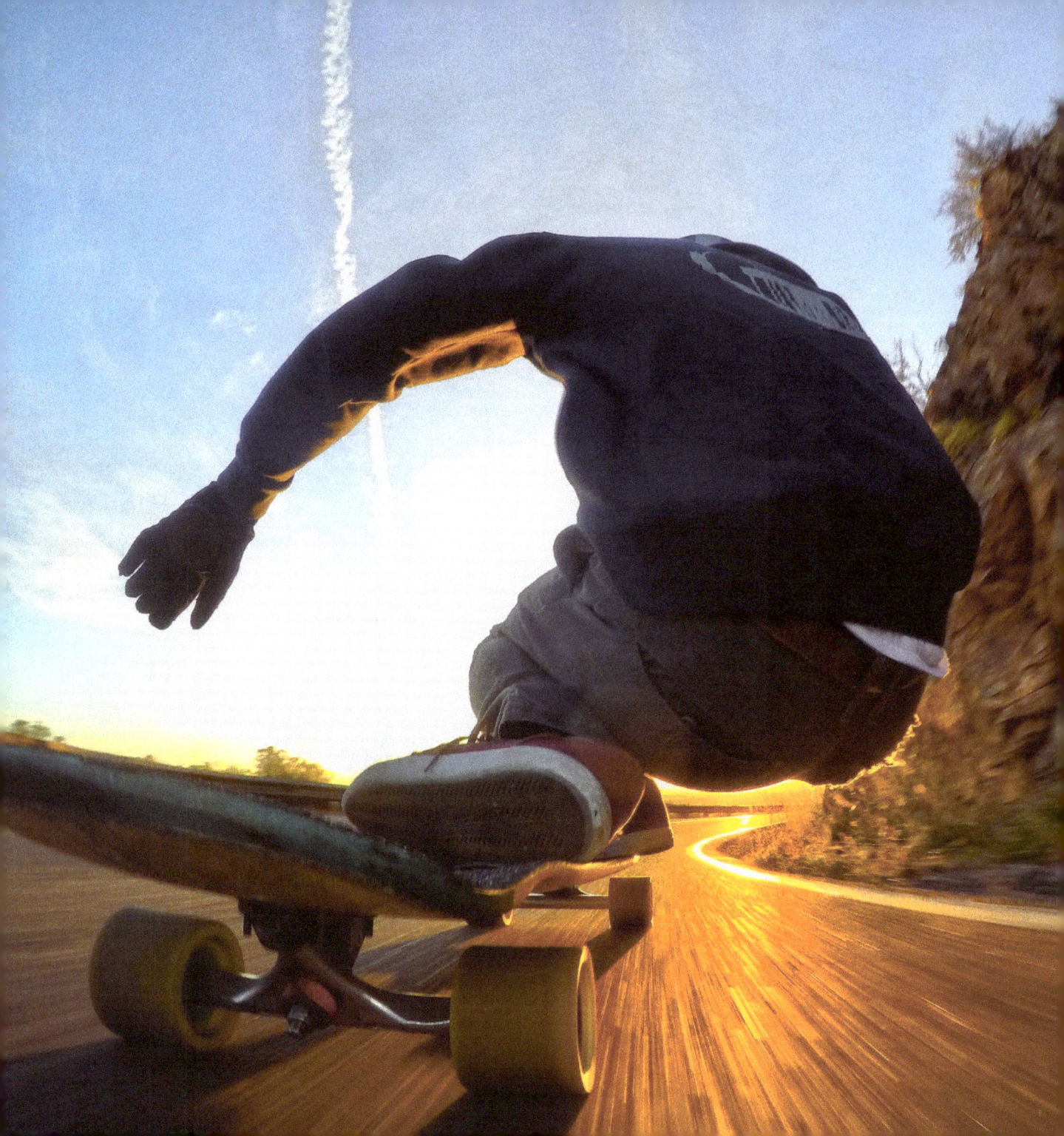

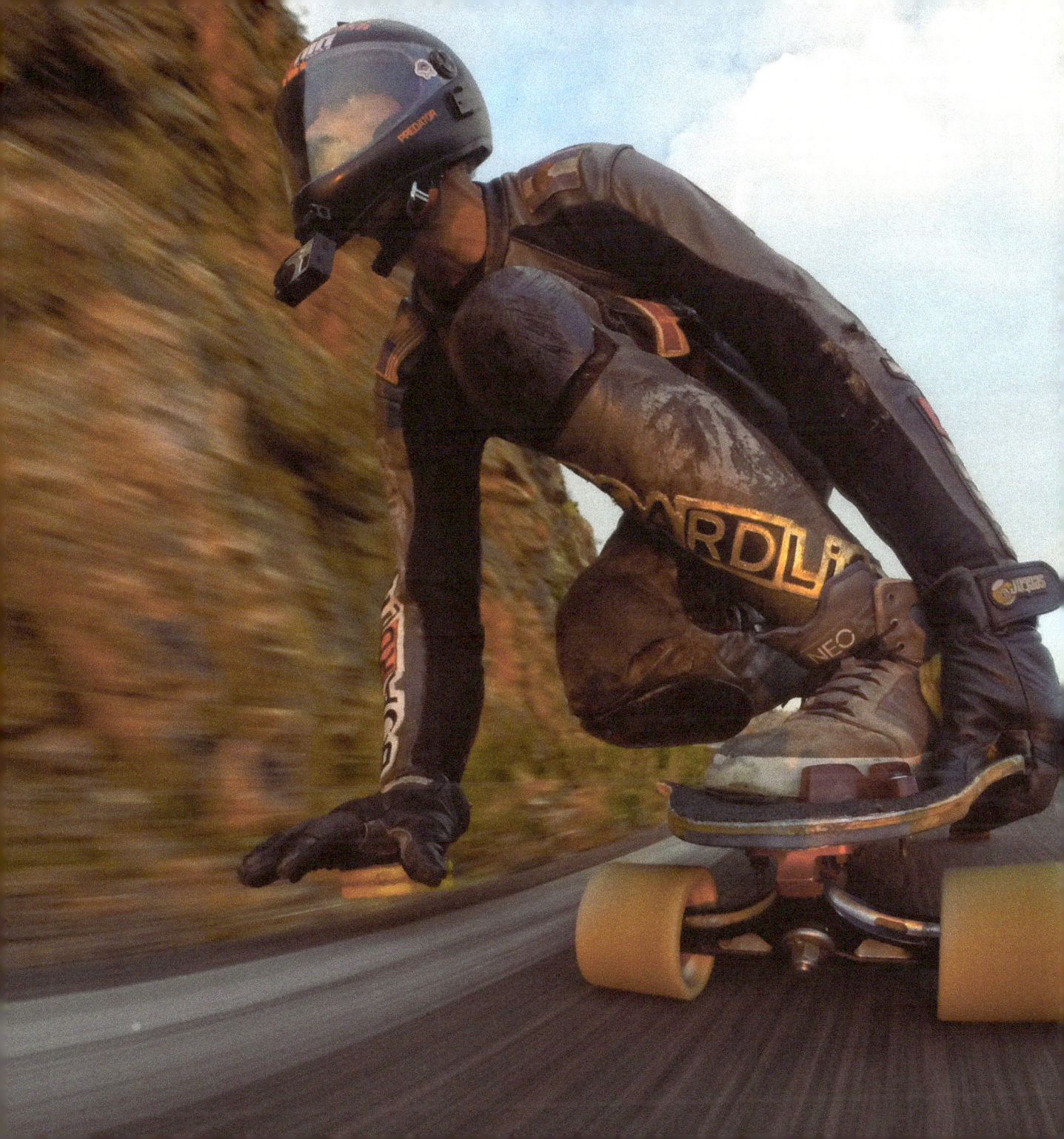

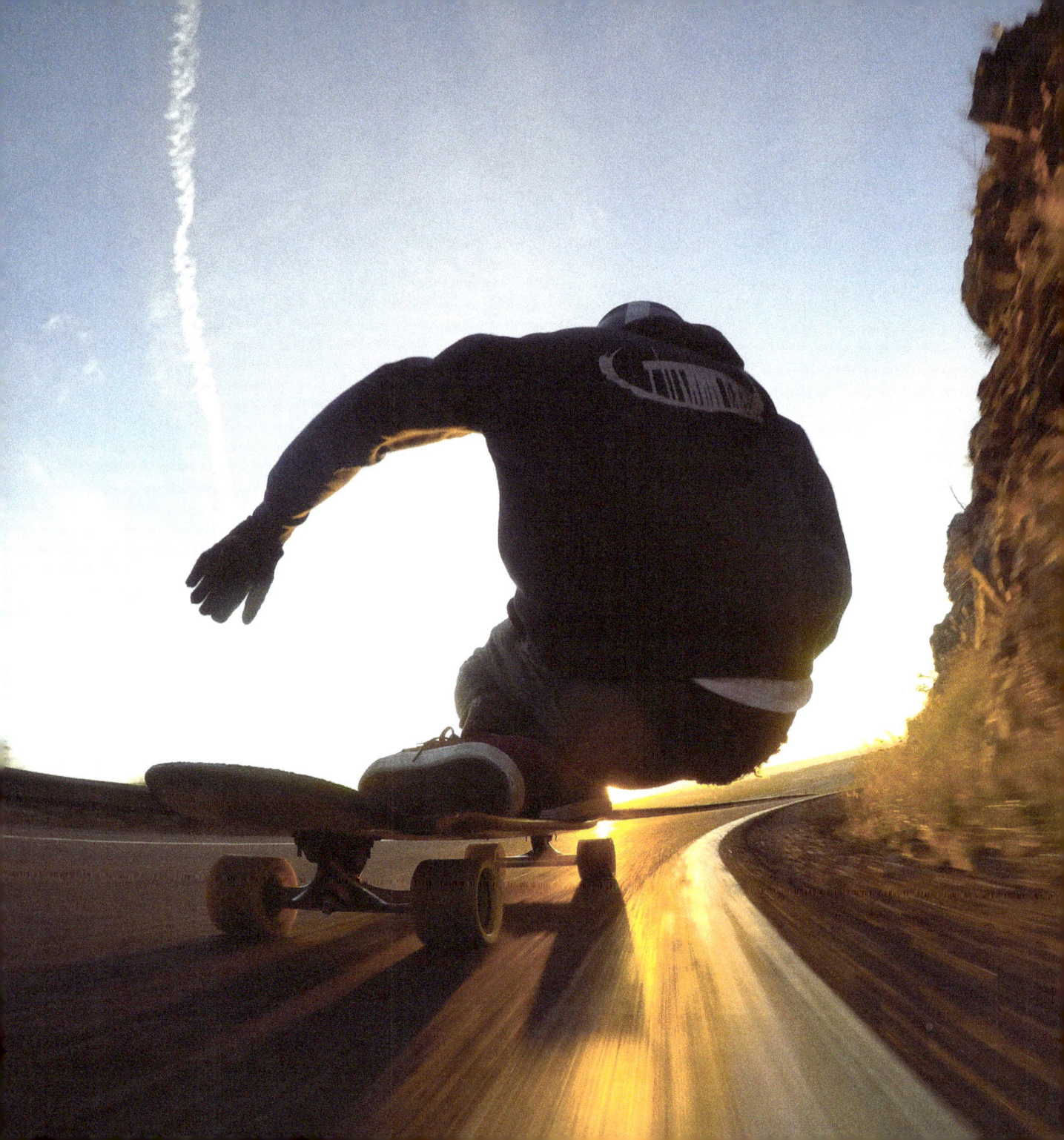

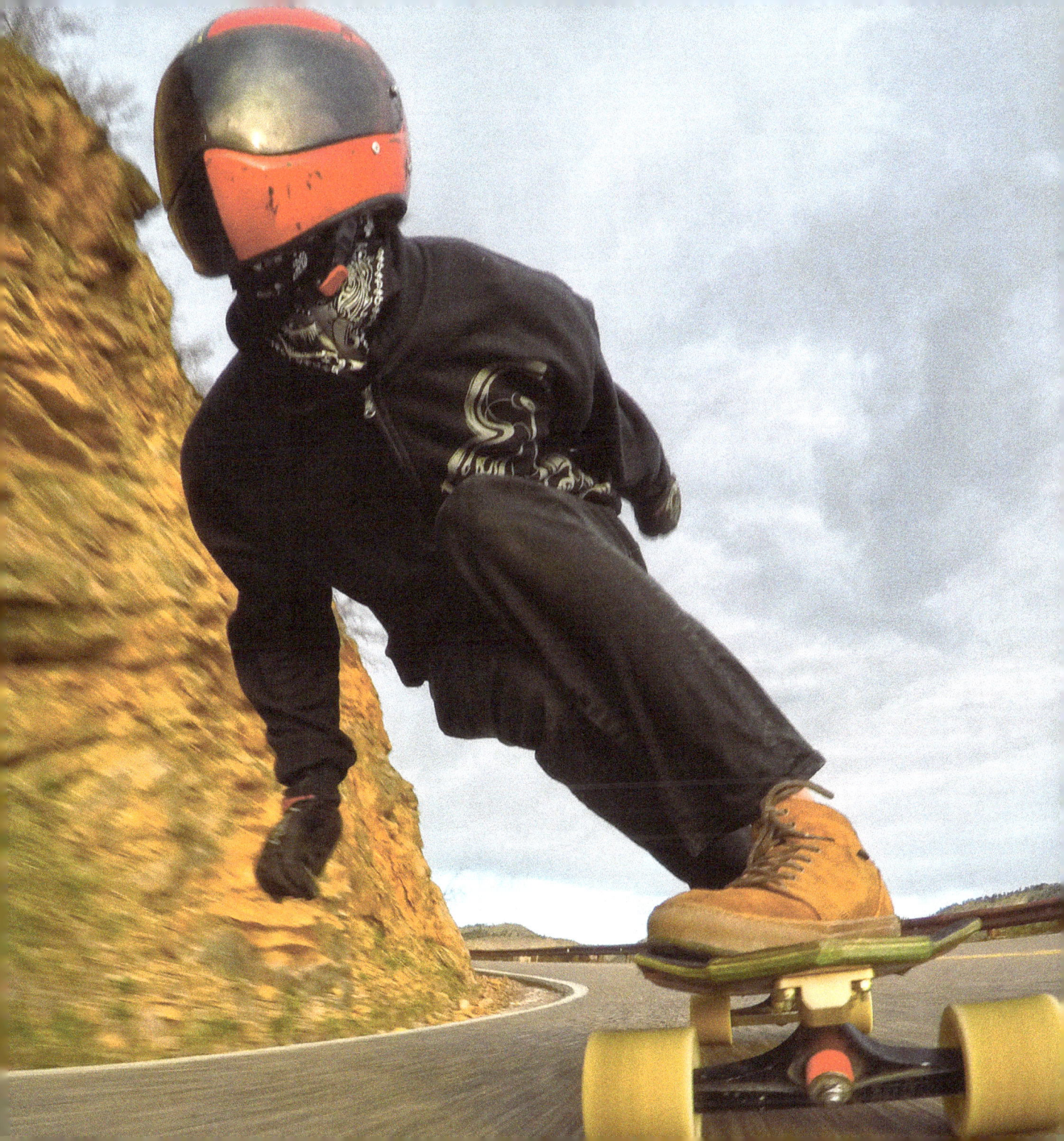

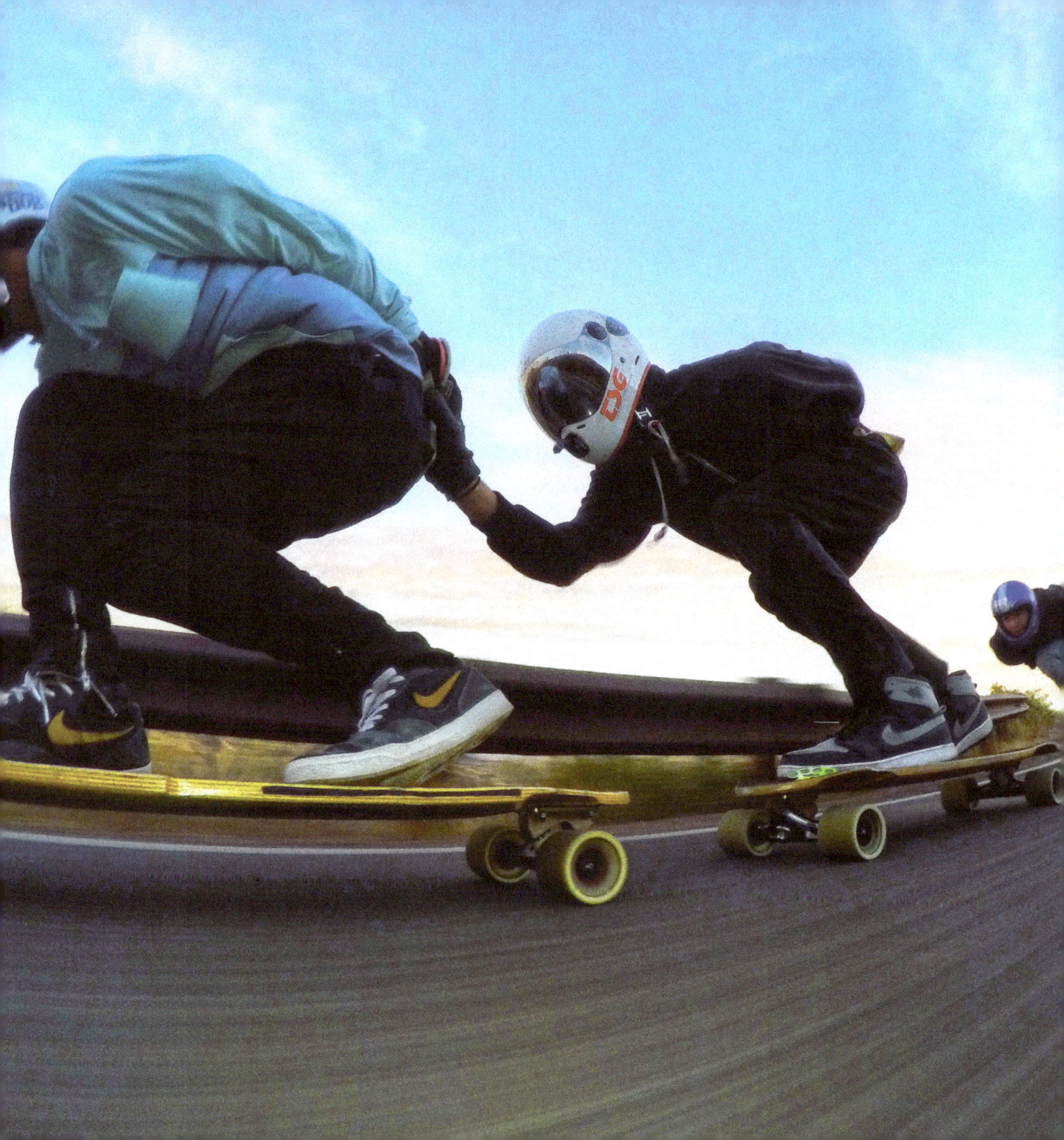

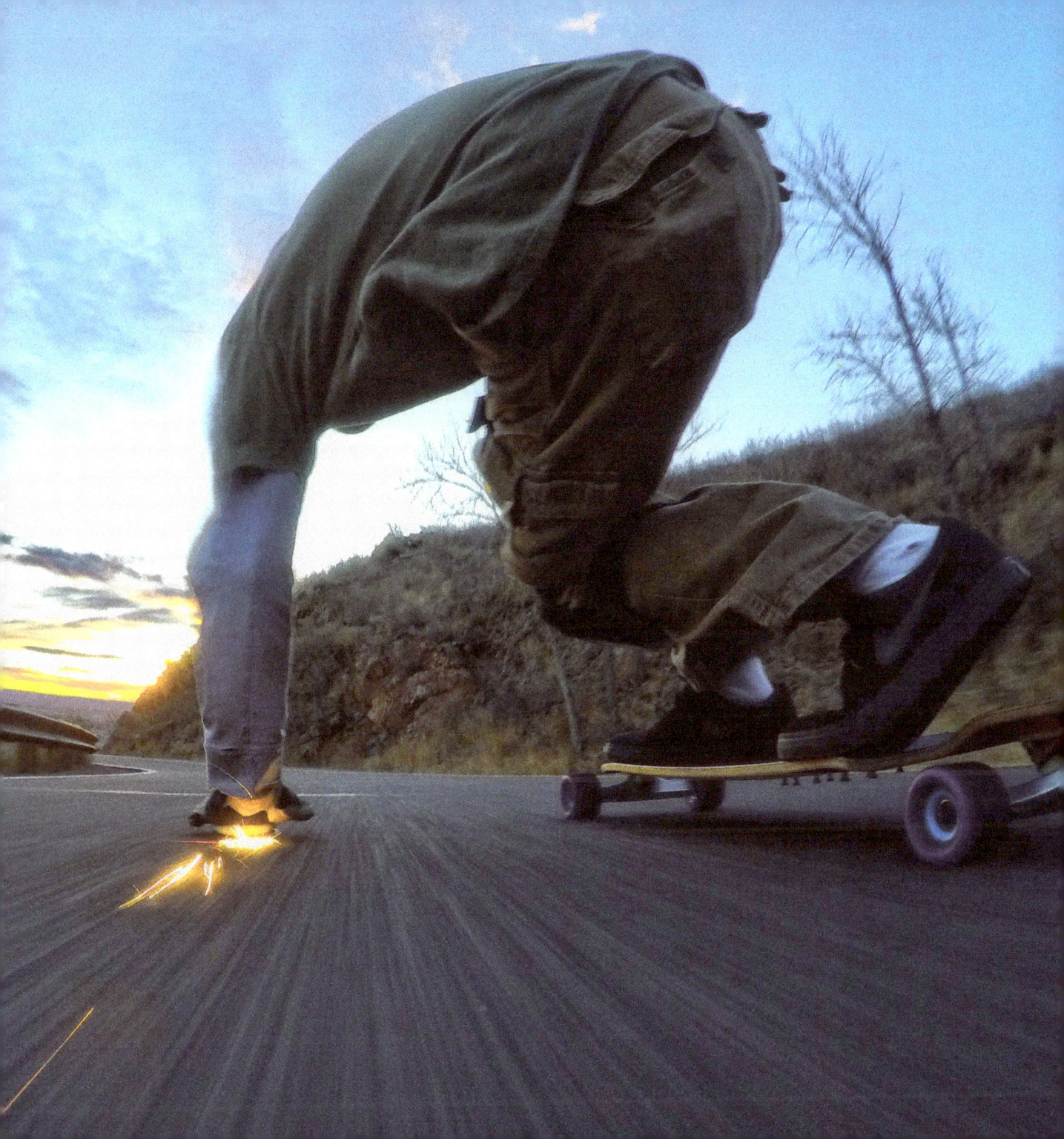

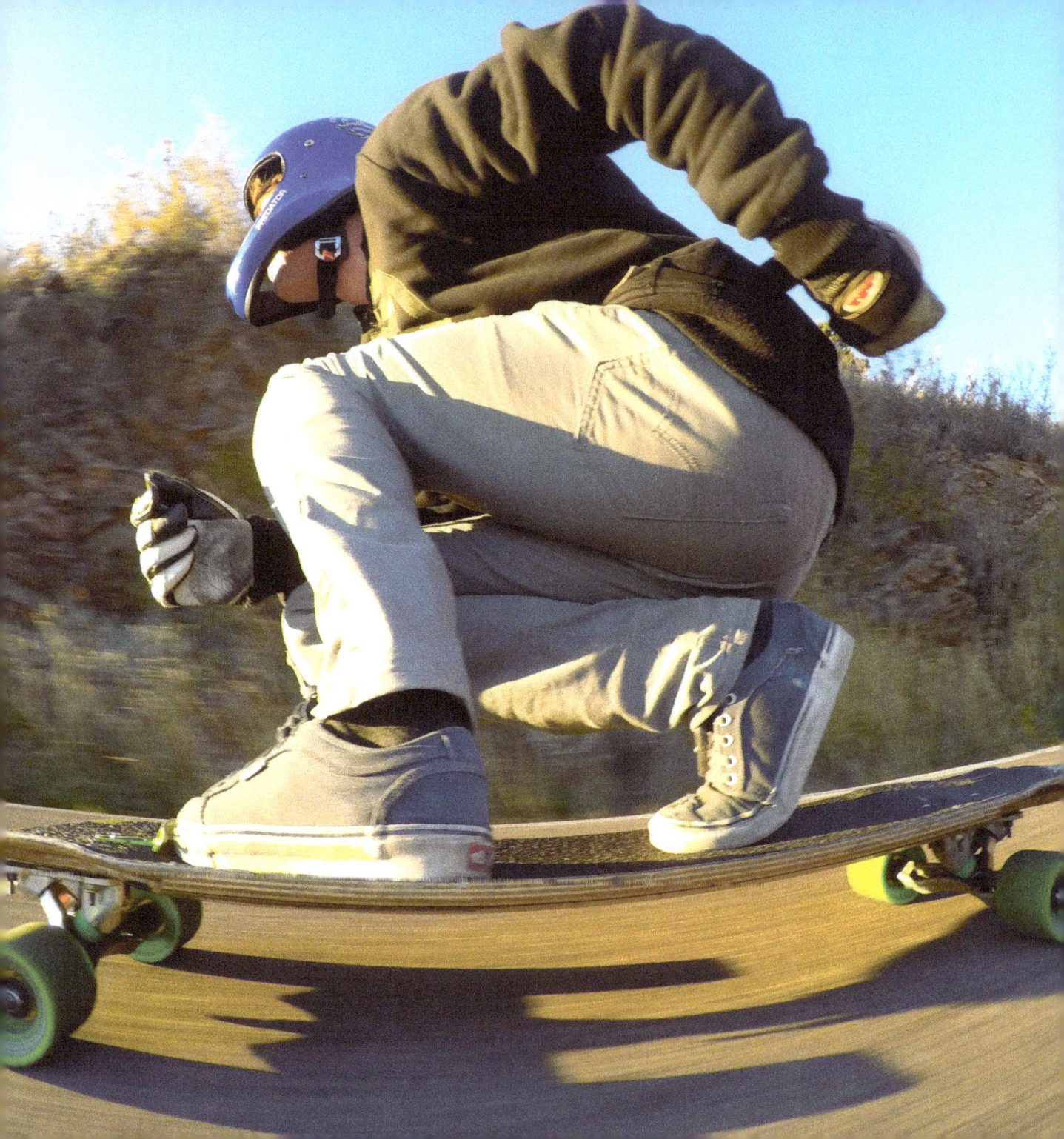

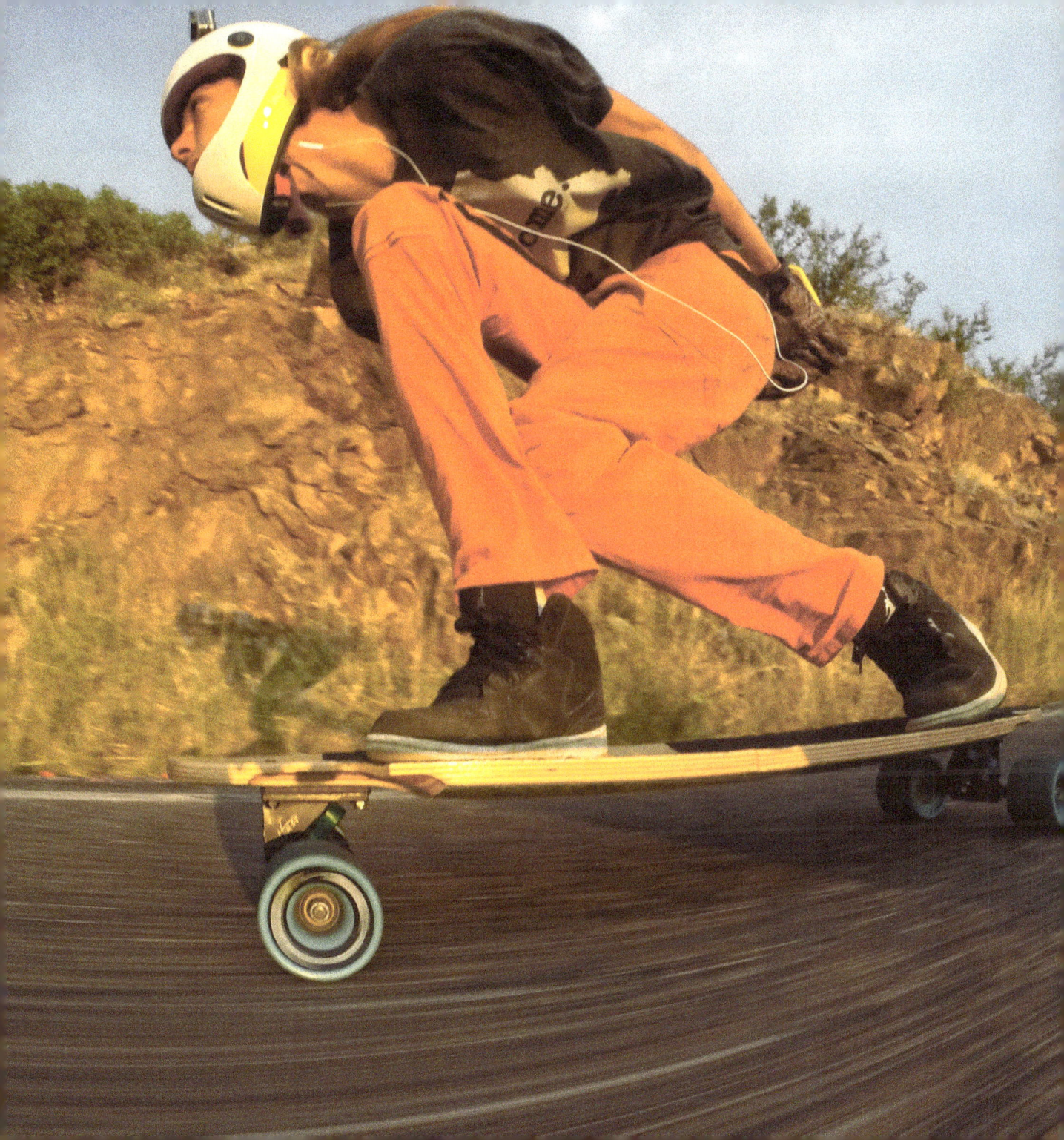

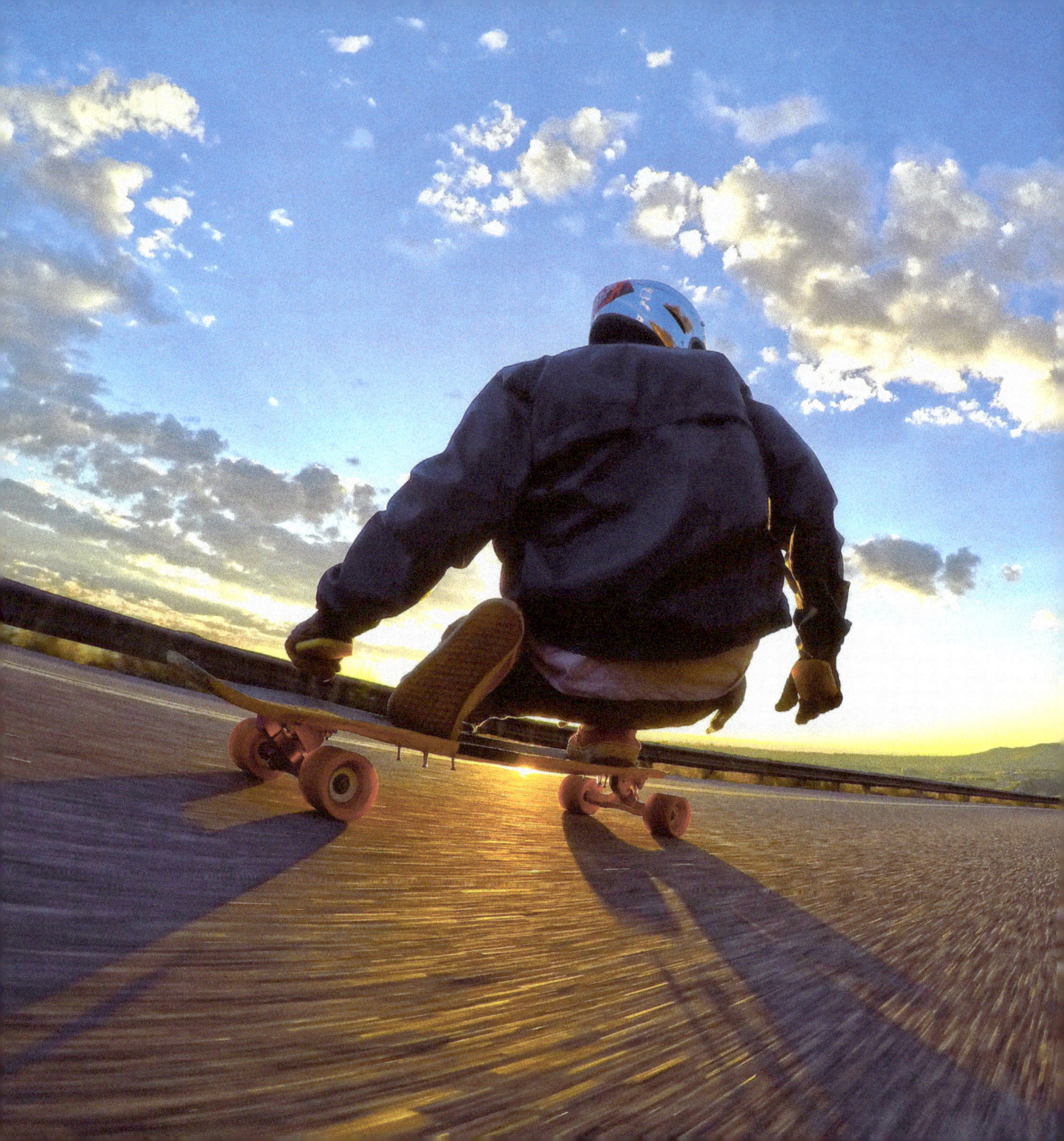

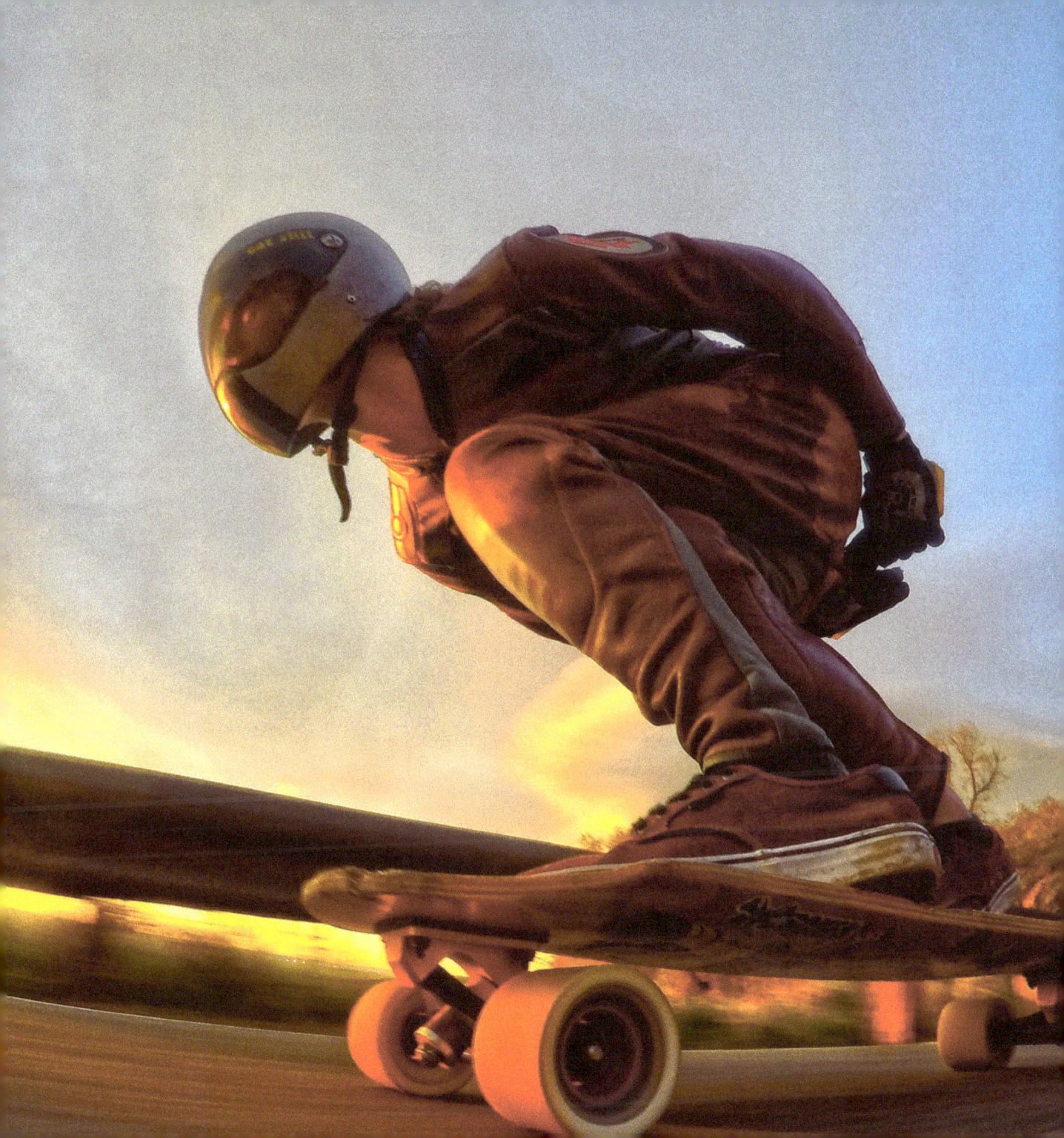

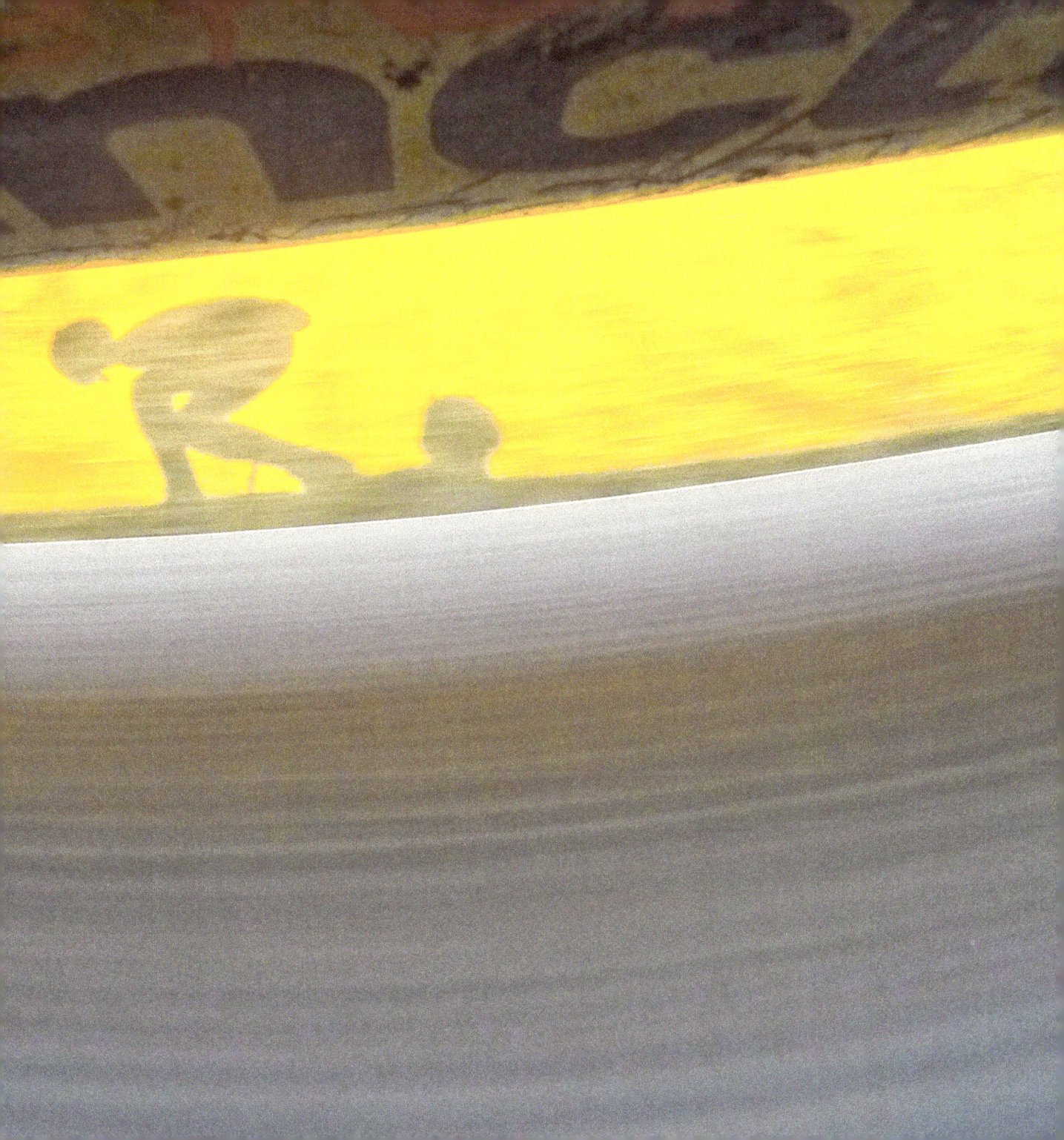

#Sk8face

You know how people have their selfie face? Their dancing face? Their concentration face? Well, allow me to introduce you to the latest in all the fancy faces: The Sk8face. What is THAT LOOK? (Sheer joy? Pure focus? Your brain screaming, "Holy S*%$! This might hurt!"?) It doesn't really matter, because Sk8face is here to stay. You're welcome.

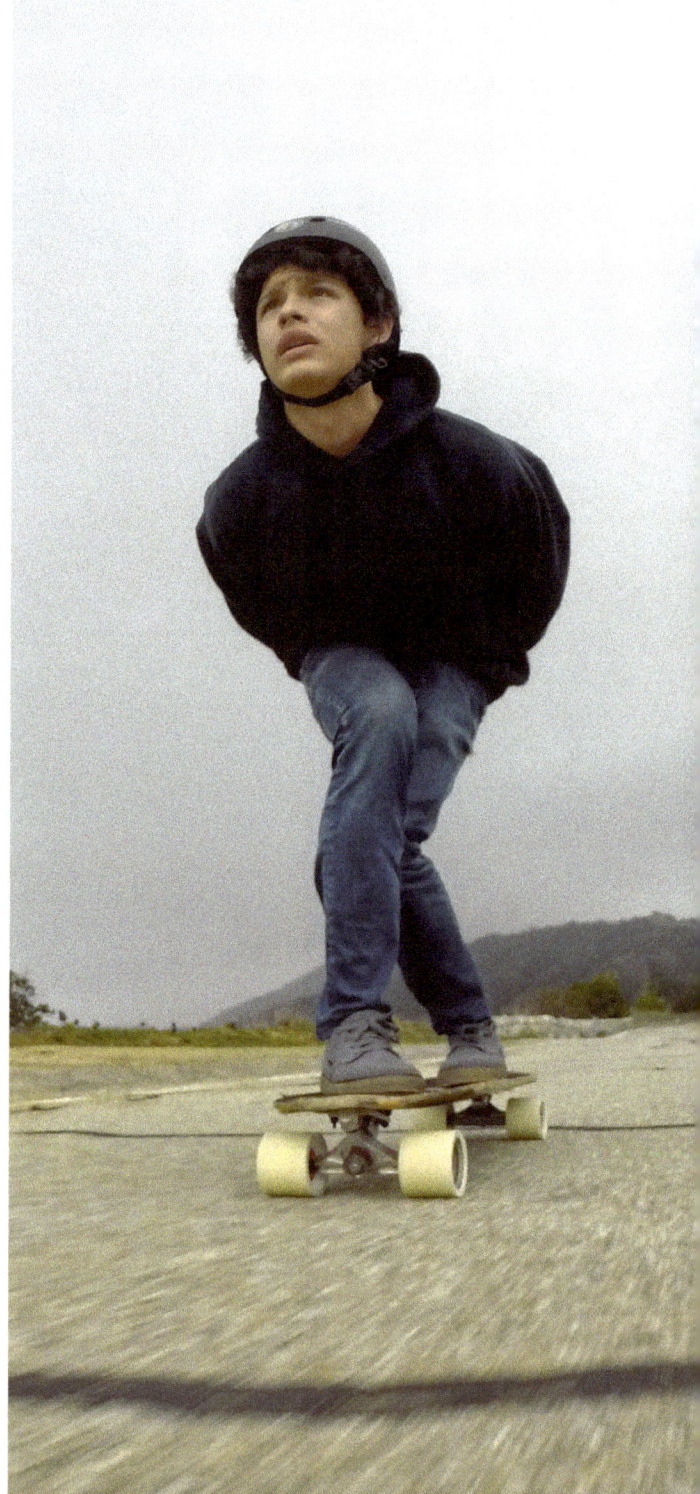

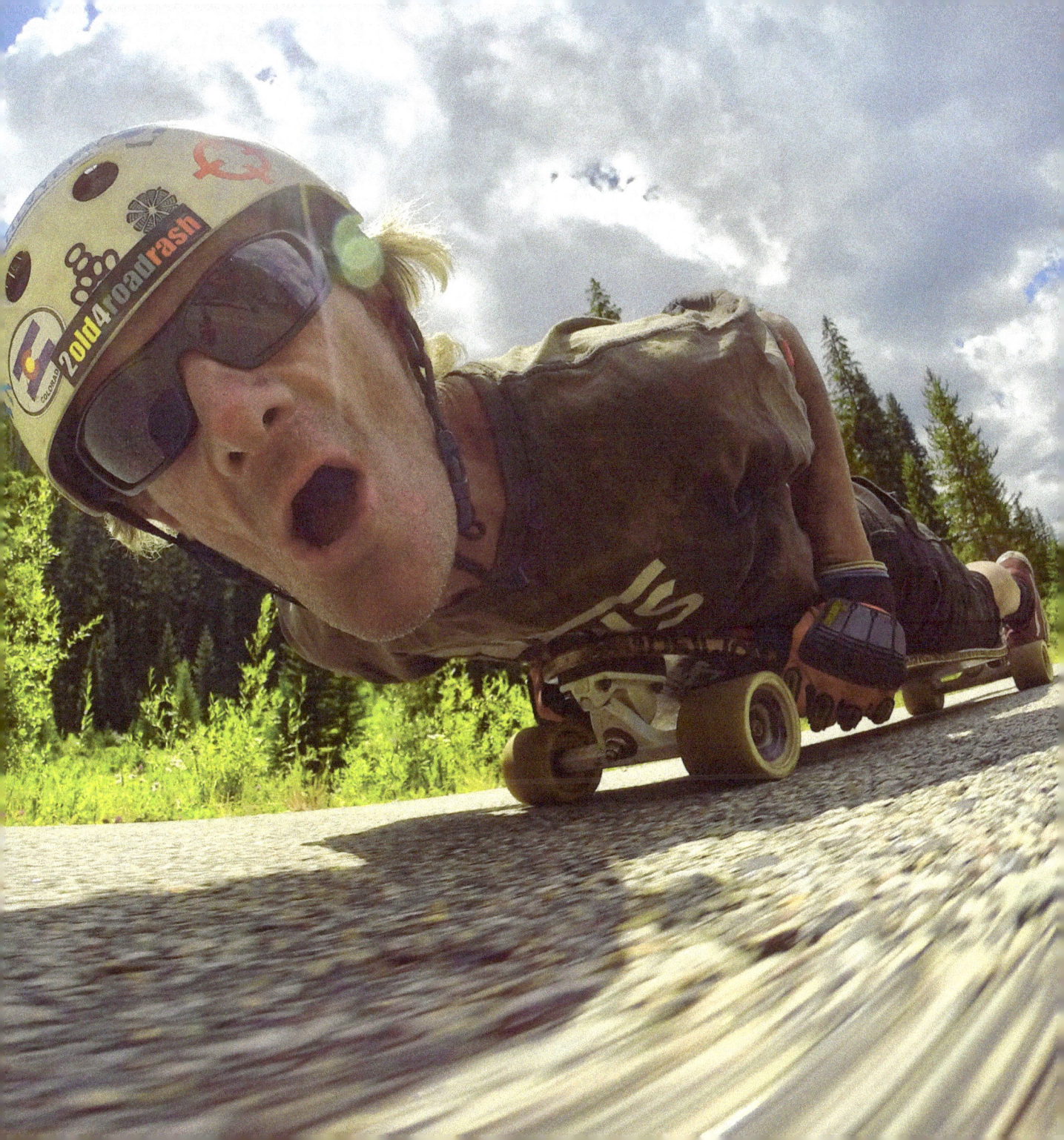

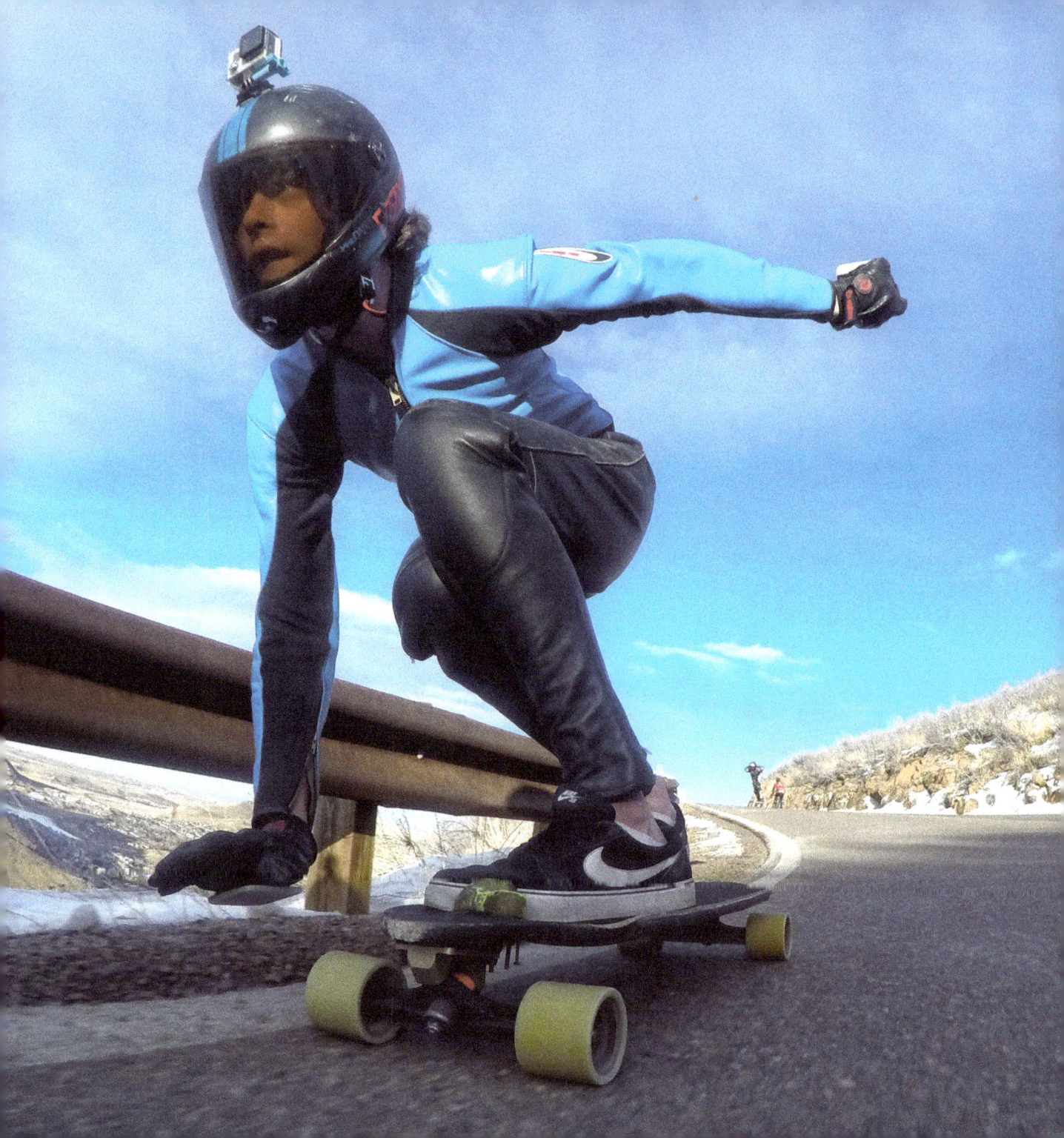

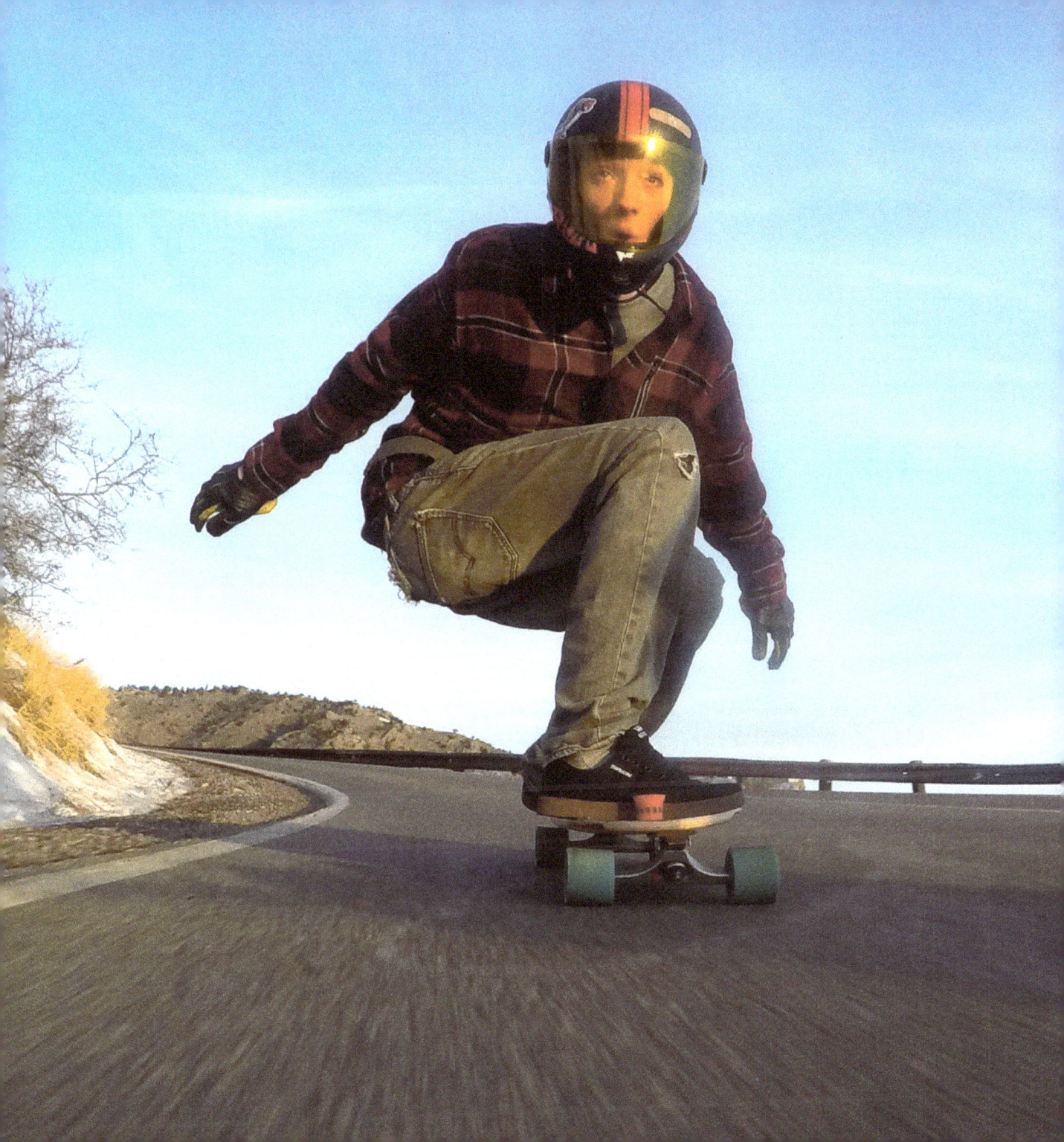

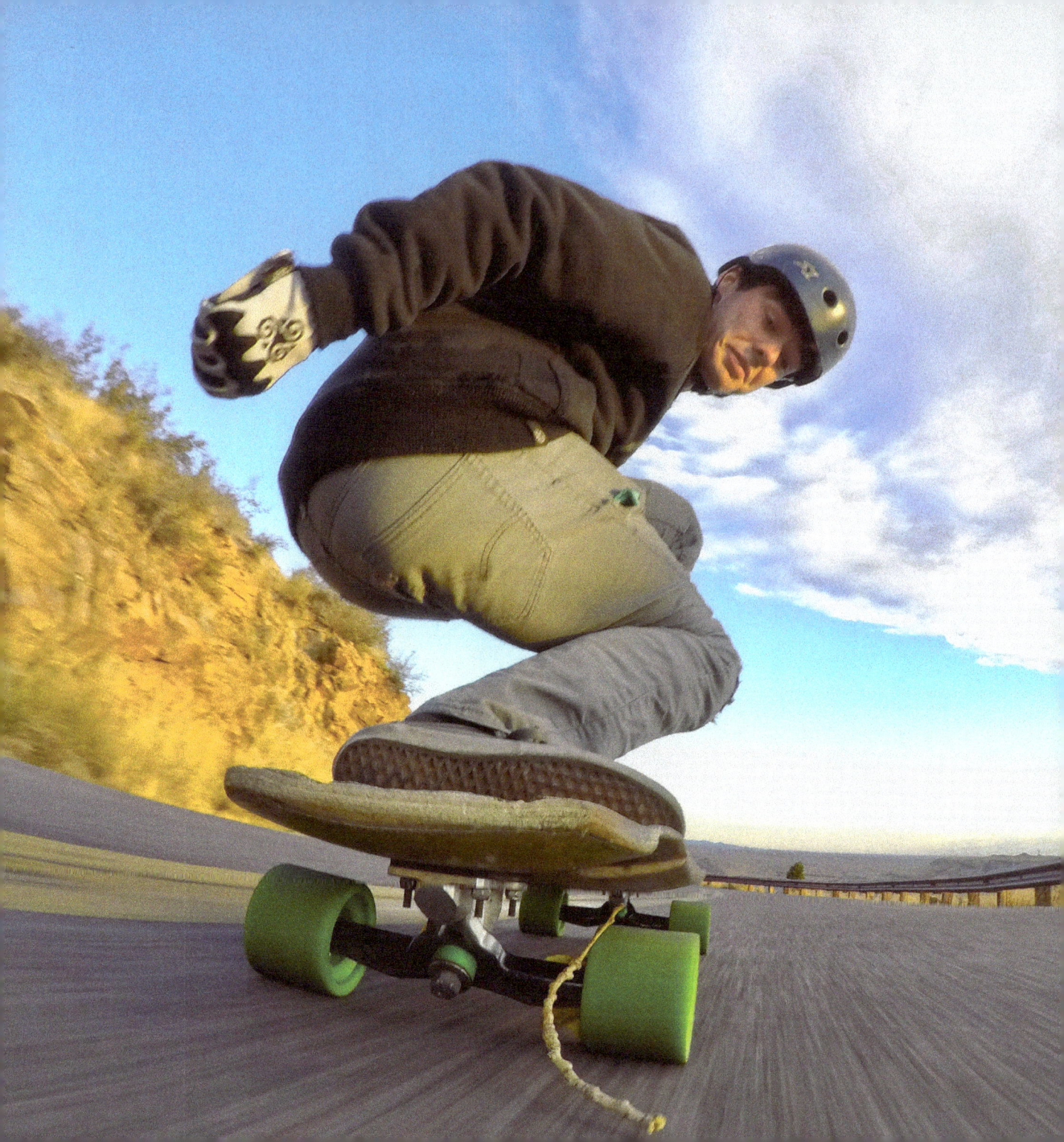

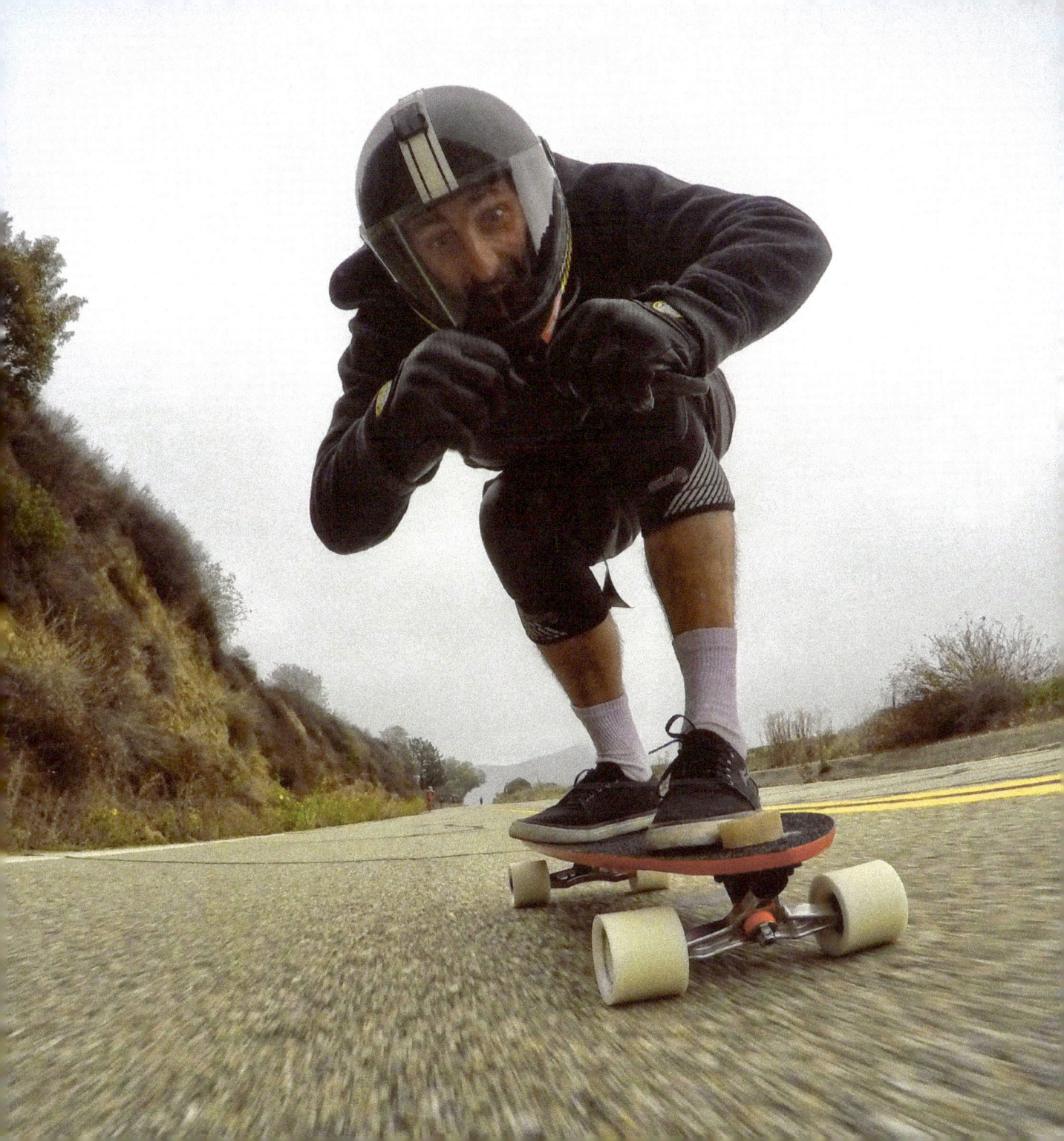

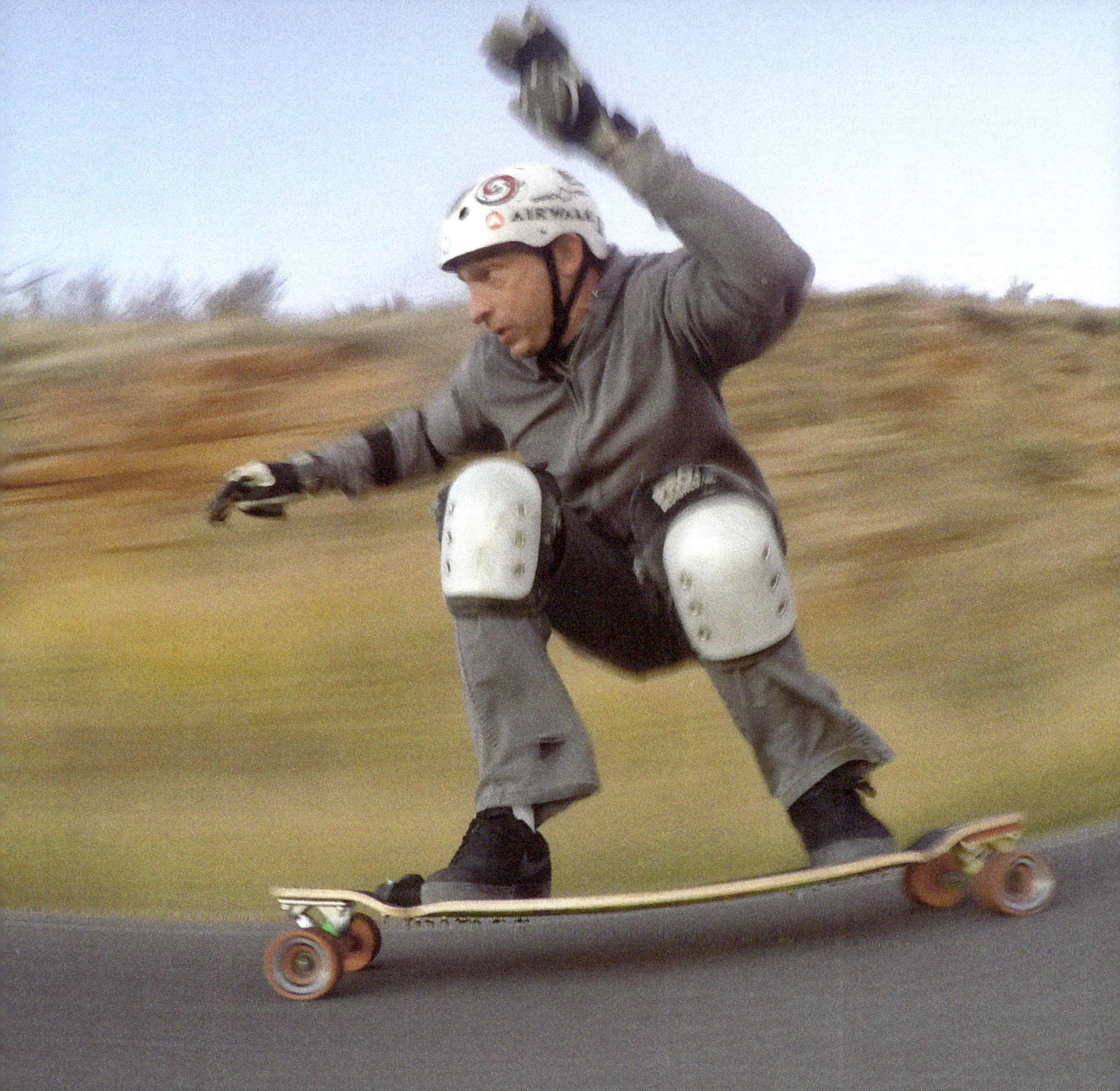

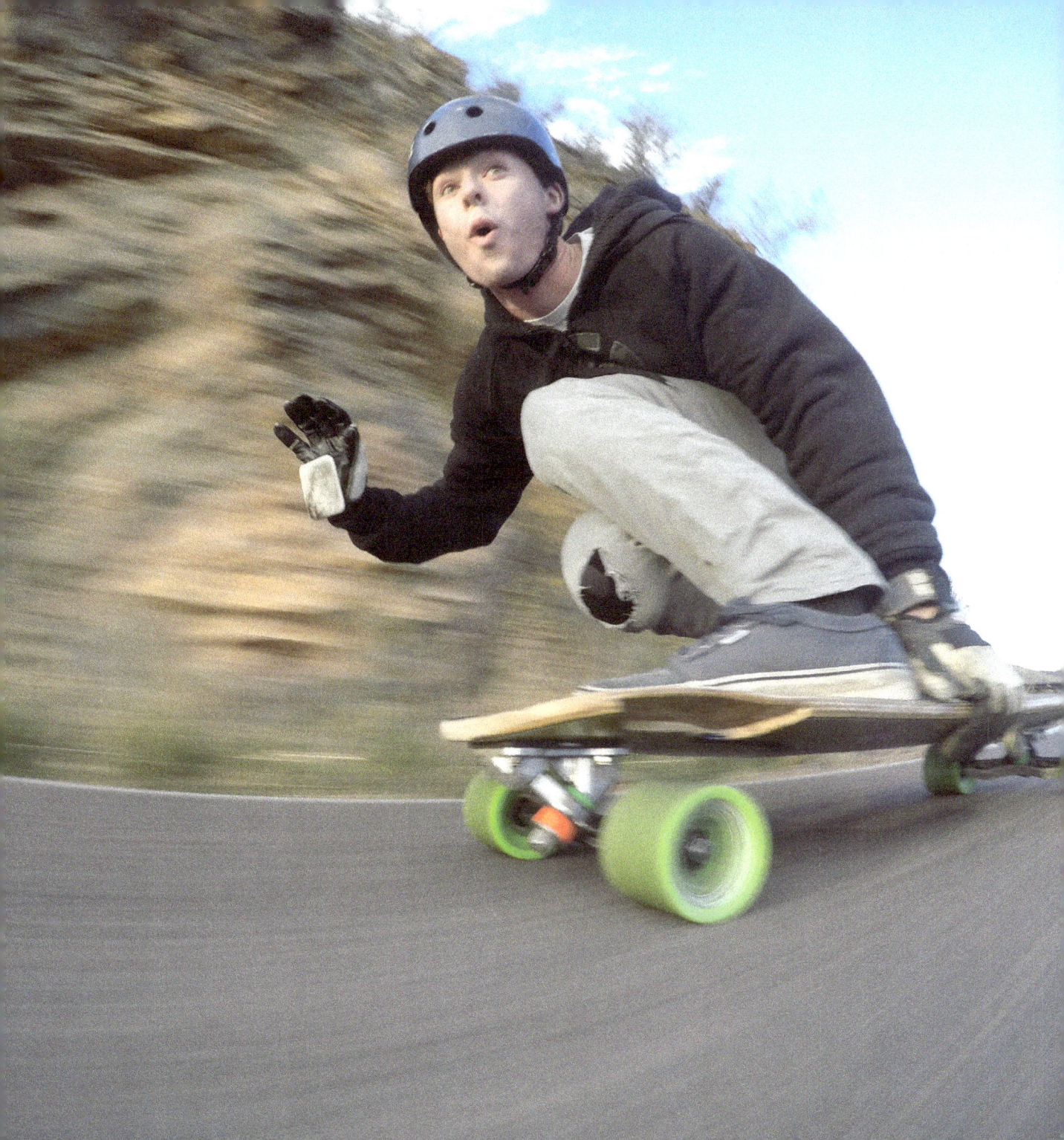

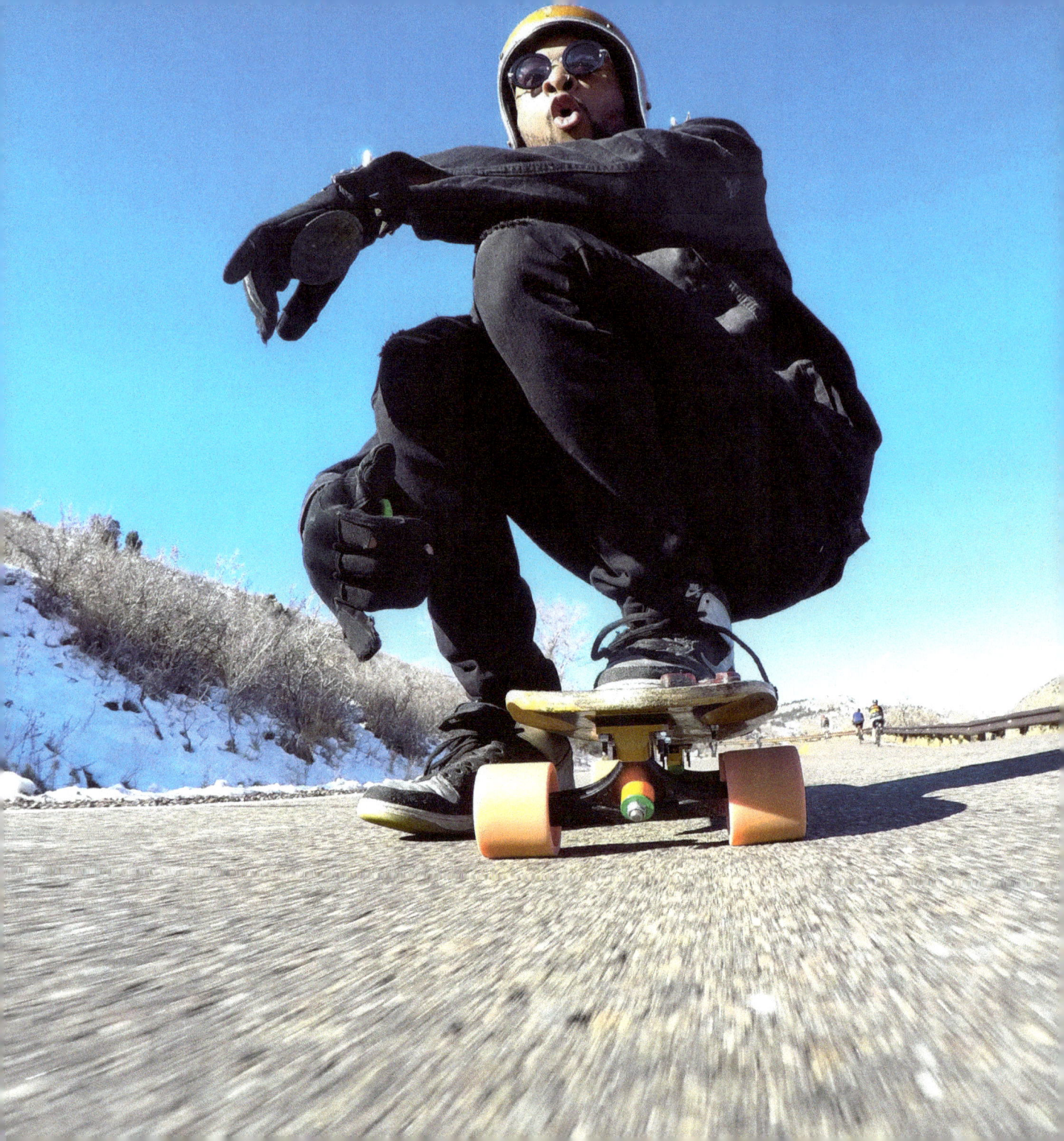

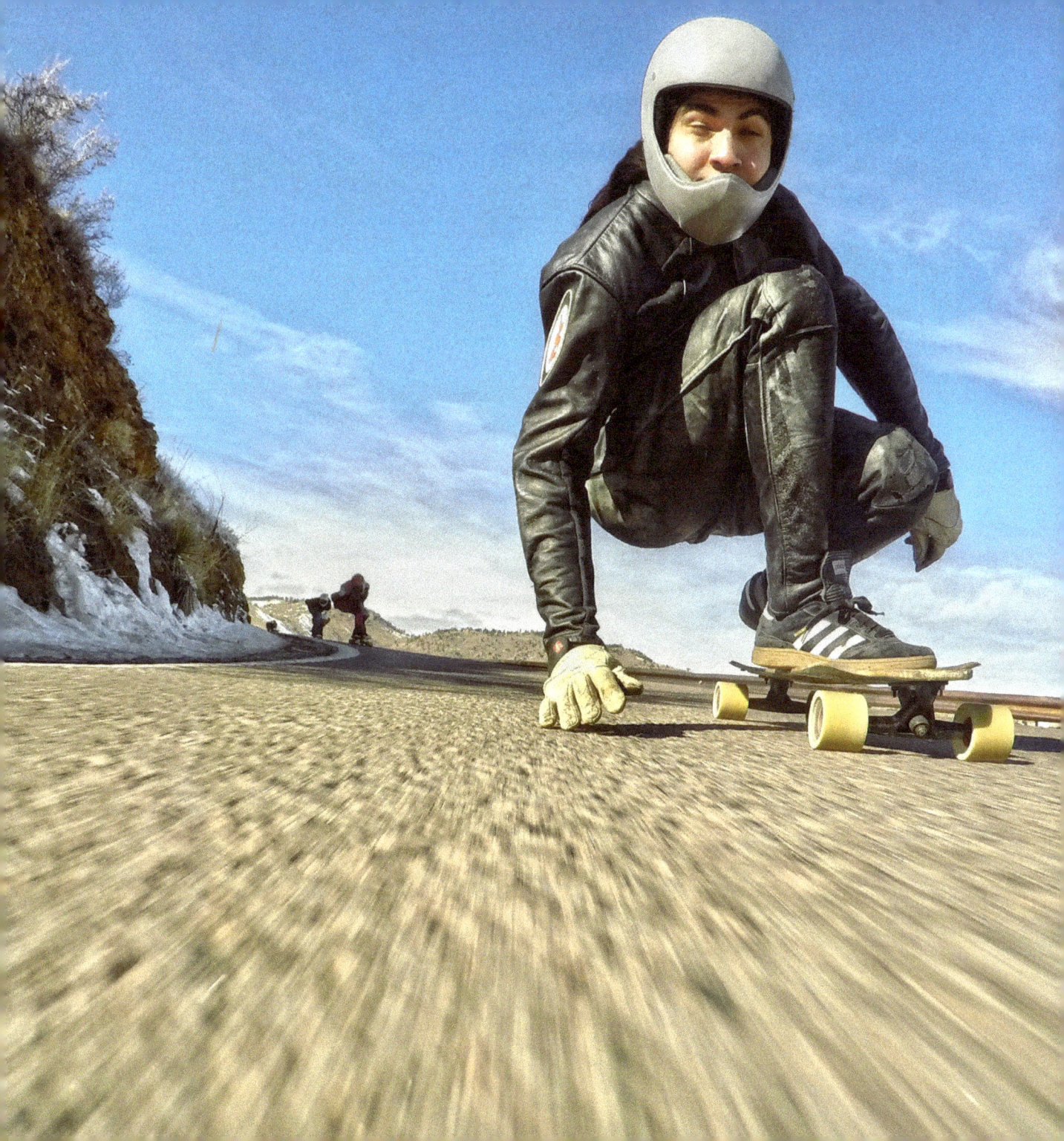

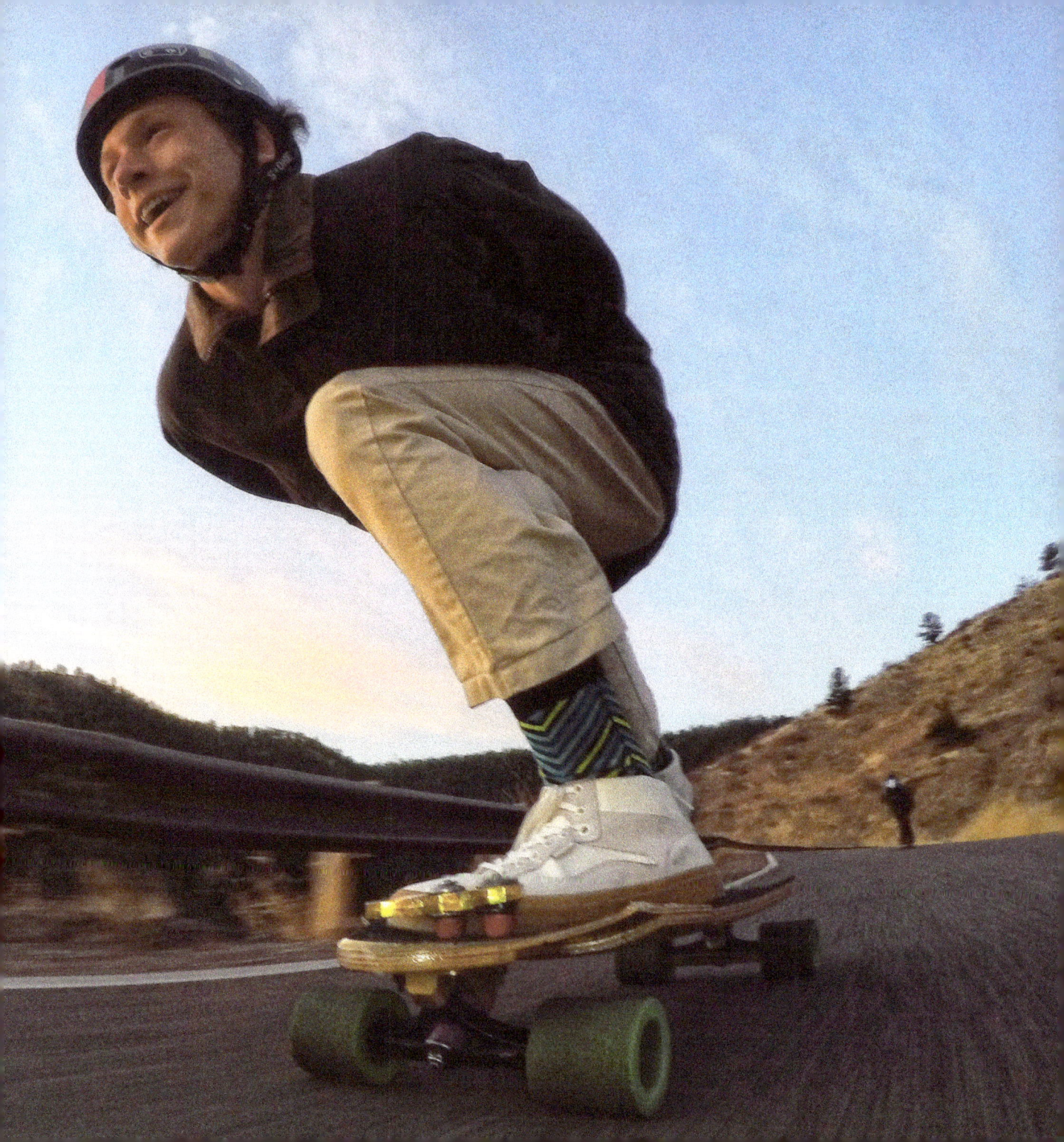

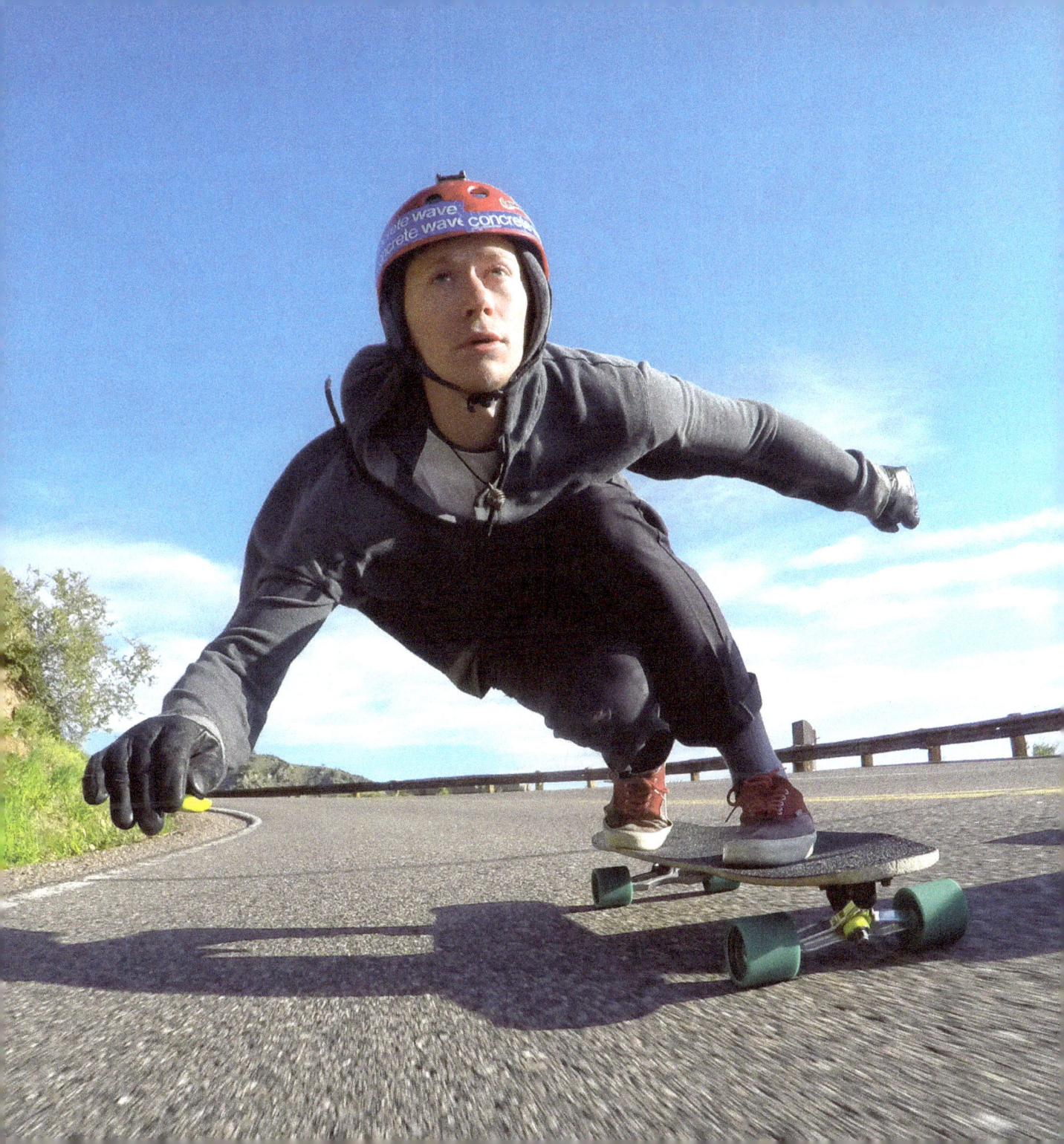

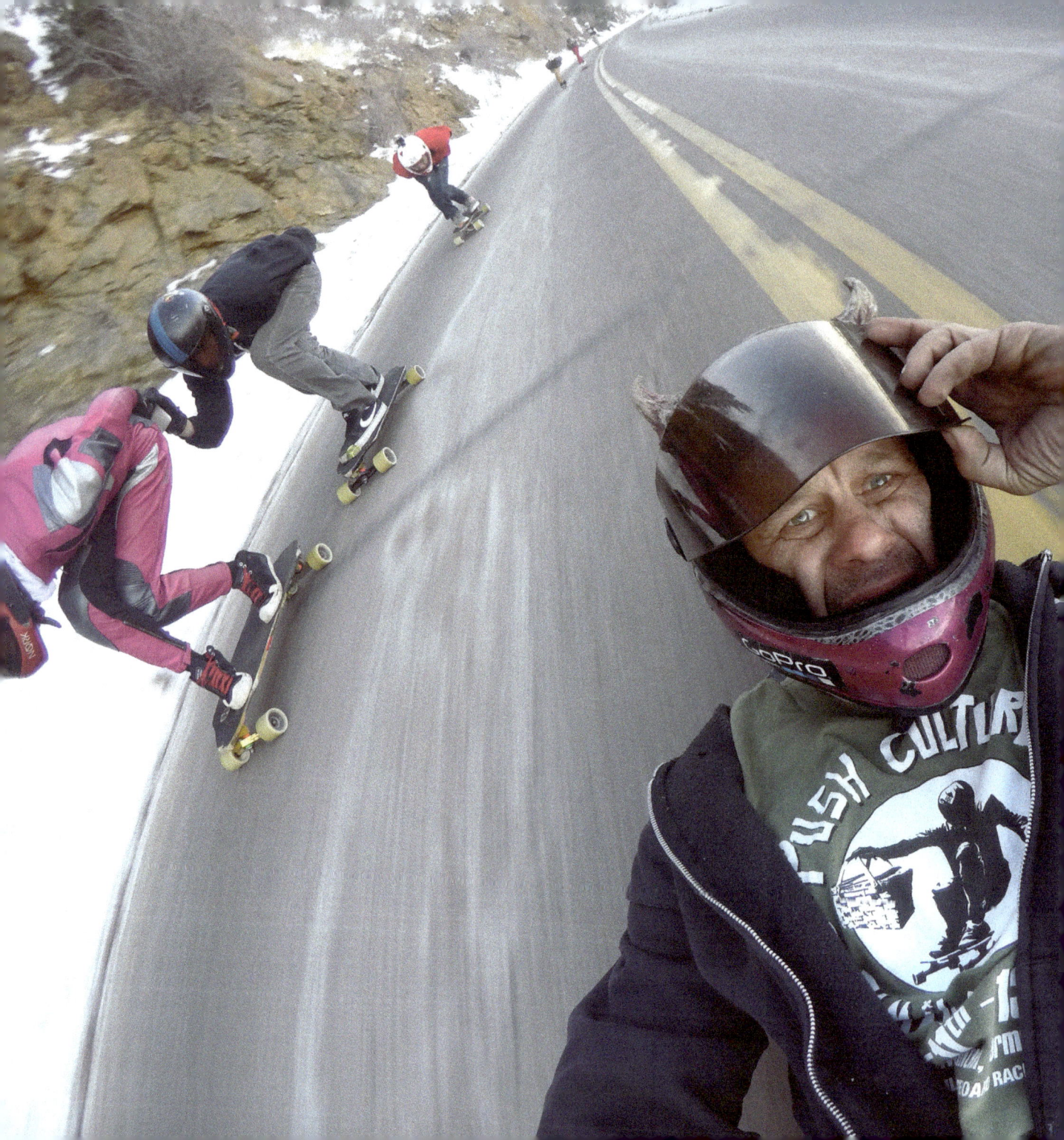

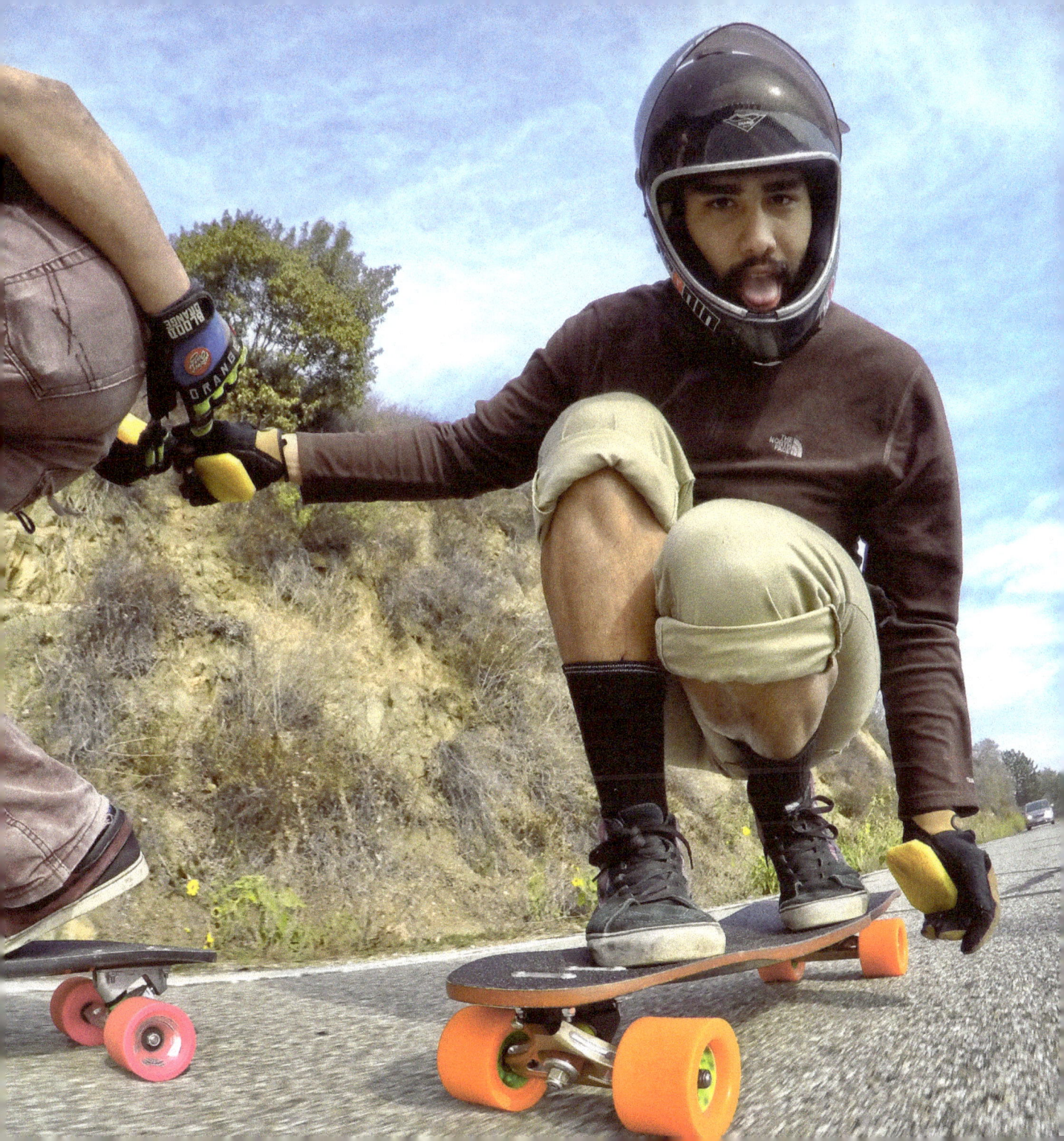

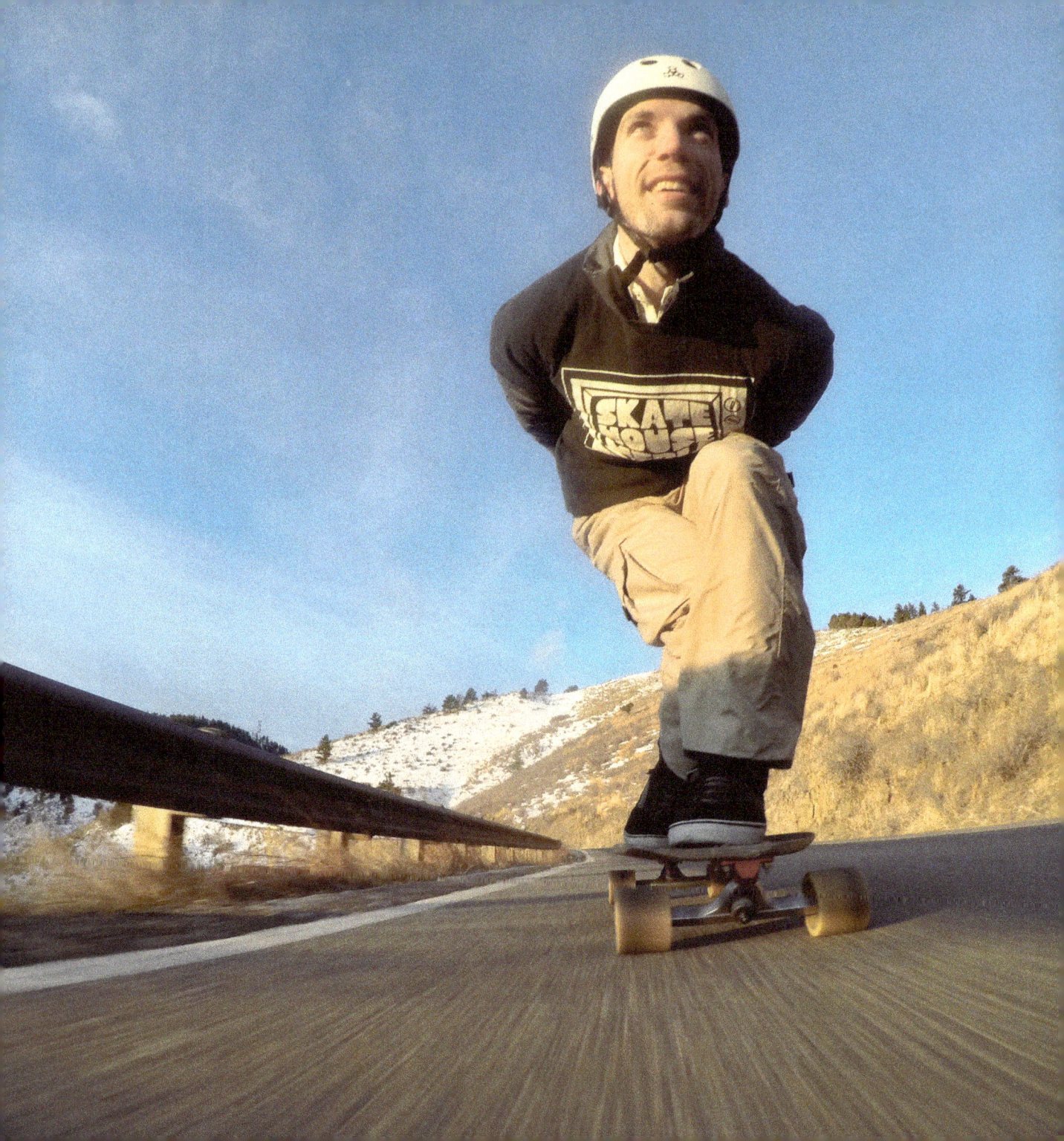

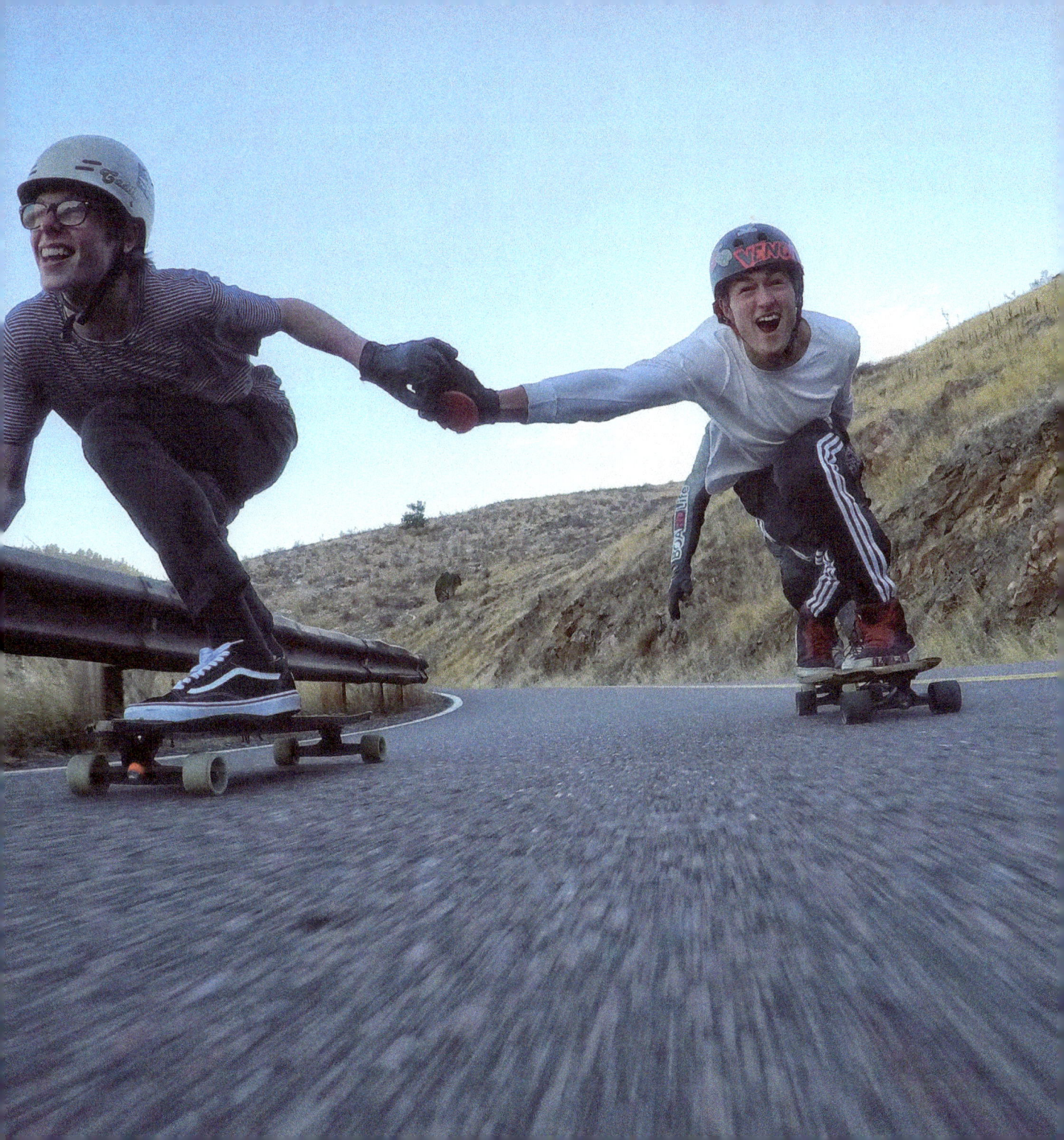

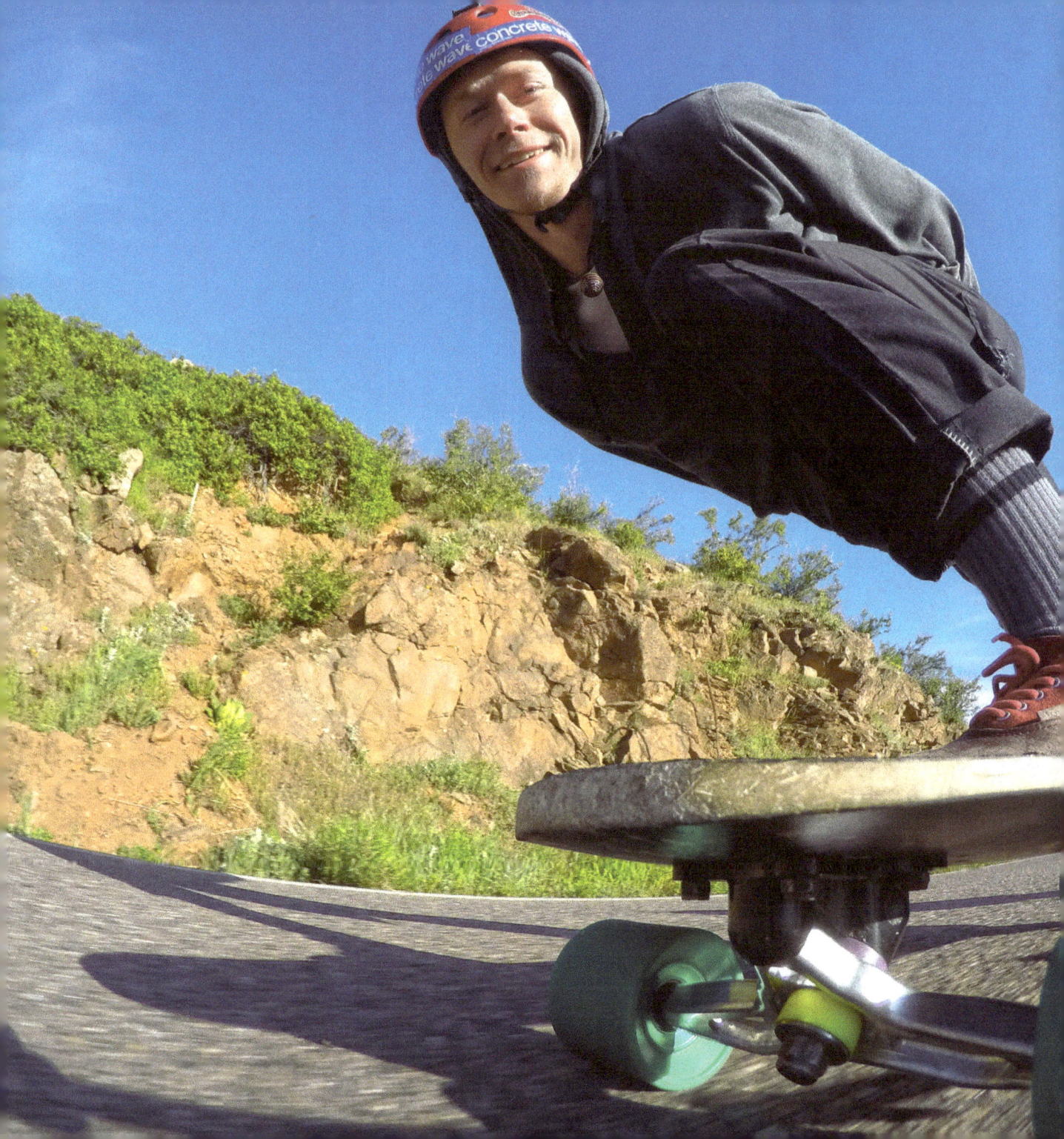

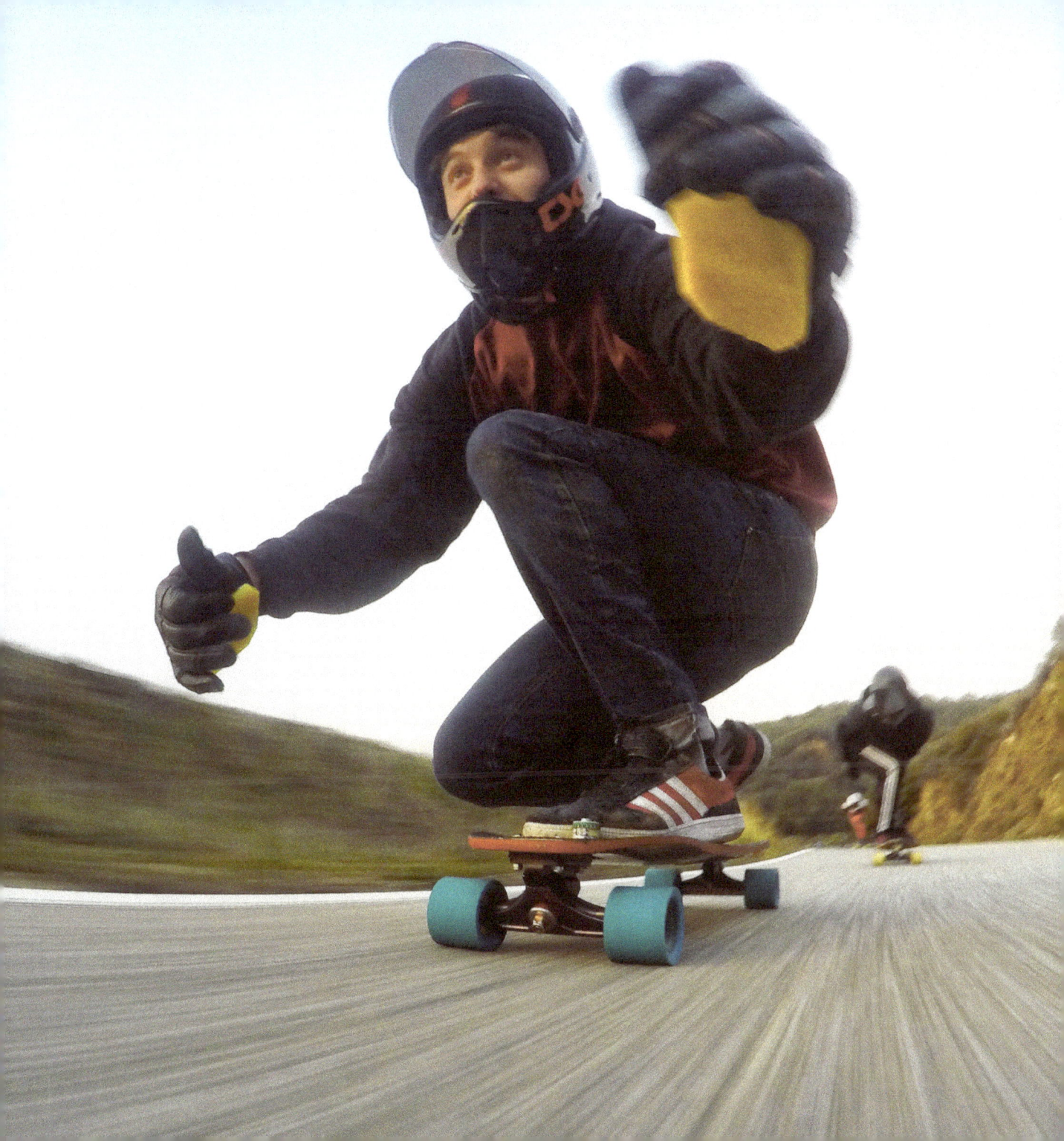

#Localsonly

Our local scene here in ColoRADo is pretty lit! We have some of the fastest and most stylish riders around! Here is a chapter dedicated to one of the most envied scenes in the world.

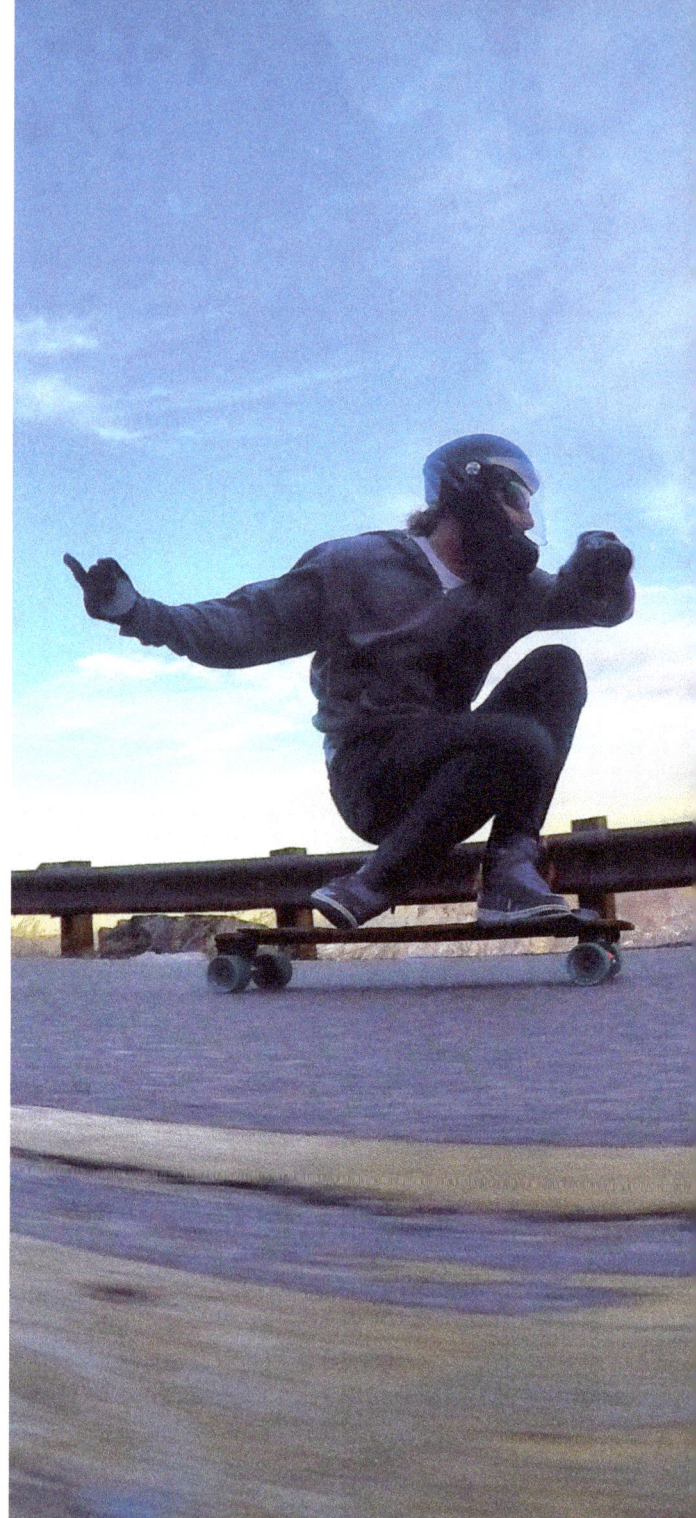

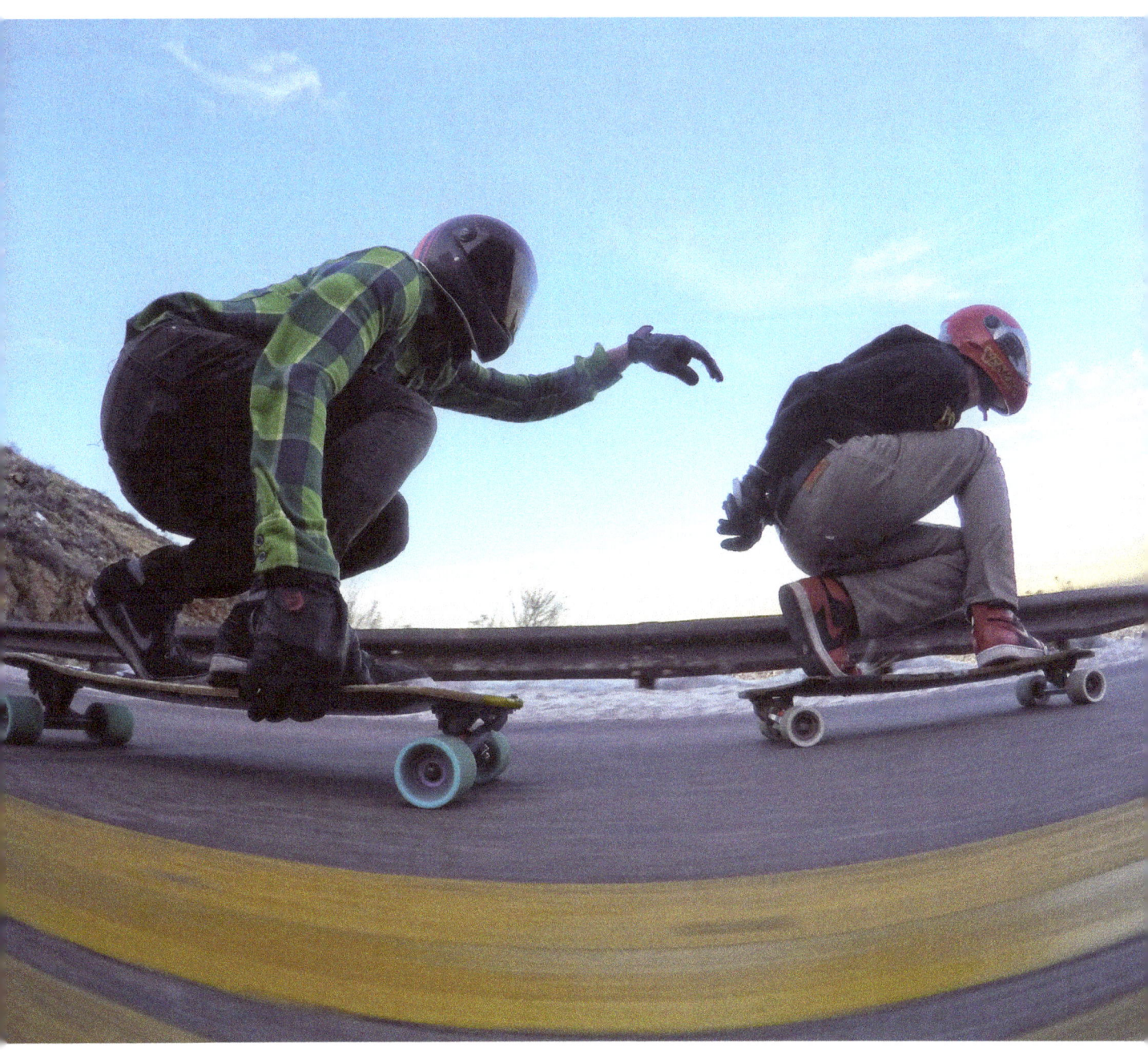

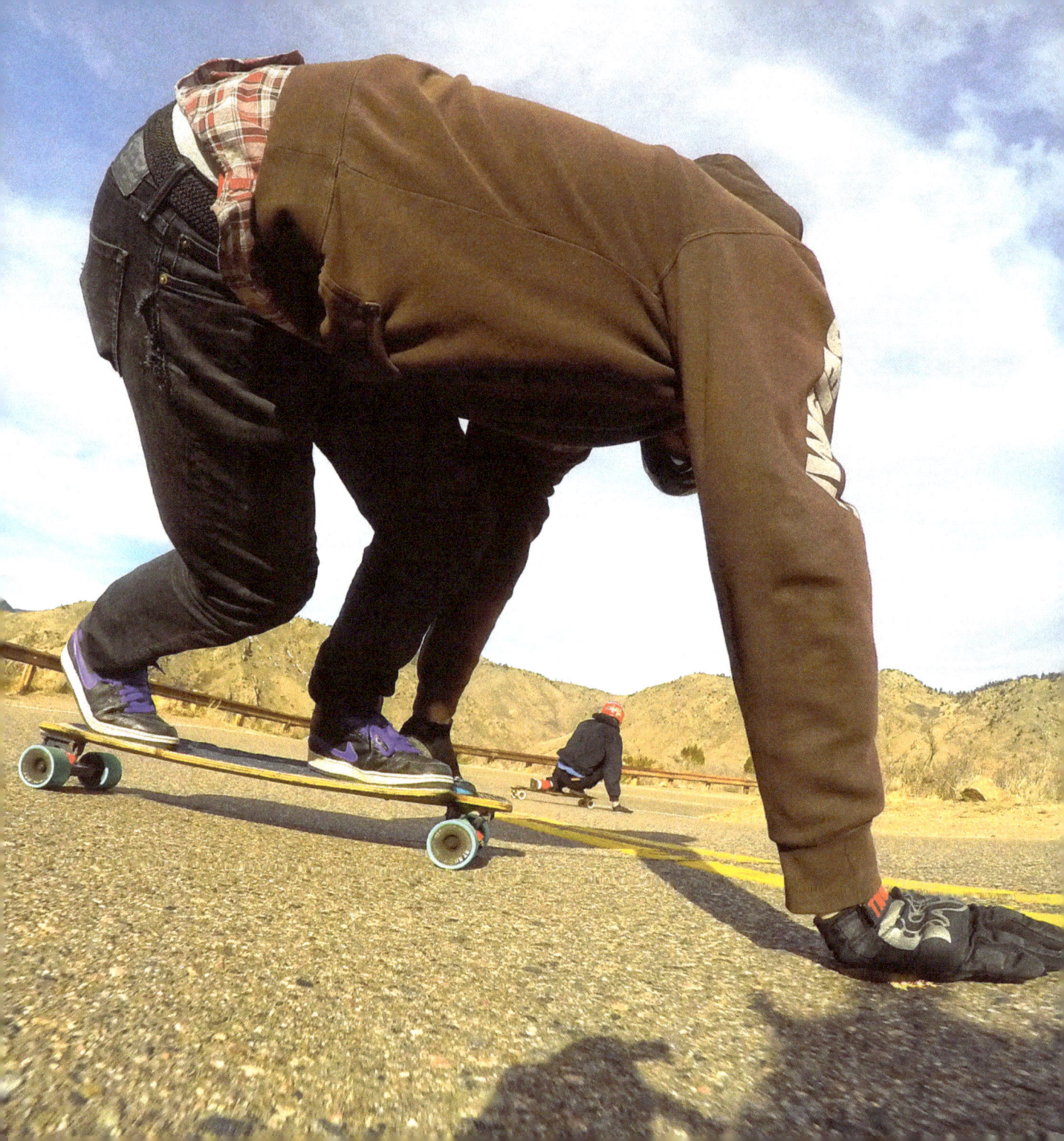

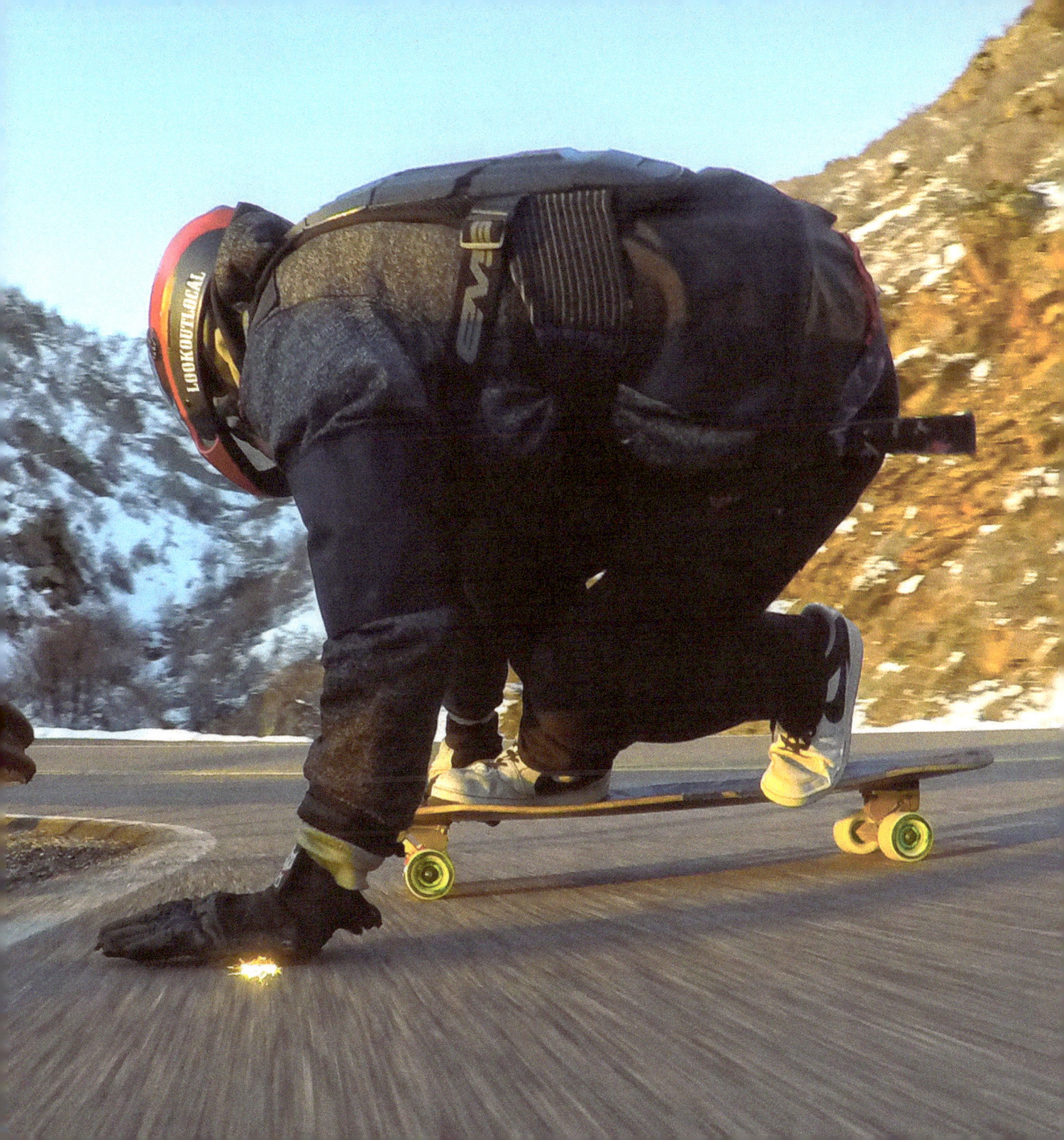

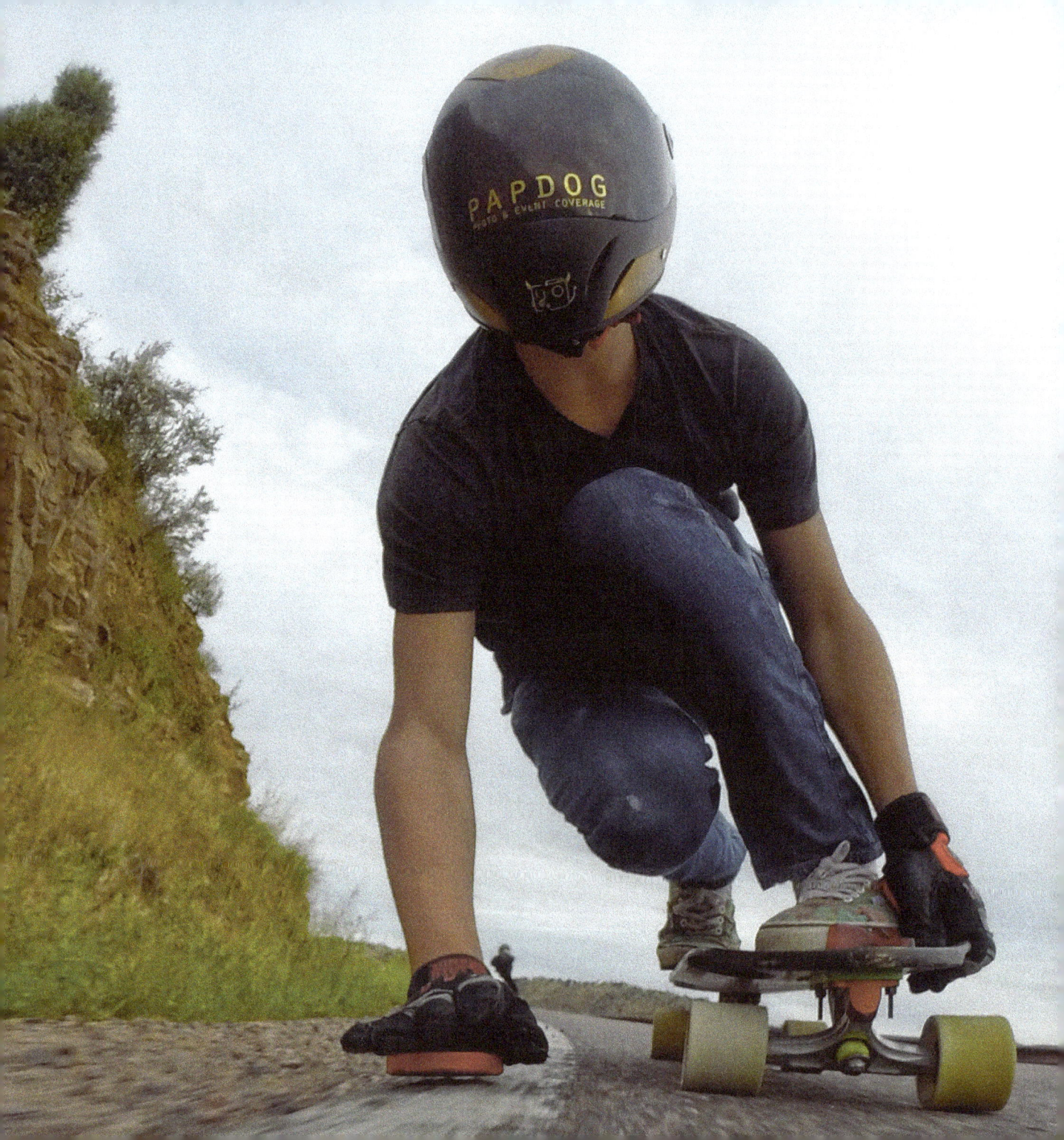

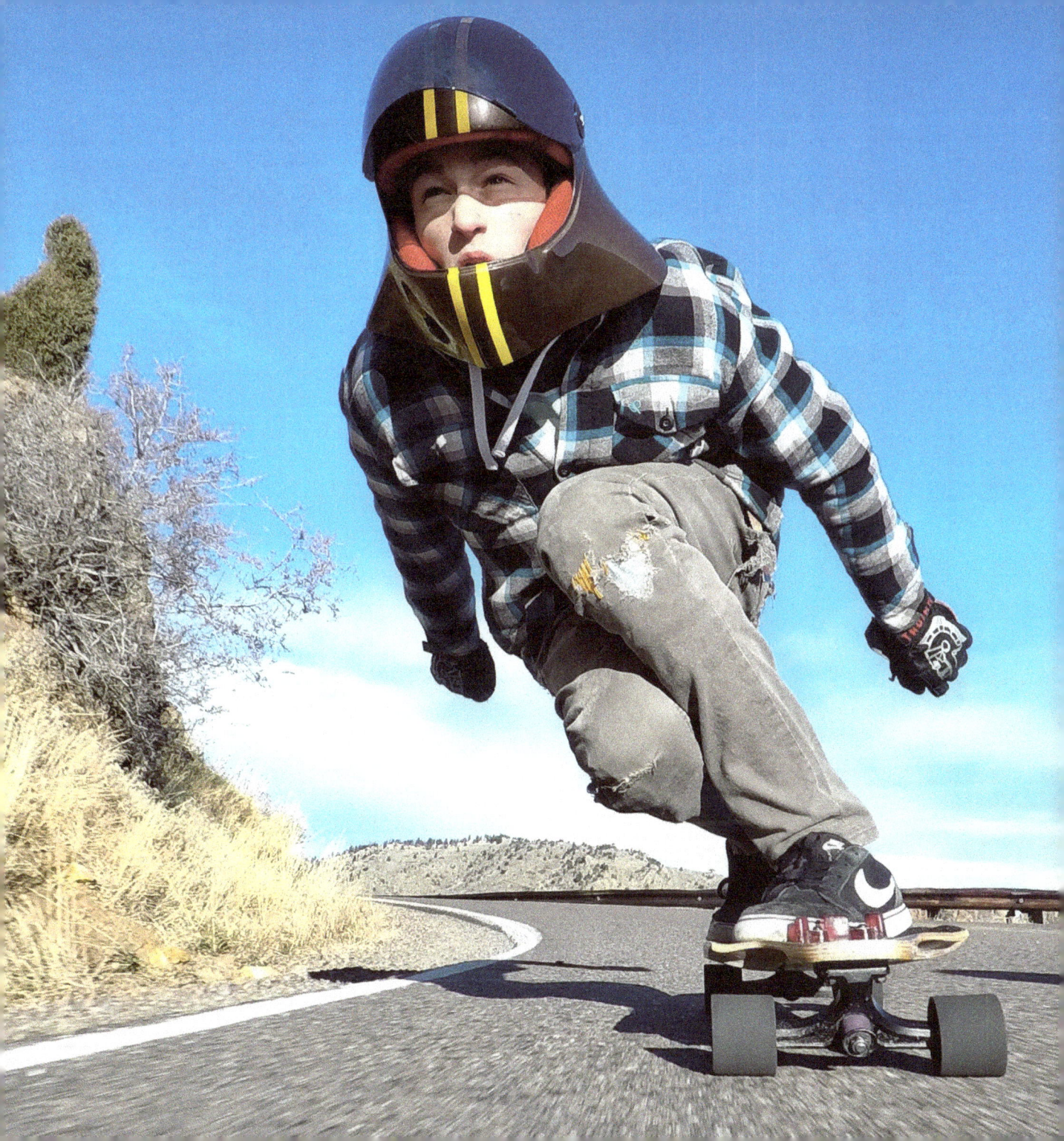

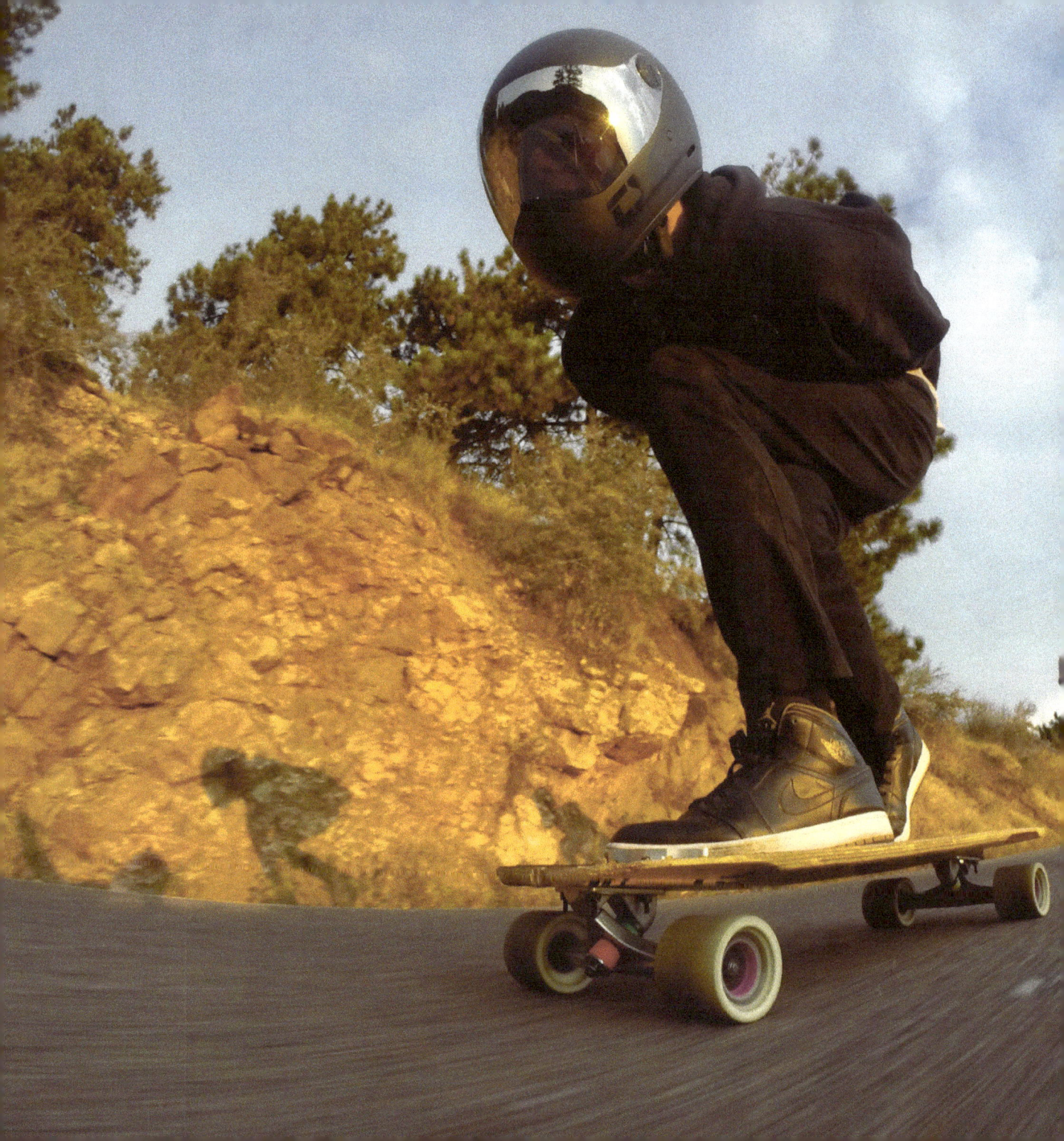

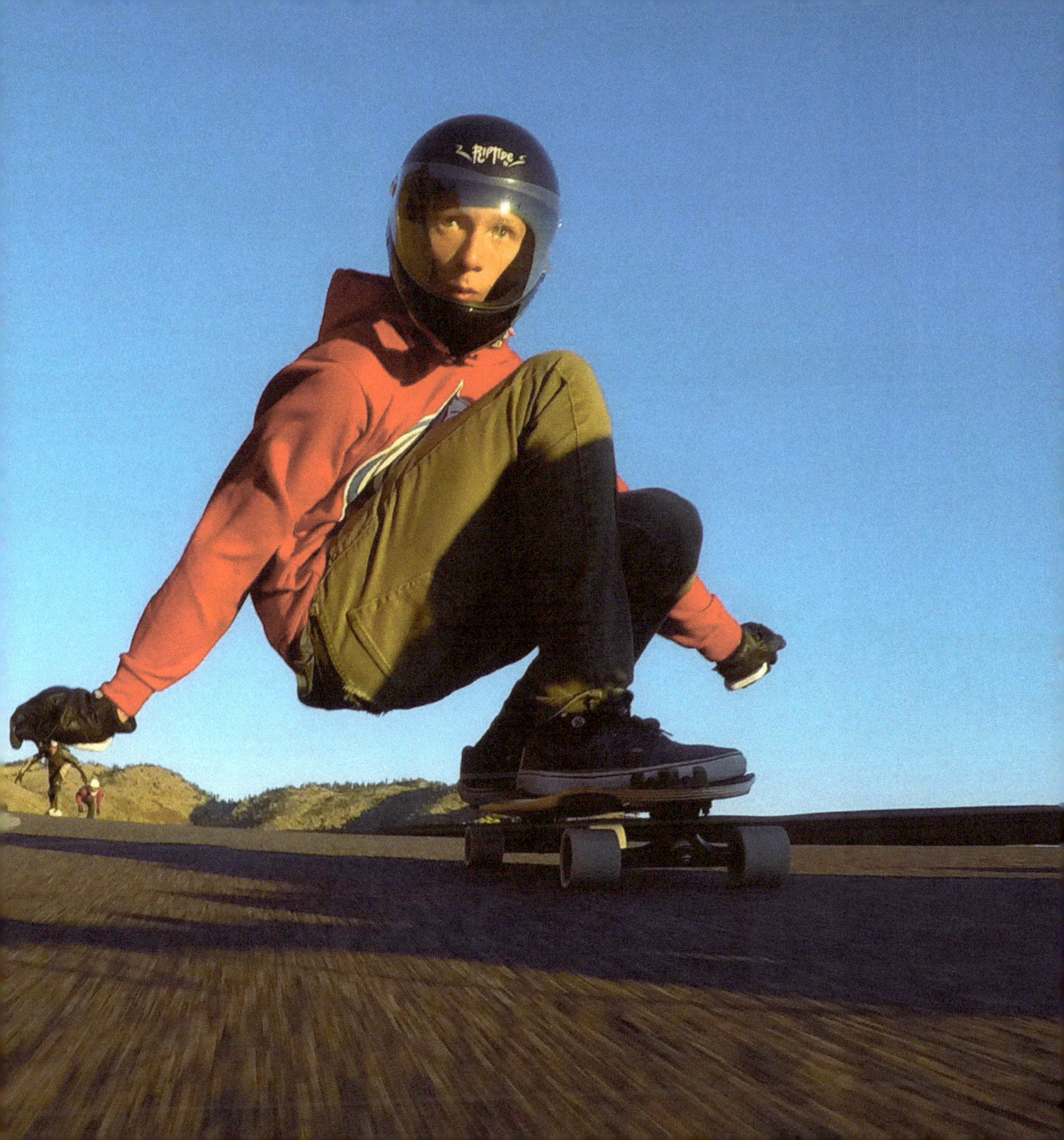

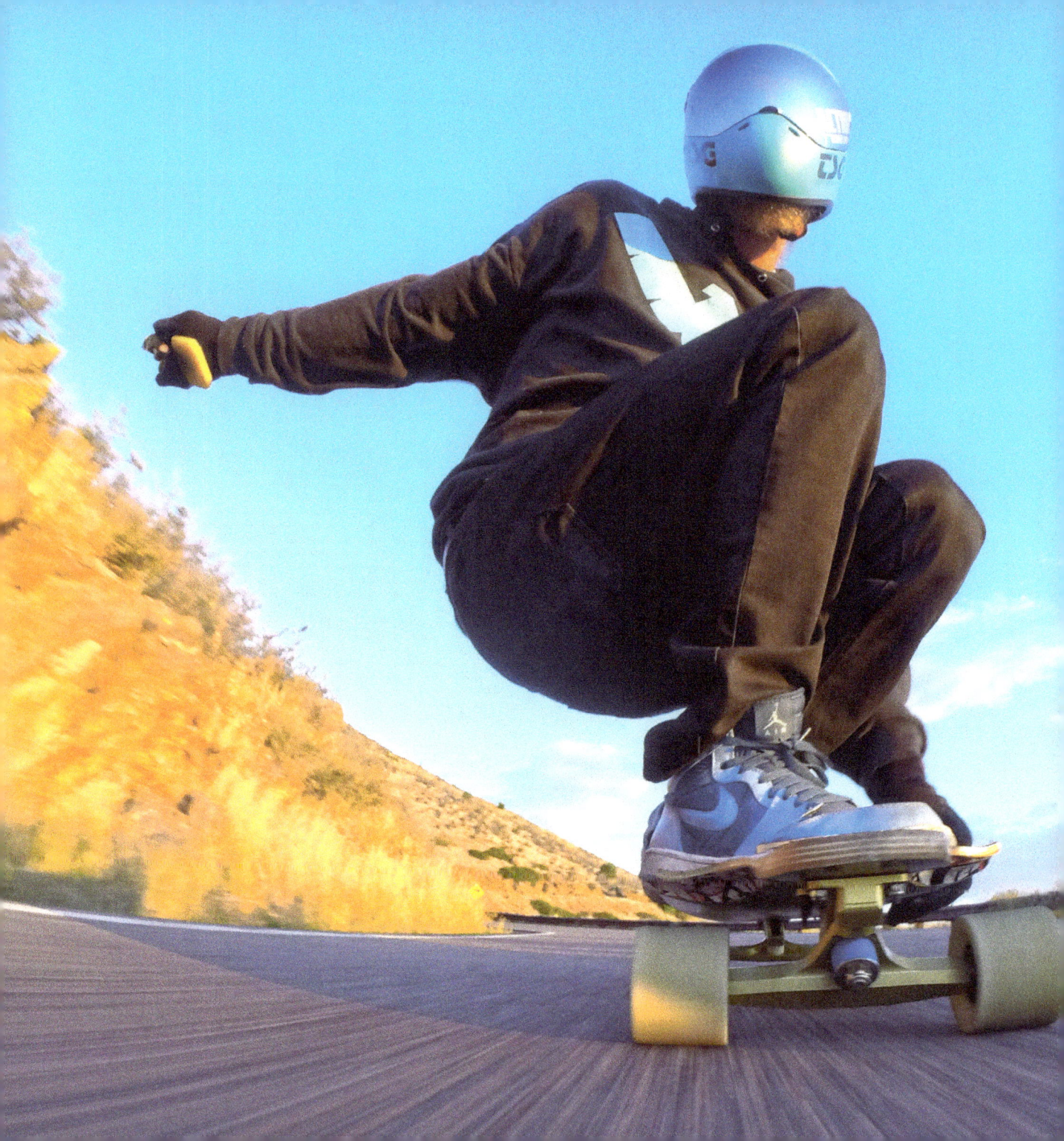

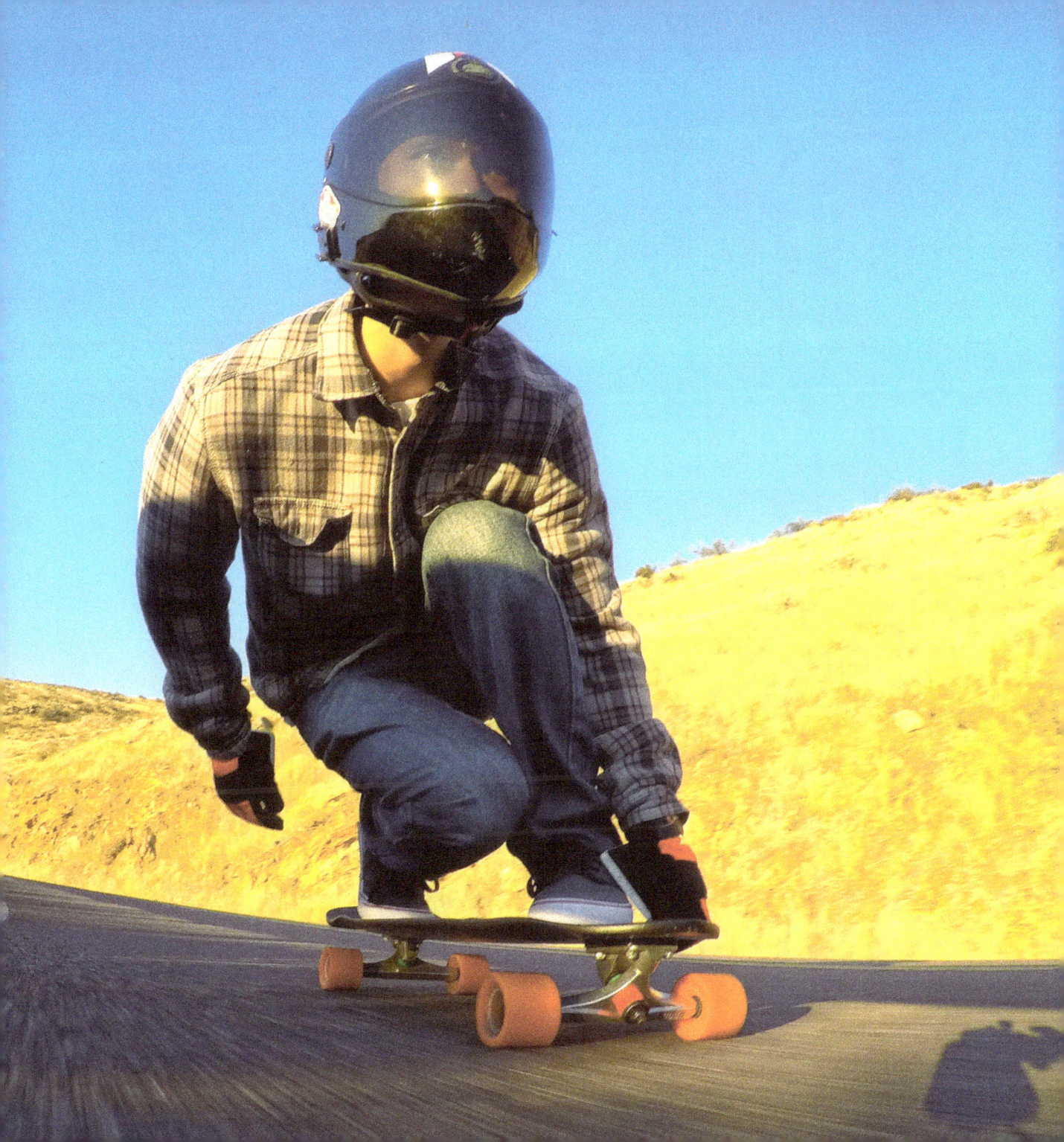

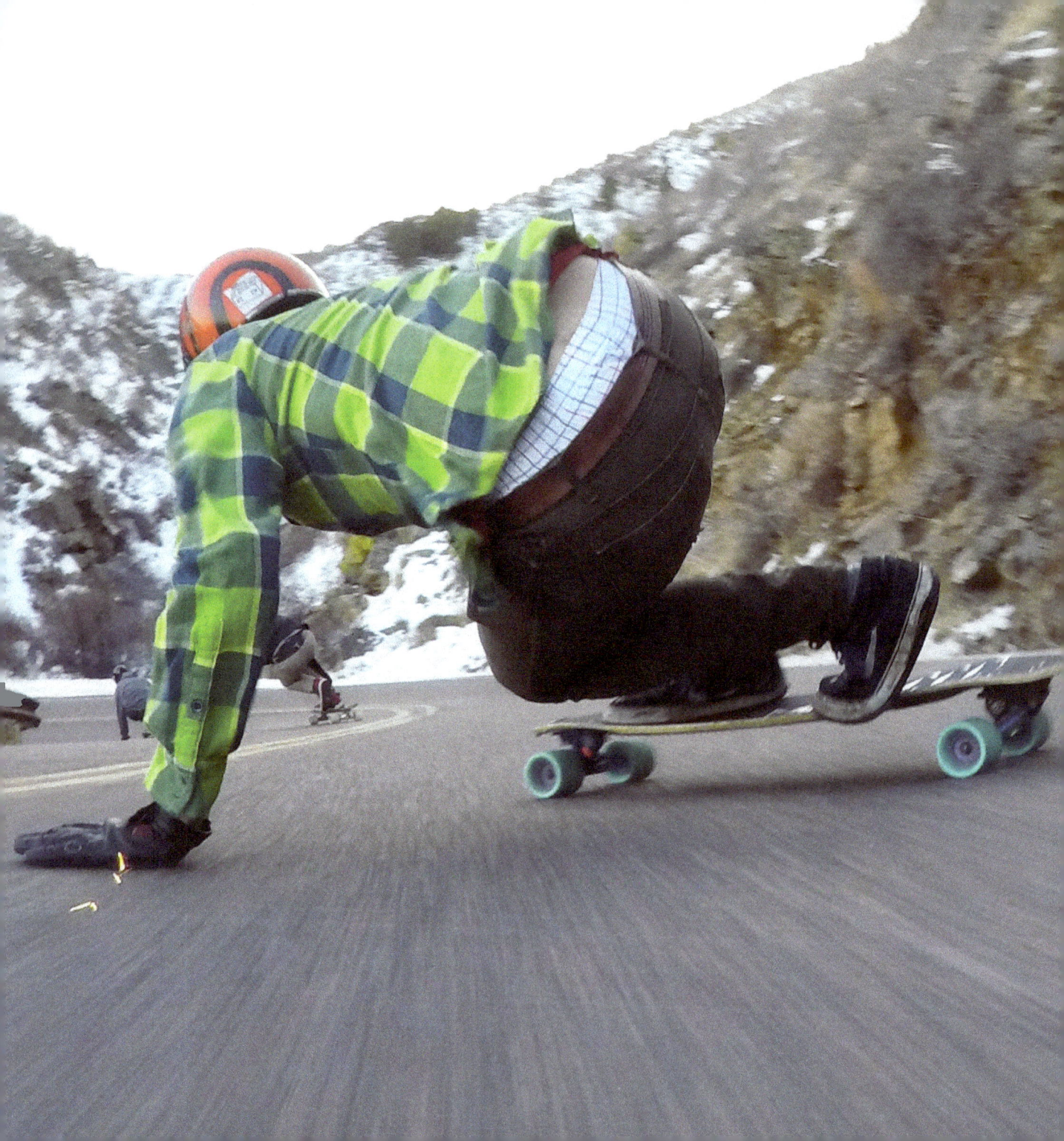

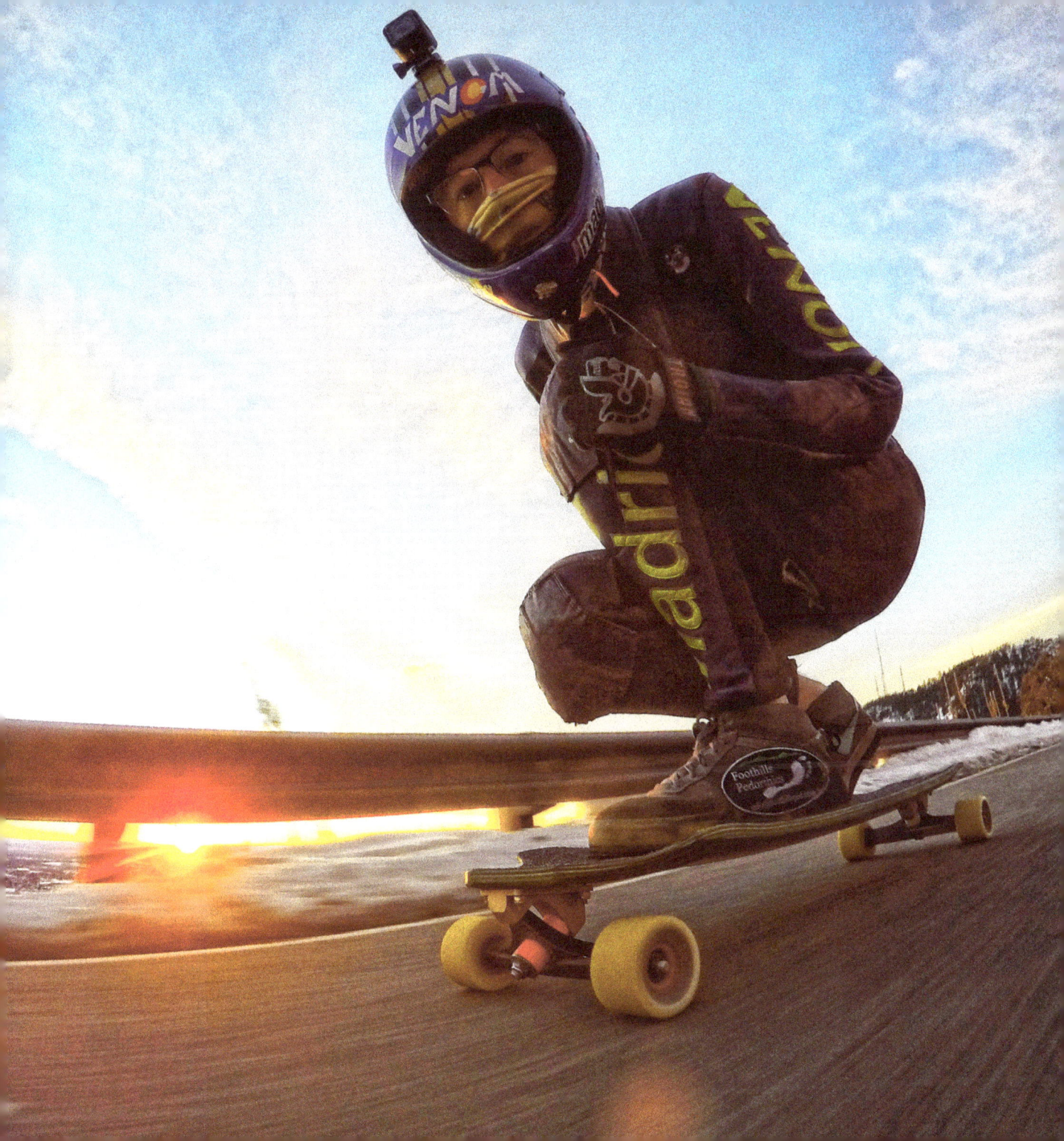

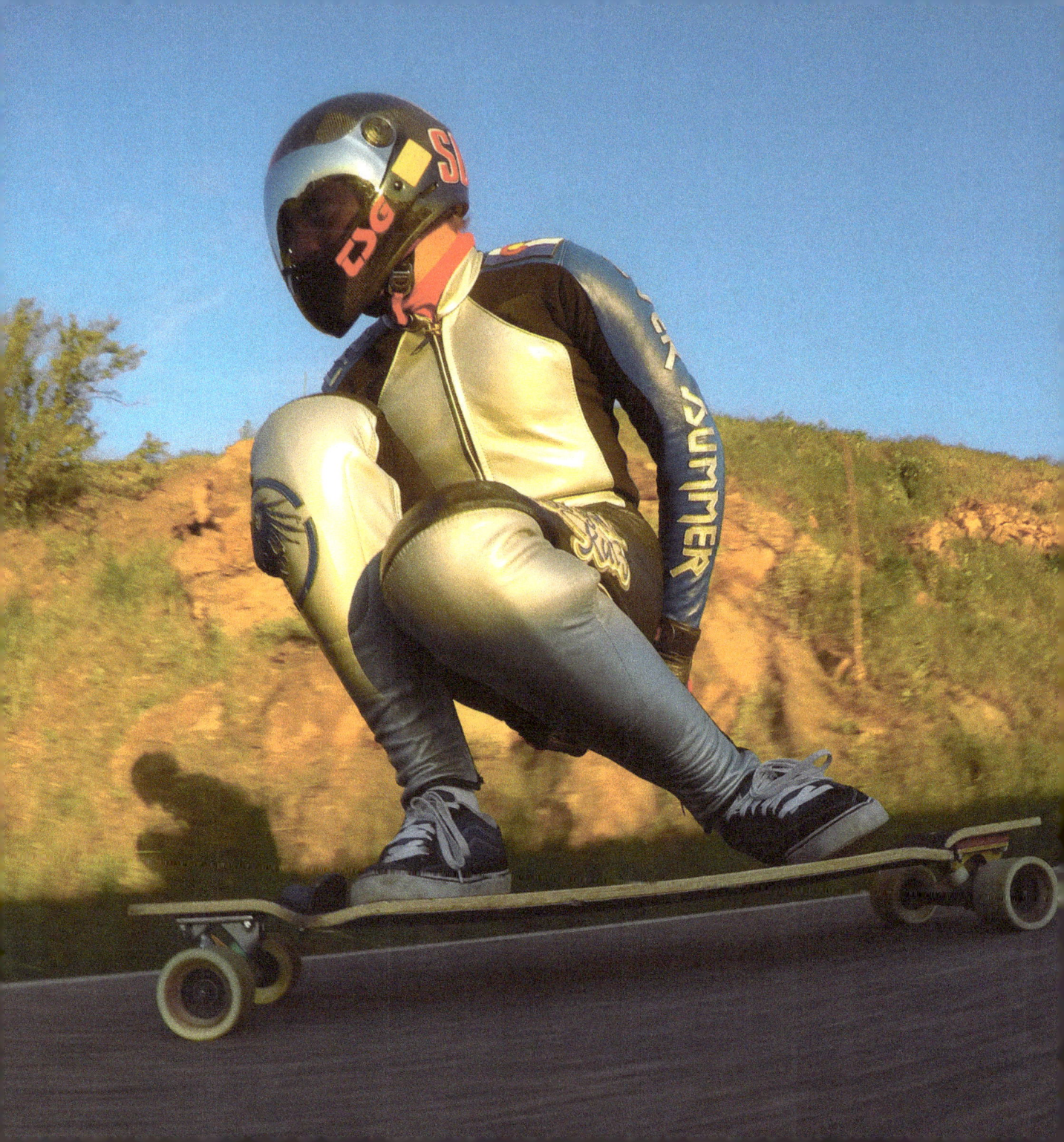

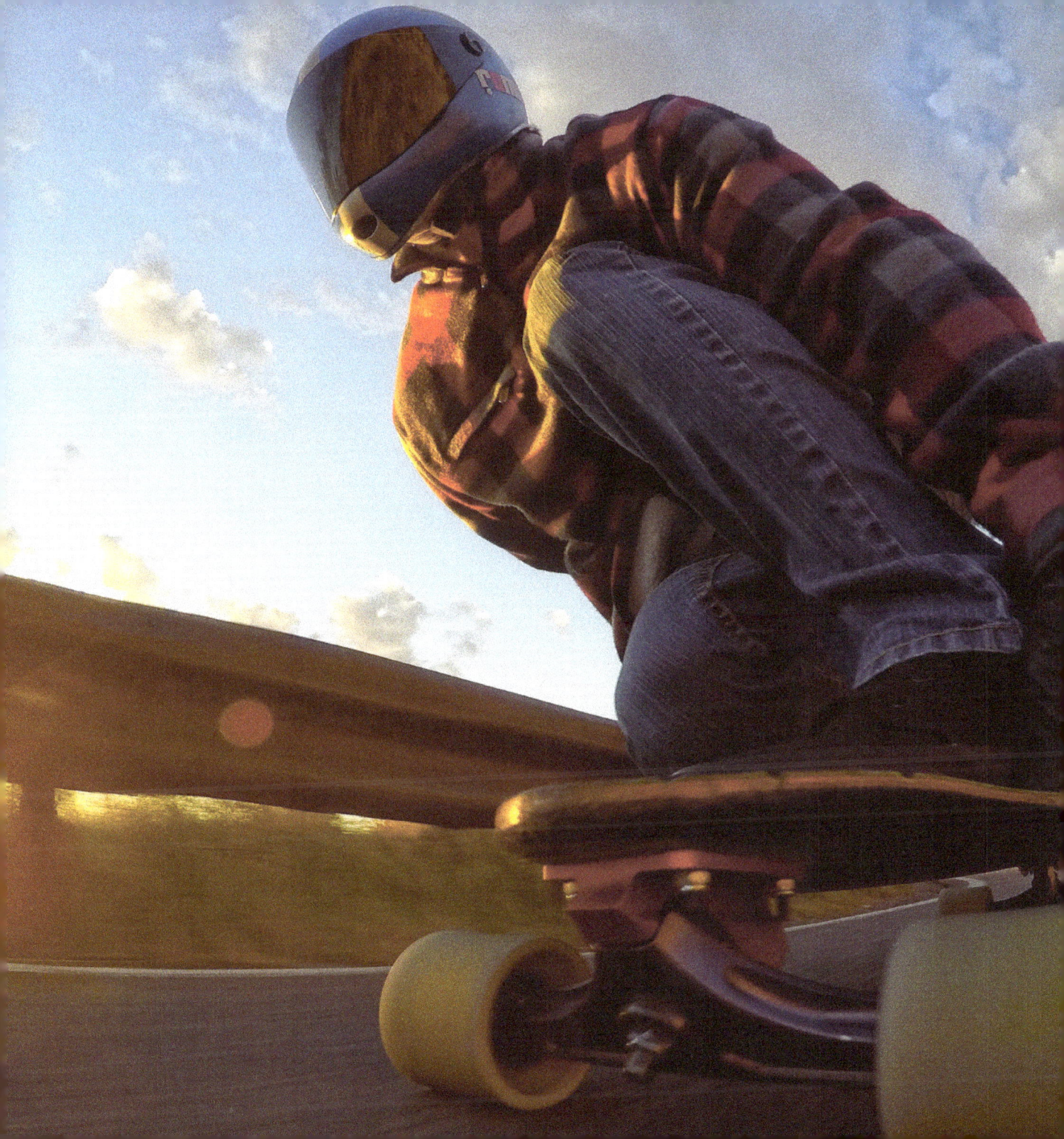

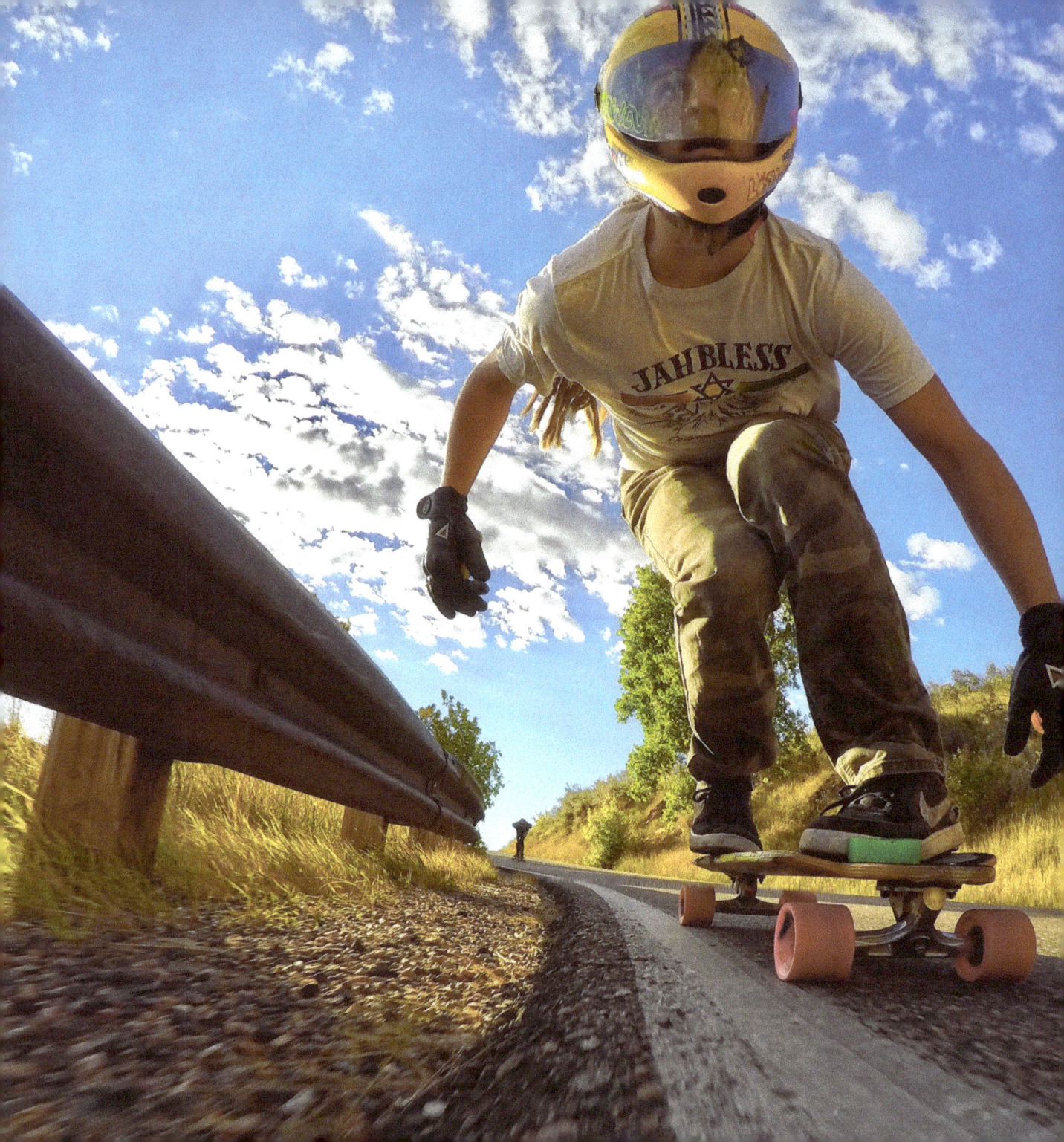

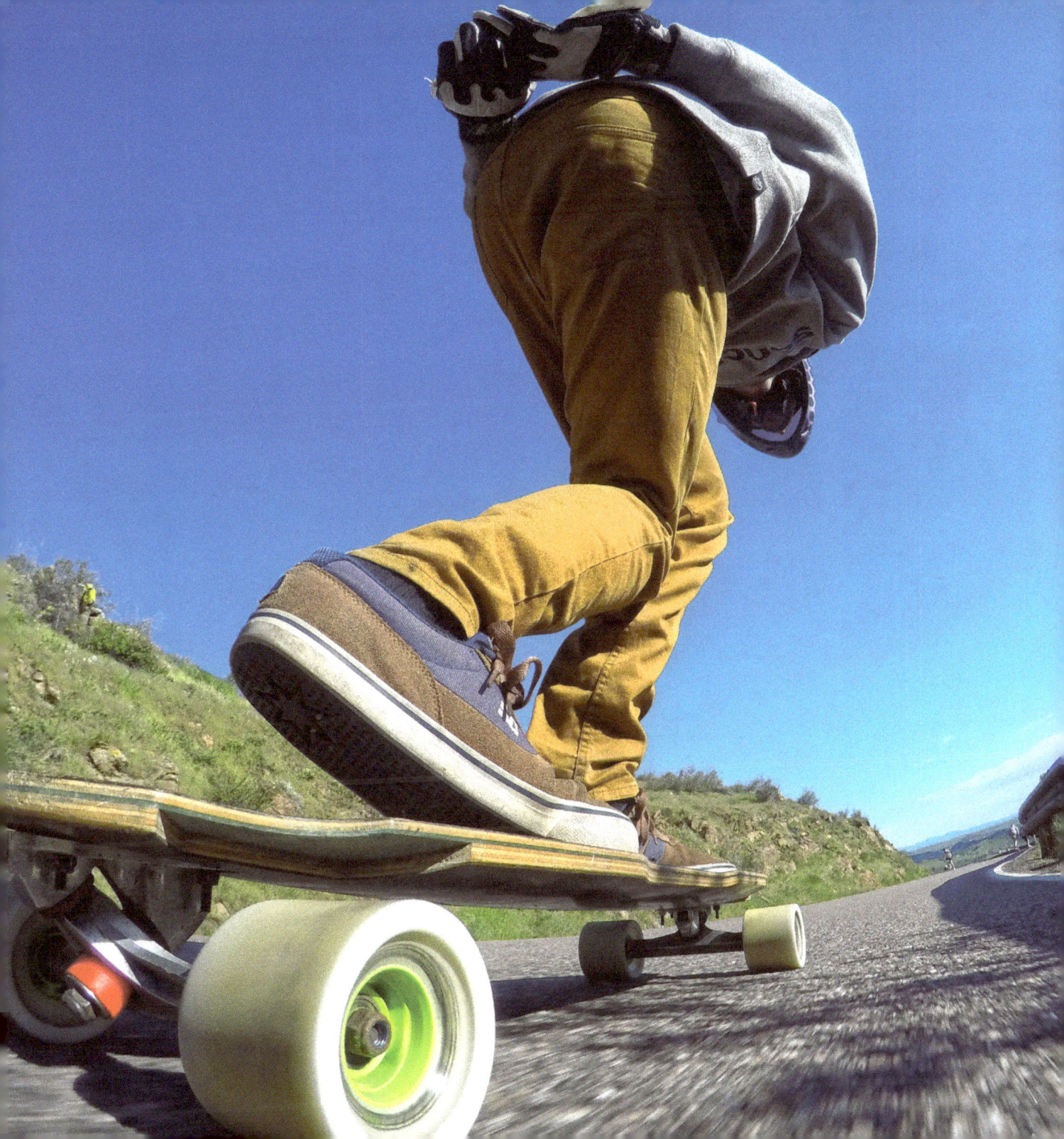

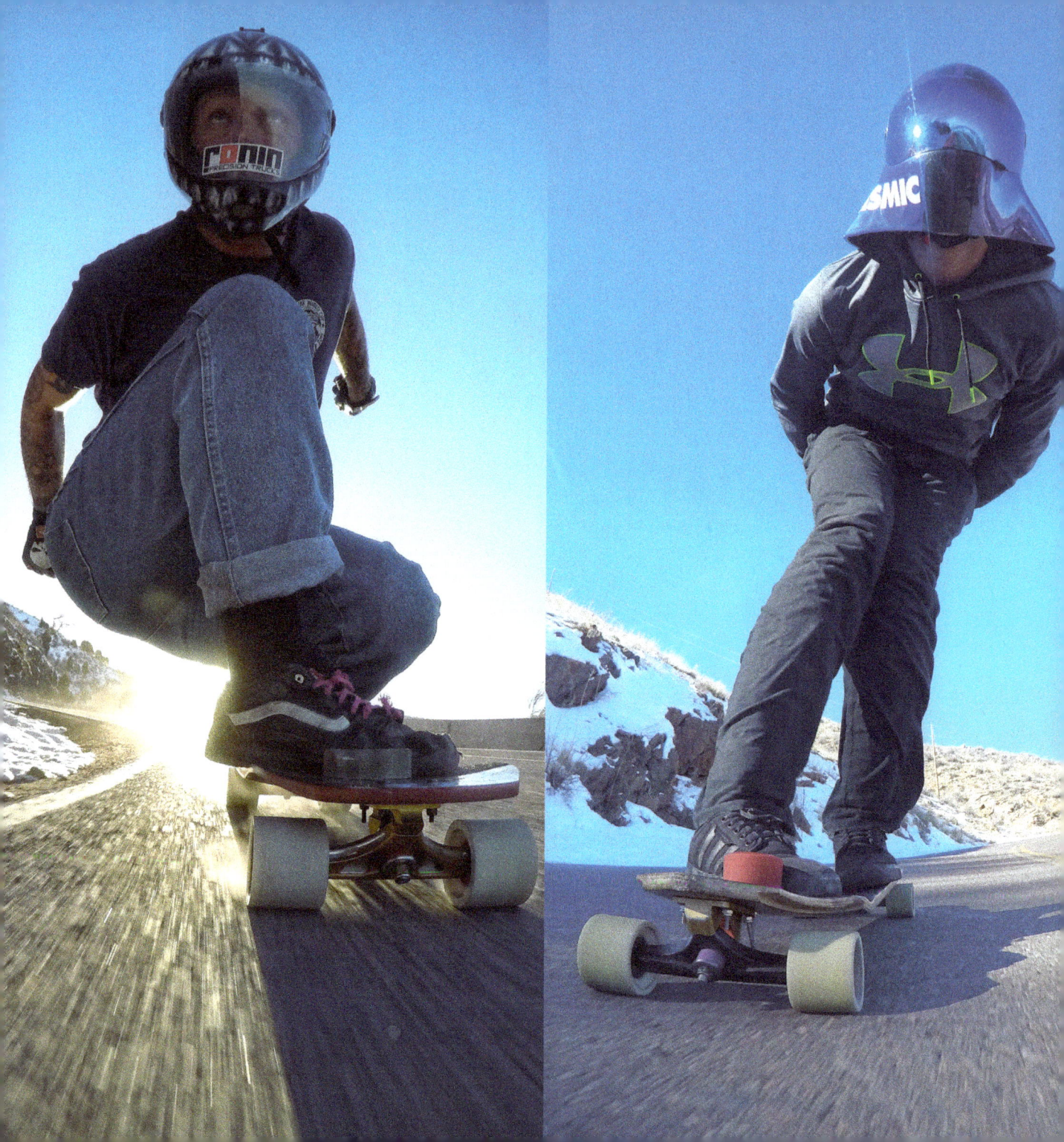

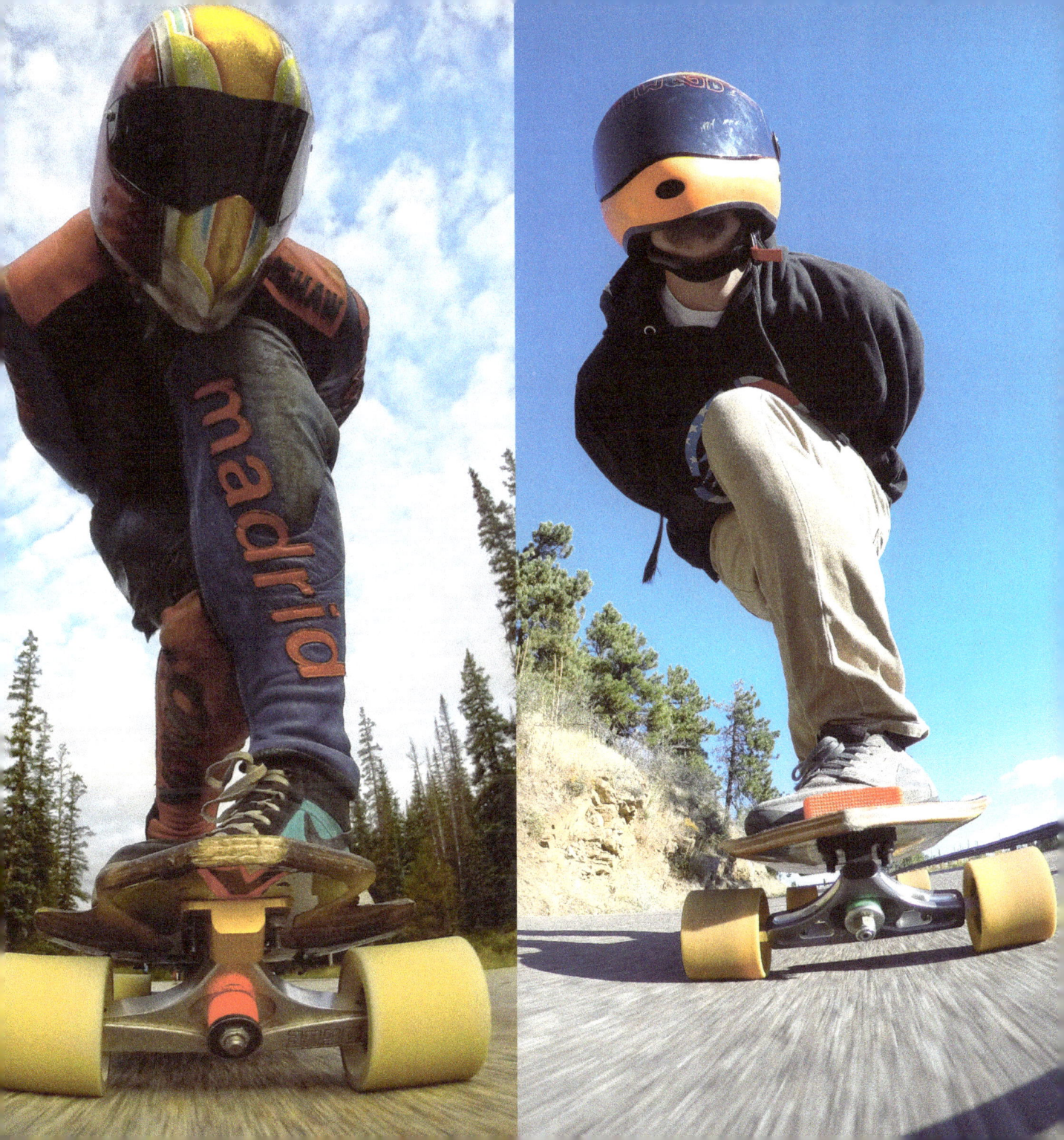

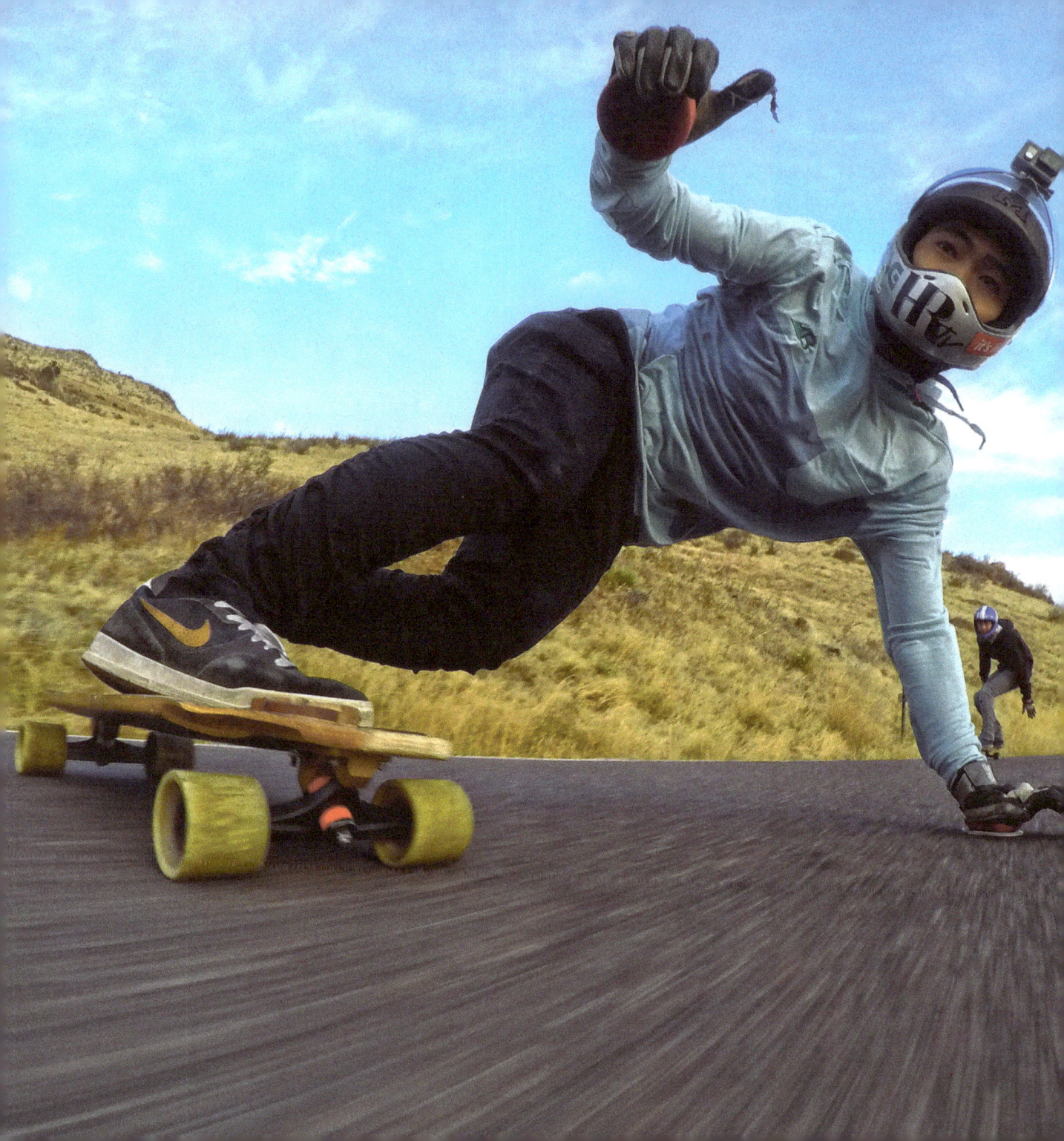

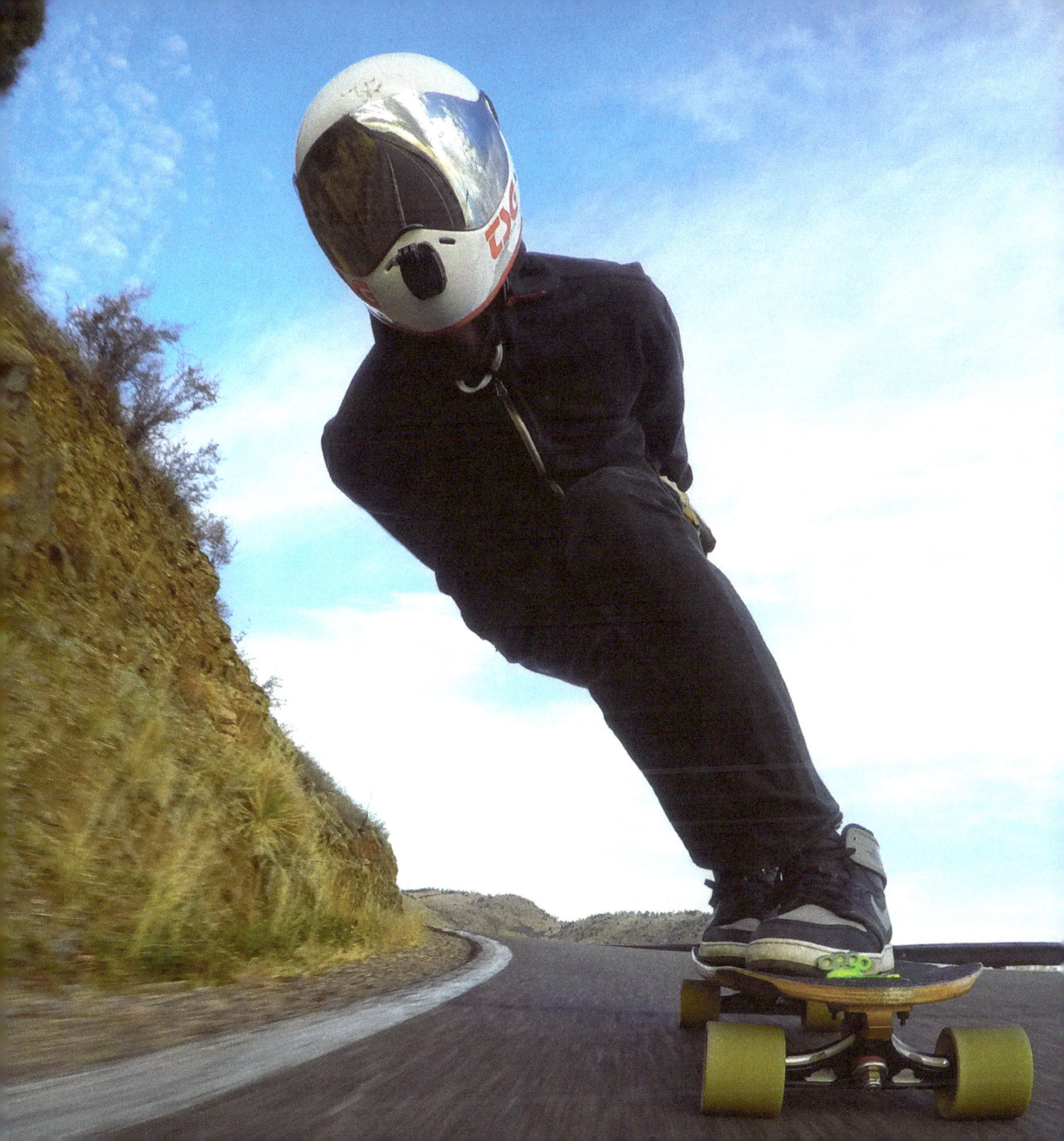

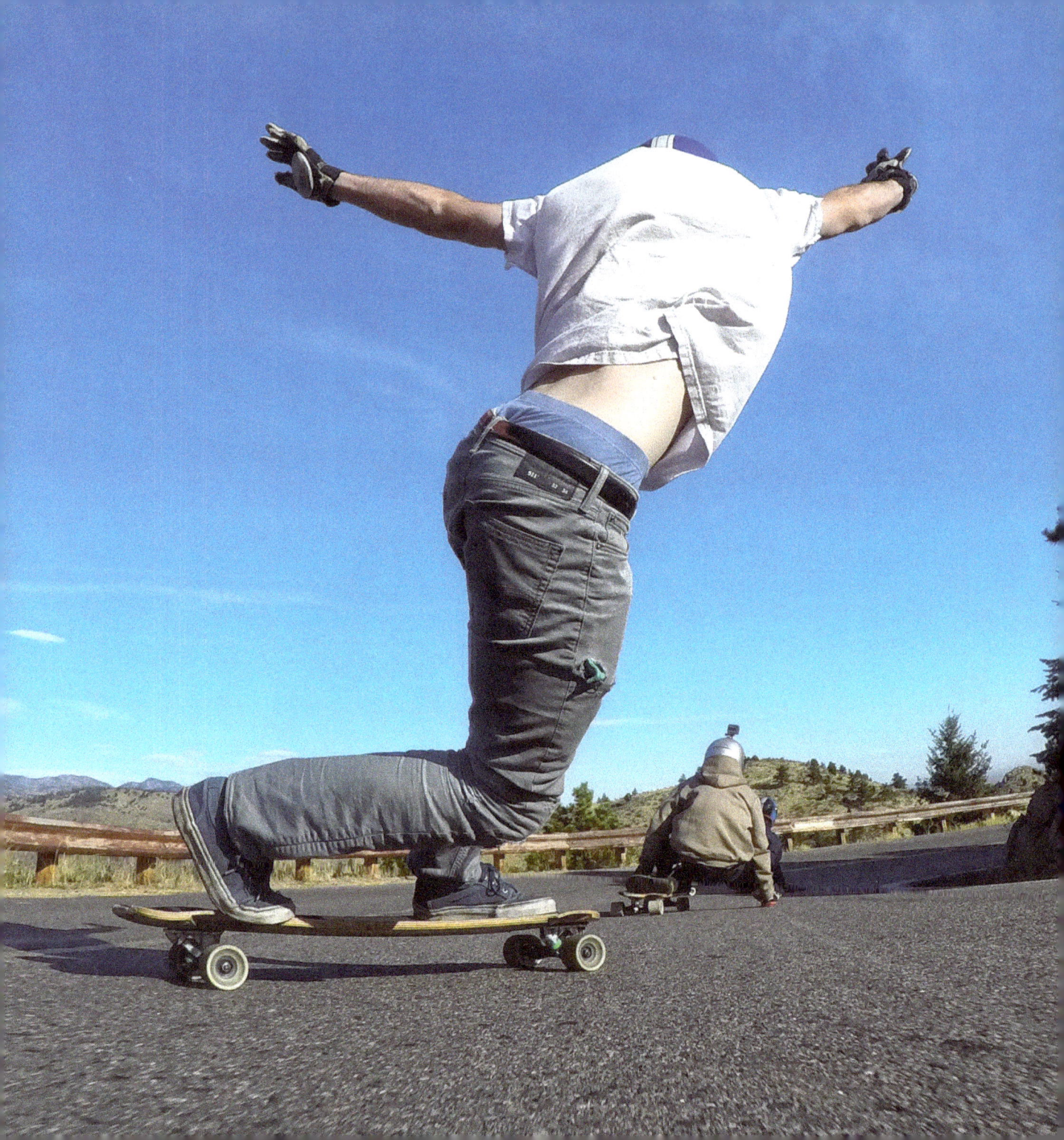

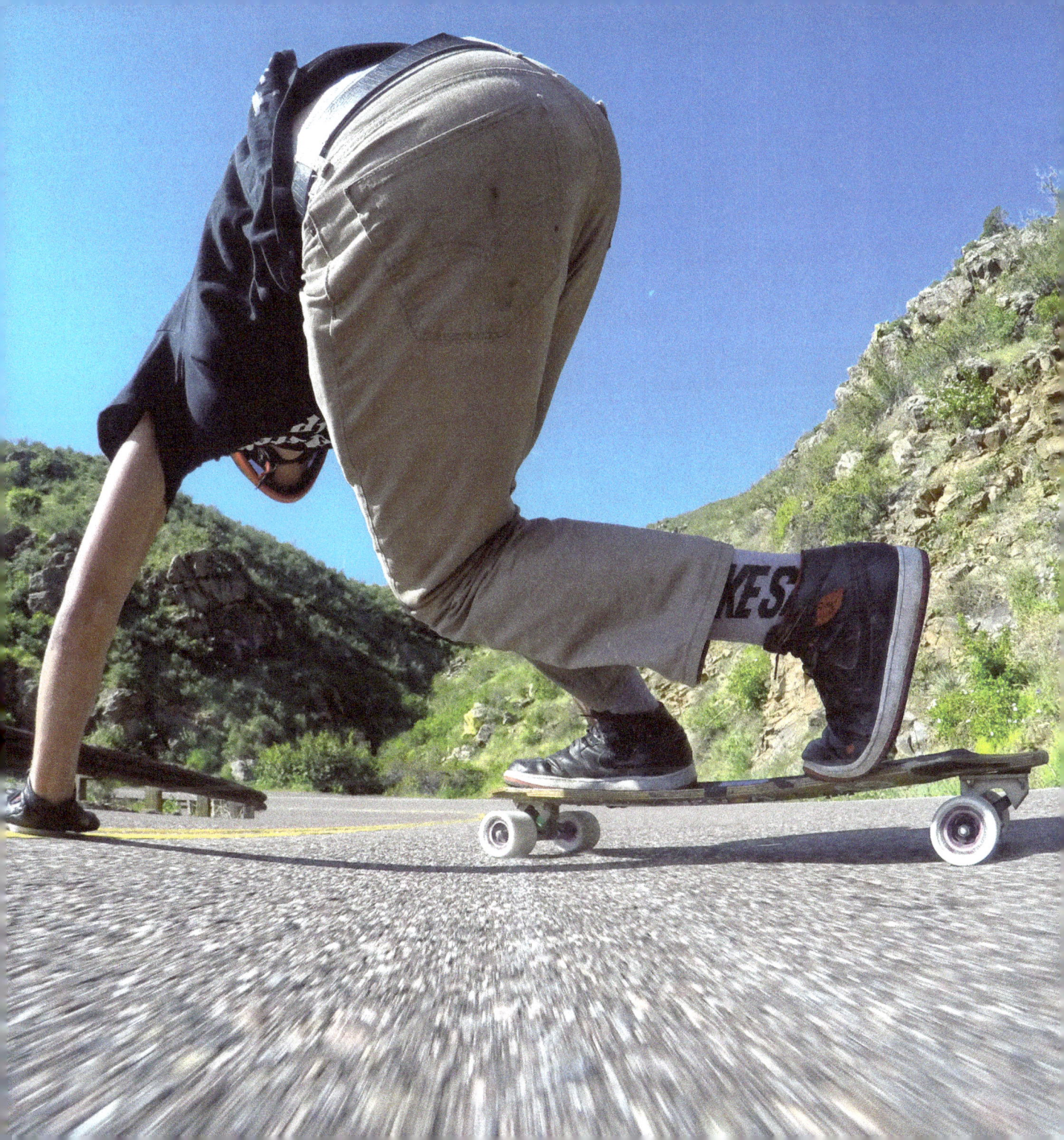

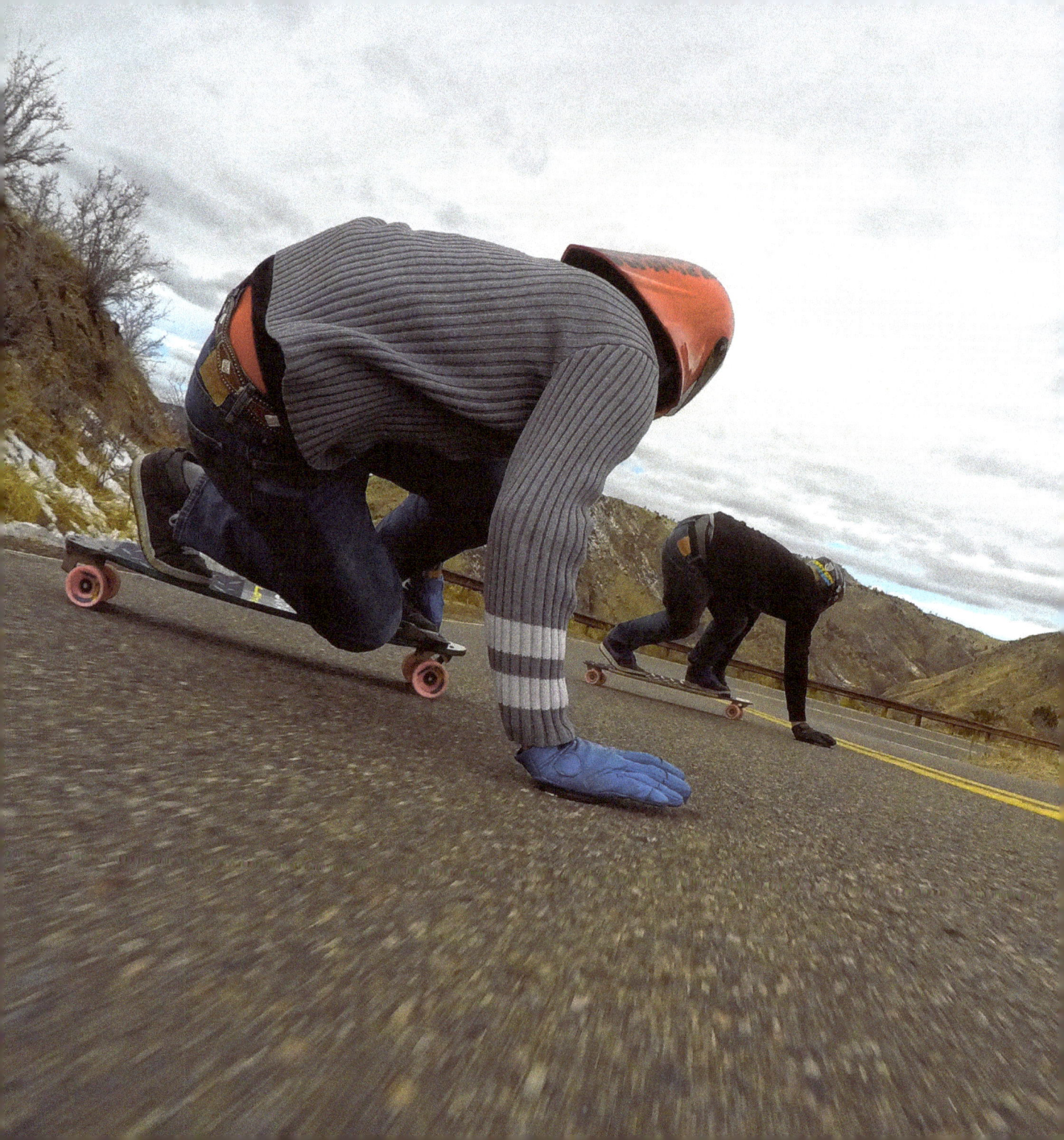

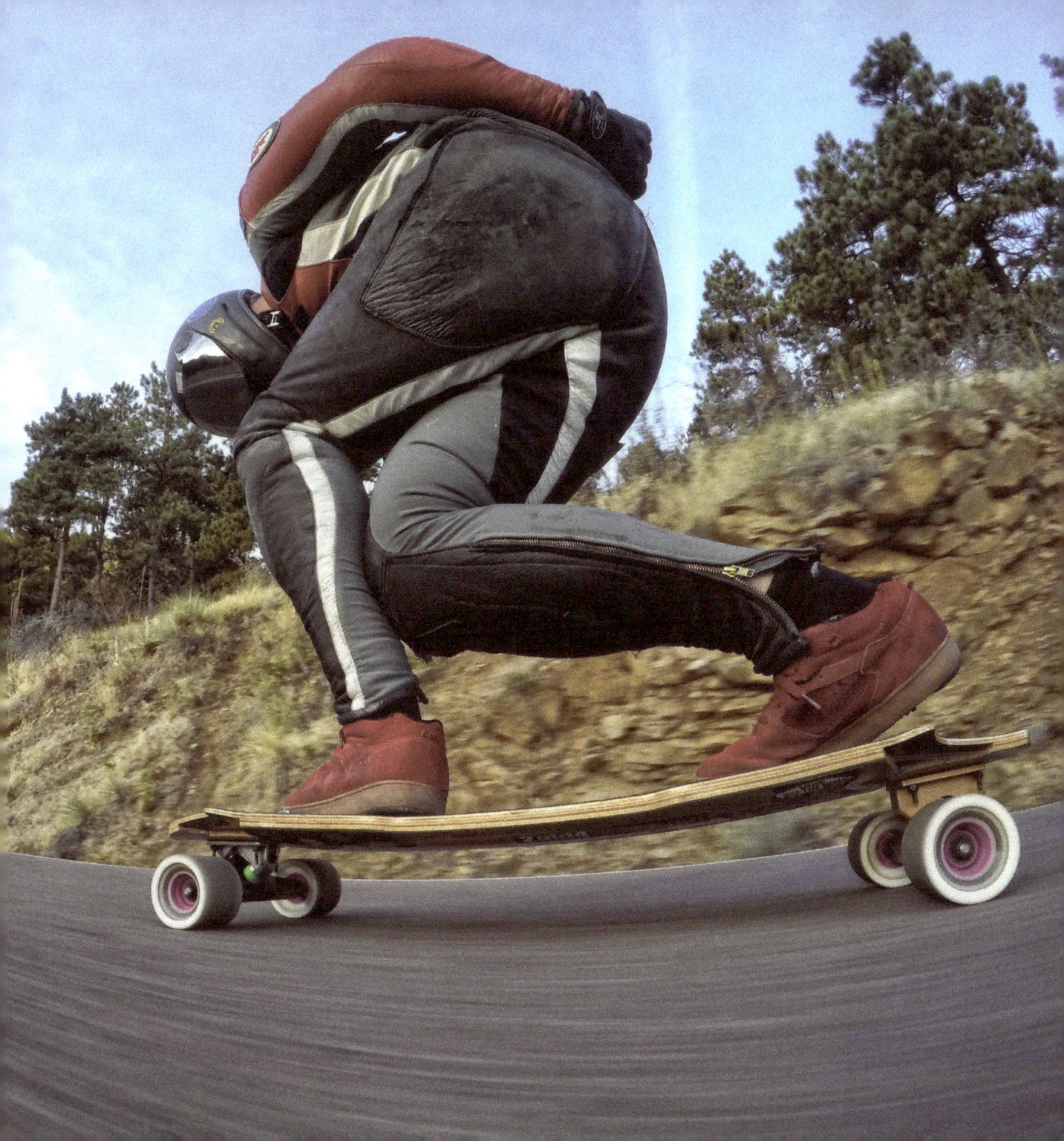

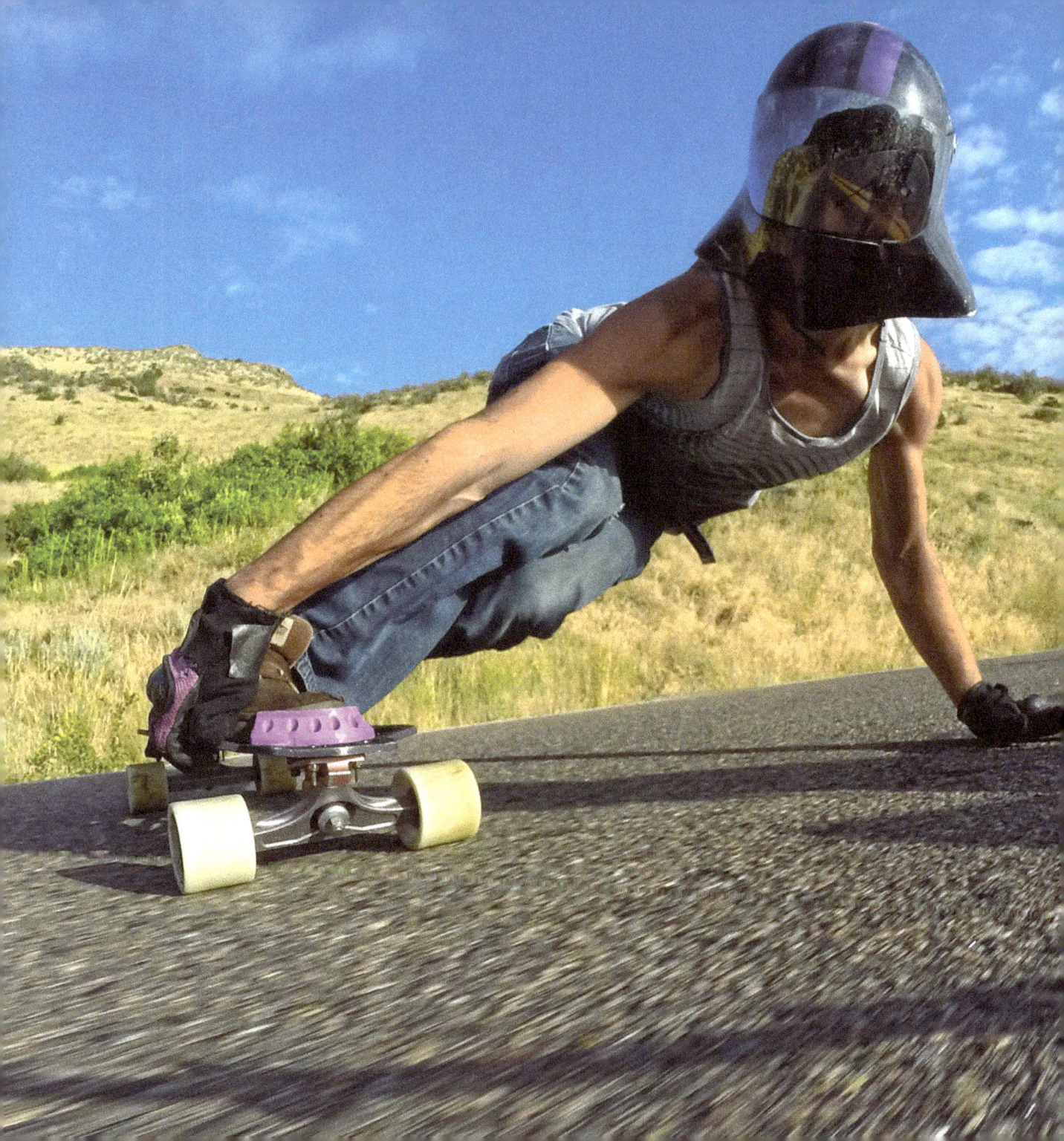

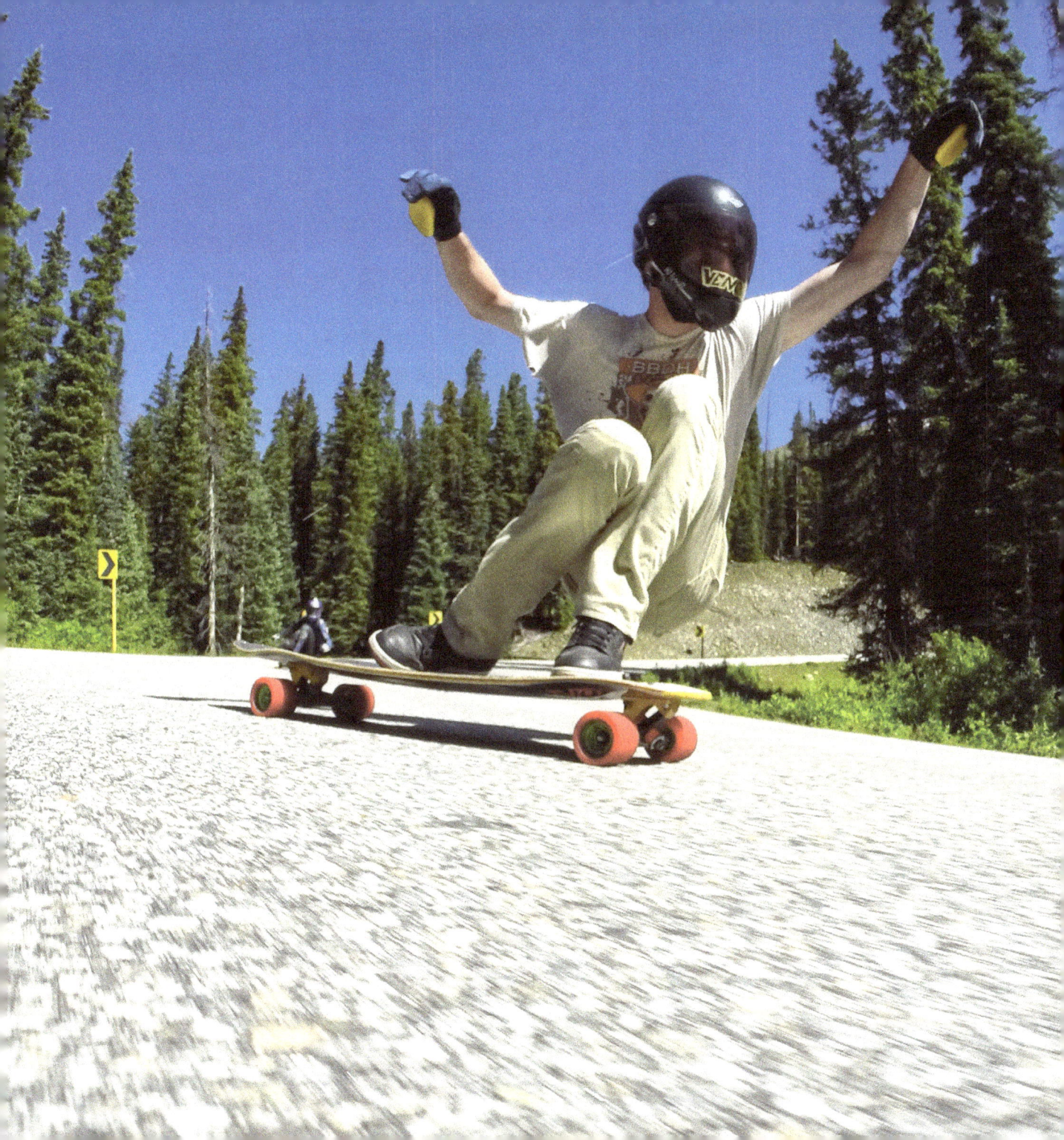

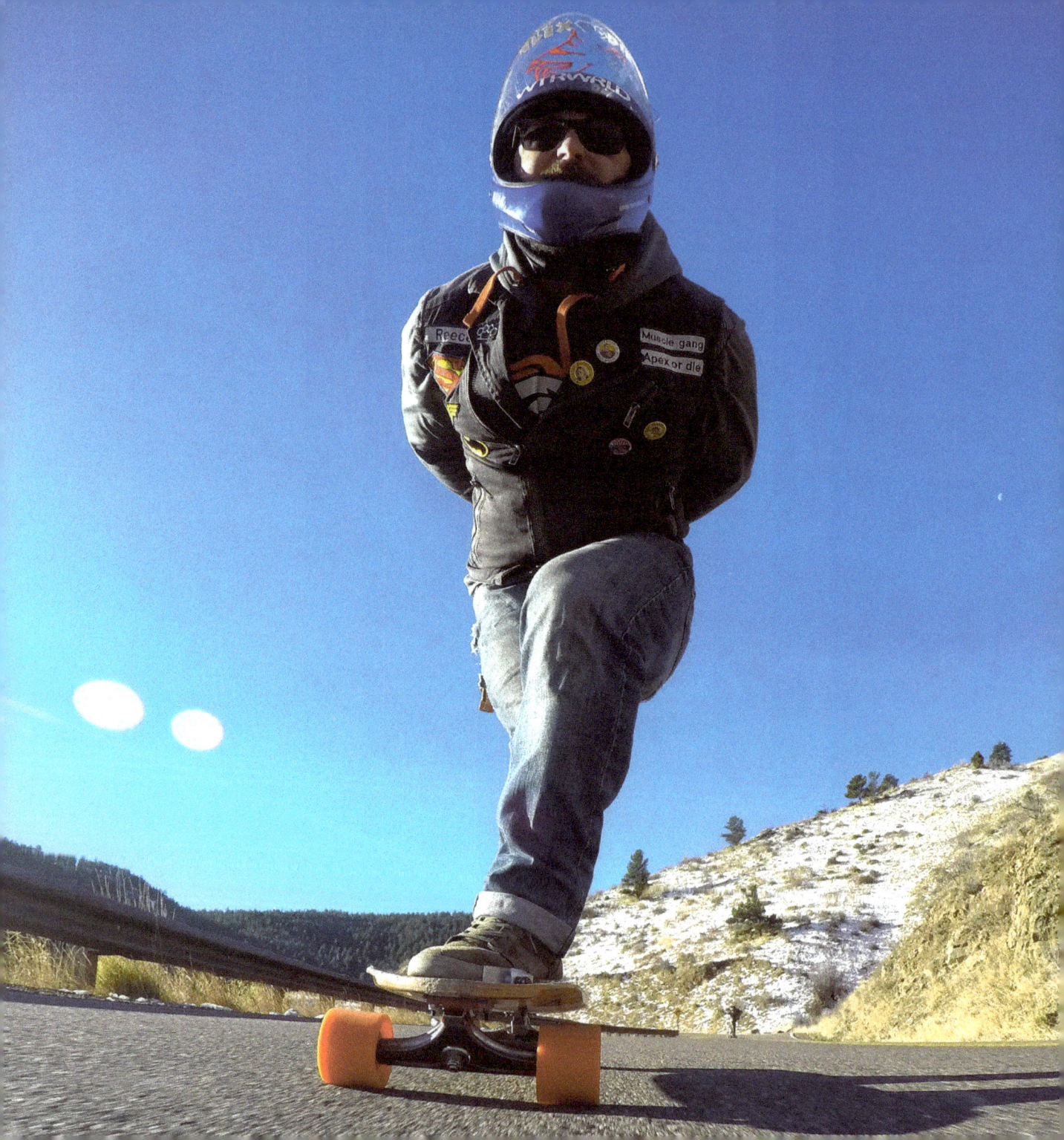

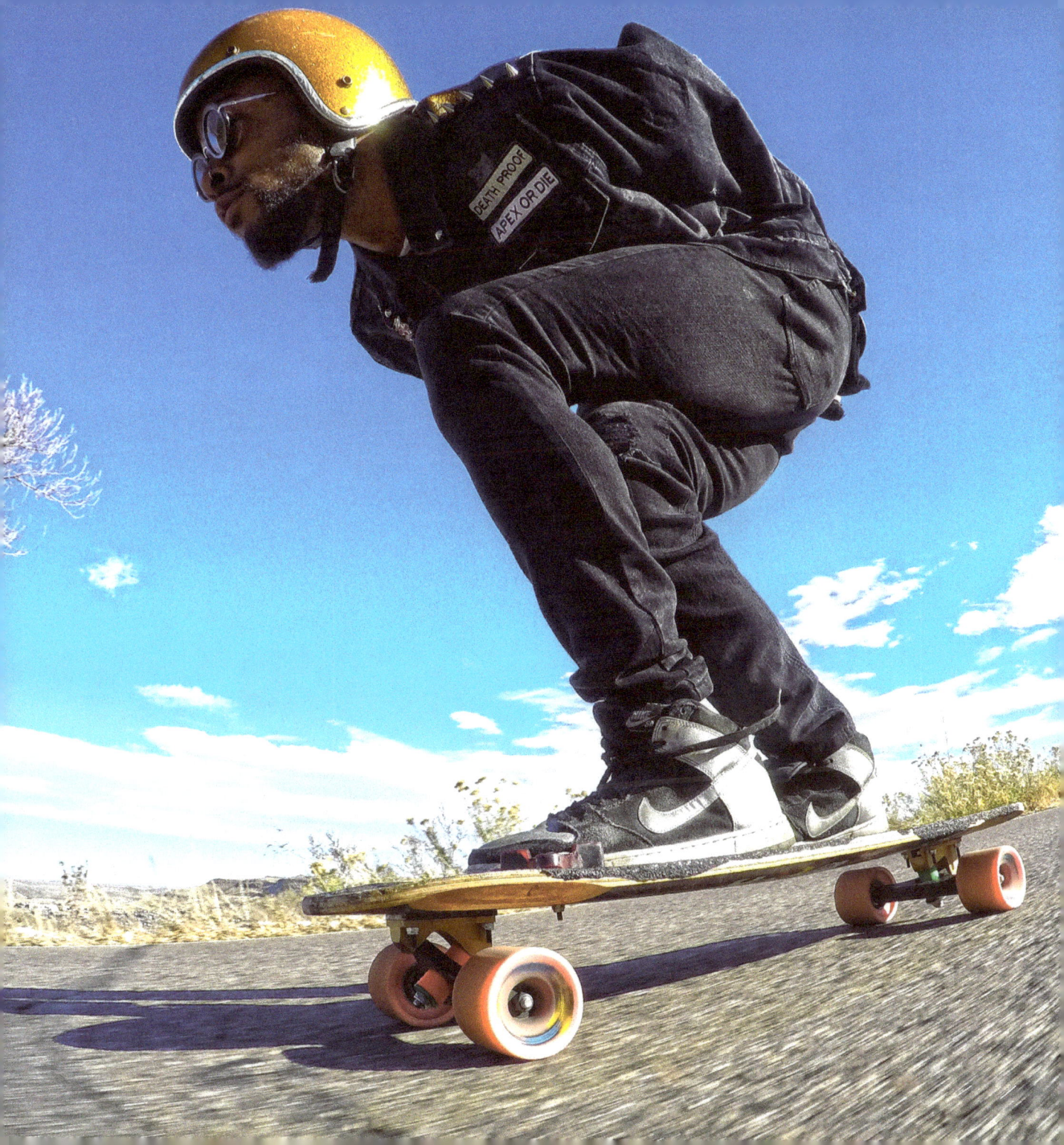

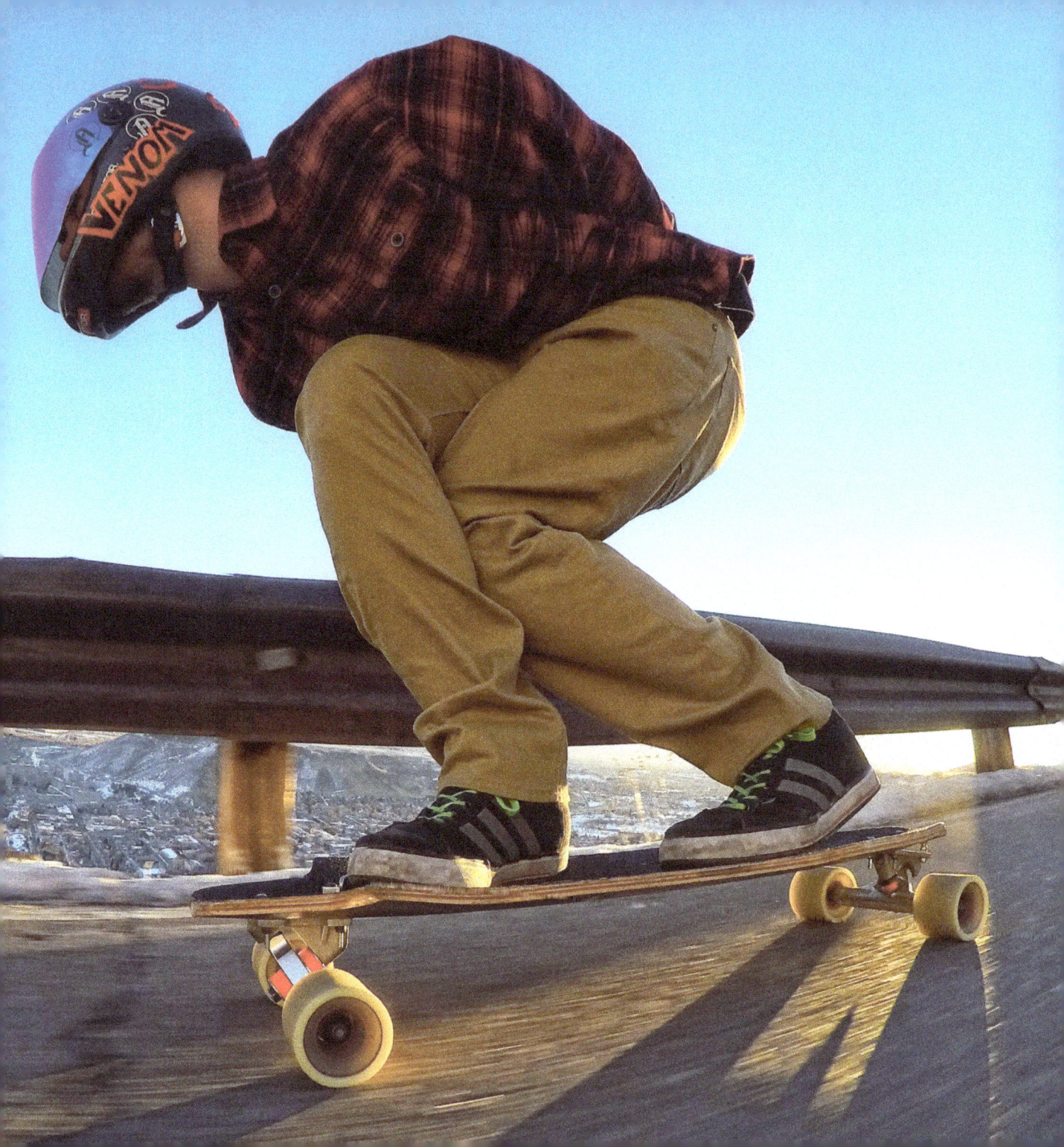

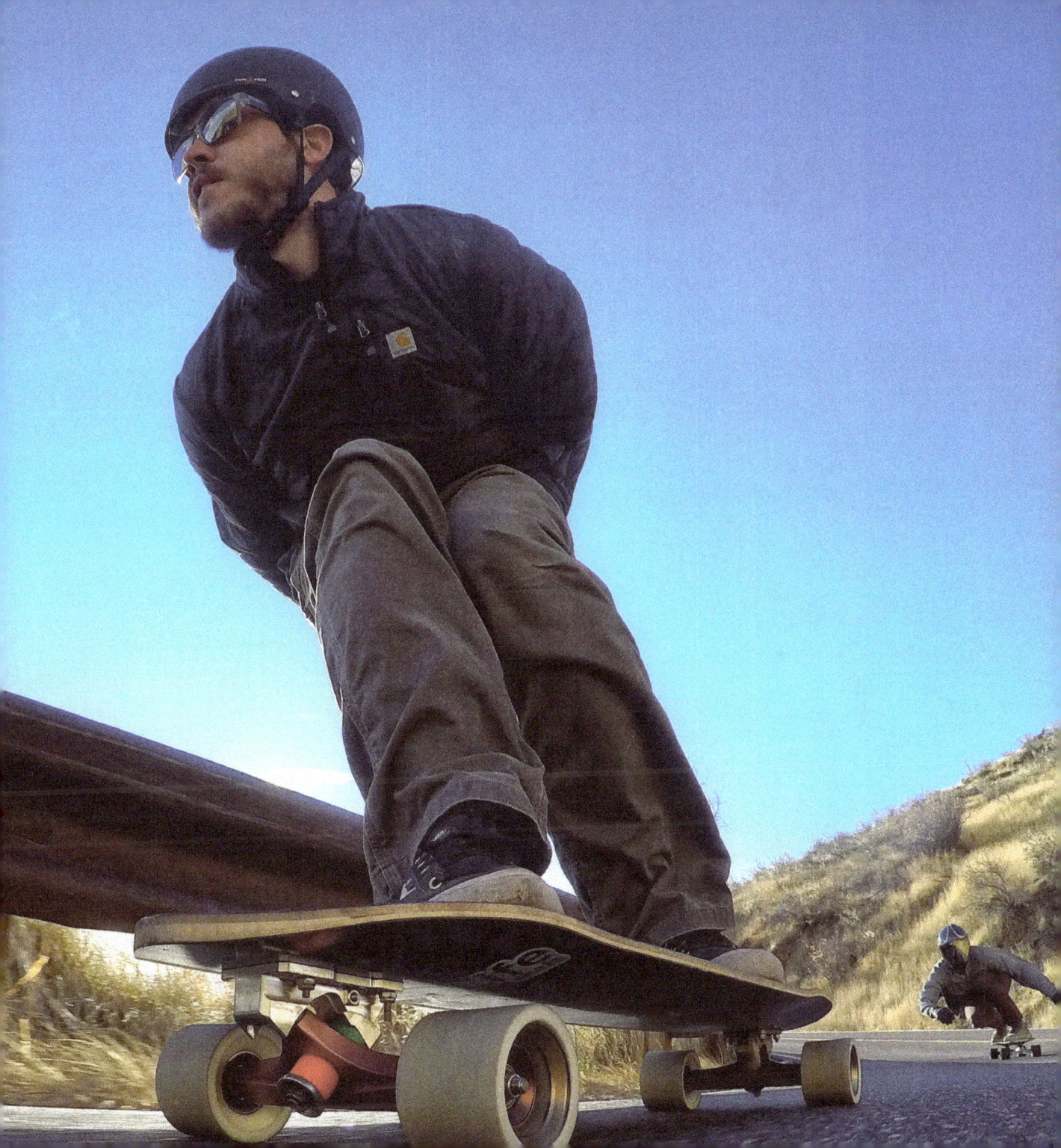

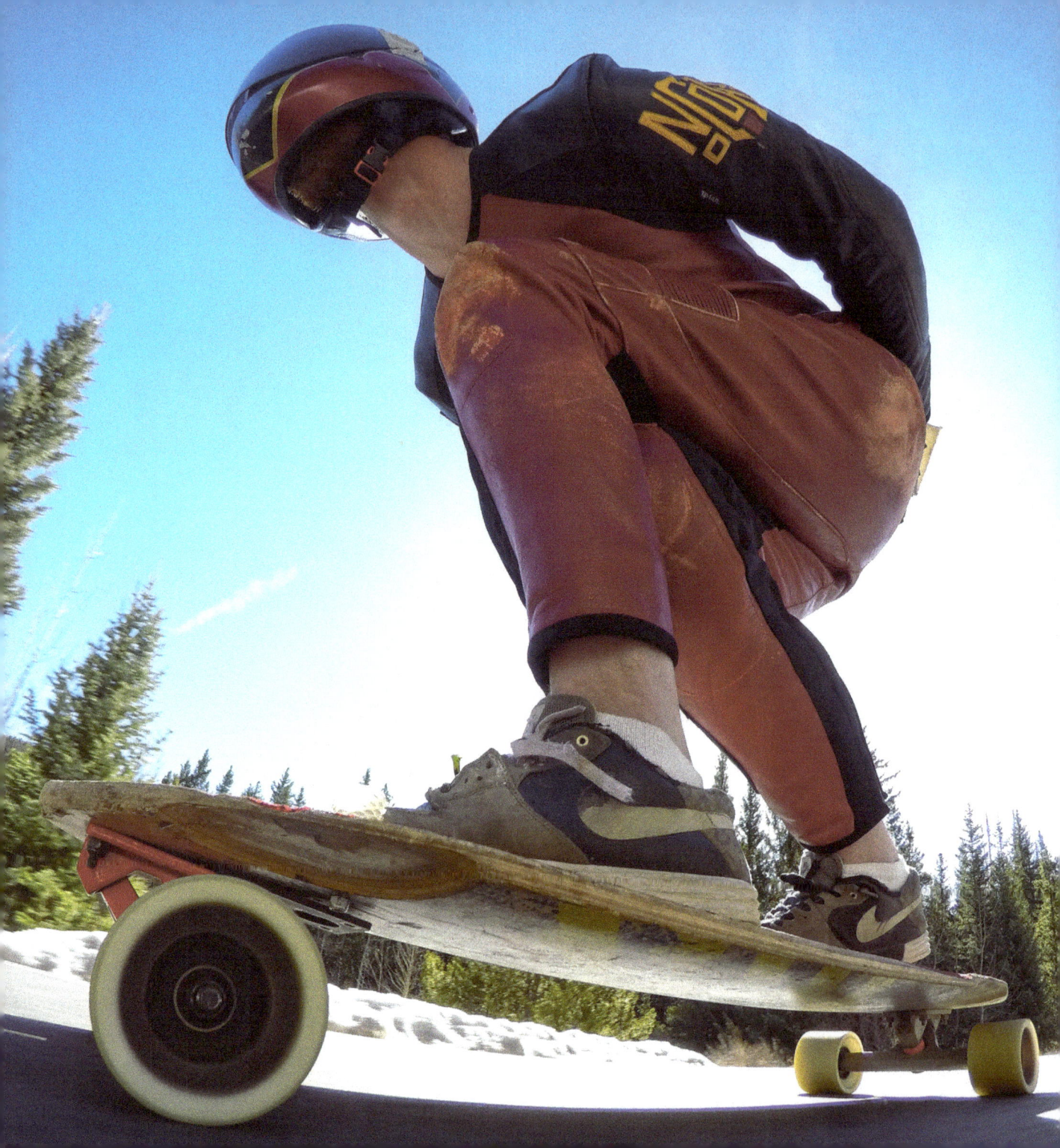

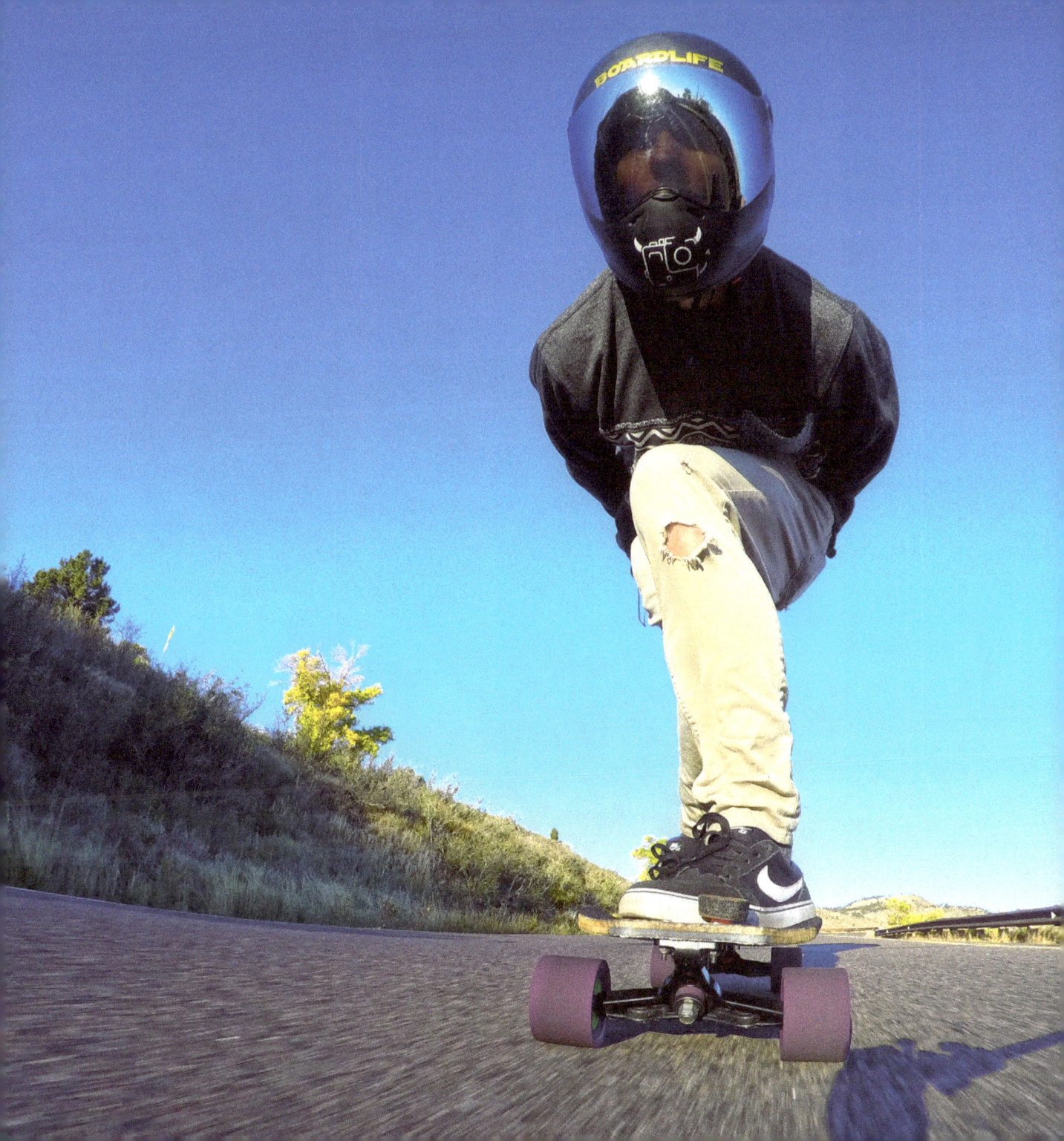

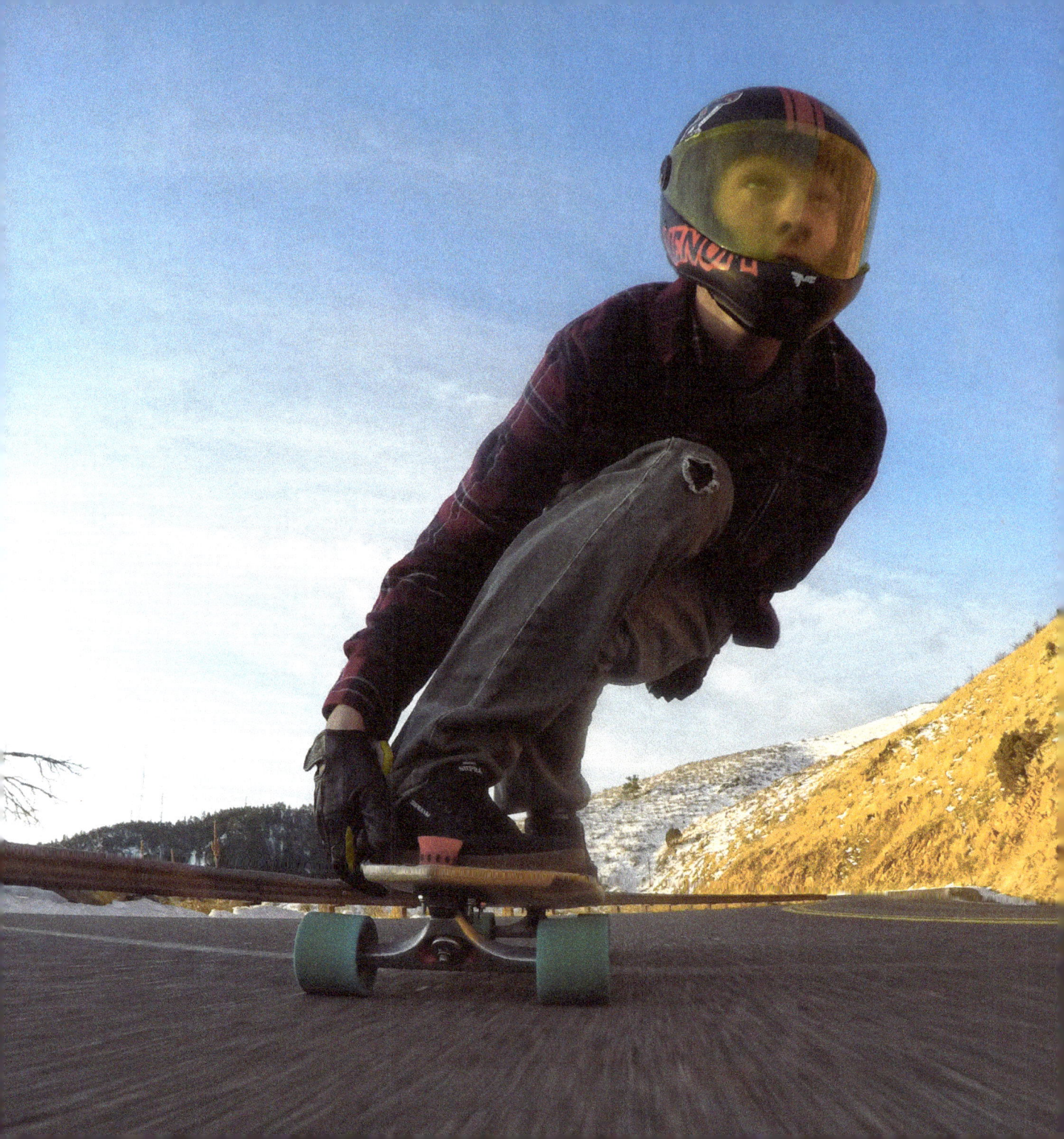

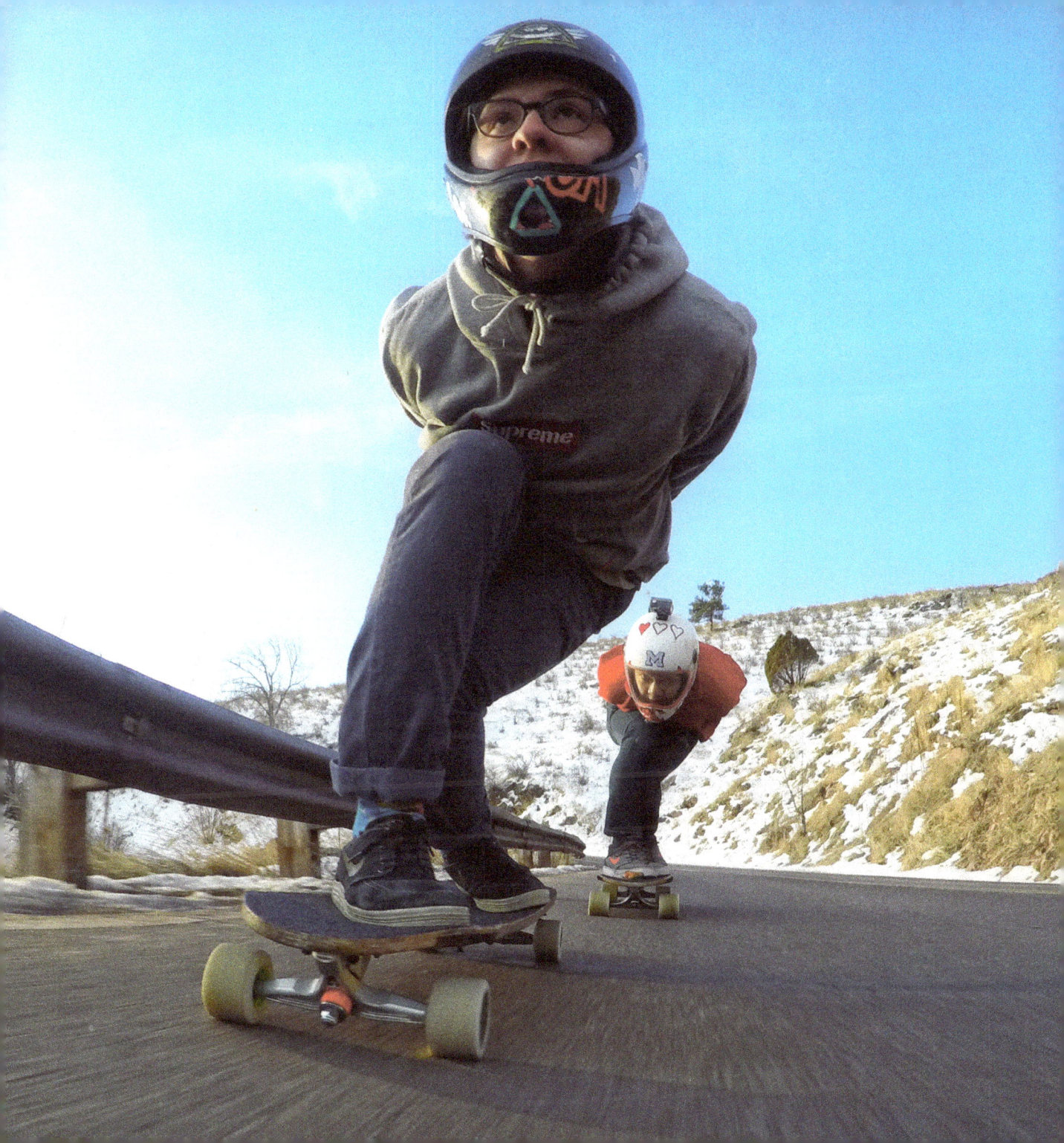

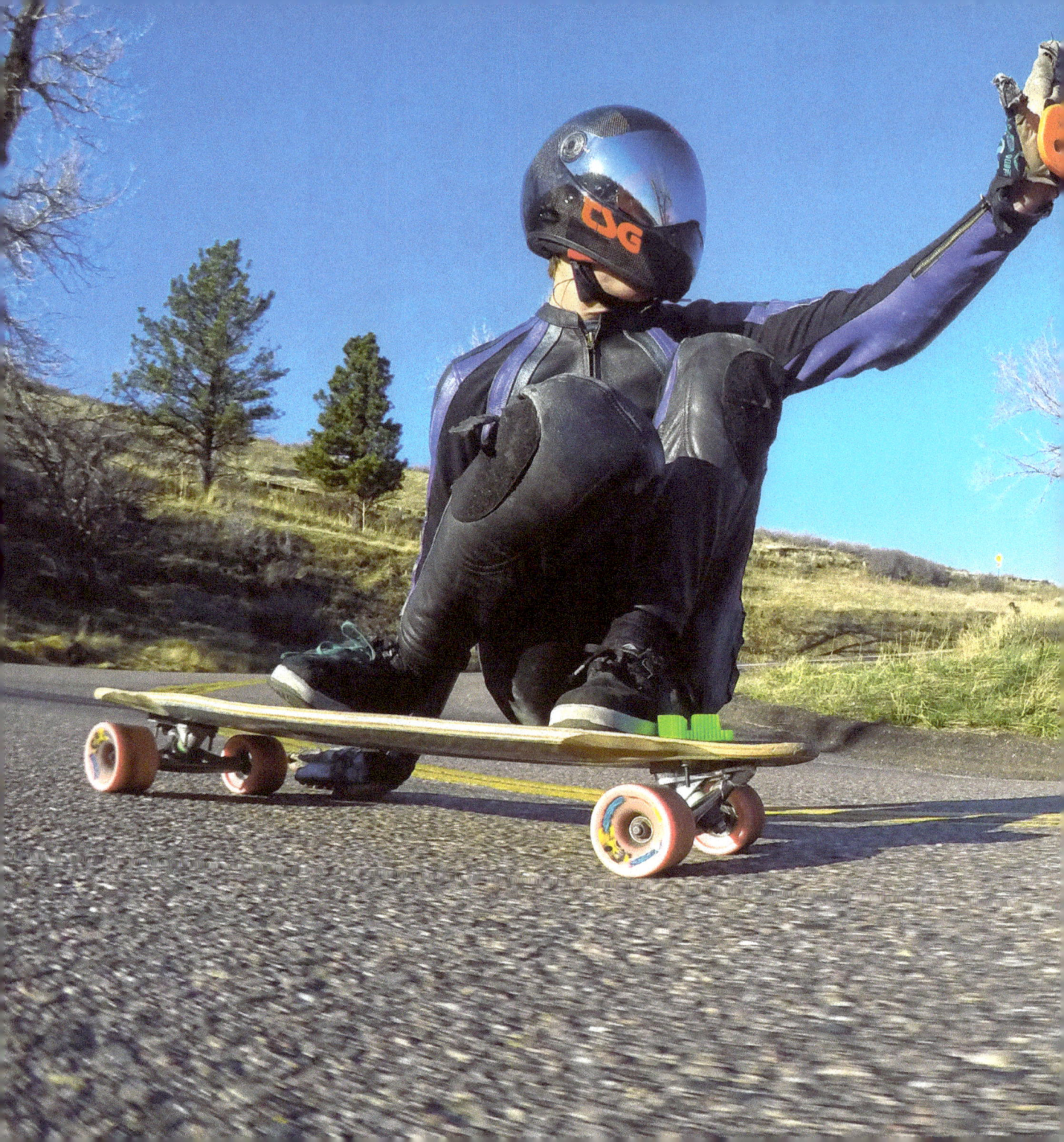

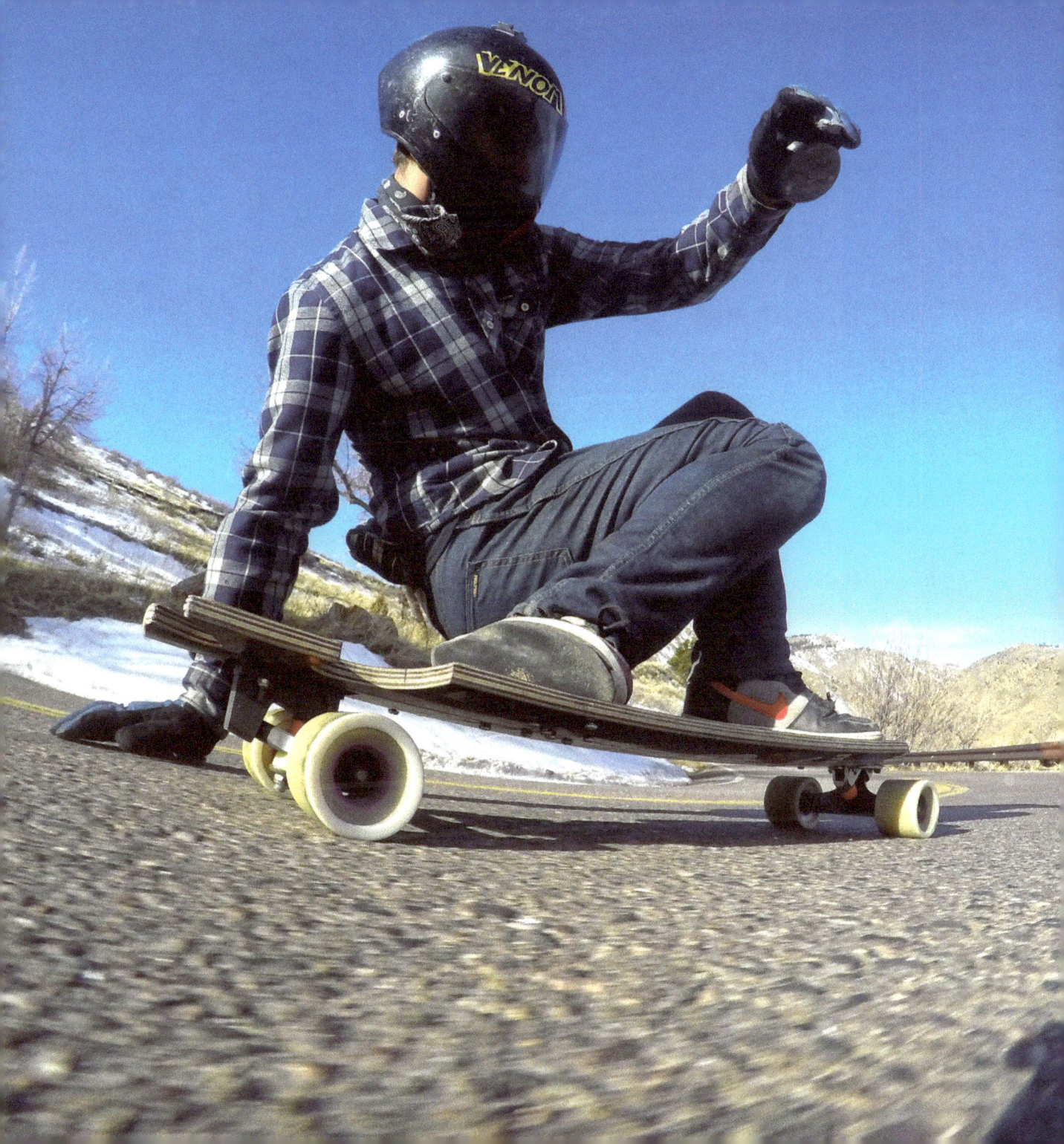

#Gloryhole

Once in a while, when I'm lucky, I manage to snap a picture-within-a-picture, which I've coined "The Gloryhole." Sometimes it's intentional, other times a happy accident…and here are a few of my favorites!

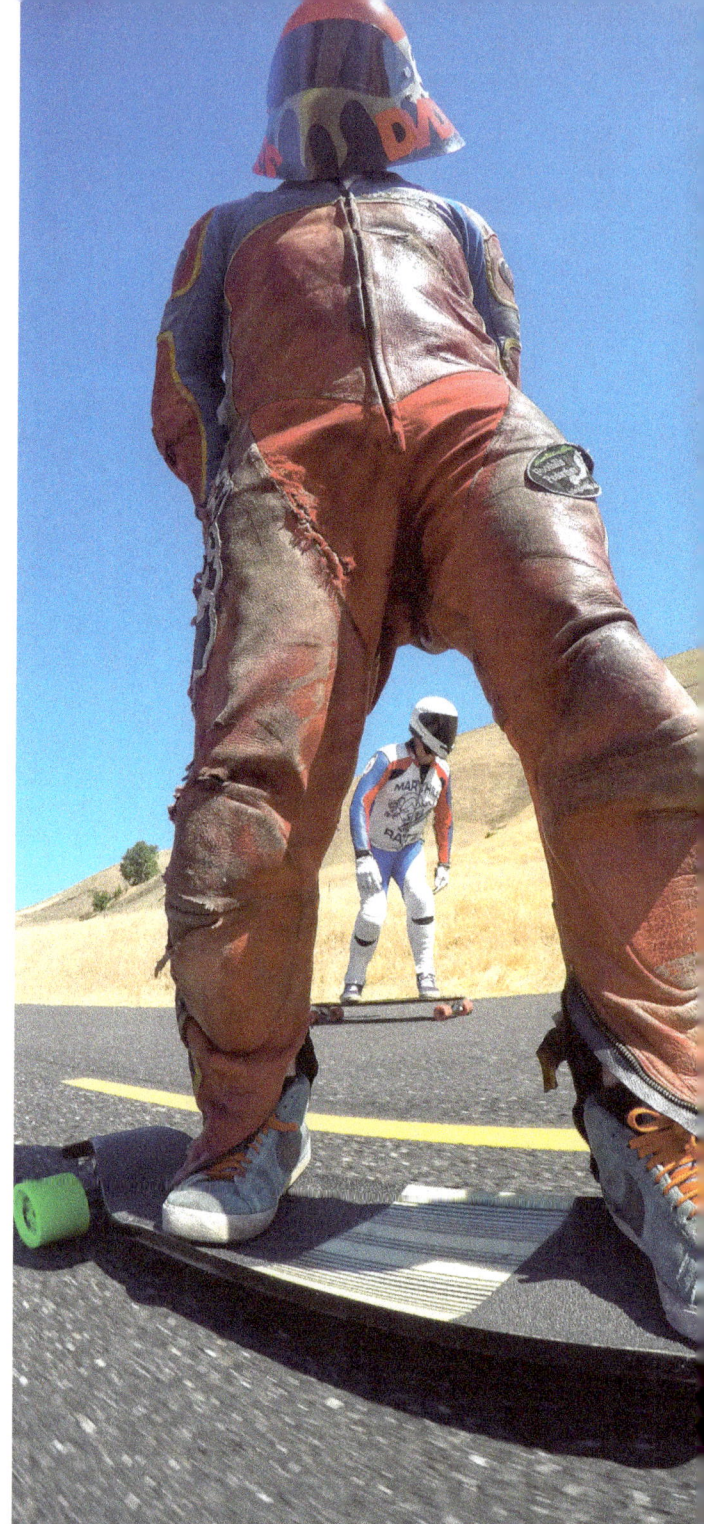

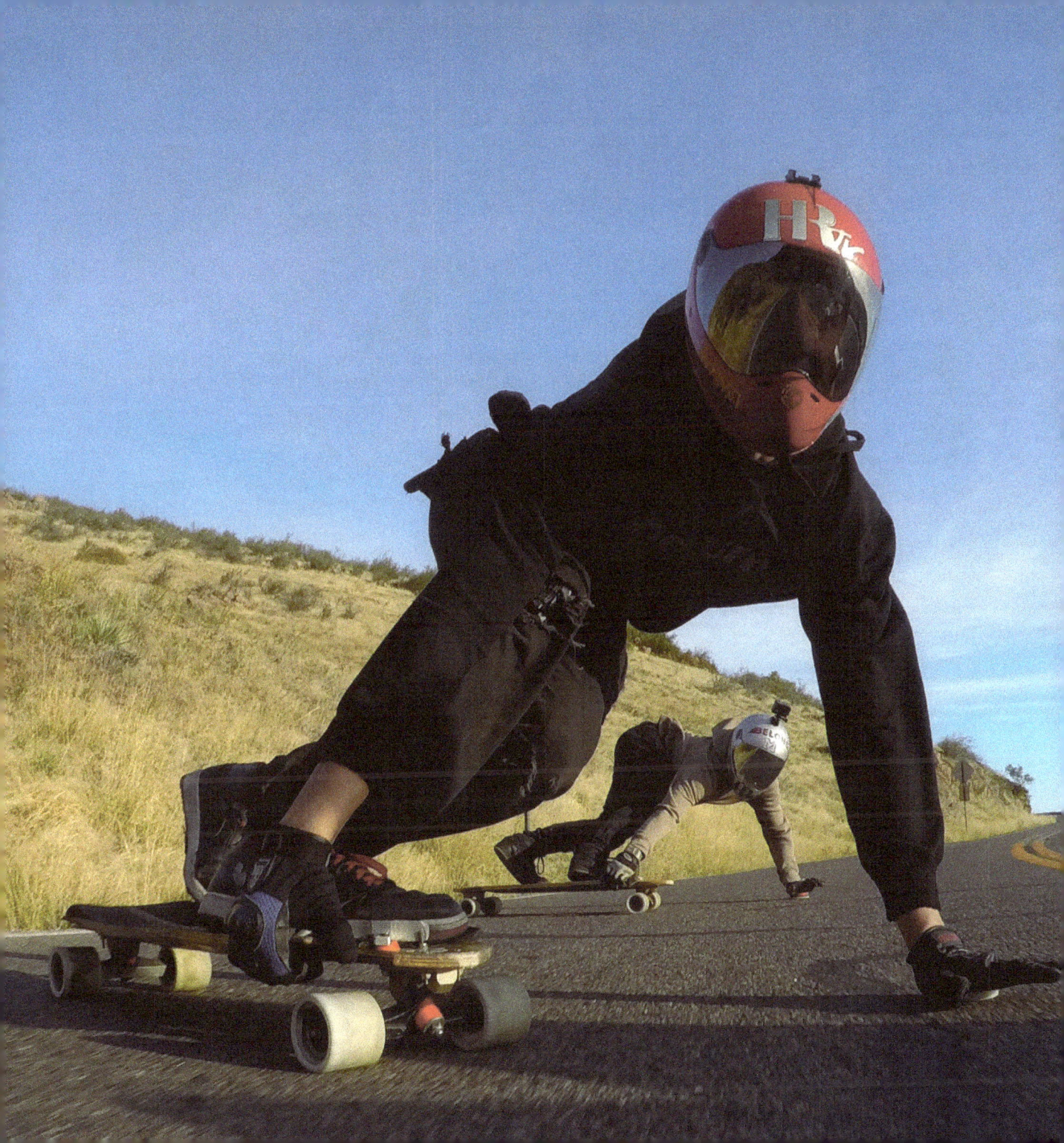

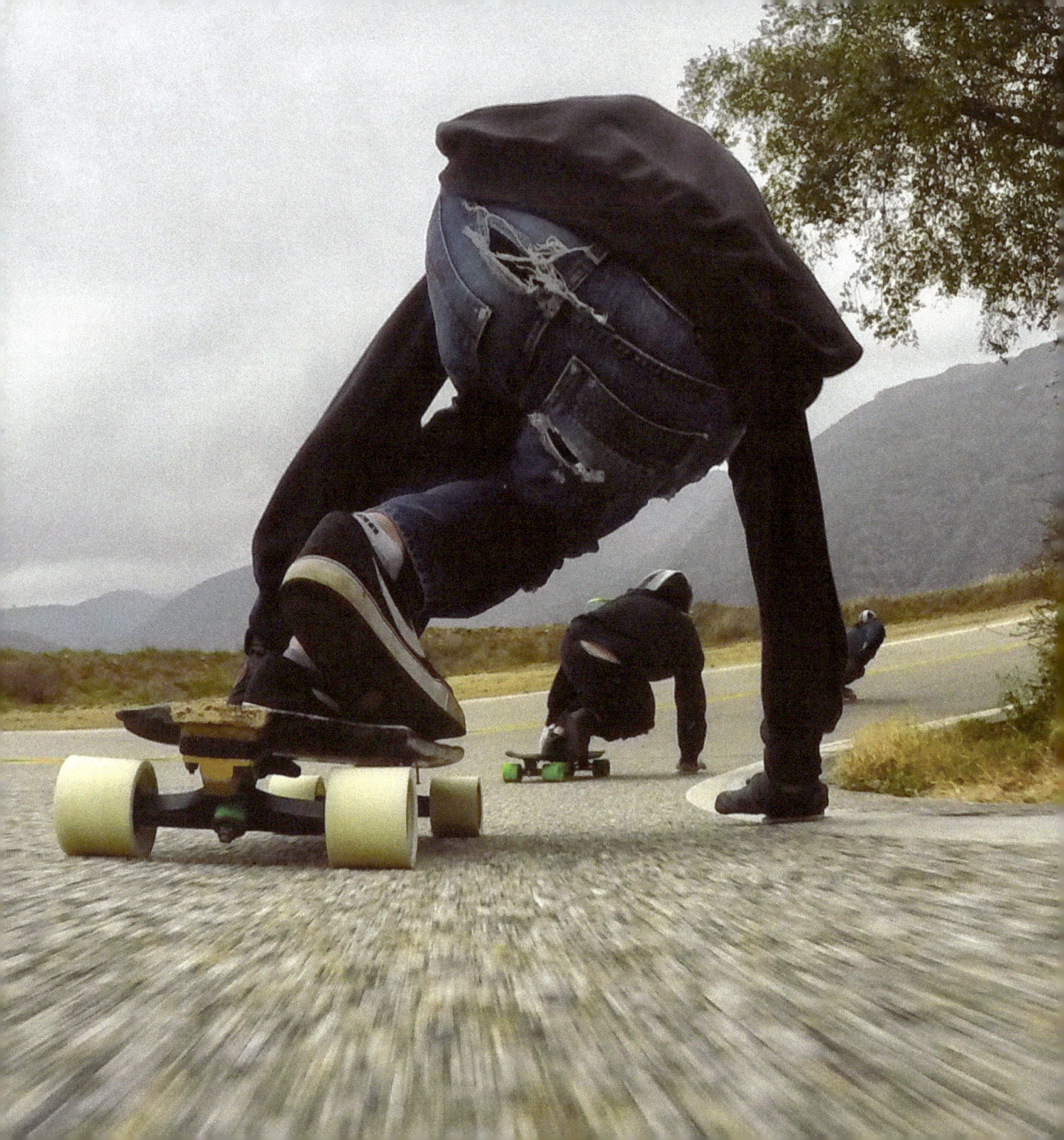

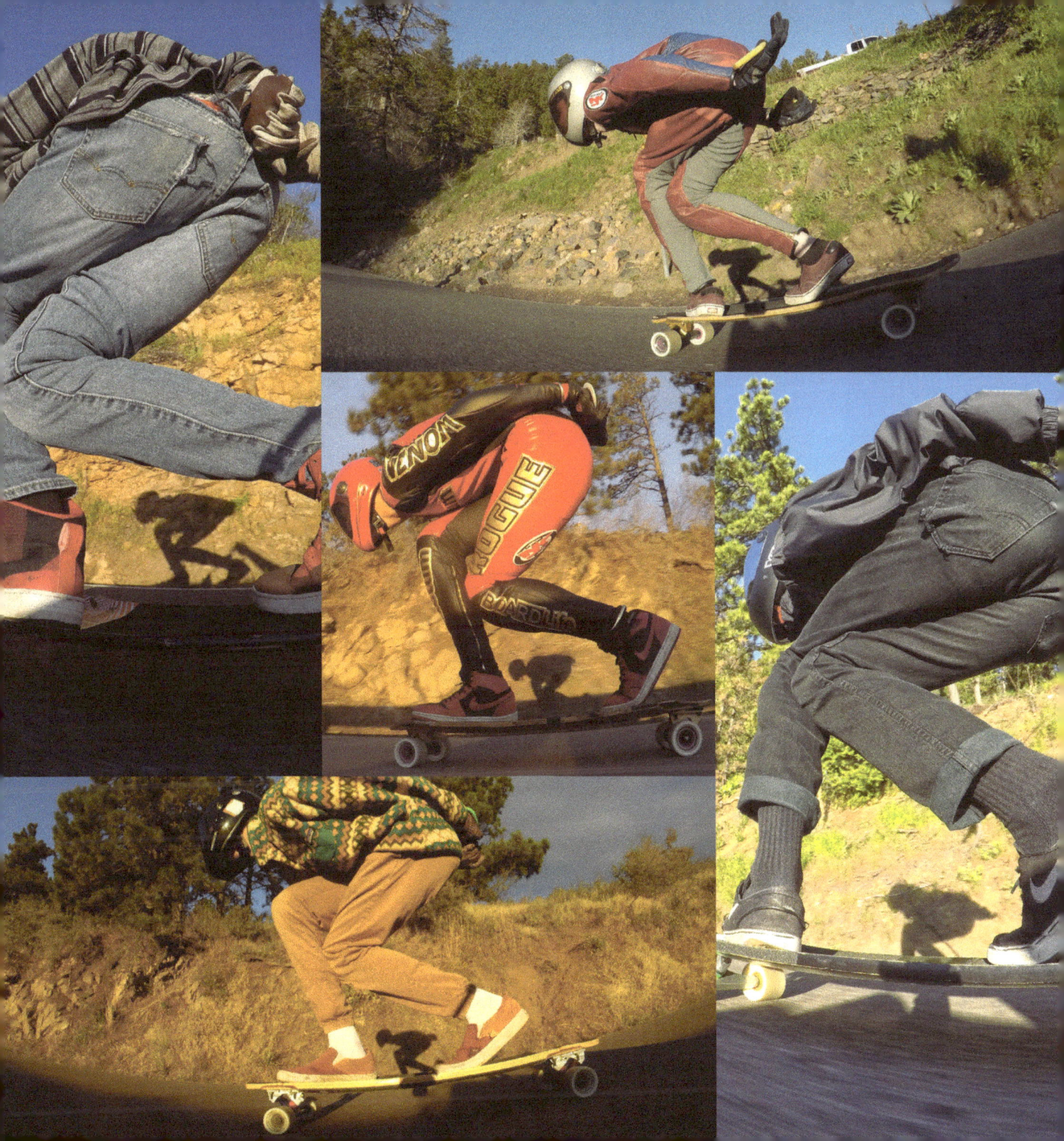

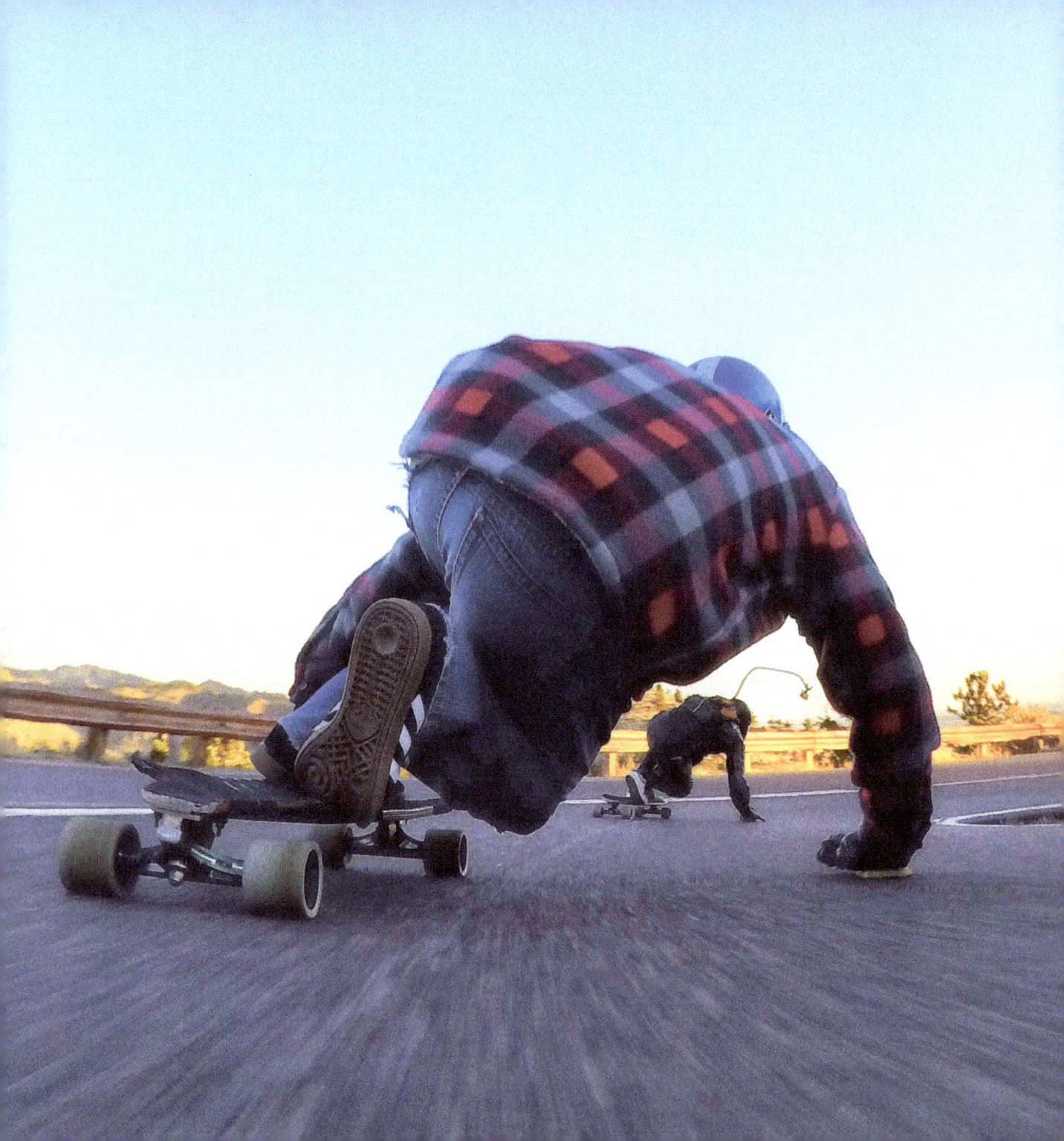

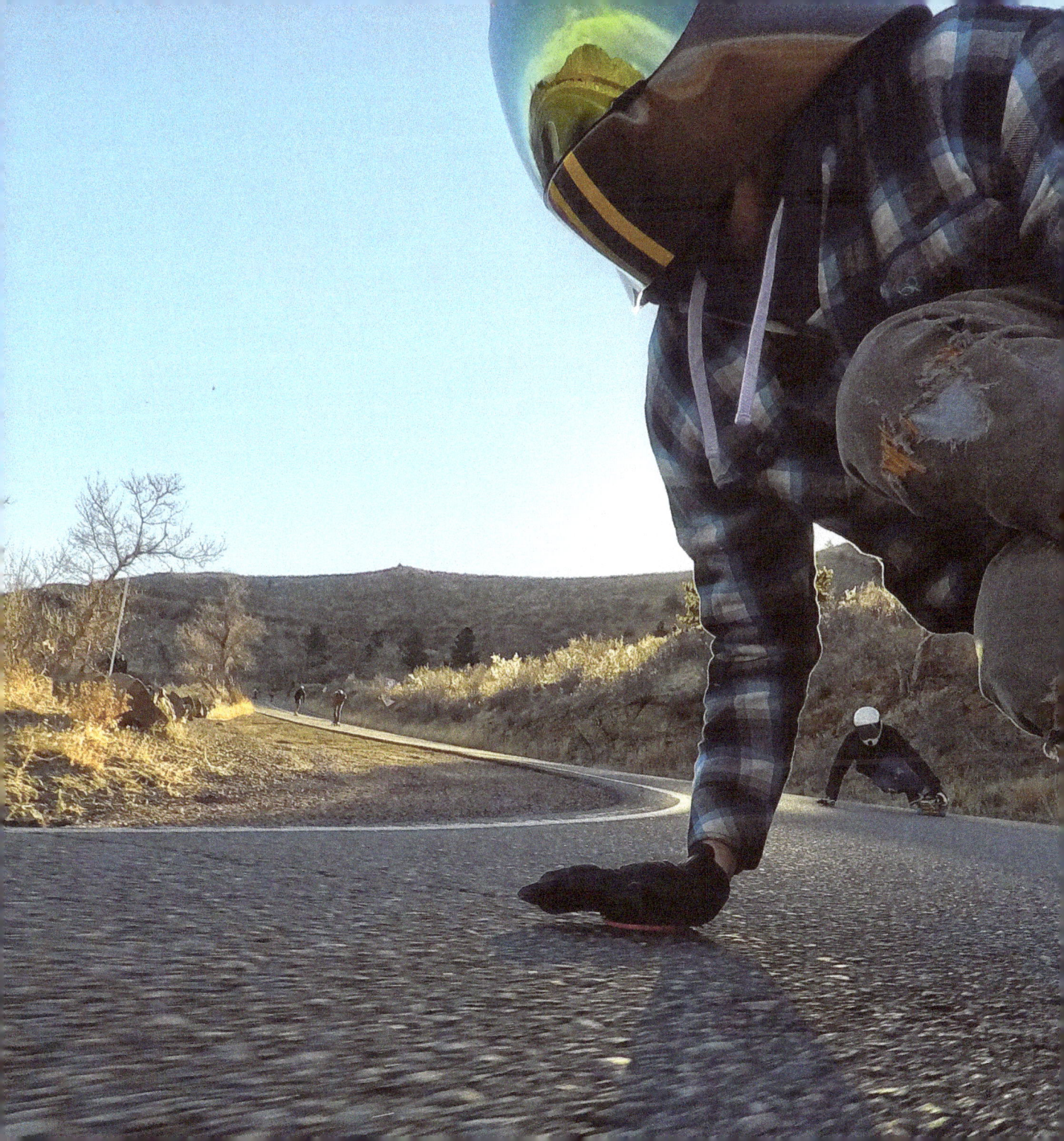

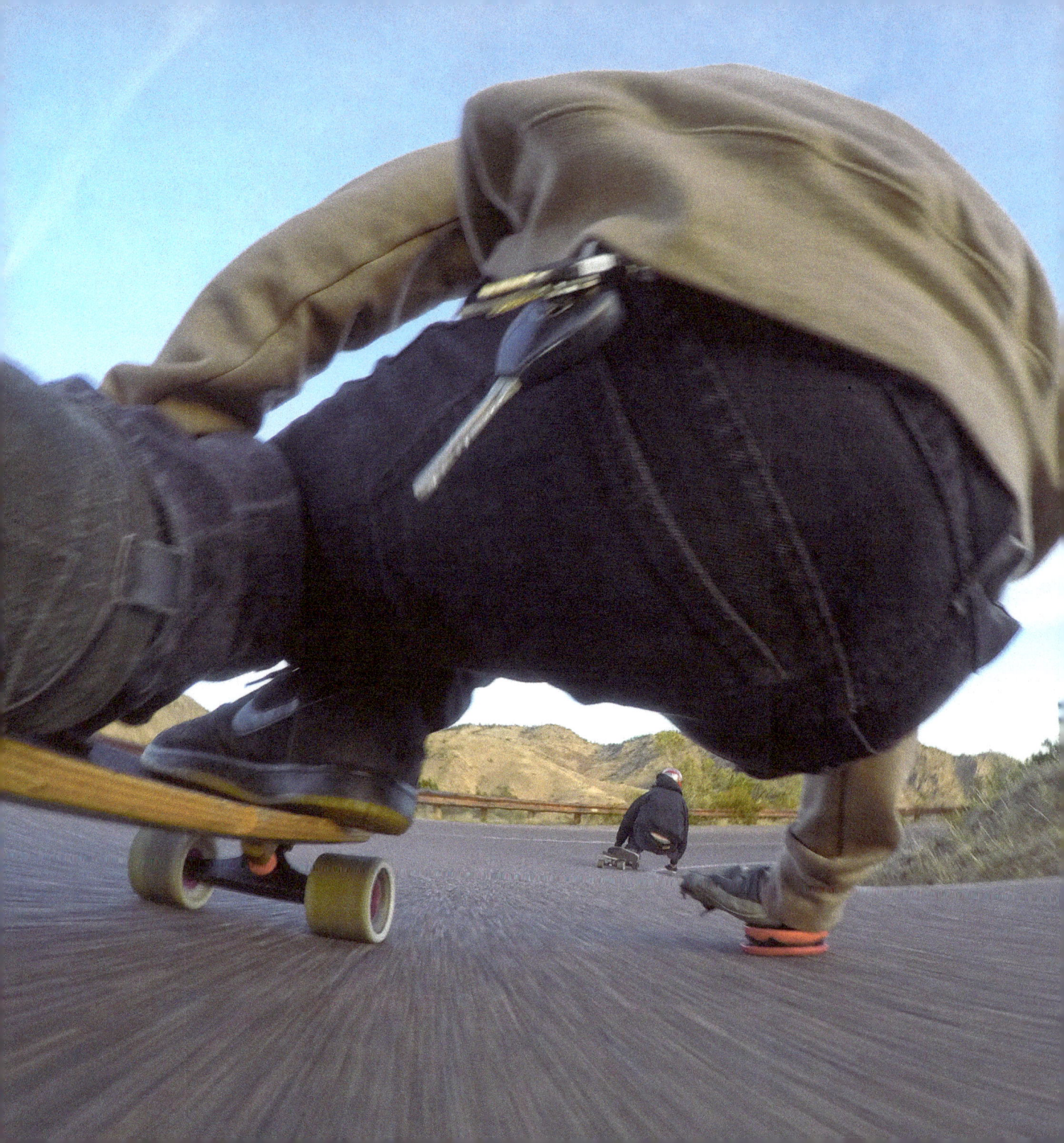

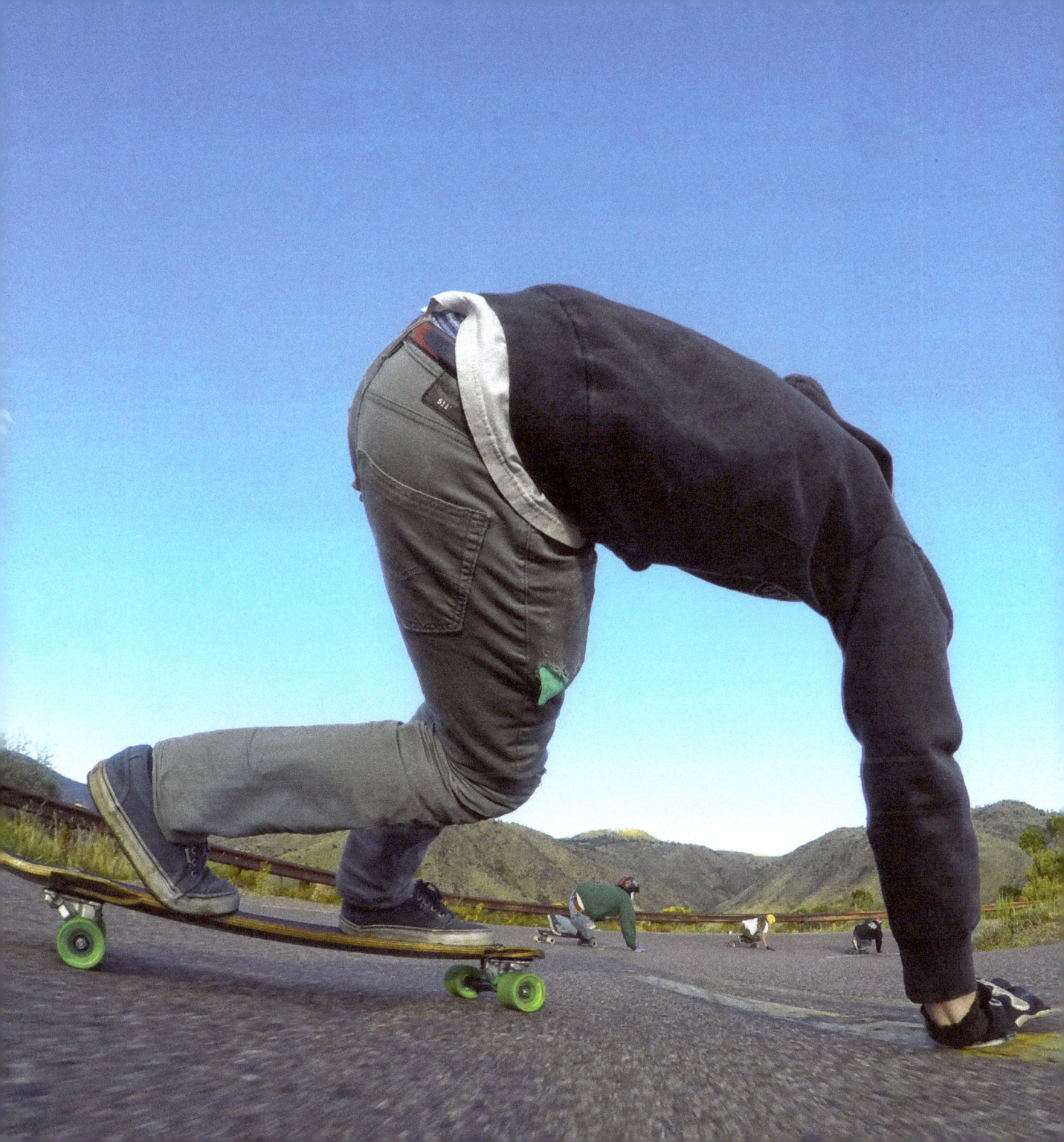

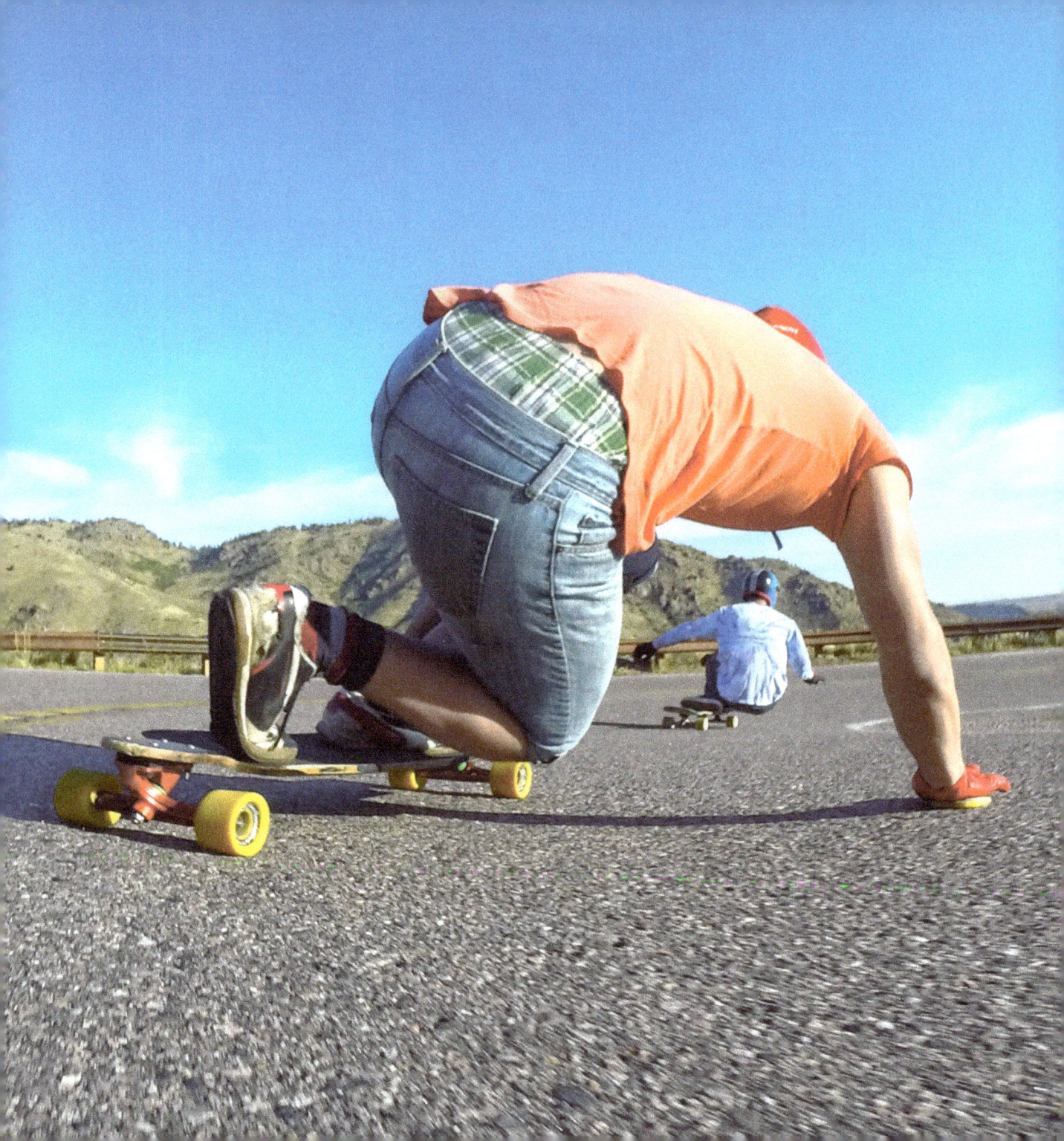

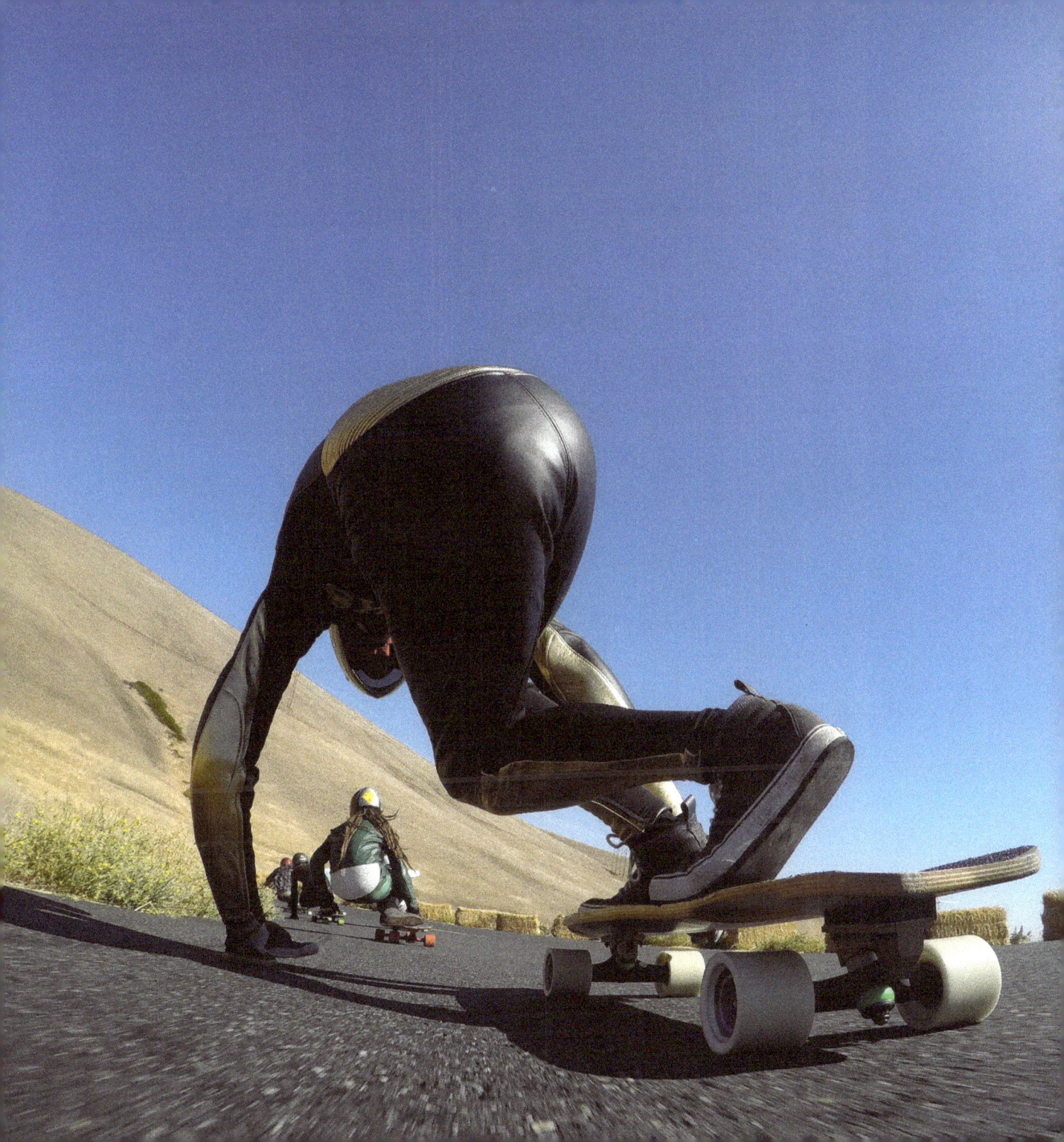

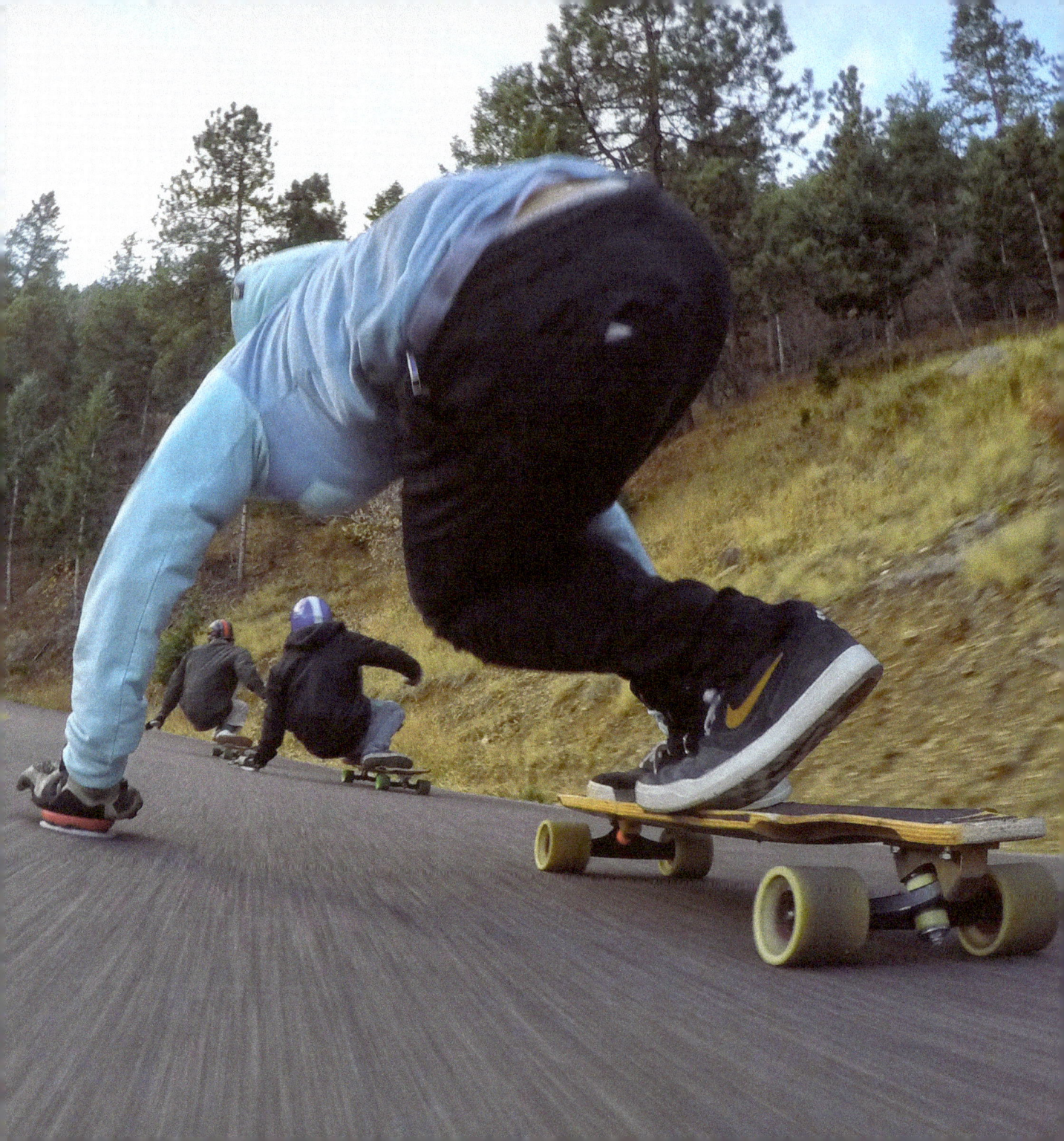

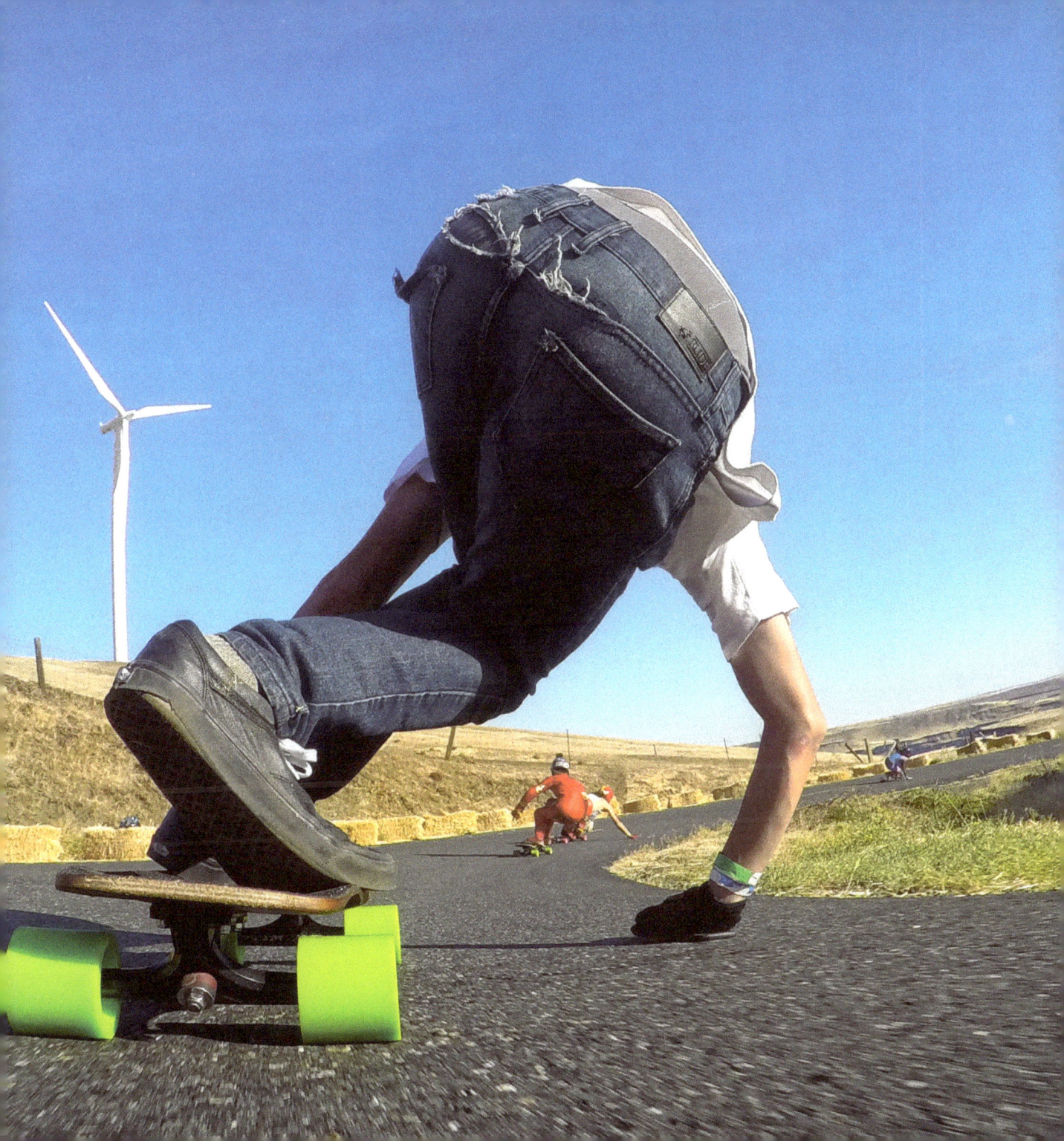

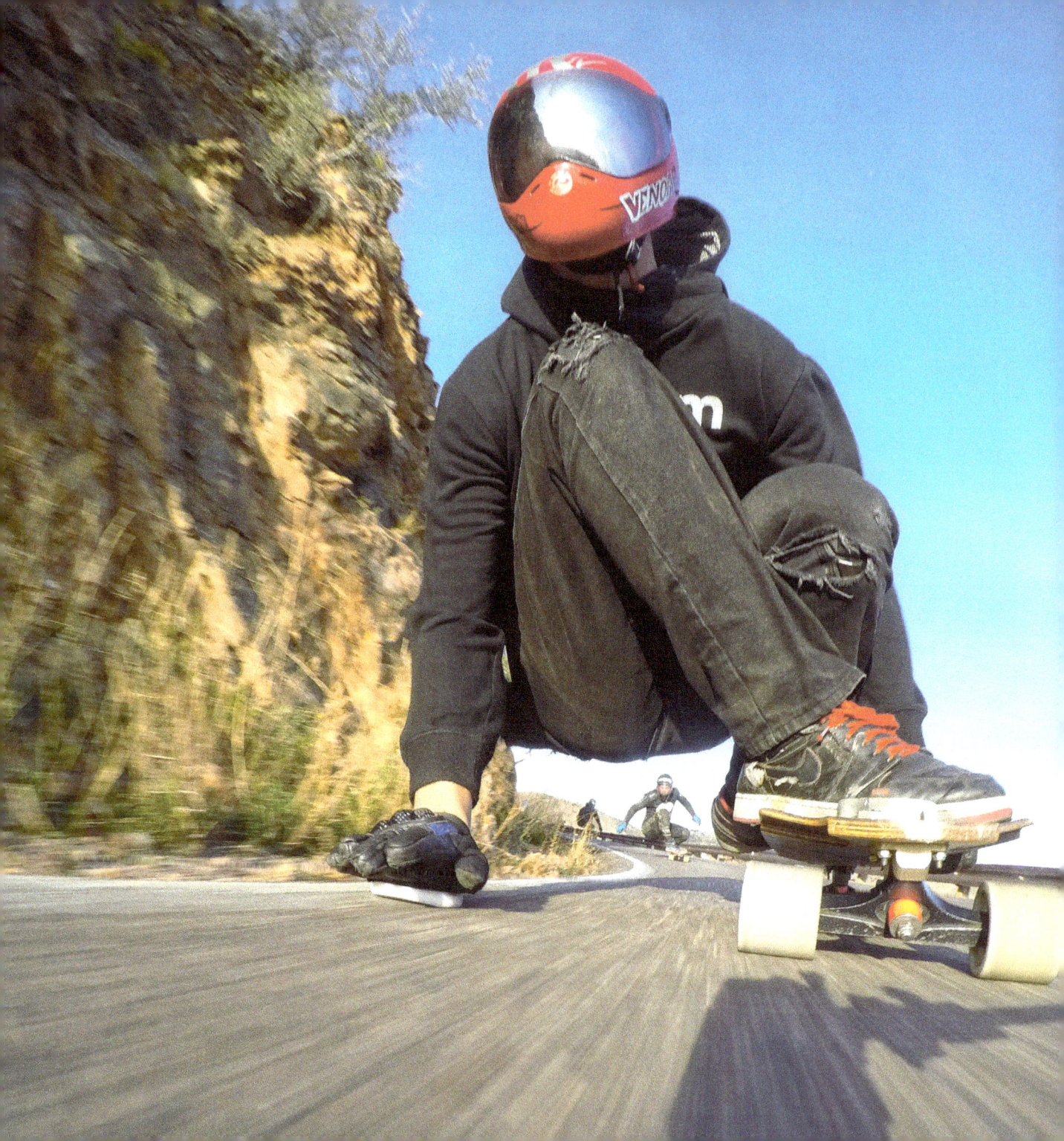

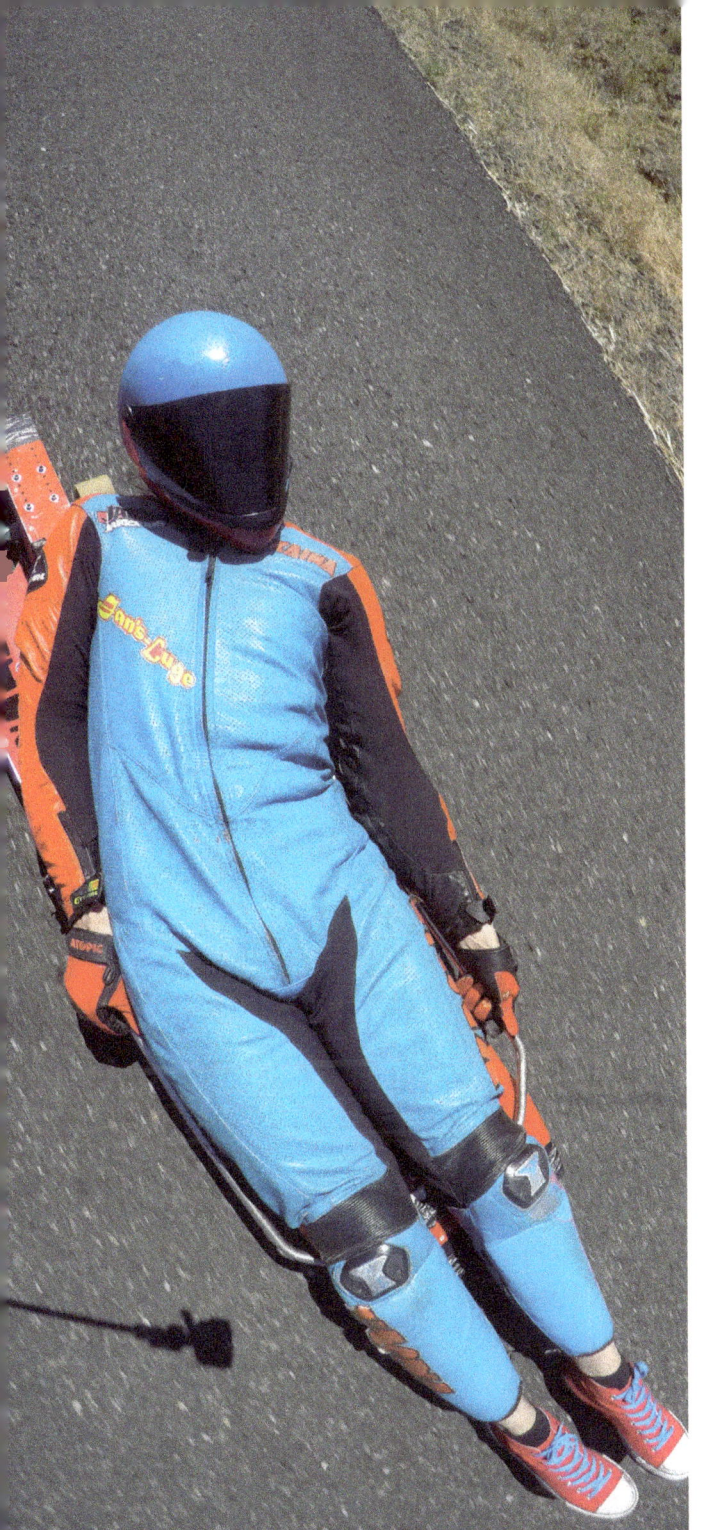

#Laydown (It's faster!)

Due to the aerodynamic superiority of the prone position, laying down is considerably faster than standing up . For that reason, the street luge is the fastest type of gravity-powered downhill machines, making it a great choice for both racing and filming.

Personally, the luge has amped up my game in so many ways, so I wanted to devote a special chapter to the beast that stole my heart.

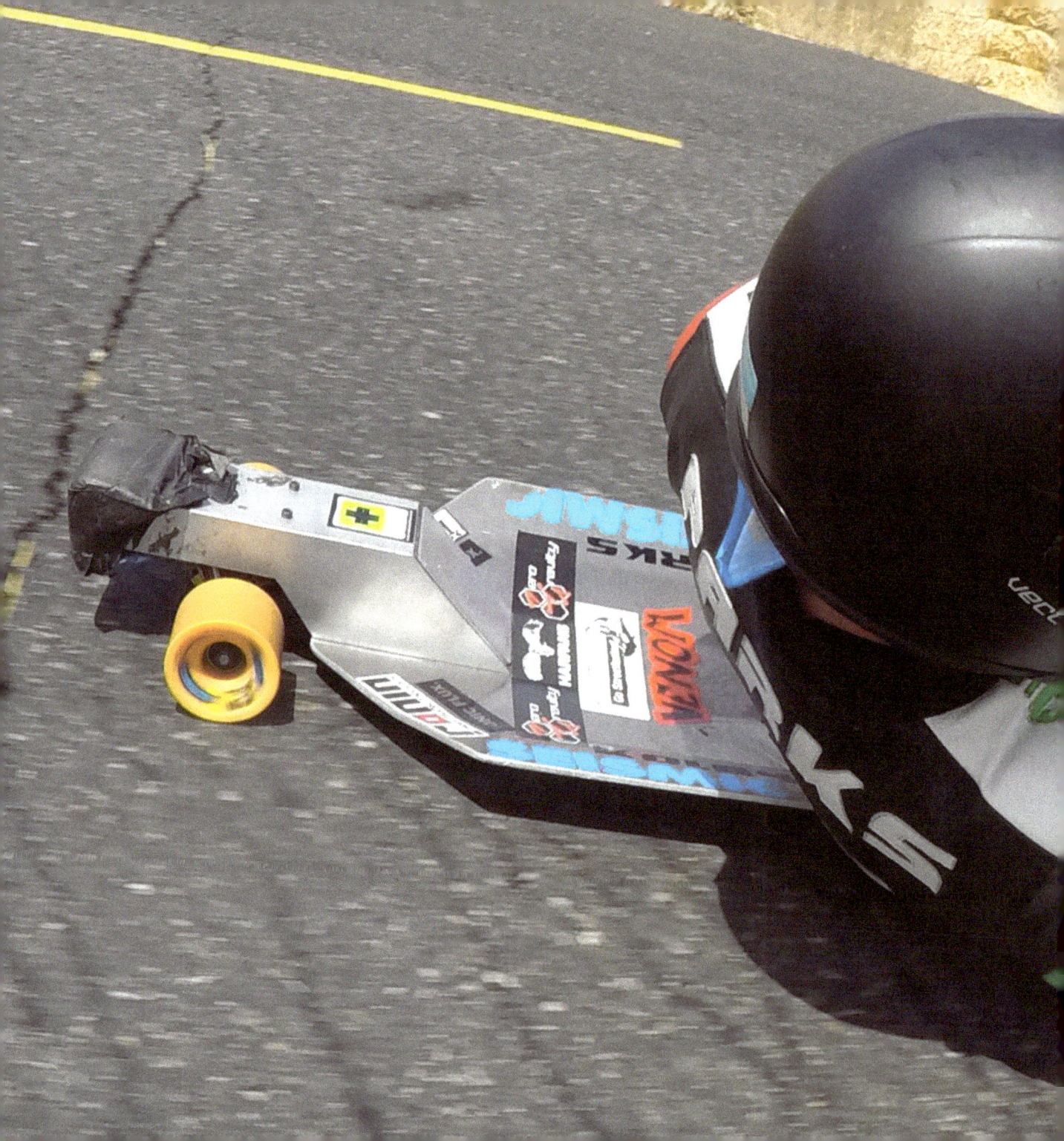

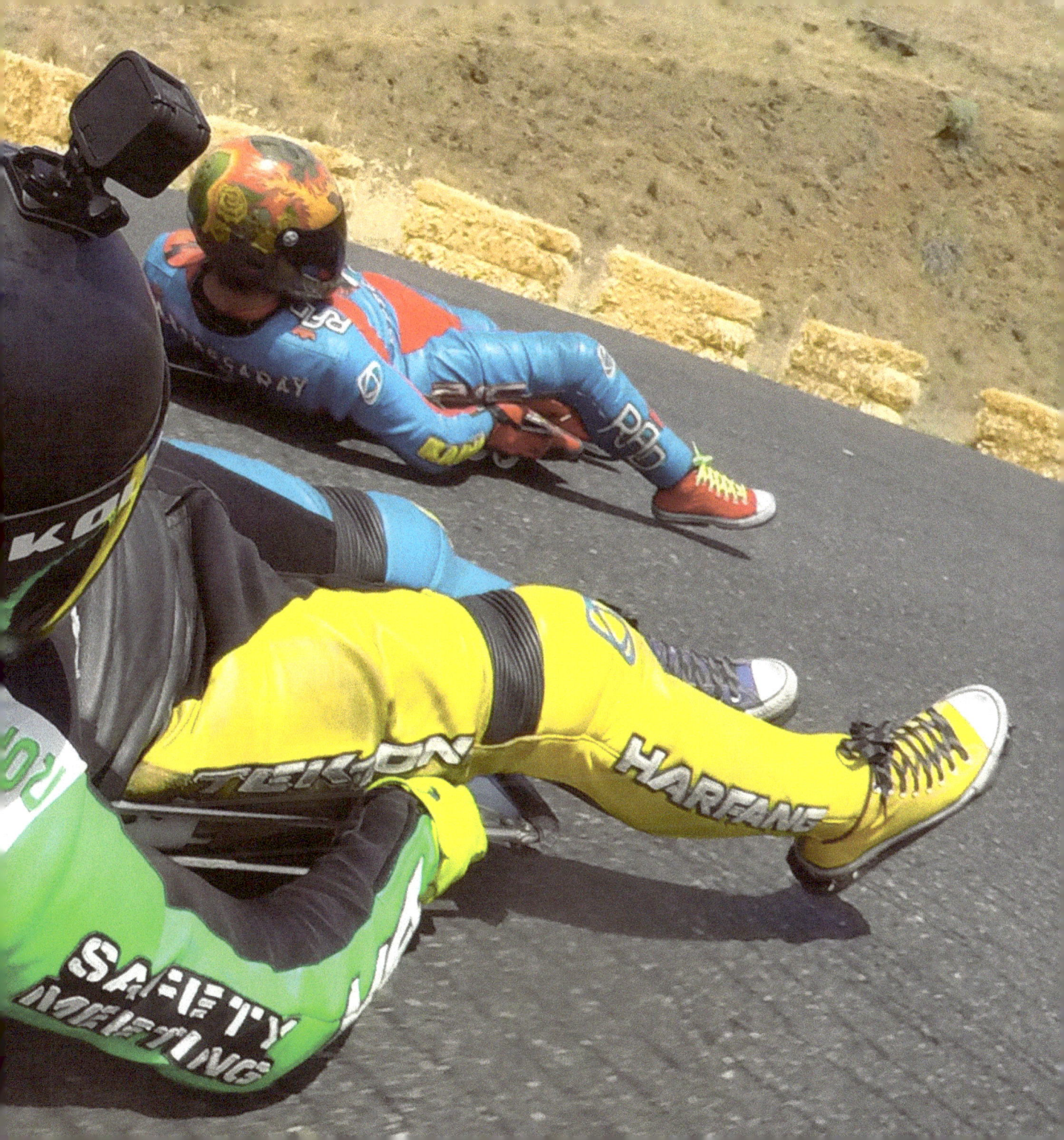

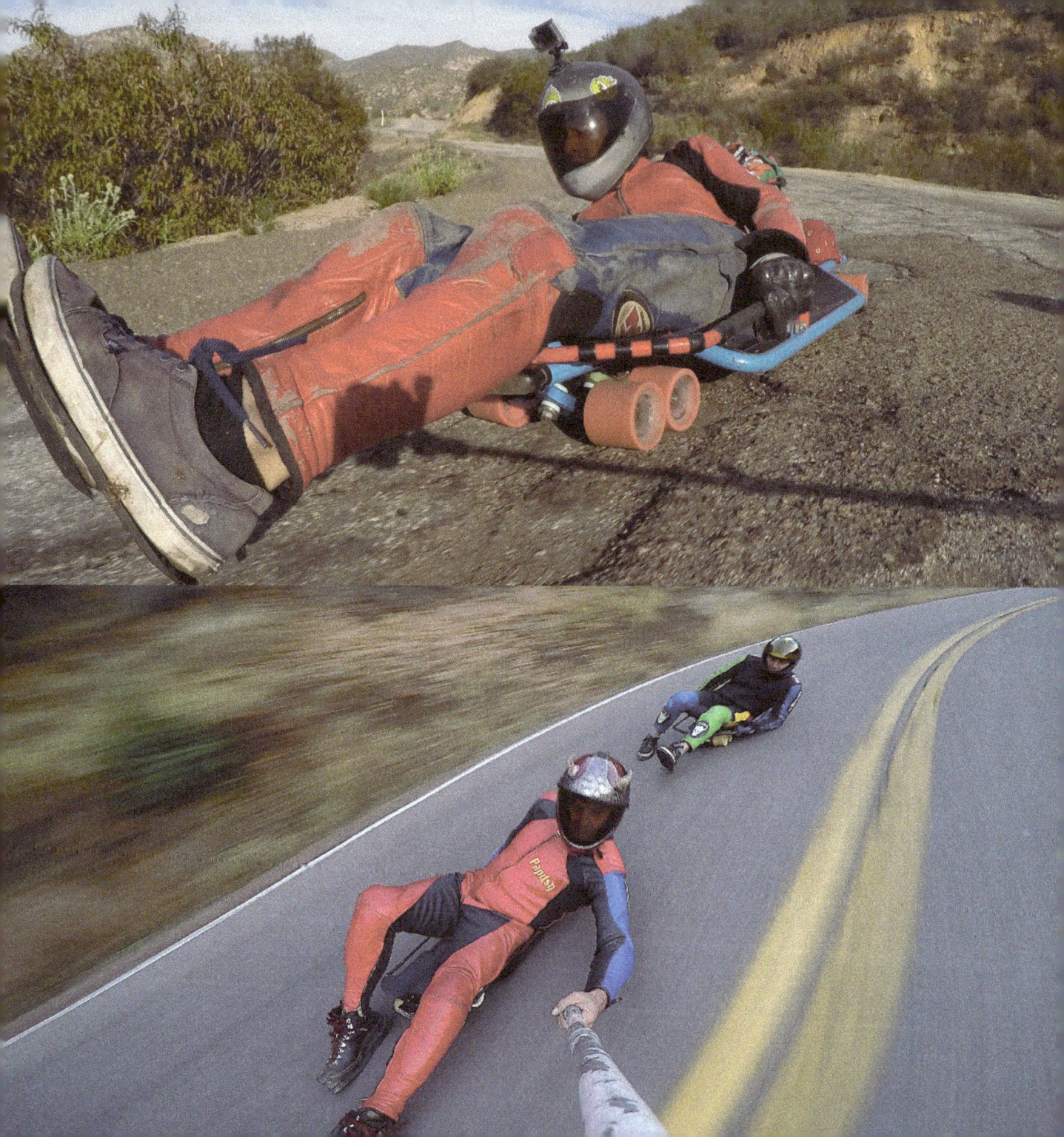

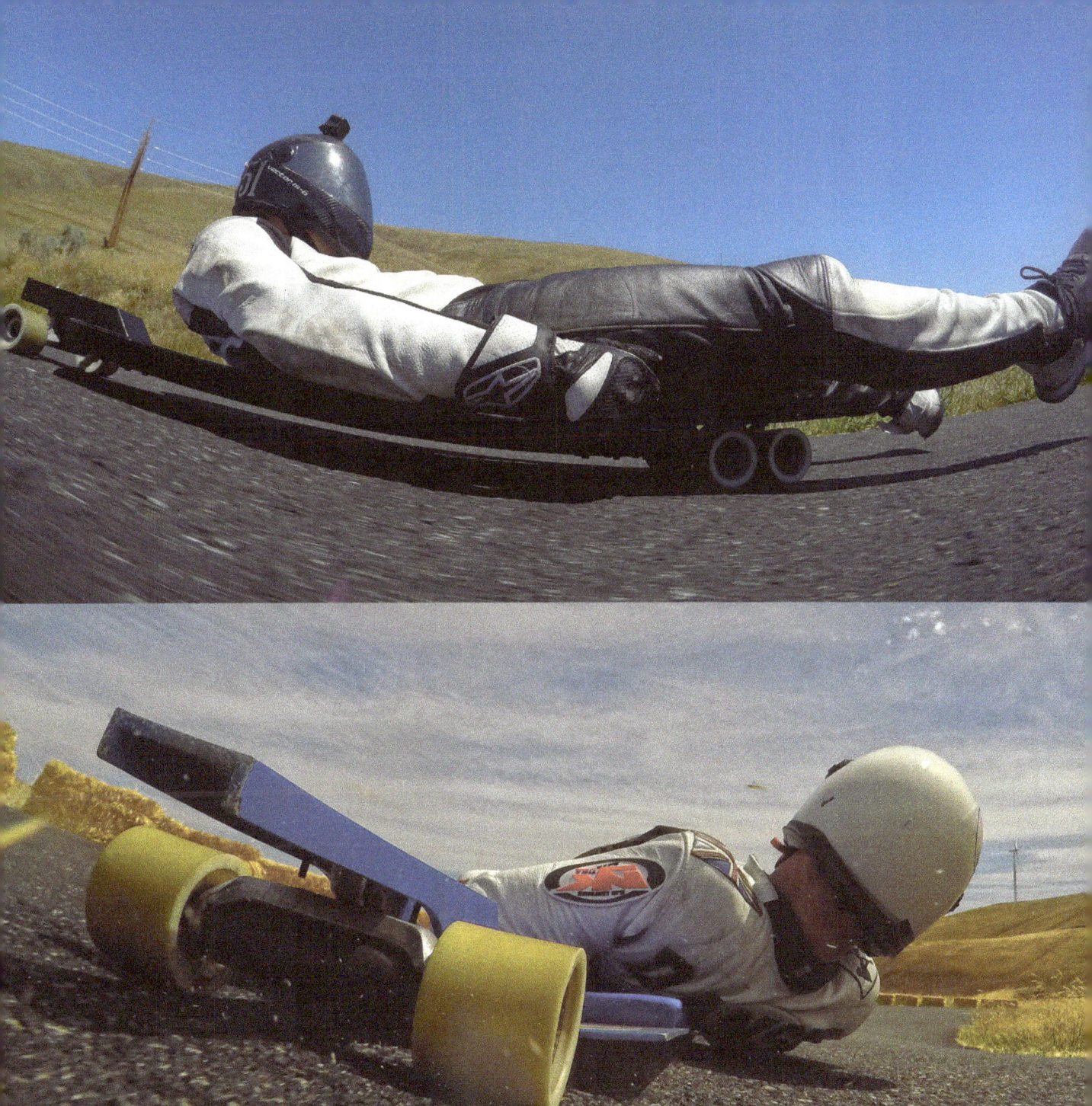

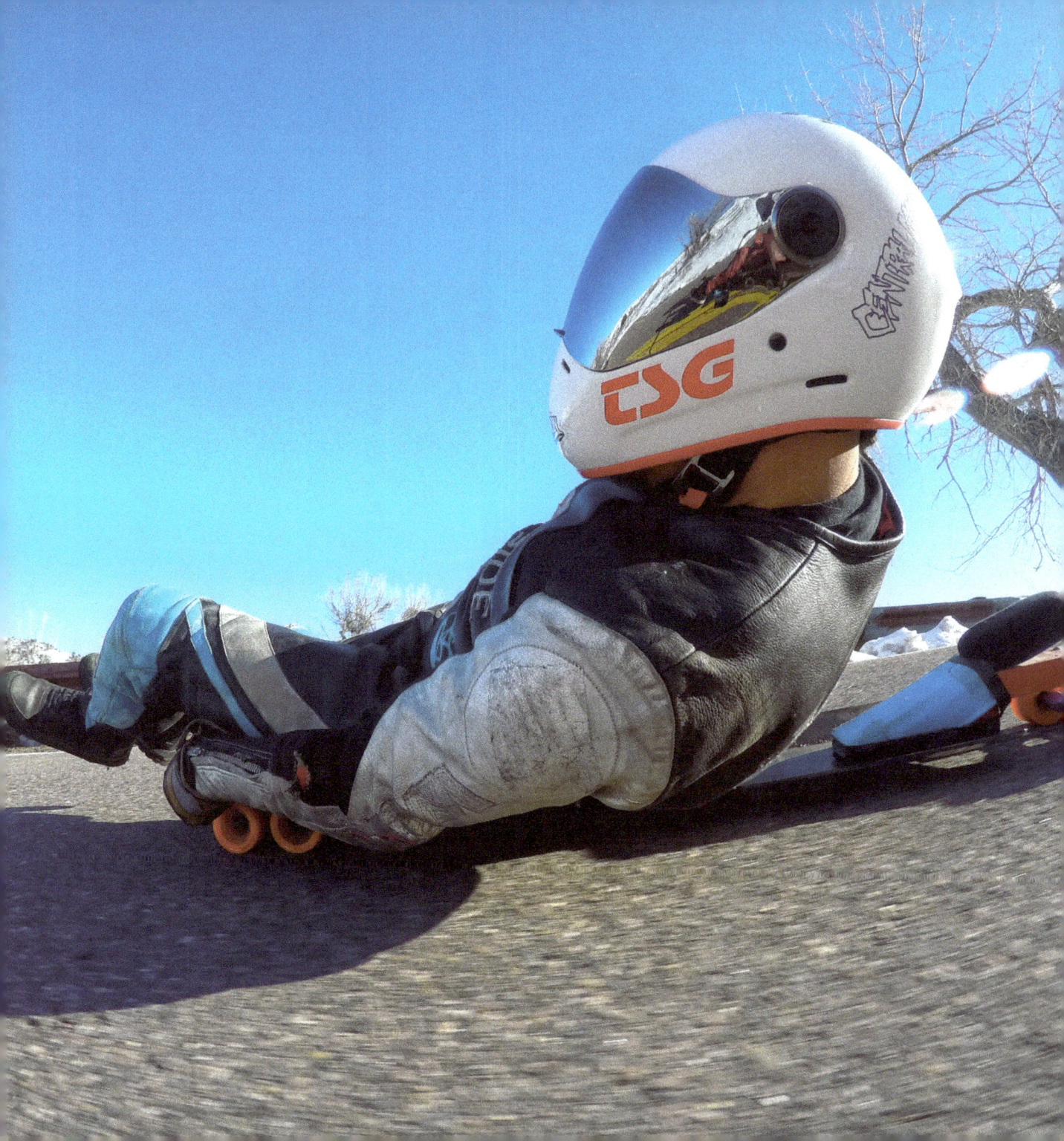

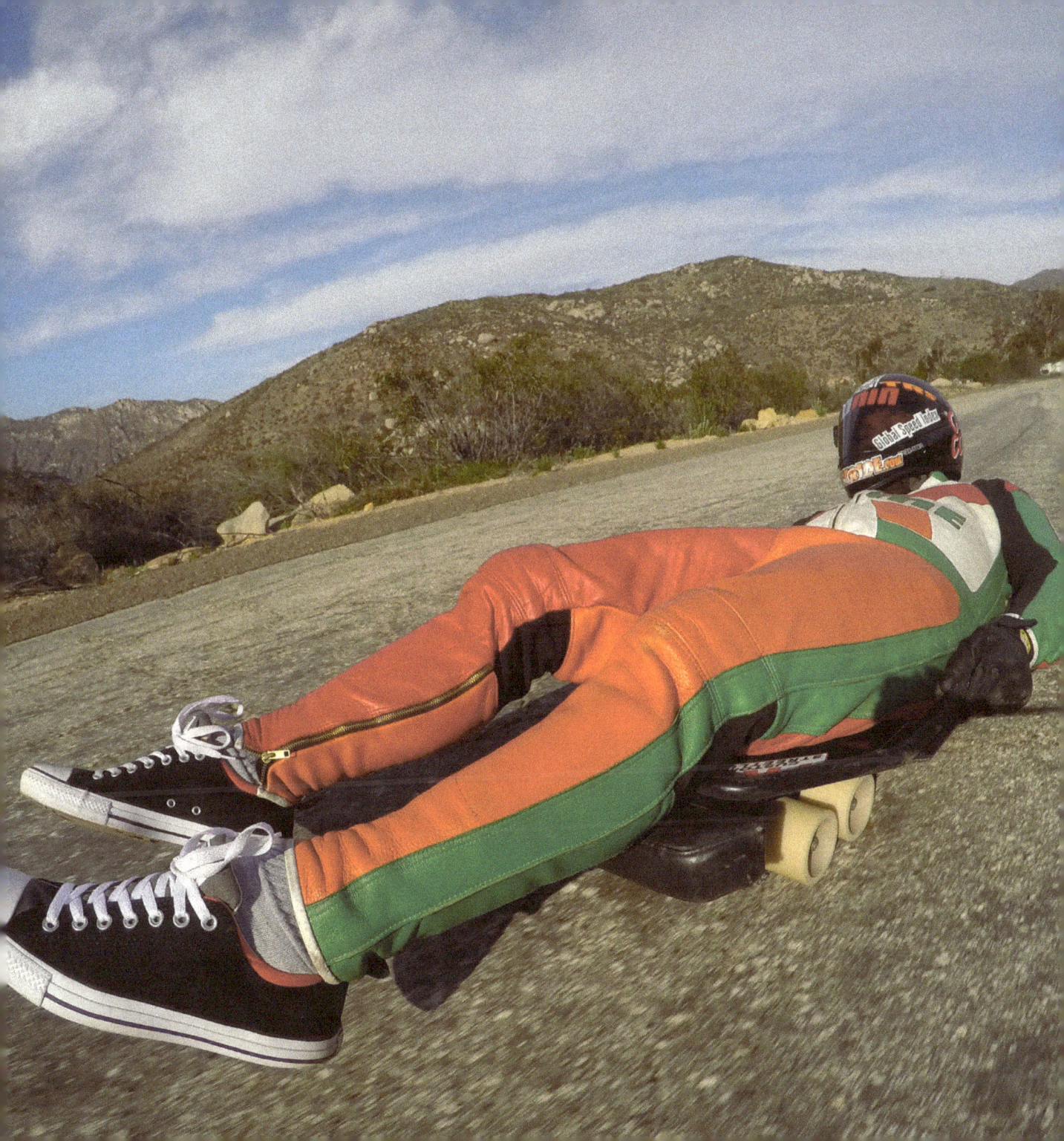

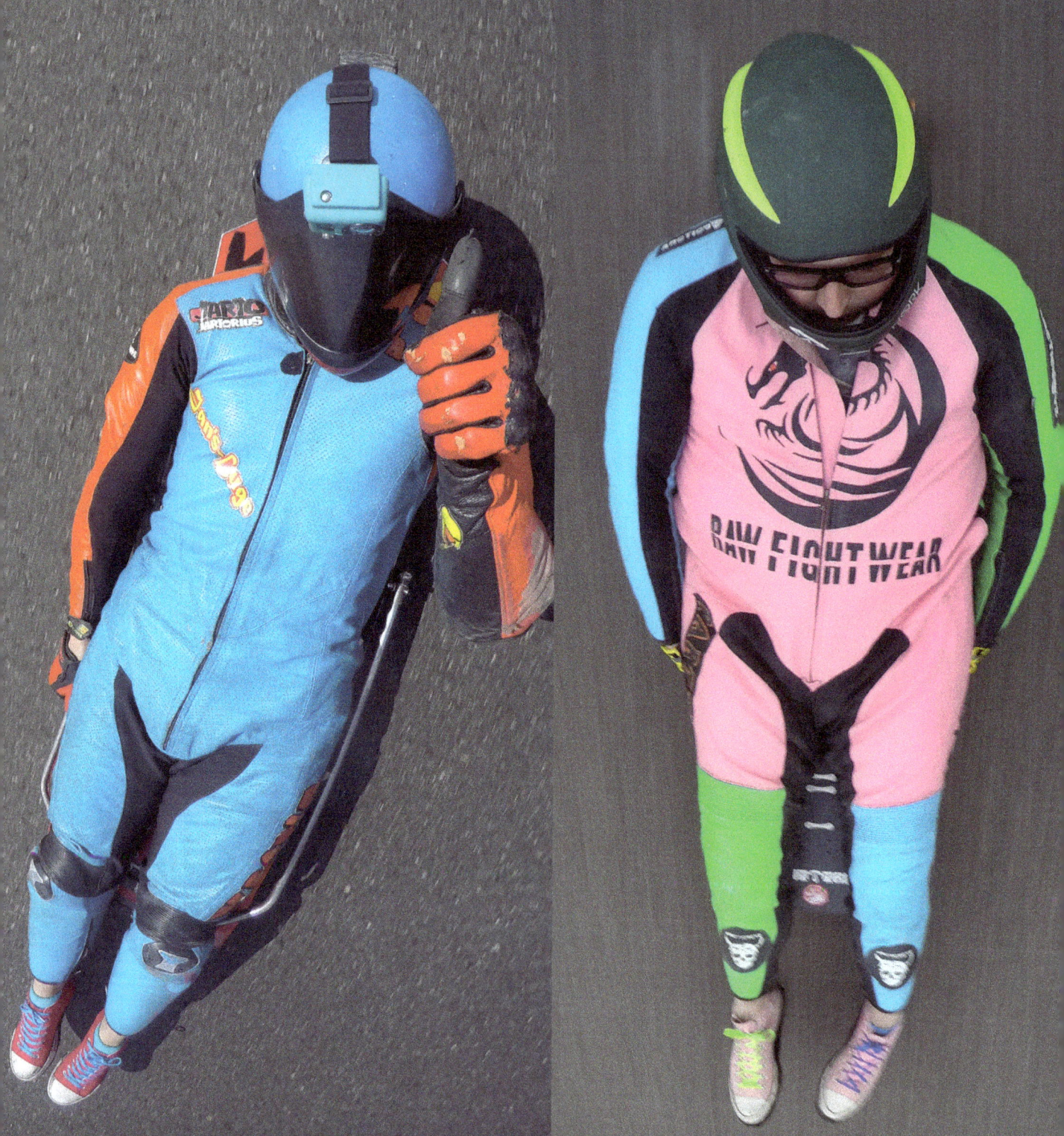

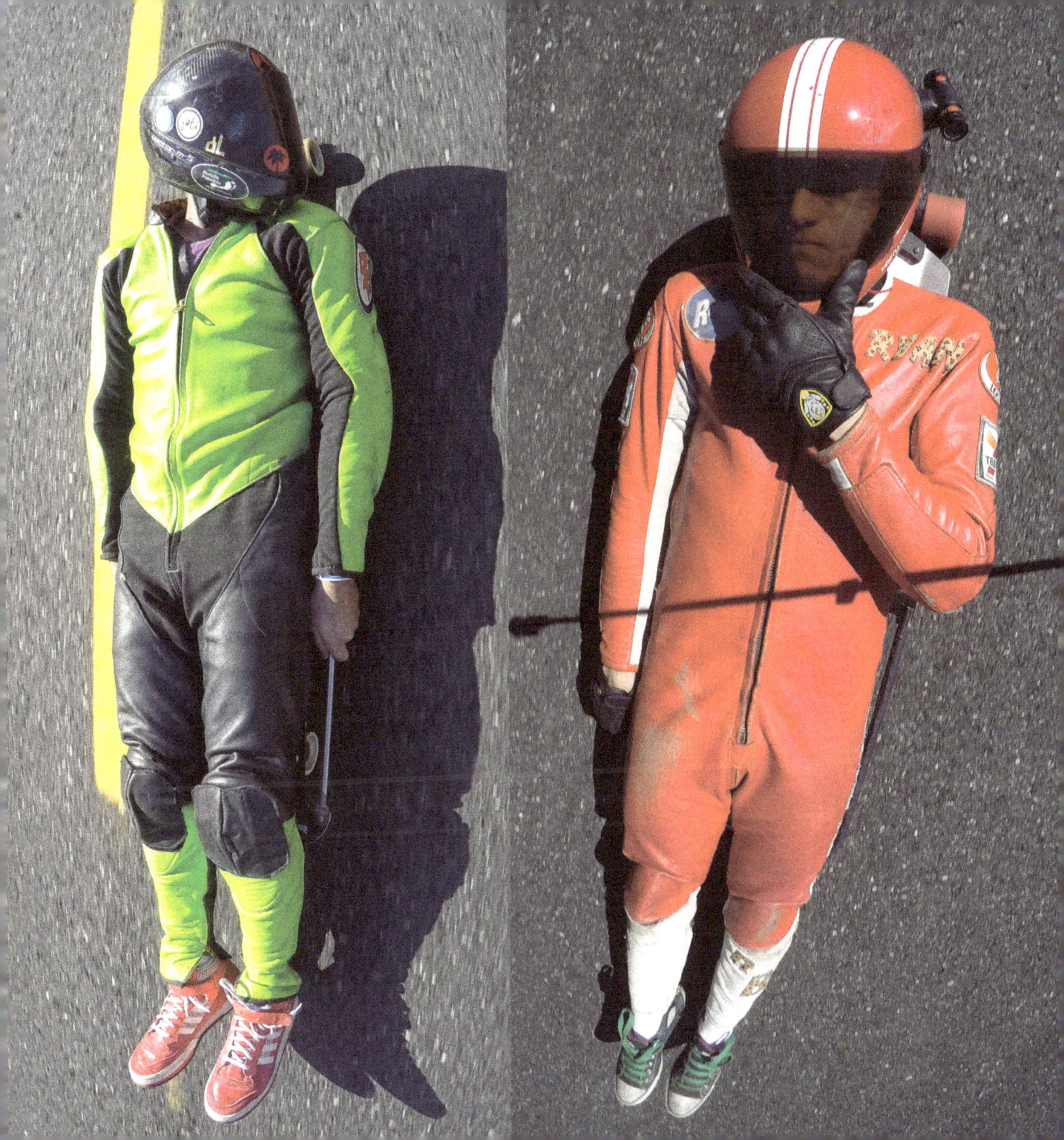

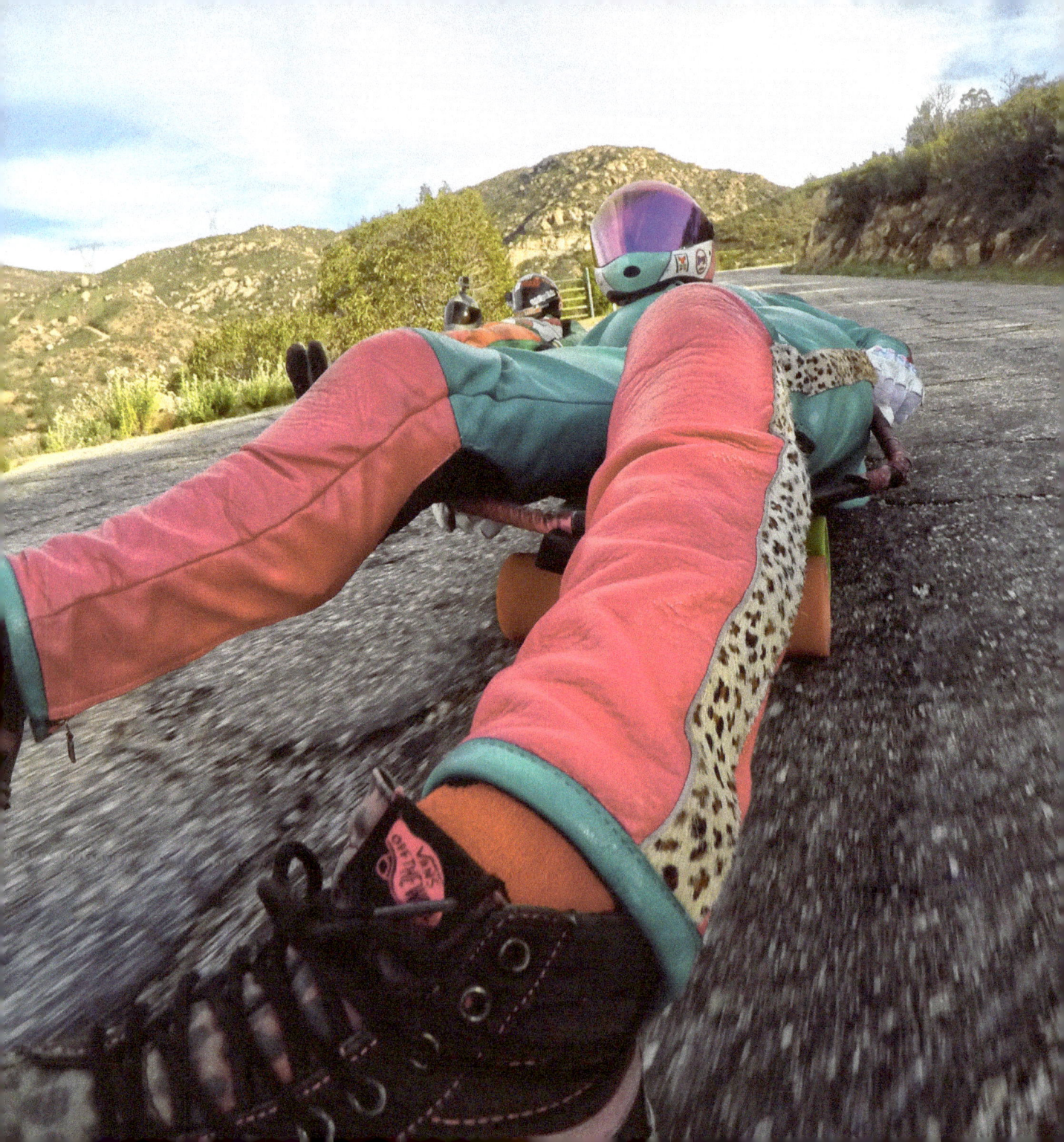

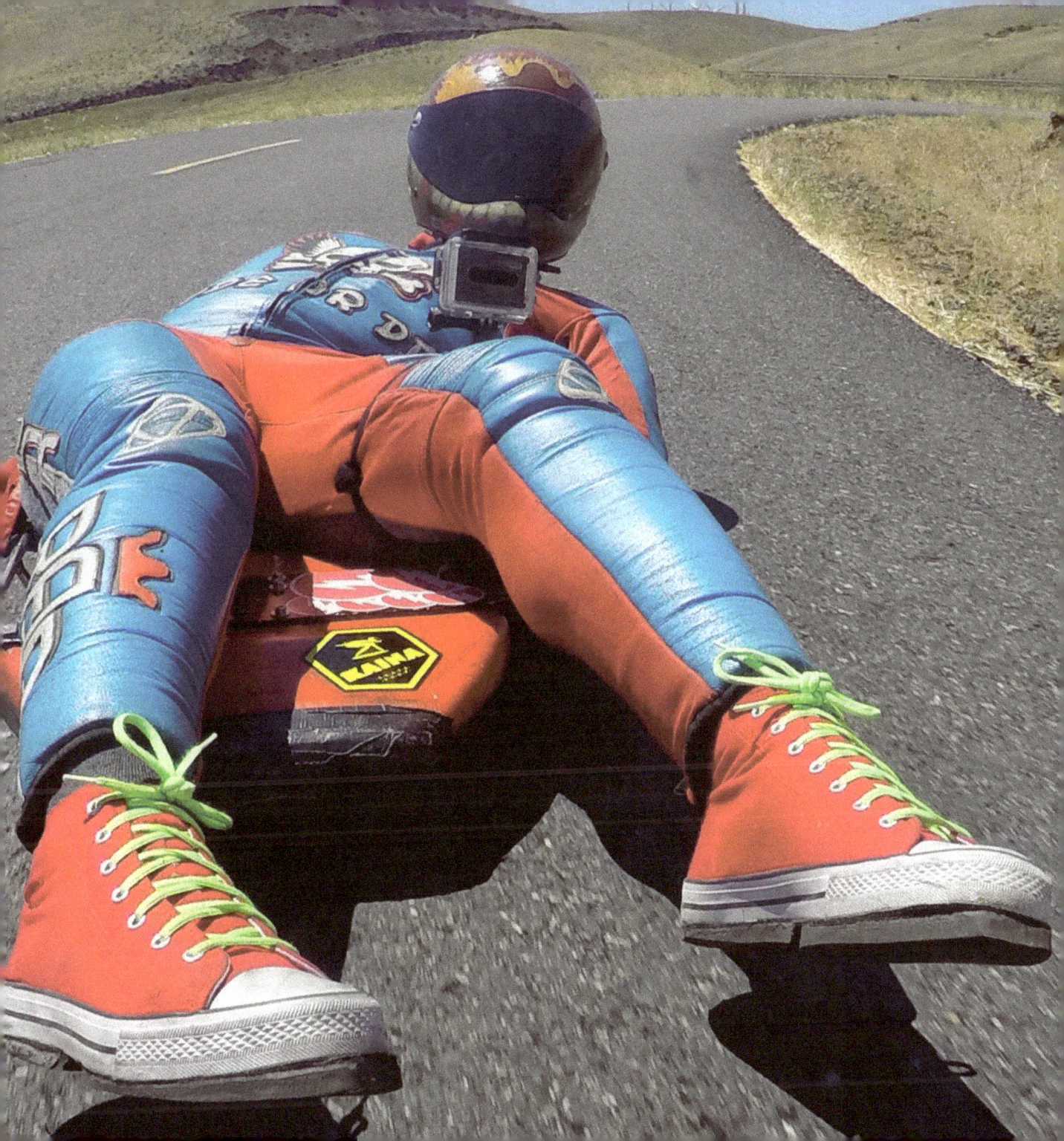

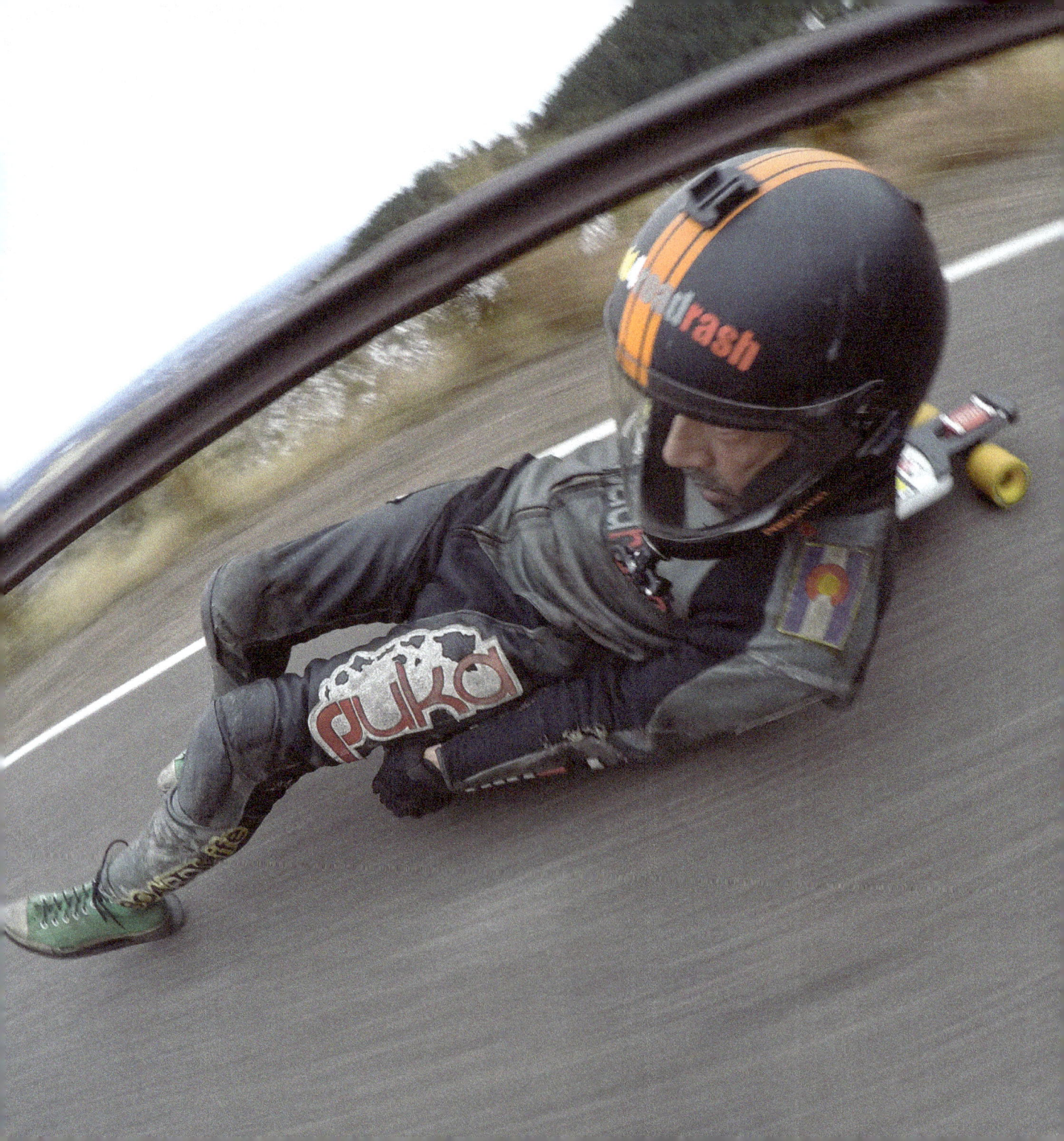

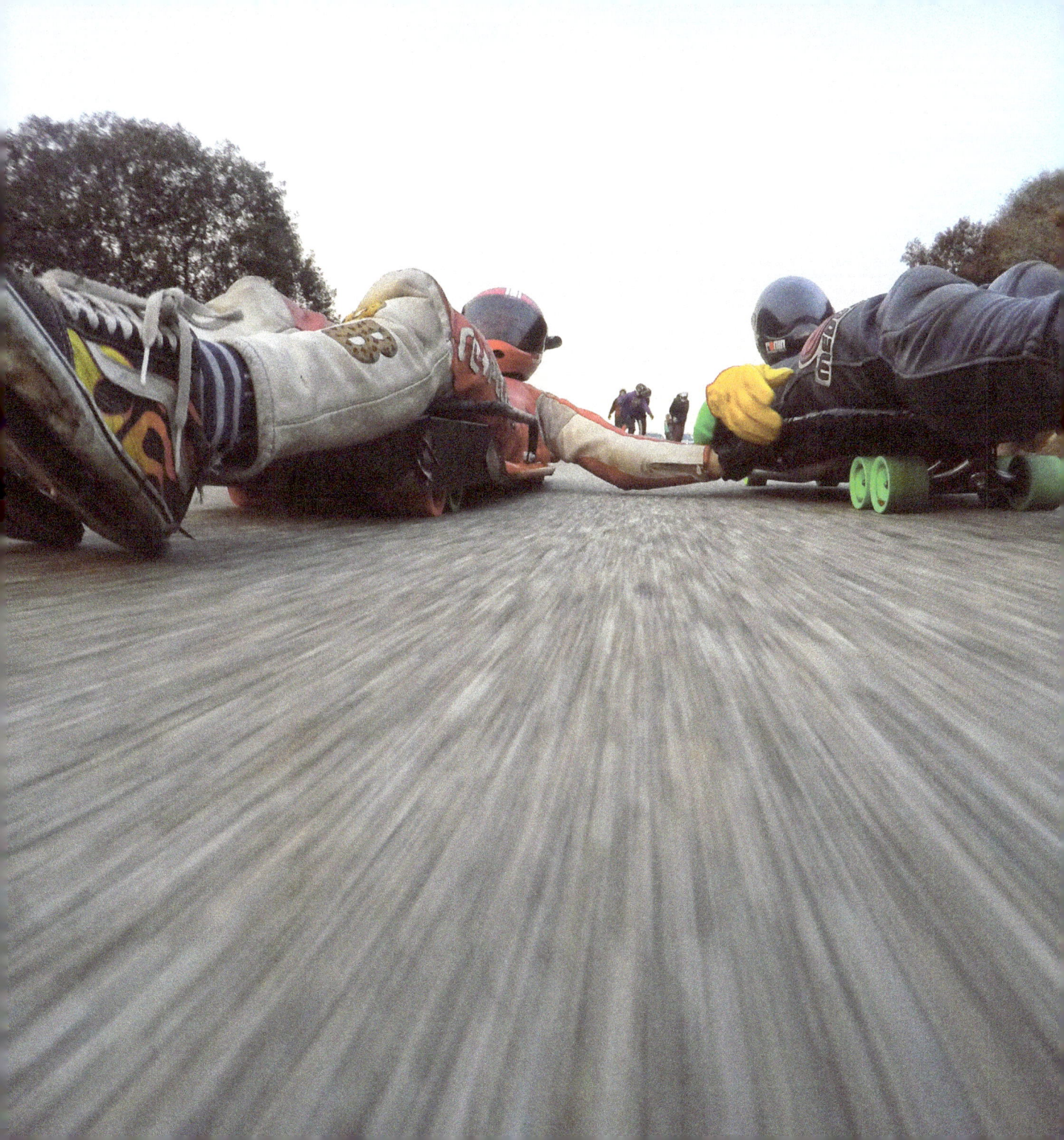

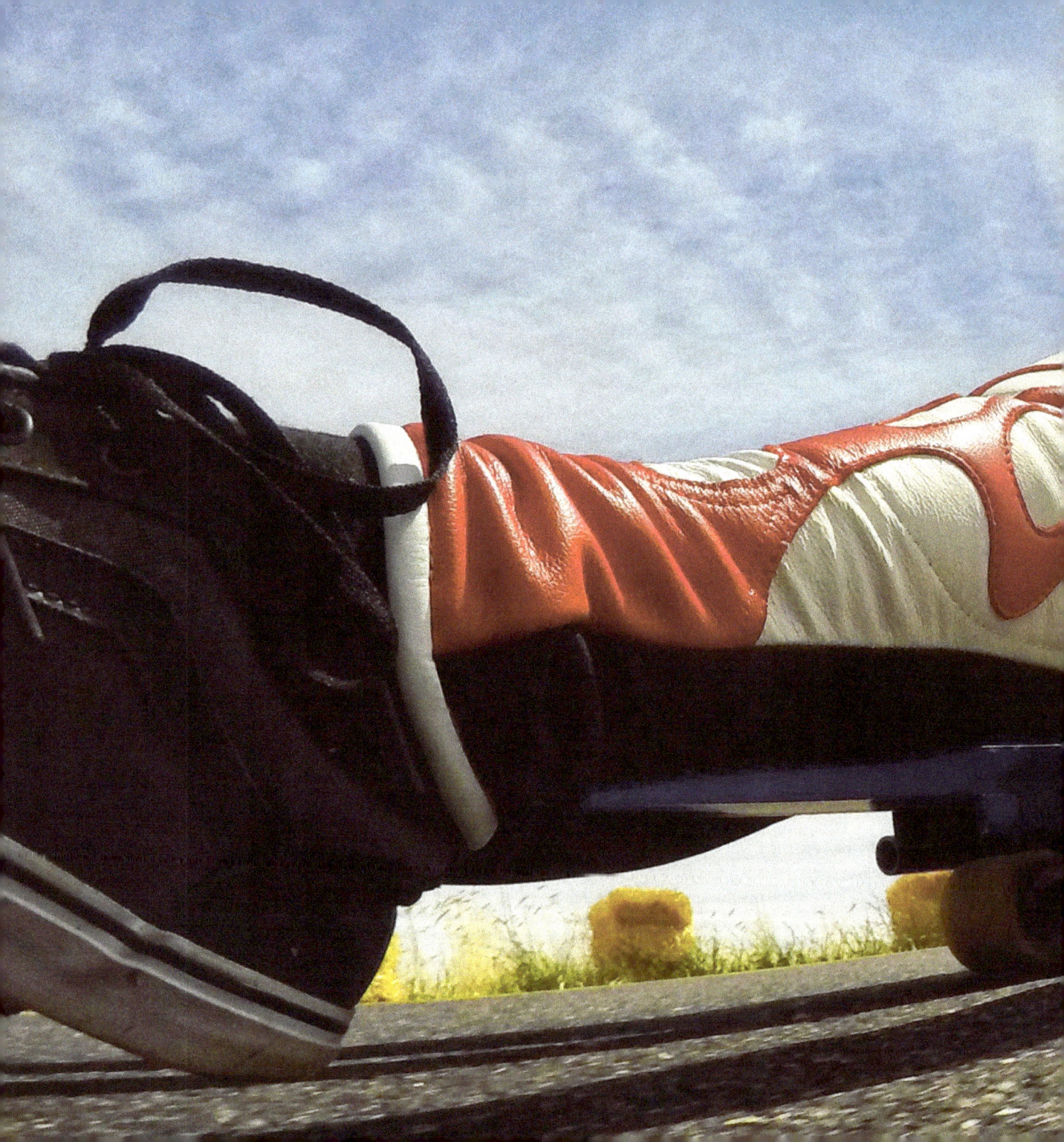

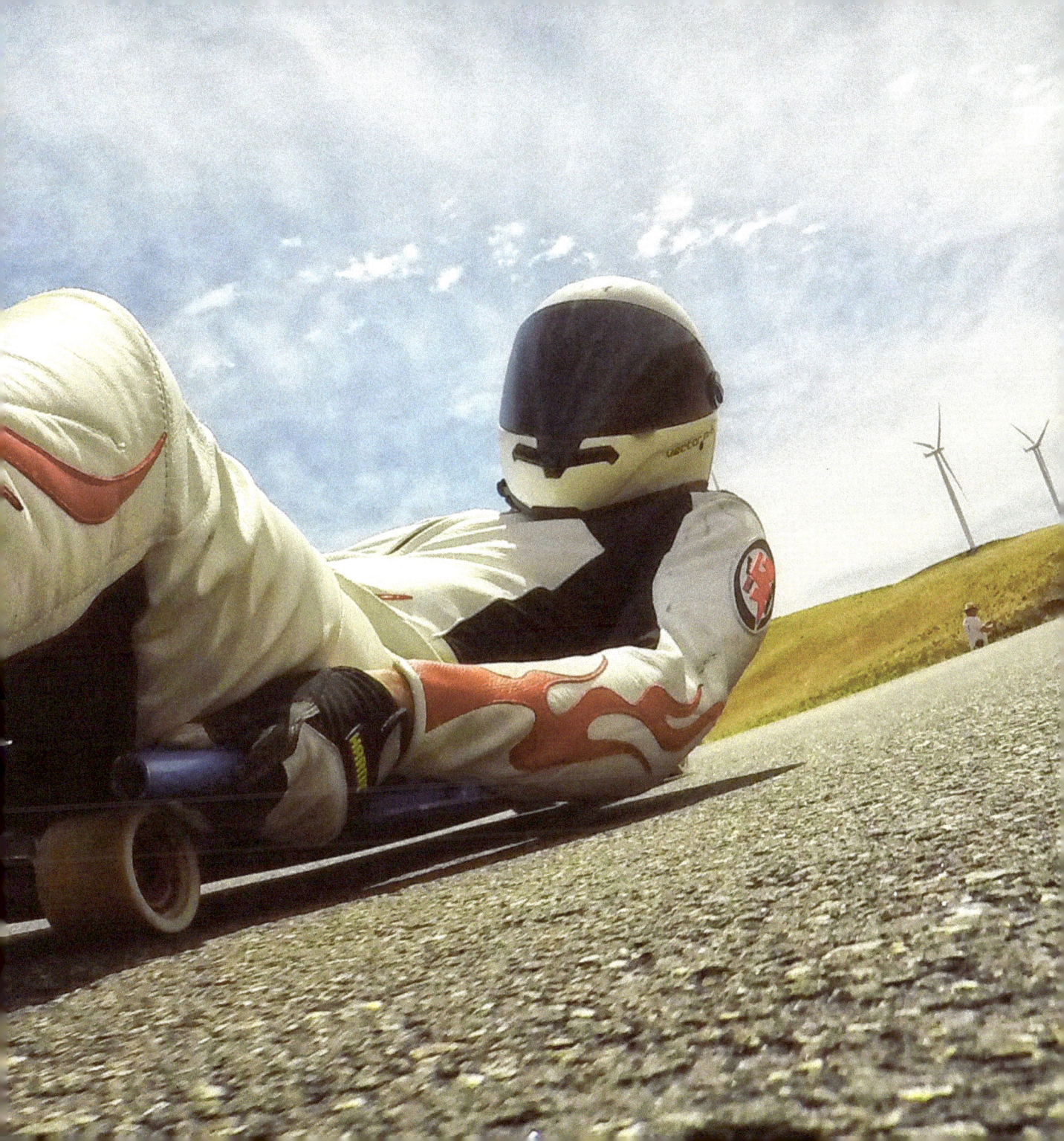

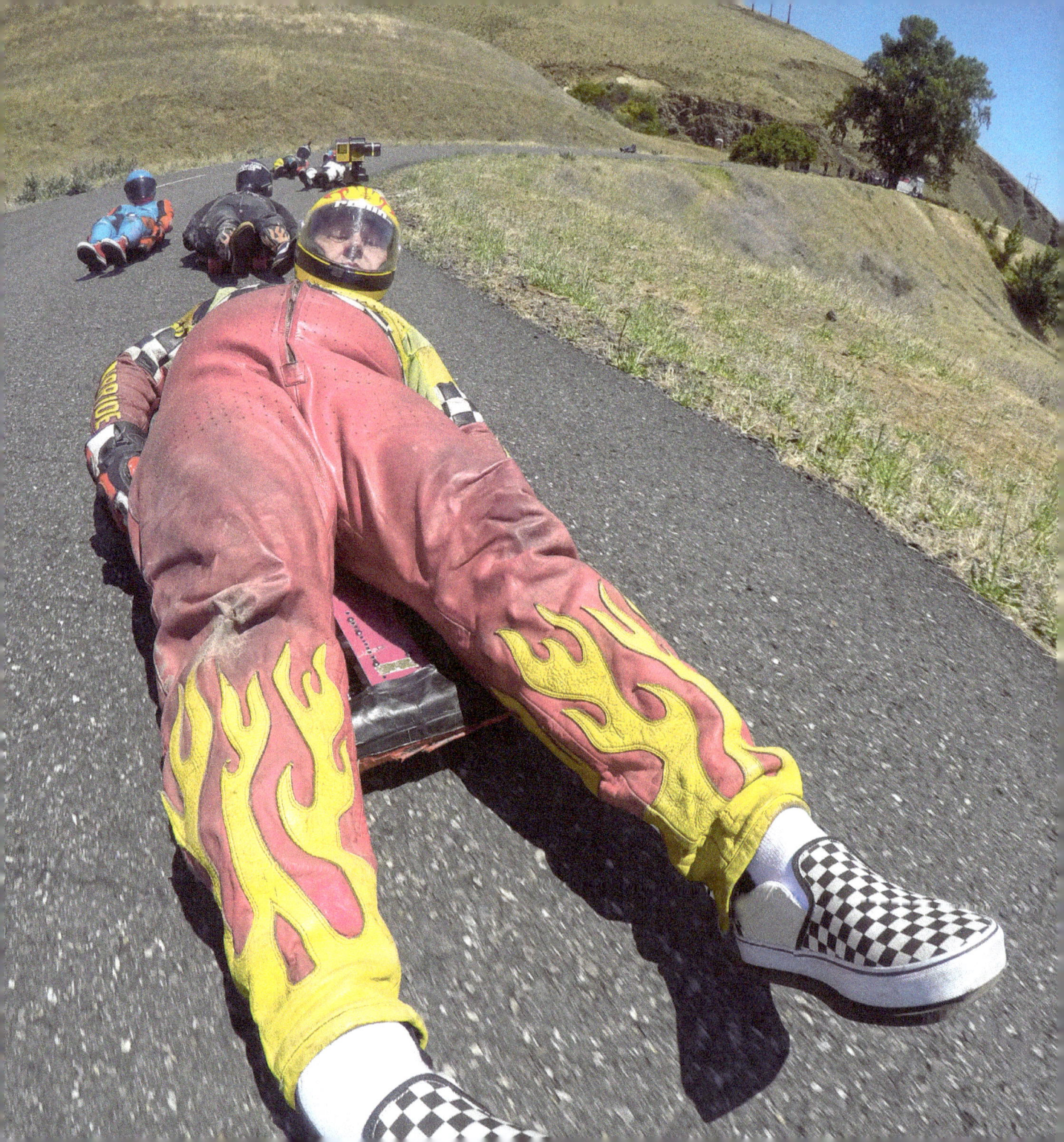

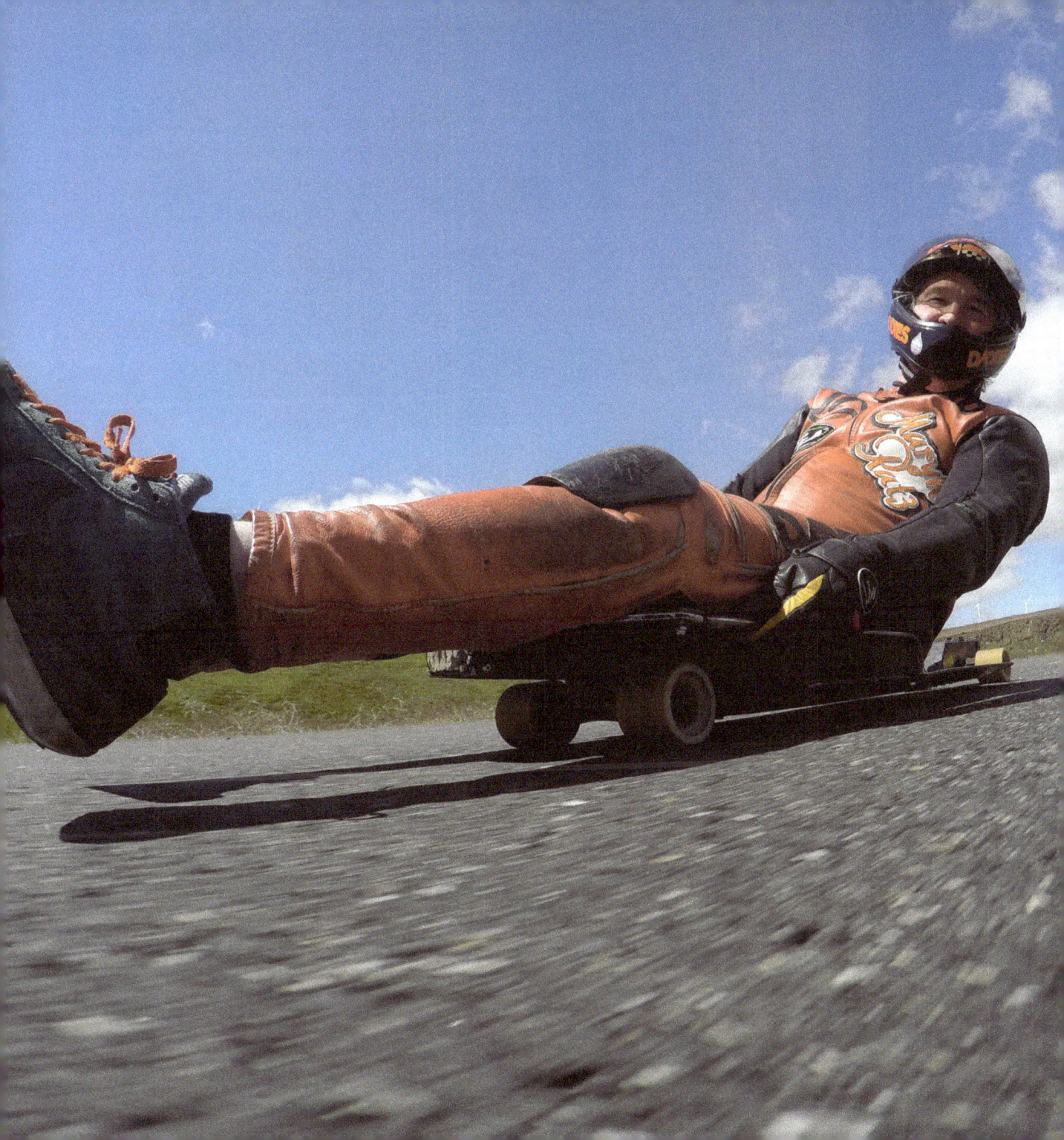

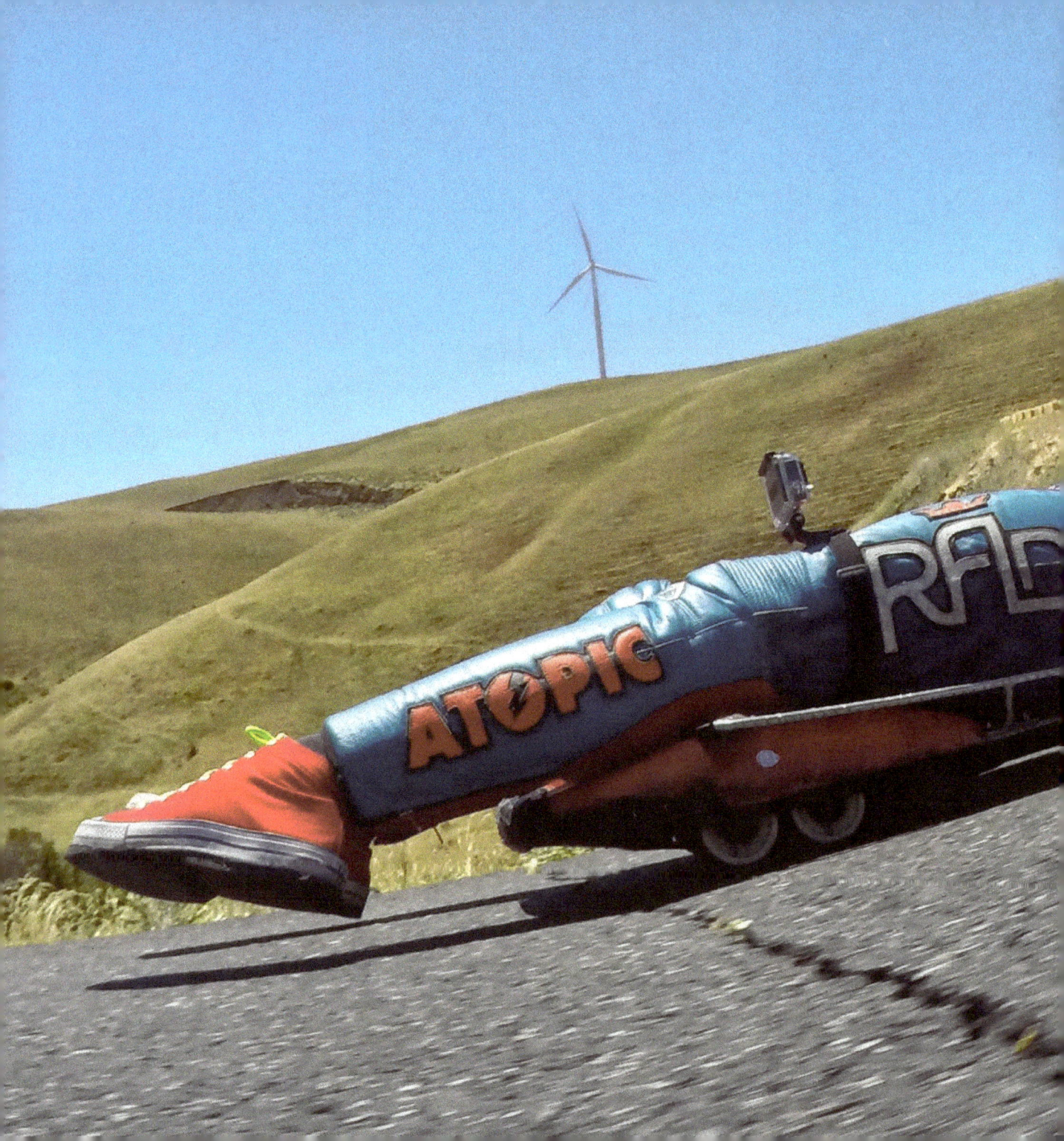

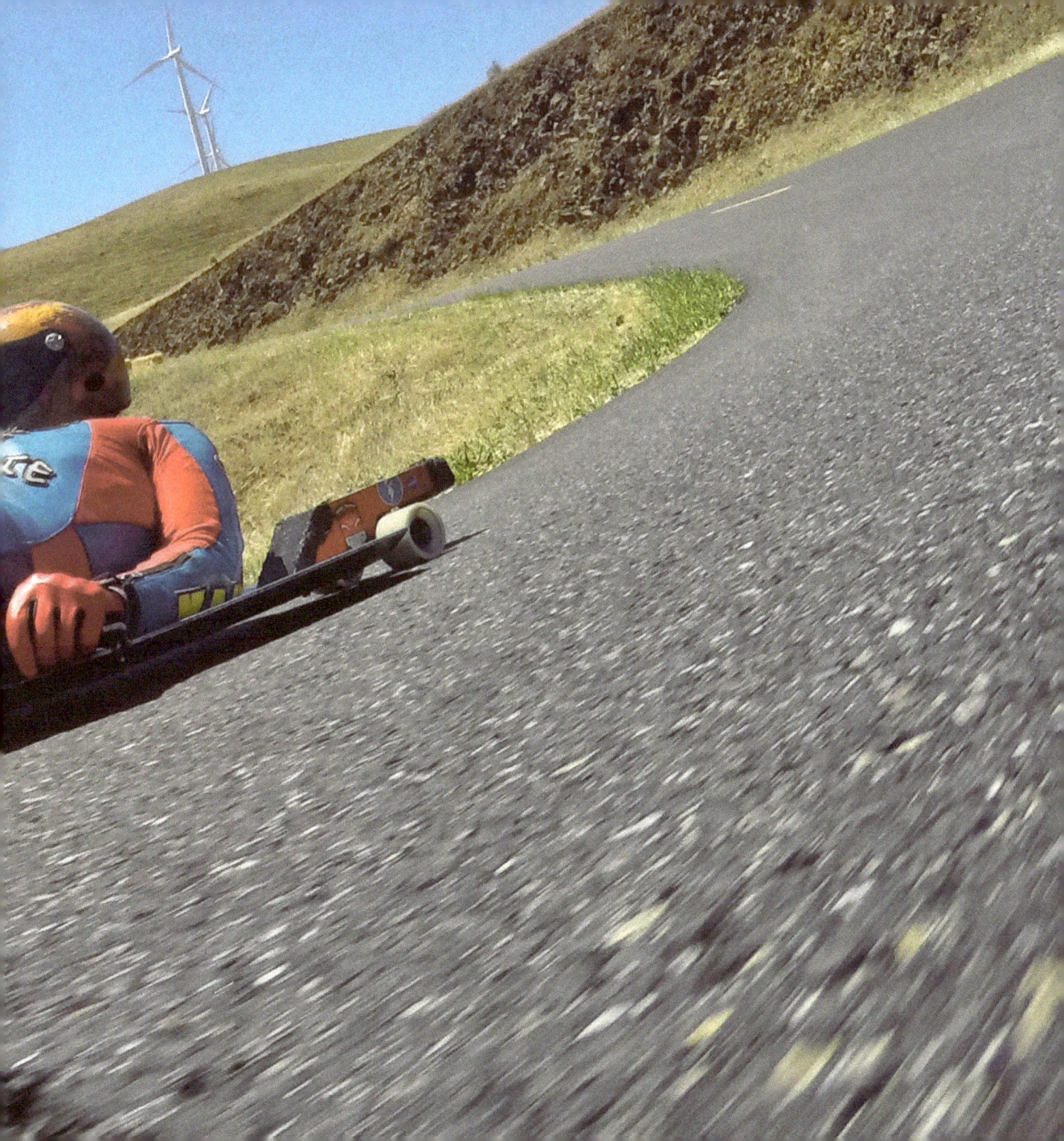

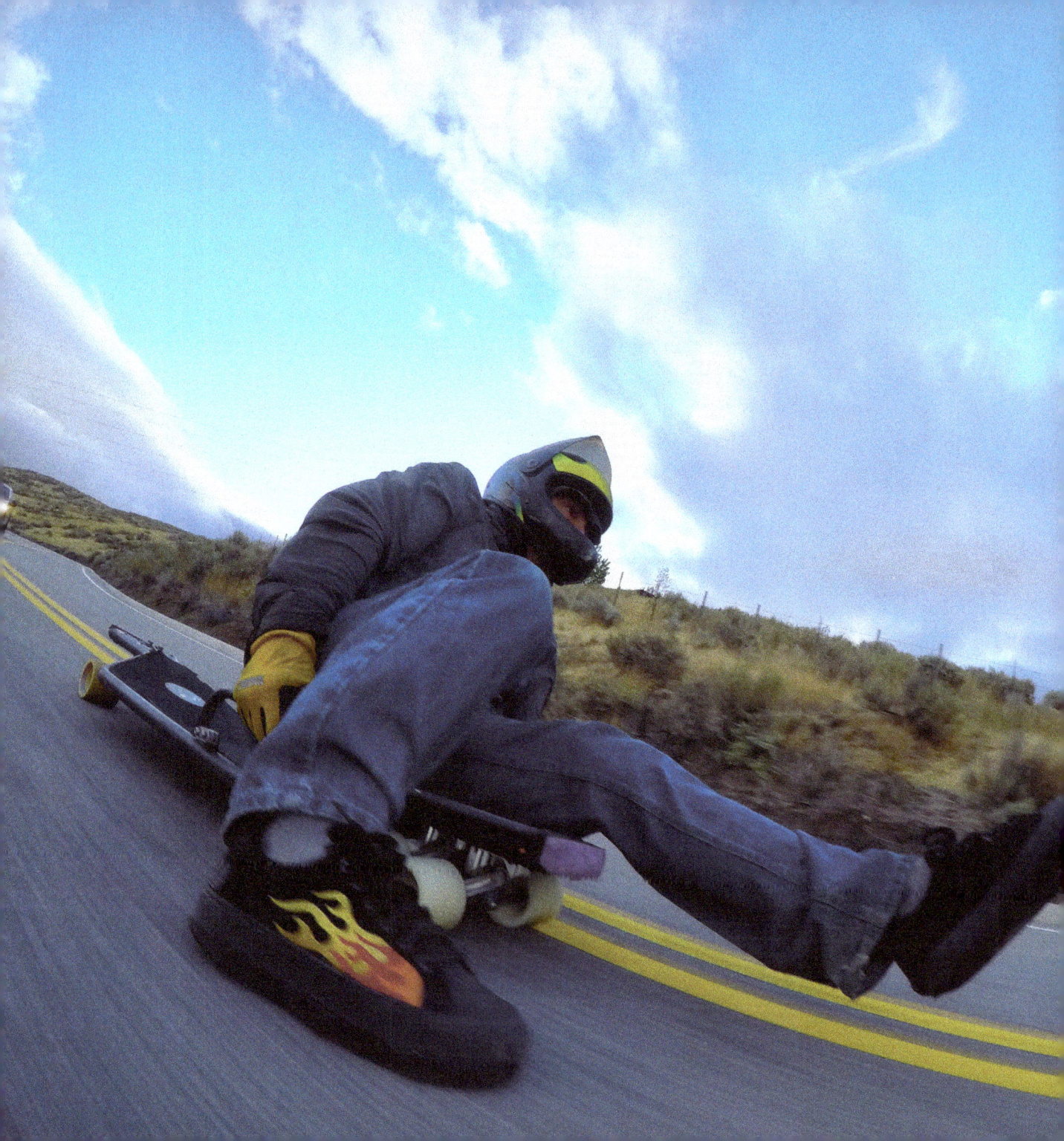

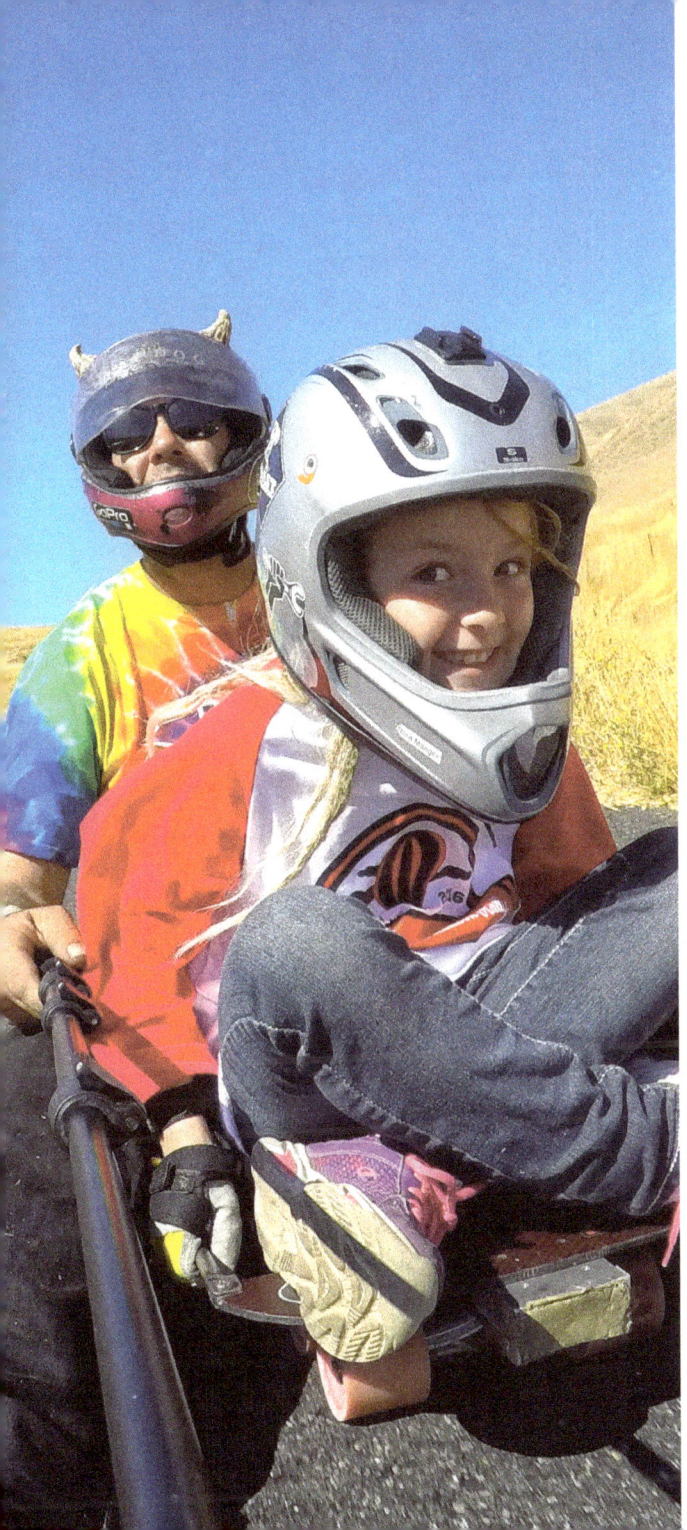

#Heyladies

Cheers to the fearless females who have stormed the scene and continue to define bravery in every sense of the word!

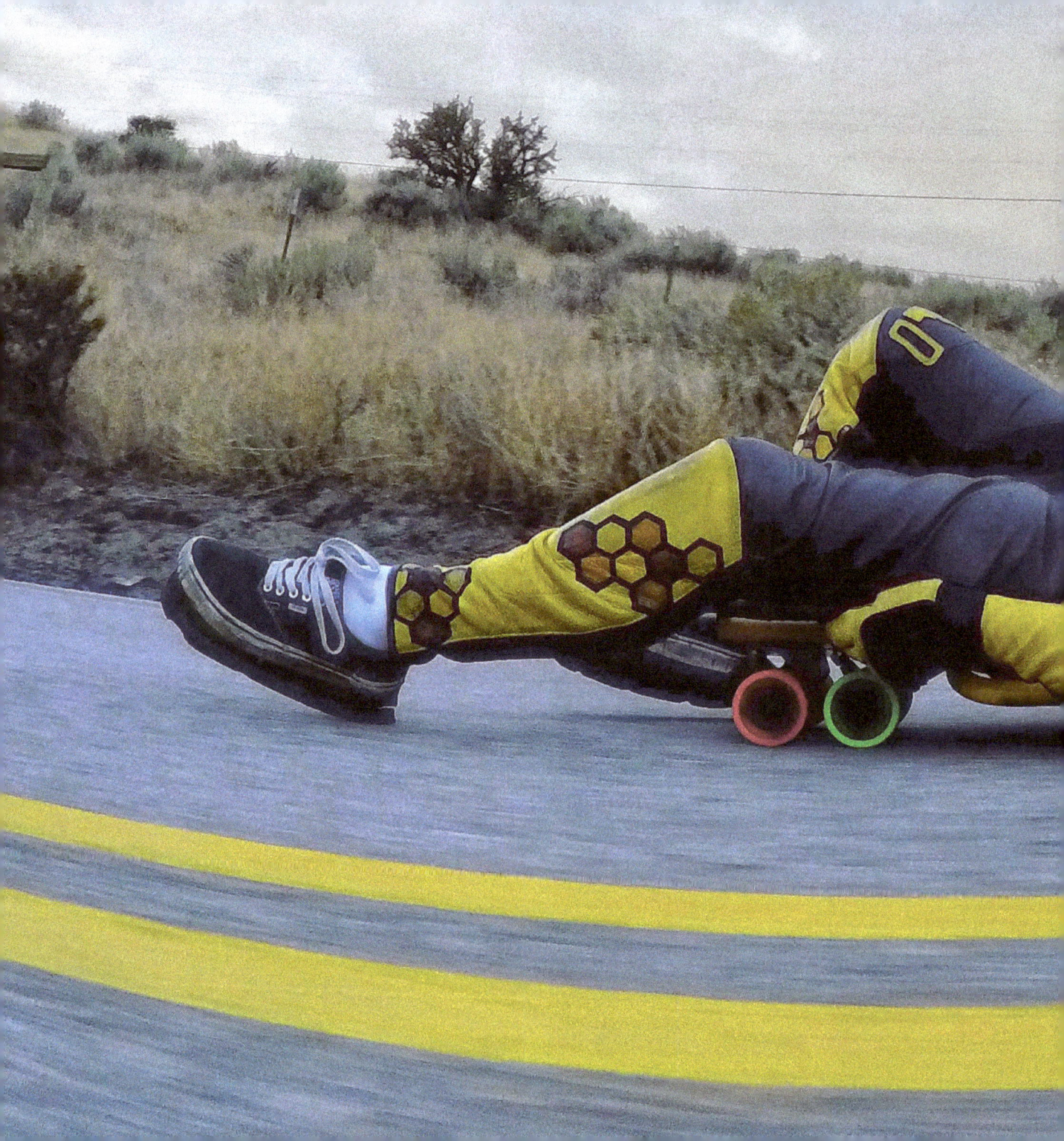

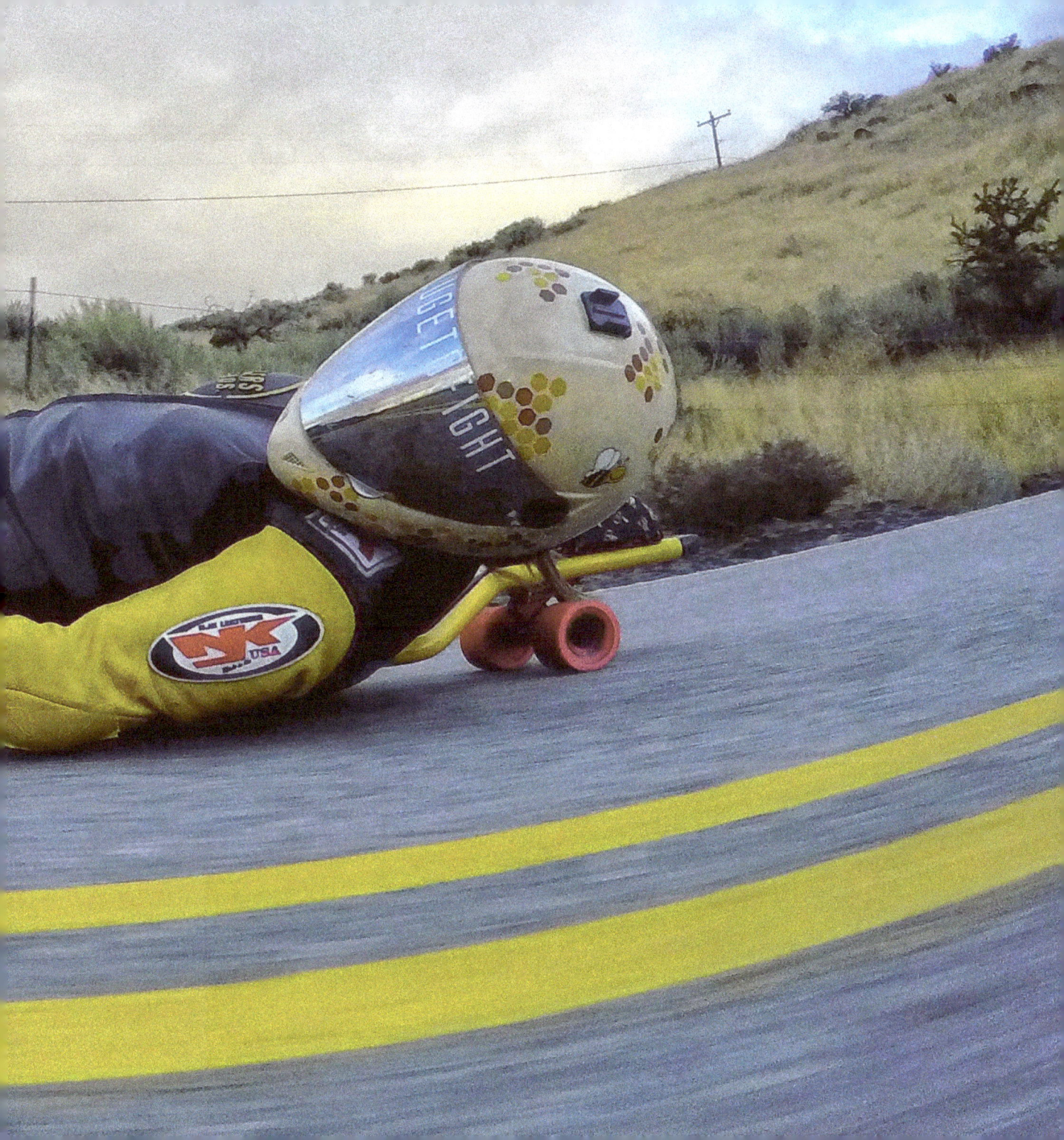

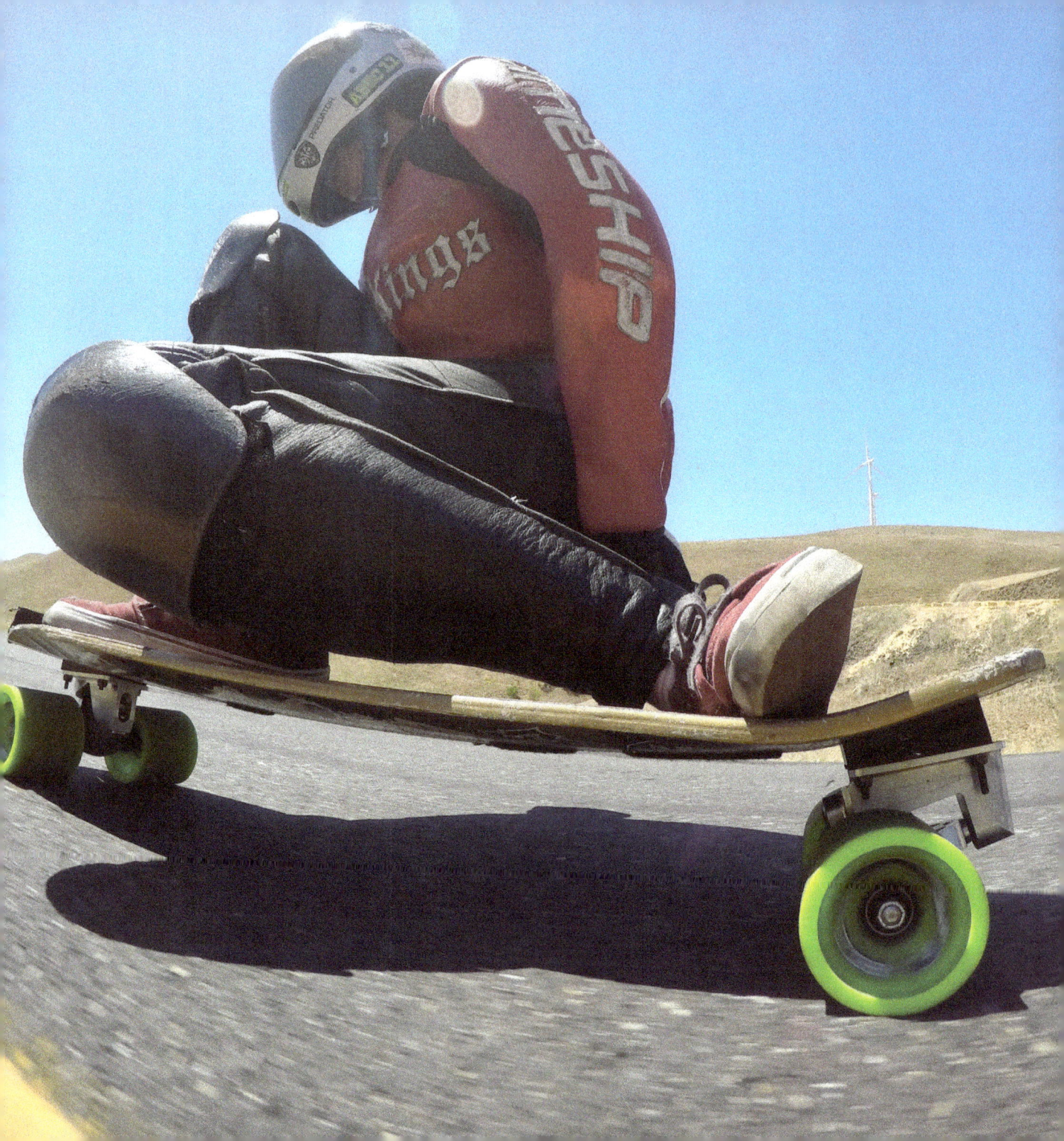

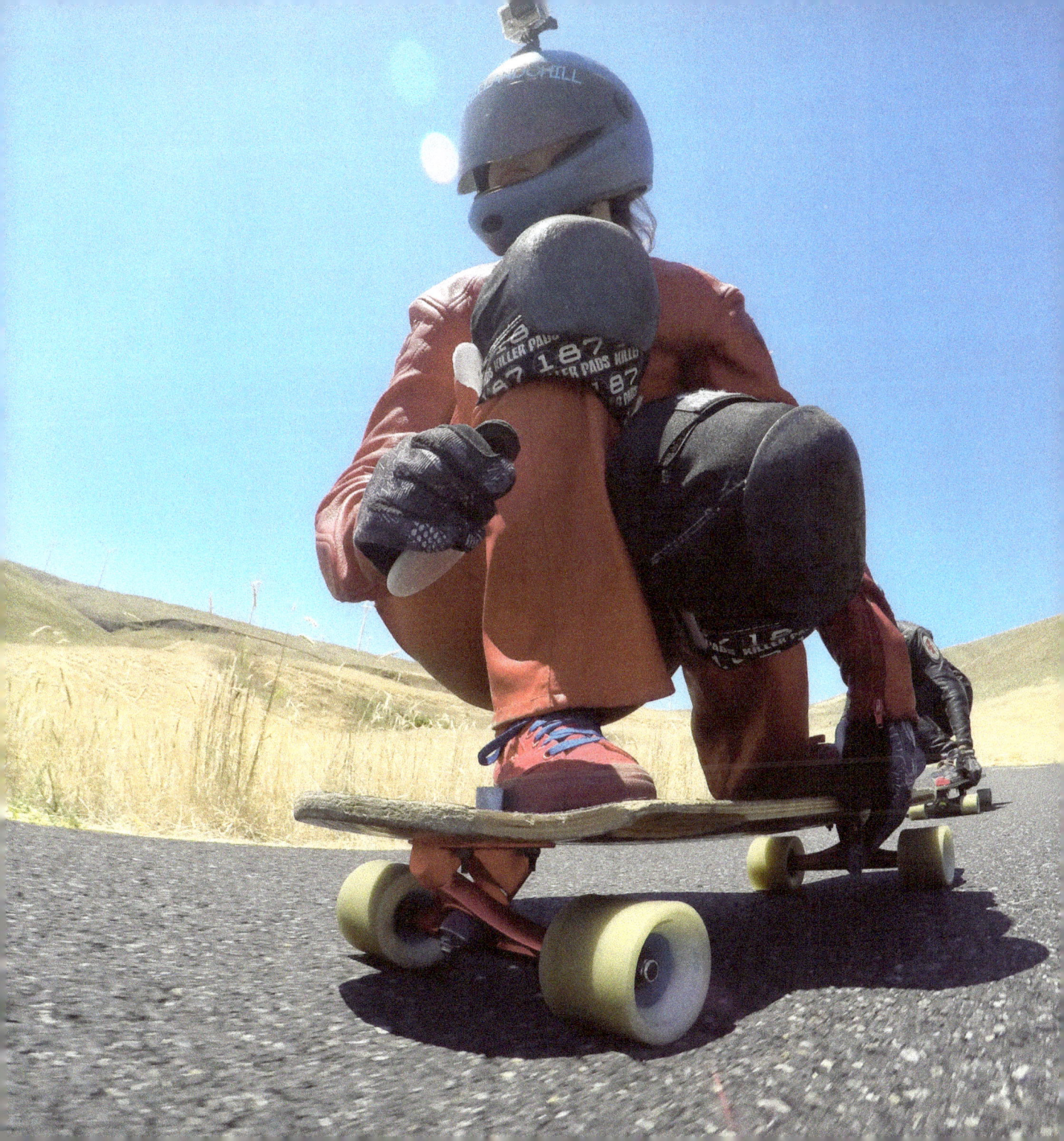

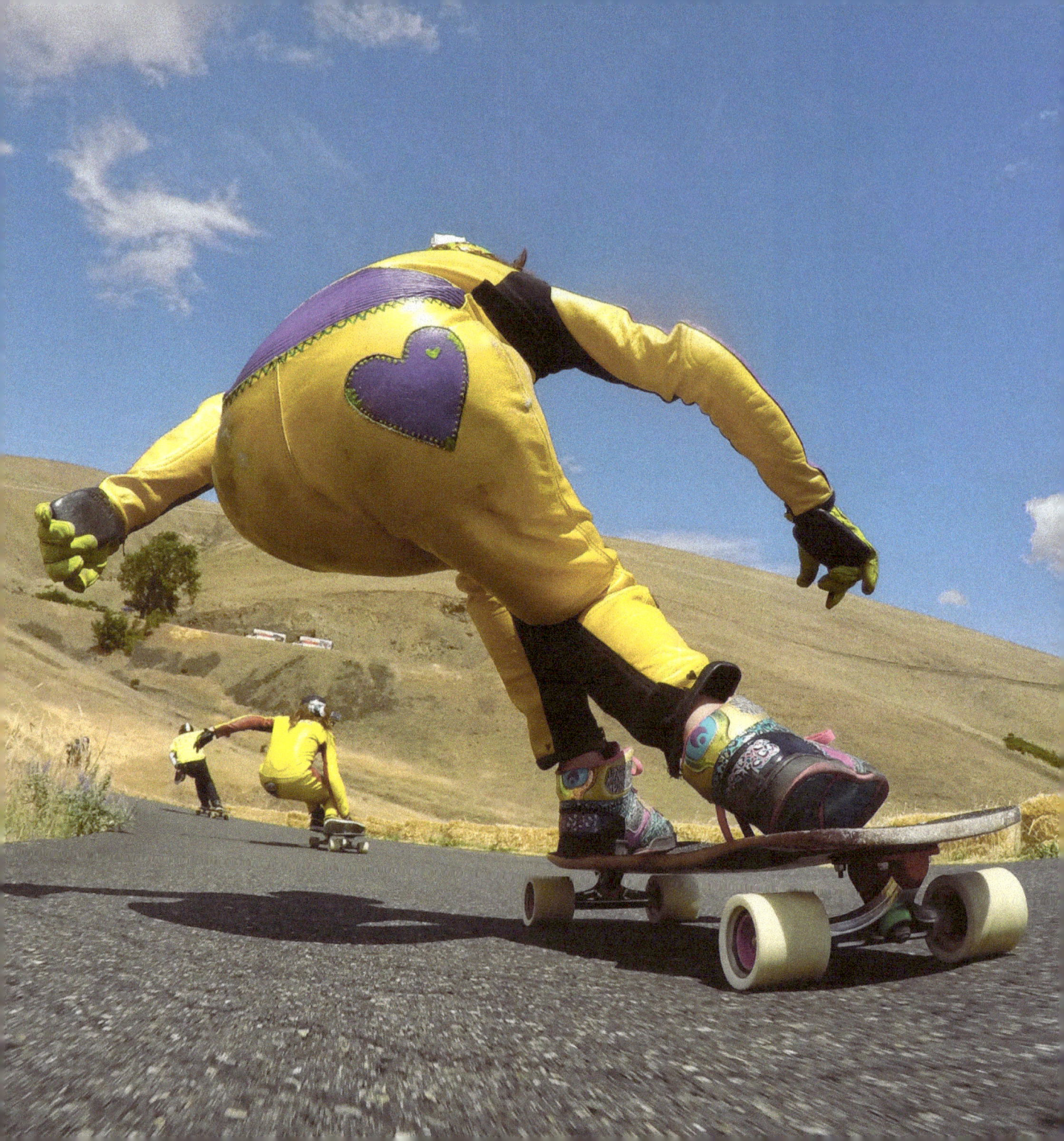

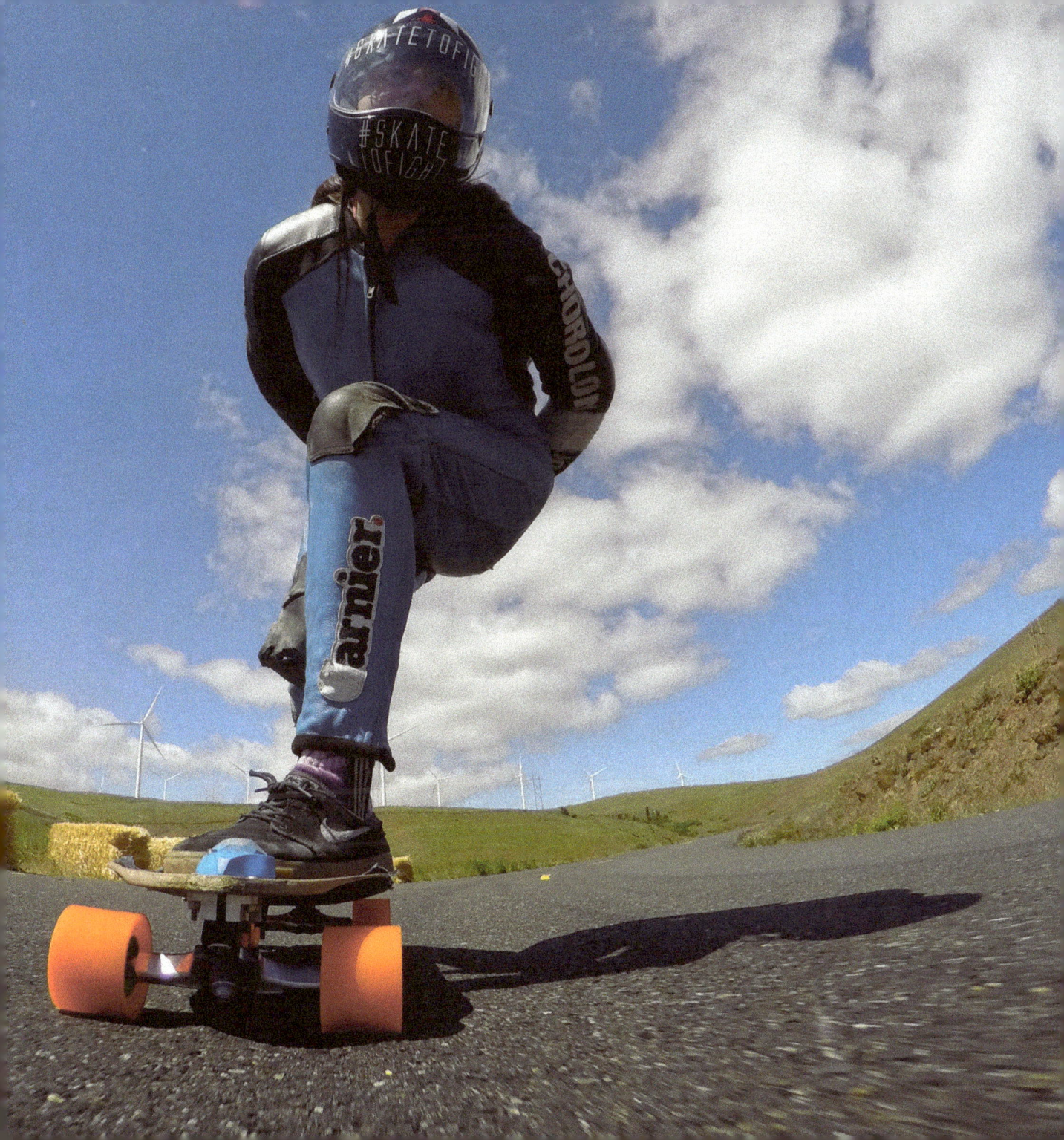

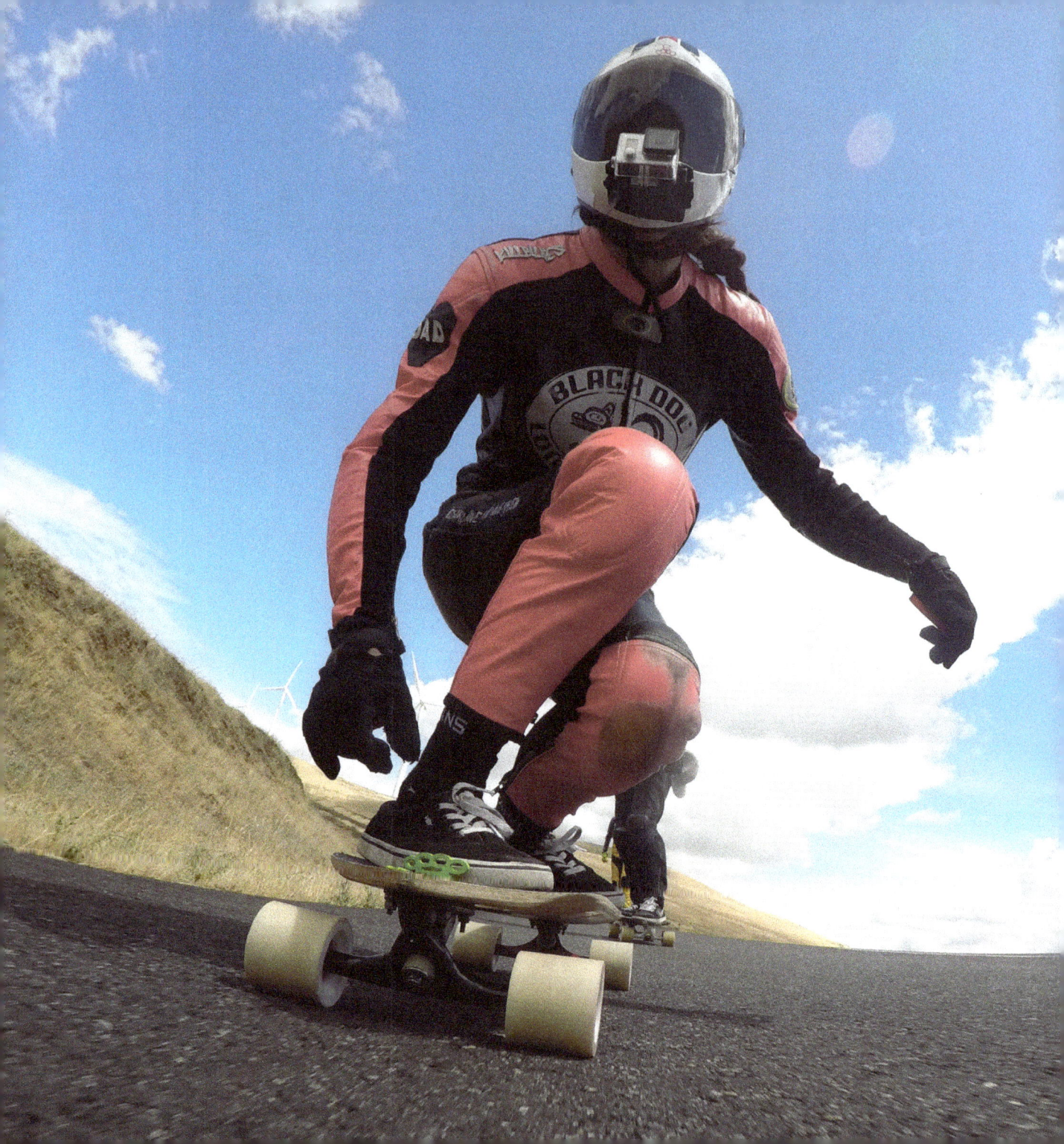

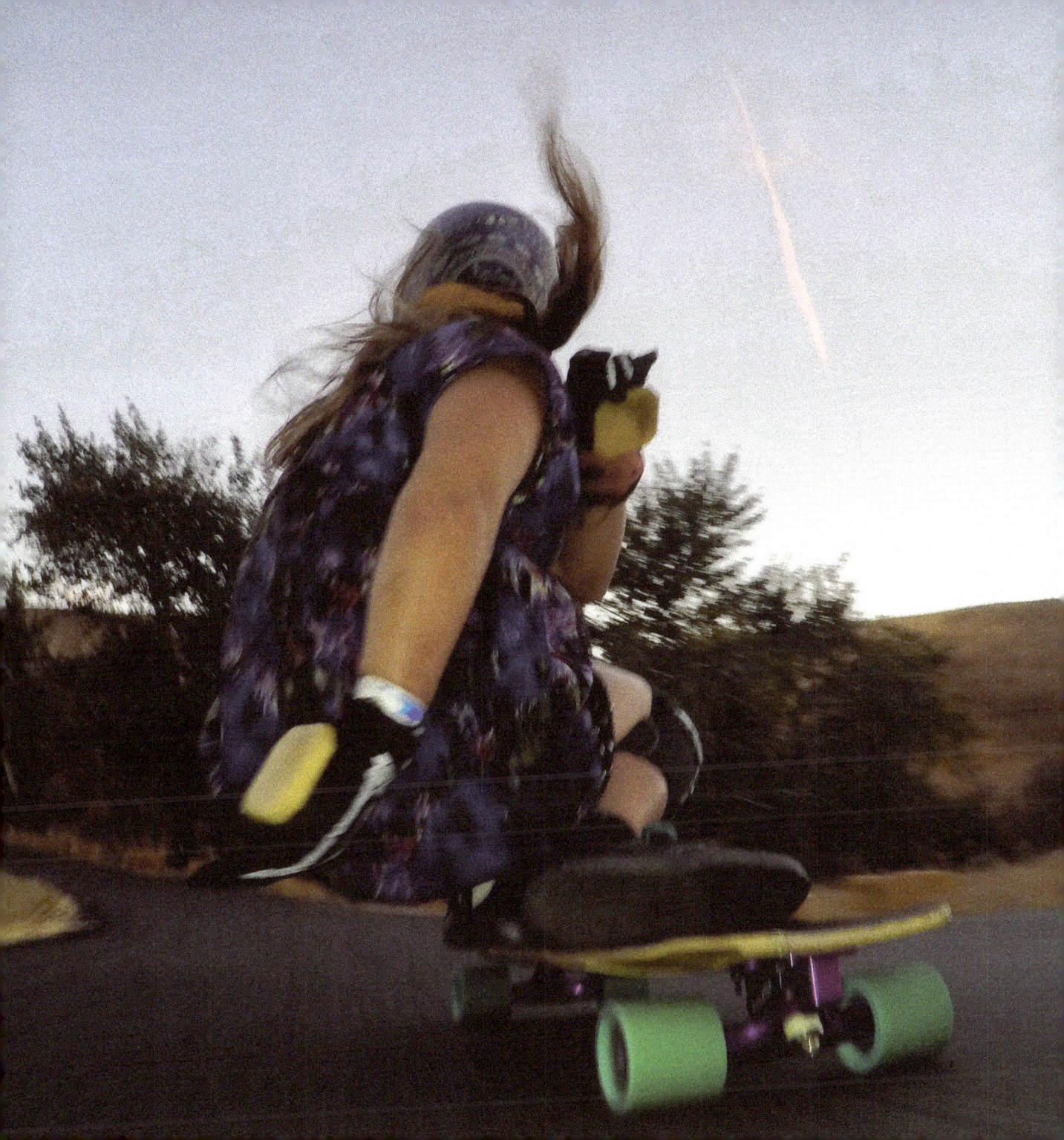

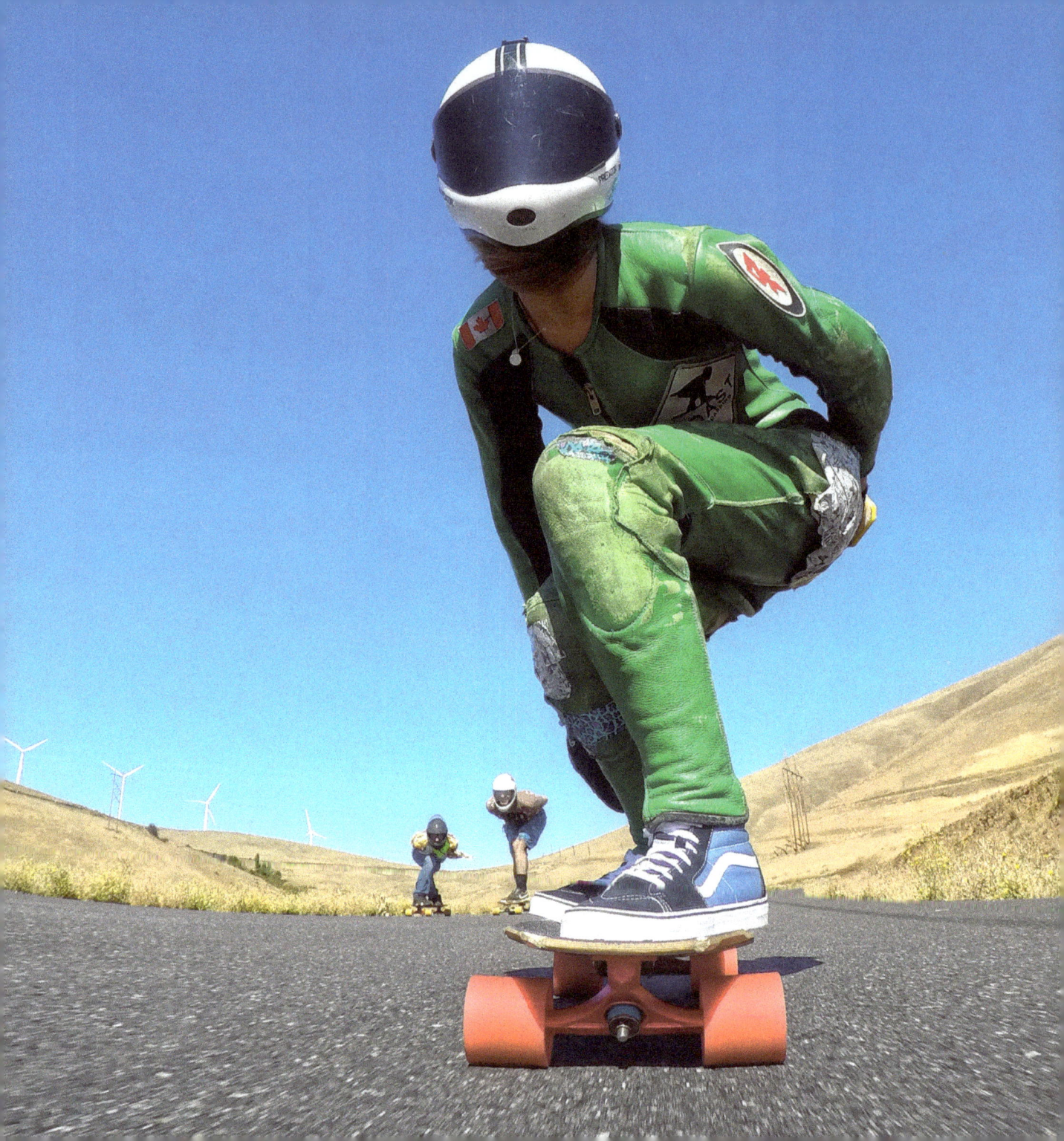

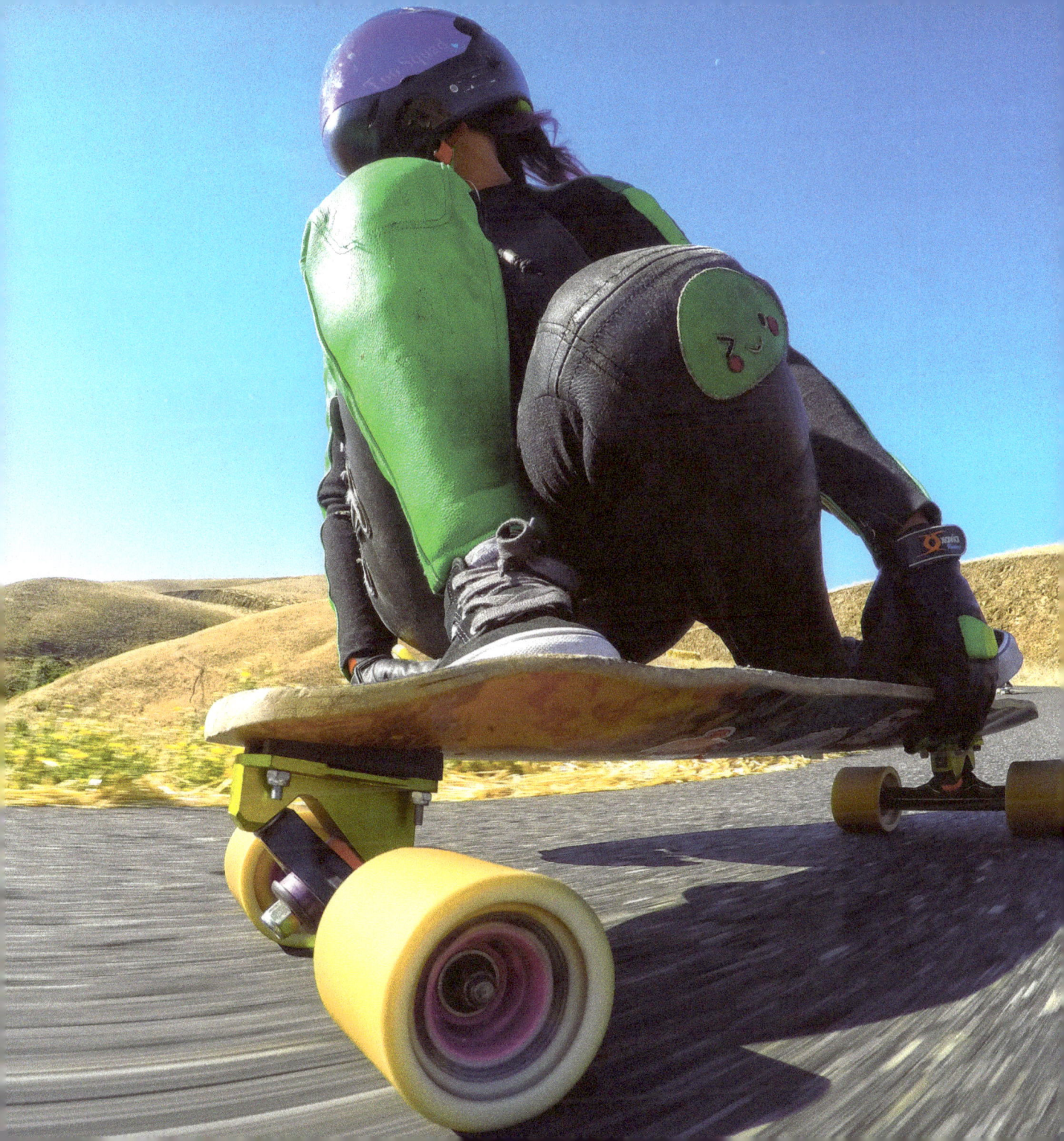

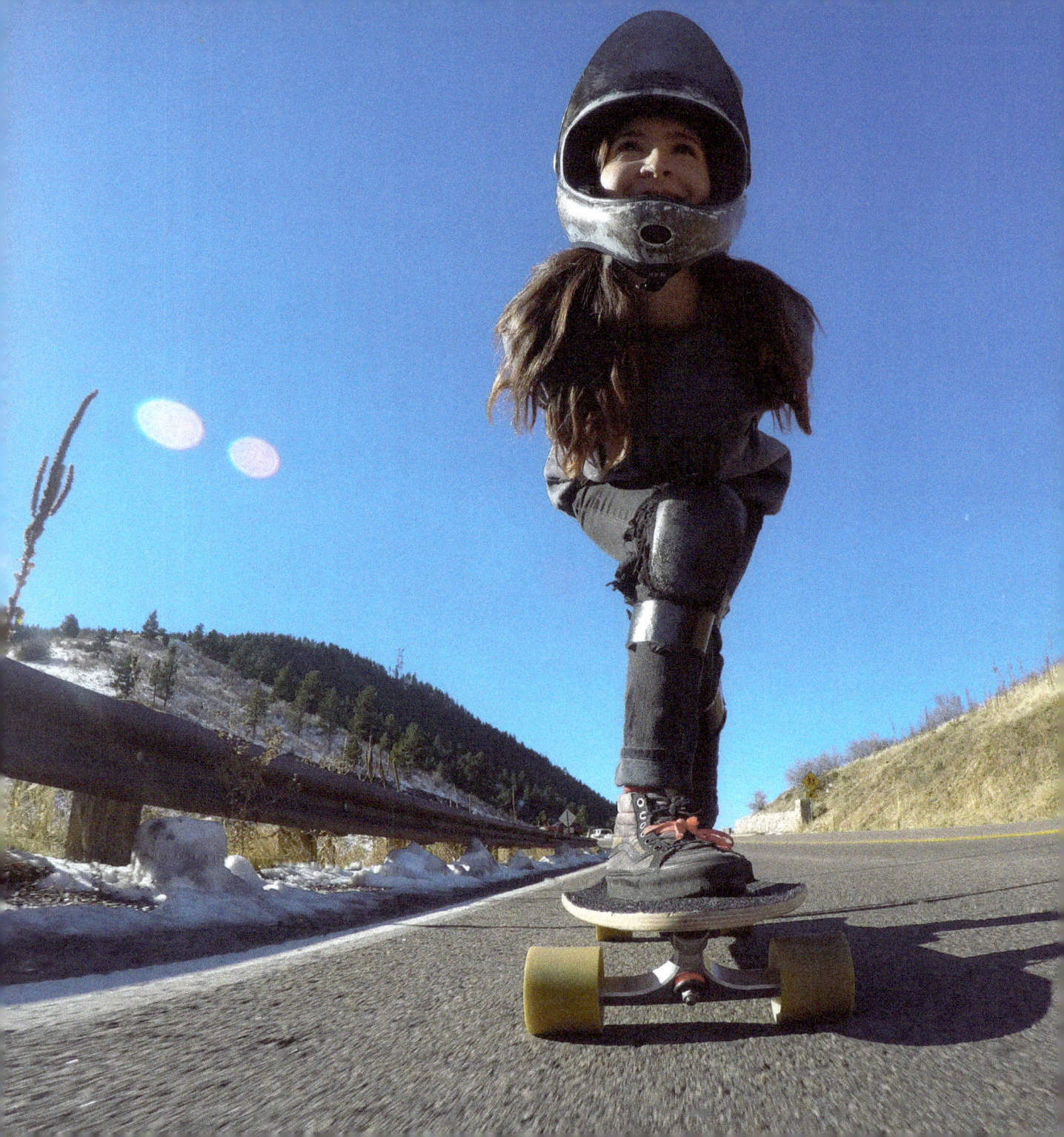

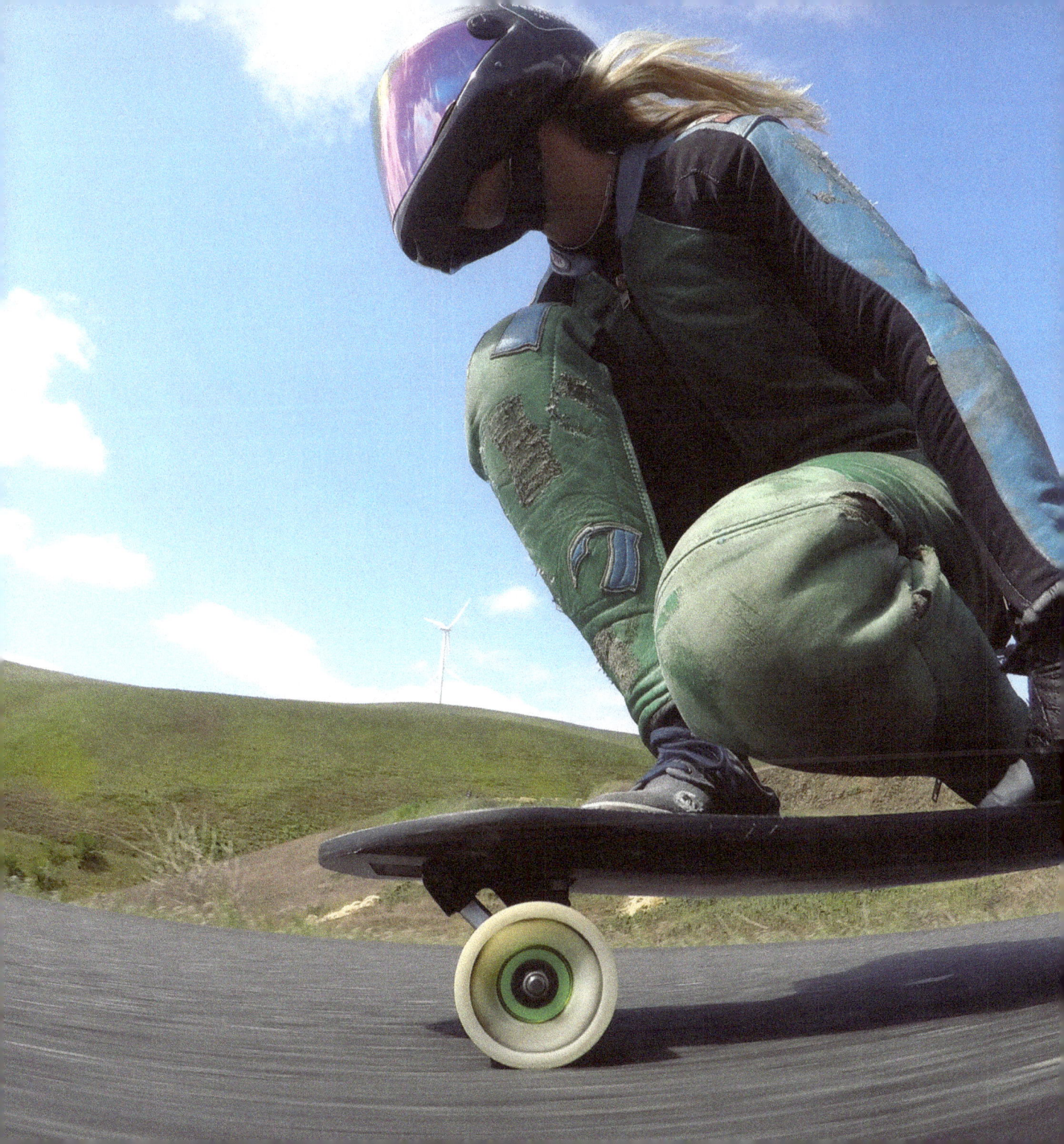

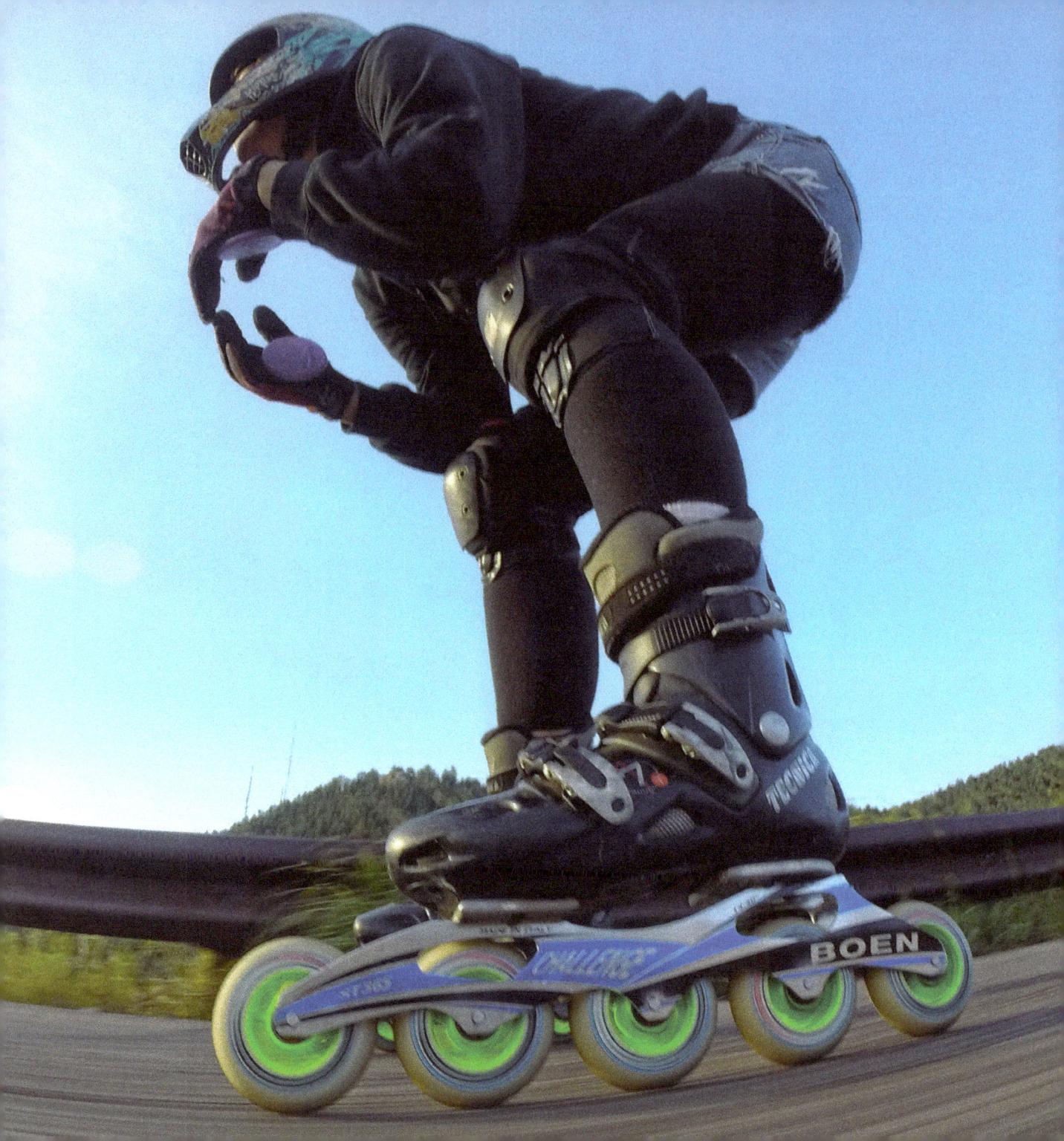

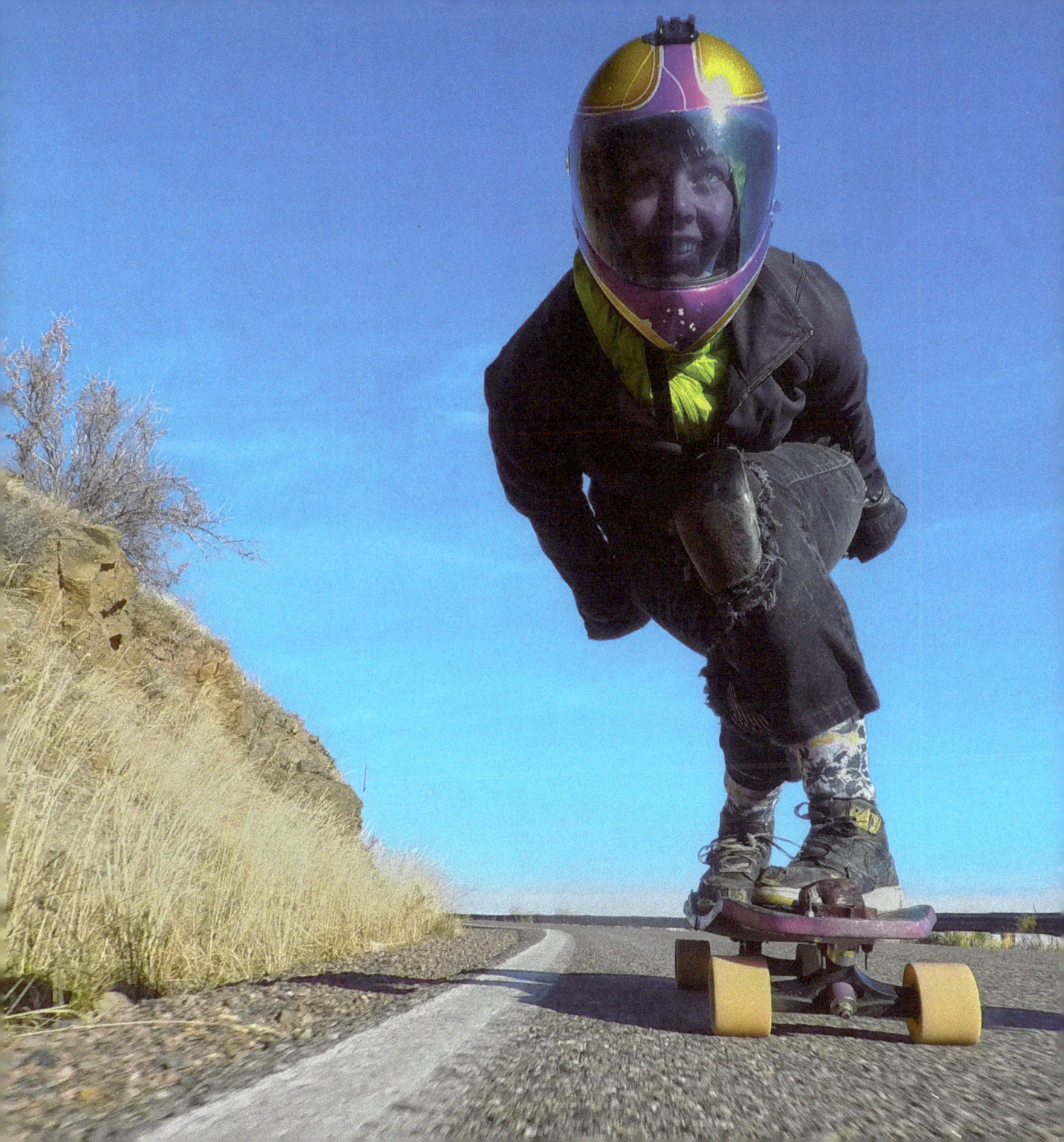

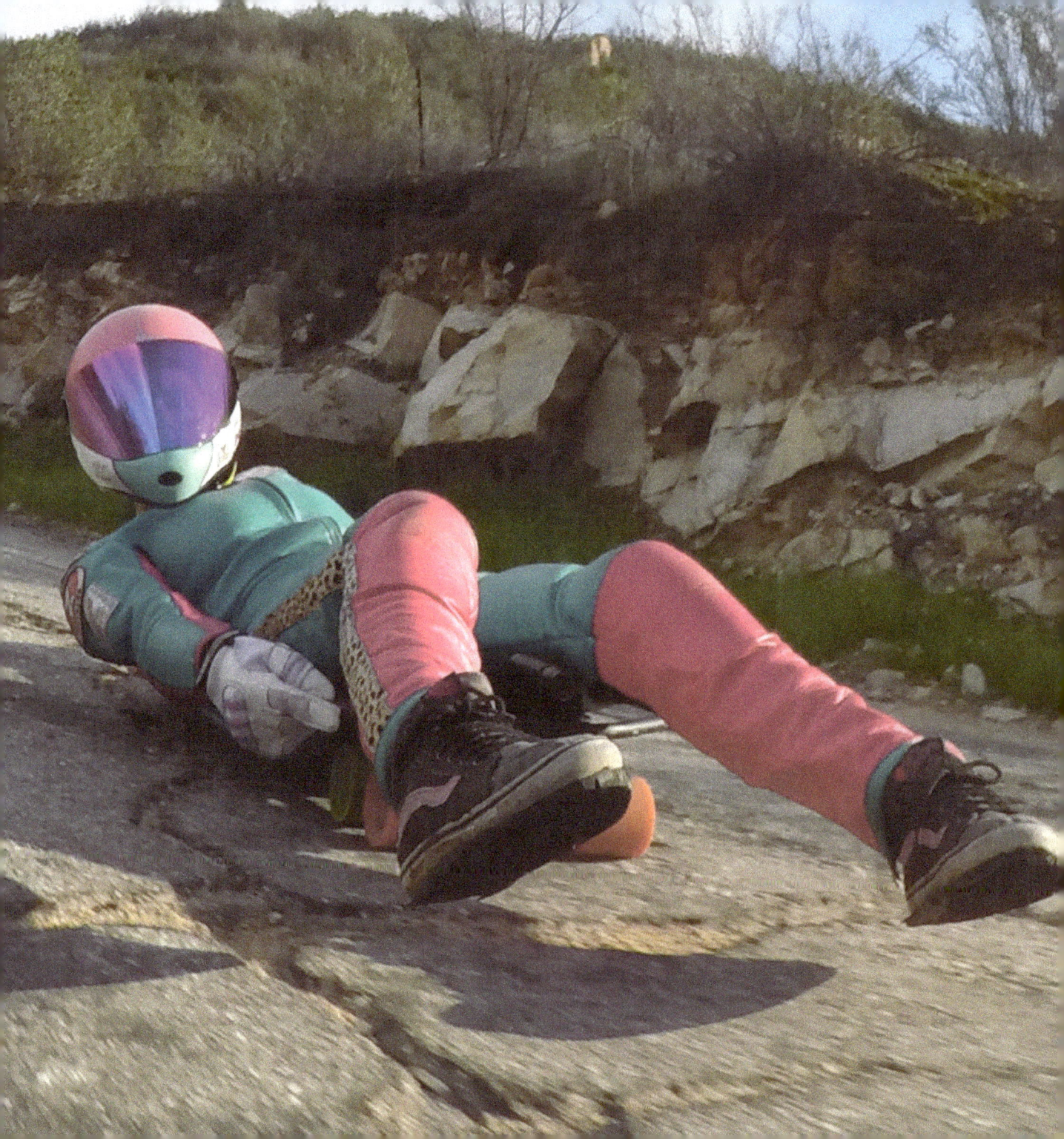

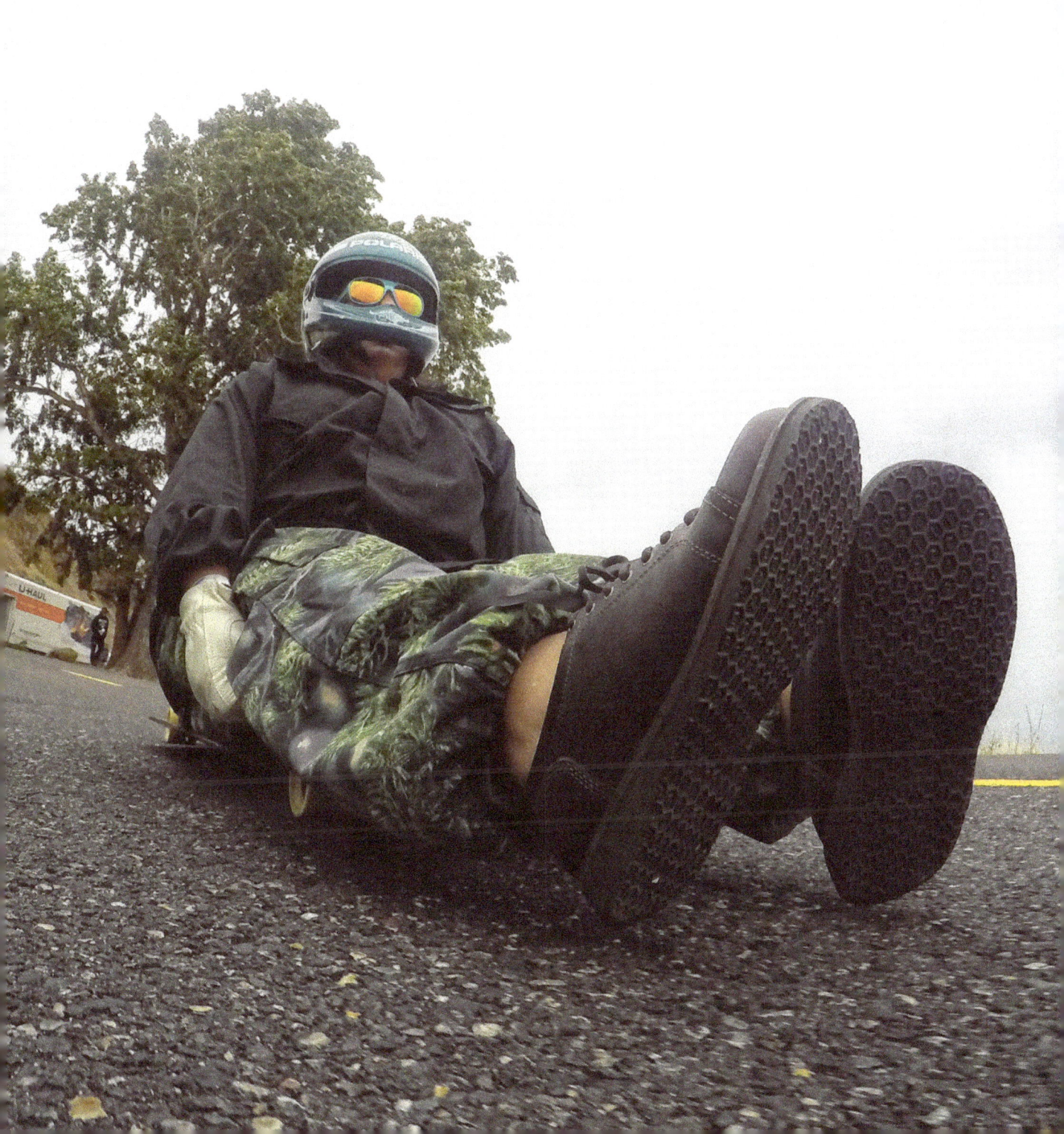

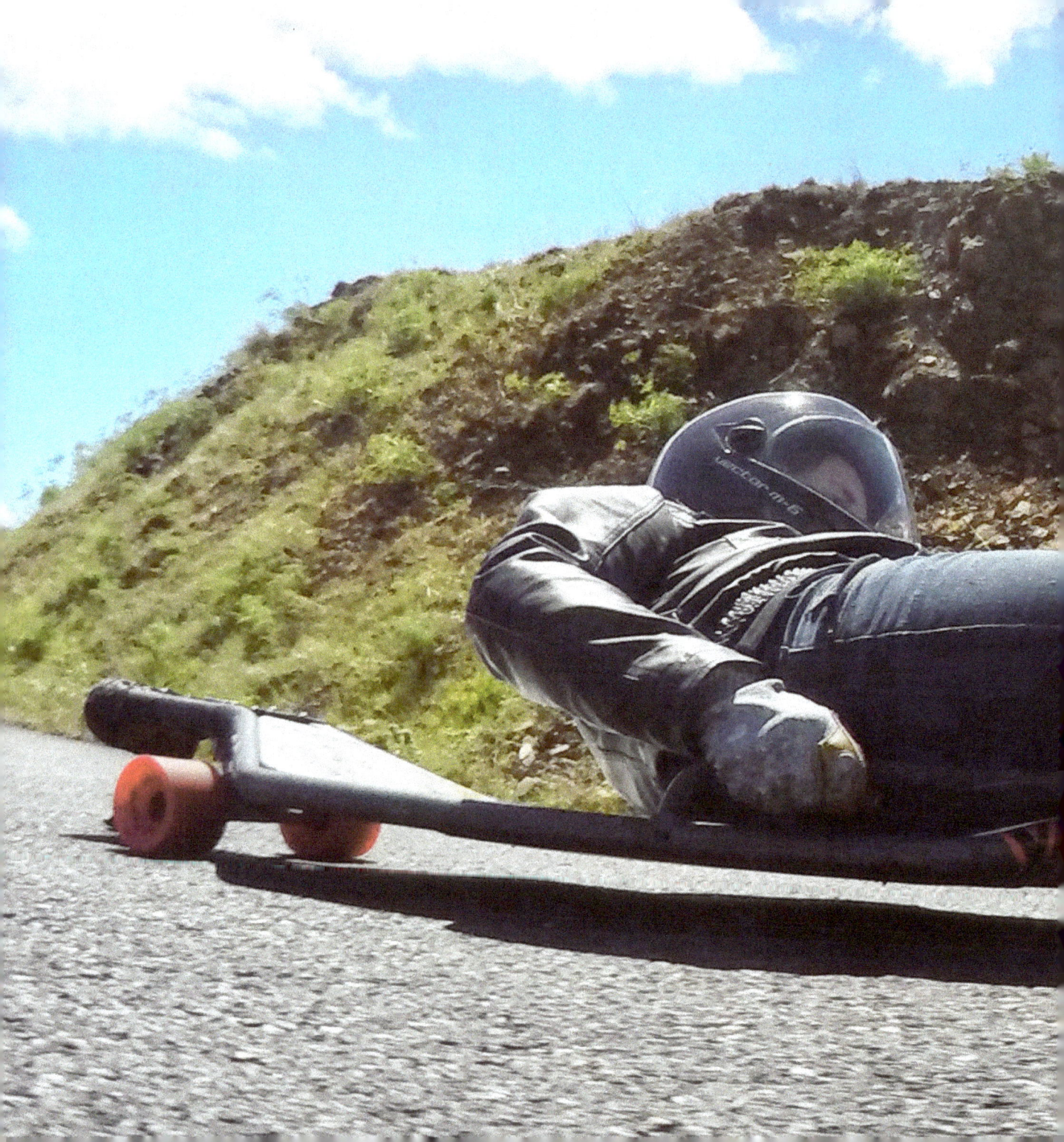

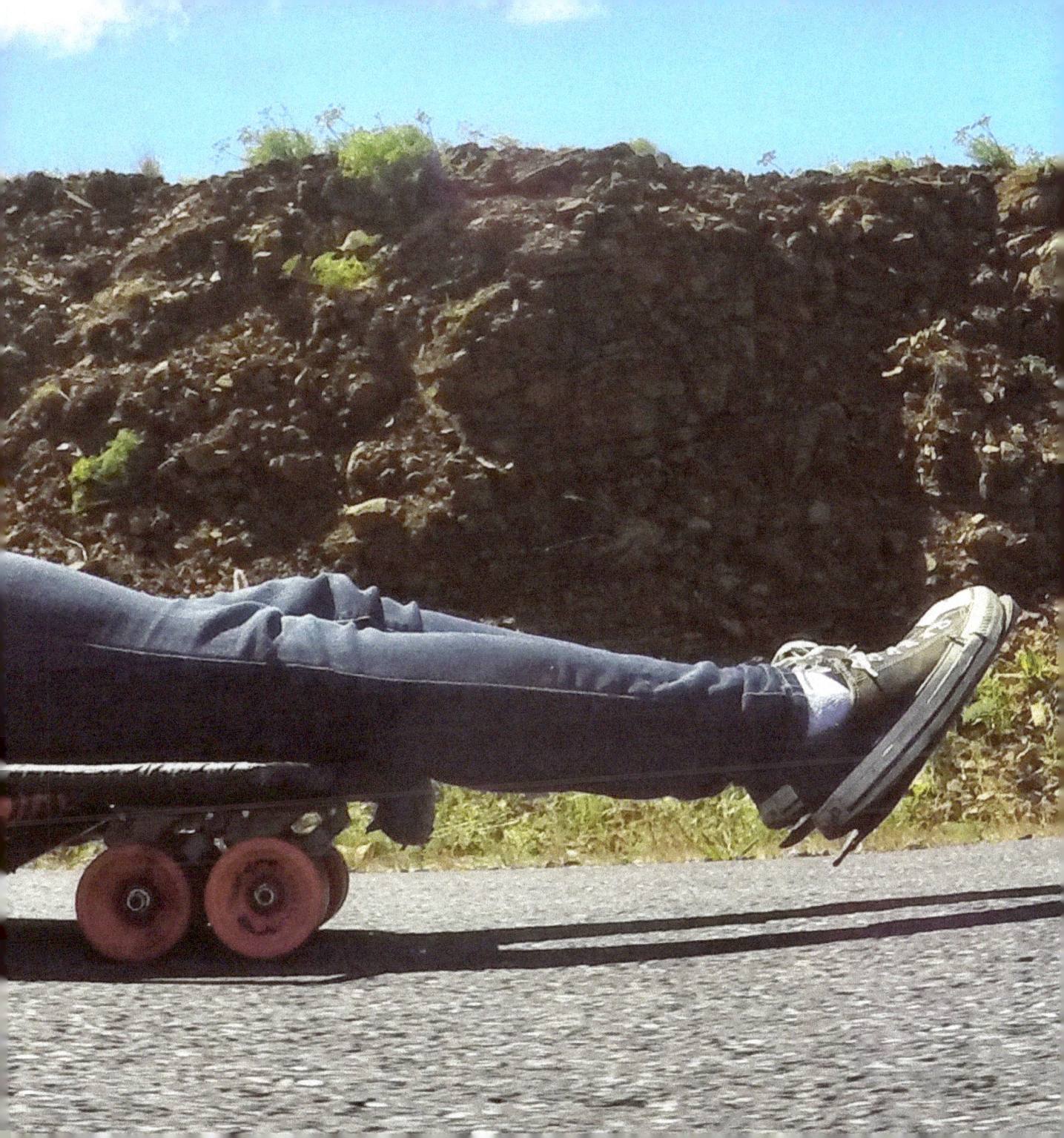

#Californication

California has some amazing roads, and the locals are fun to skate with, IF you can keep up...

We are beyond grateful for the hospitality our west coast homies have shown us when we've passed through their golden state, so I hope the following shots represent some of the rad times we have had in their presence!

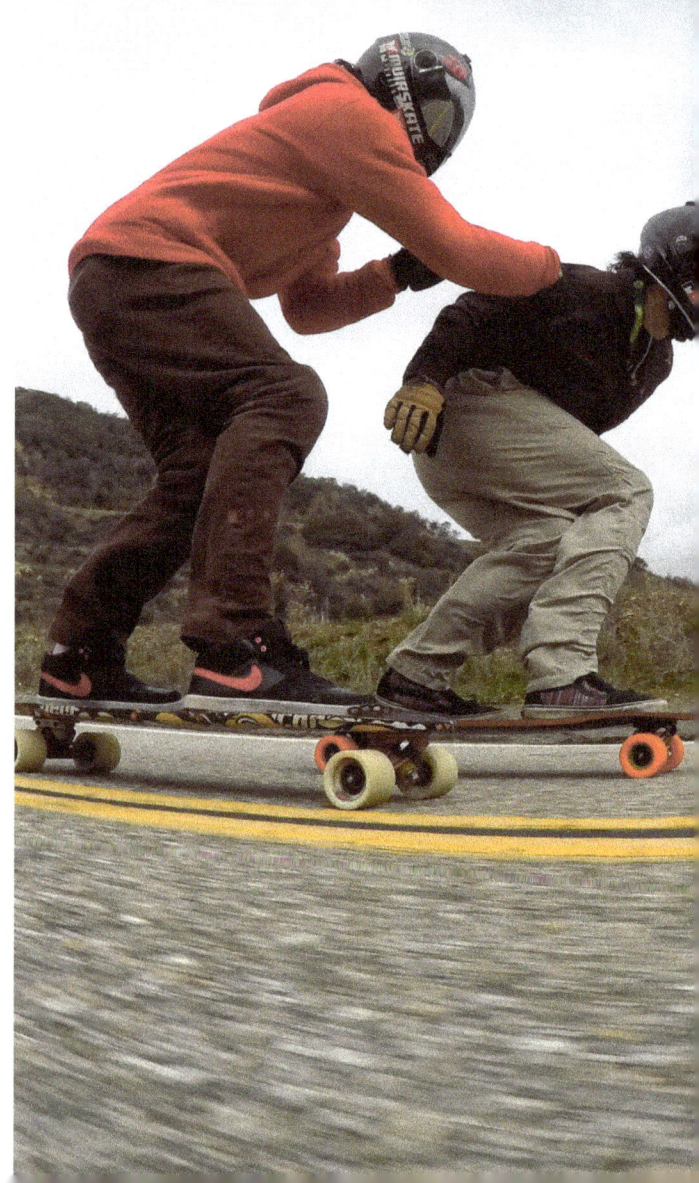

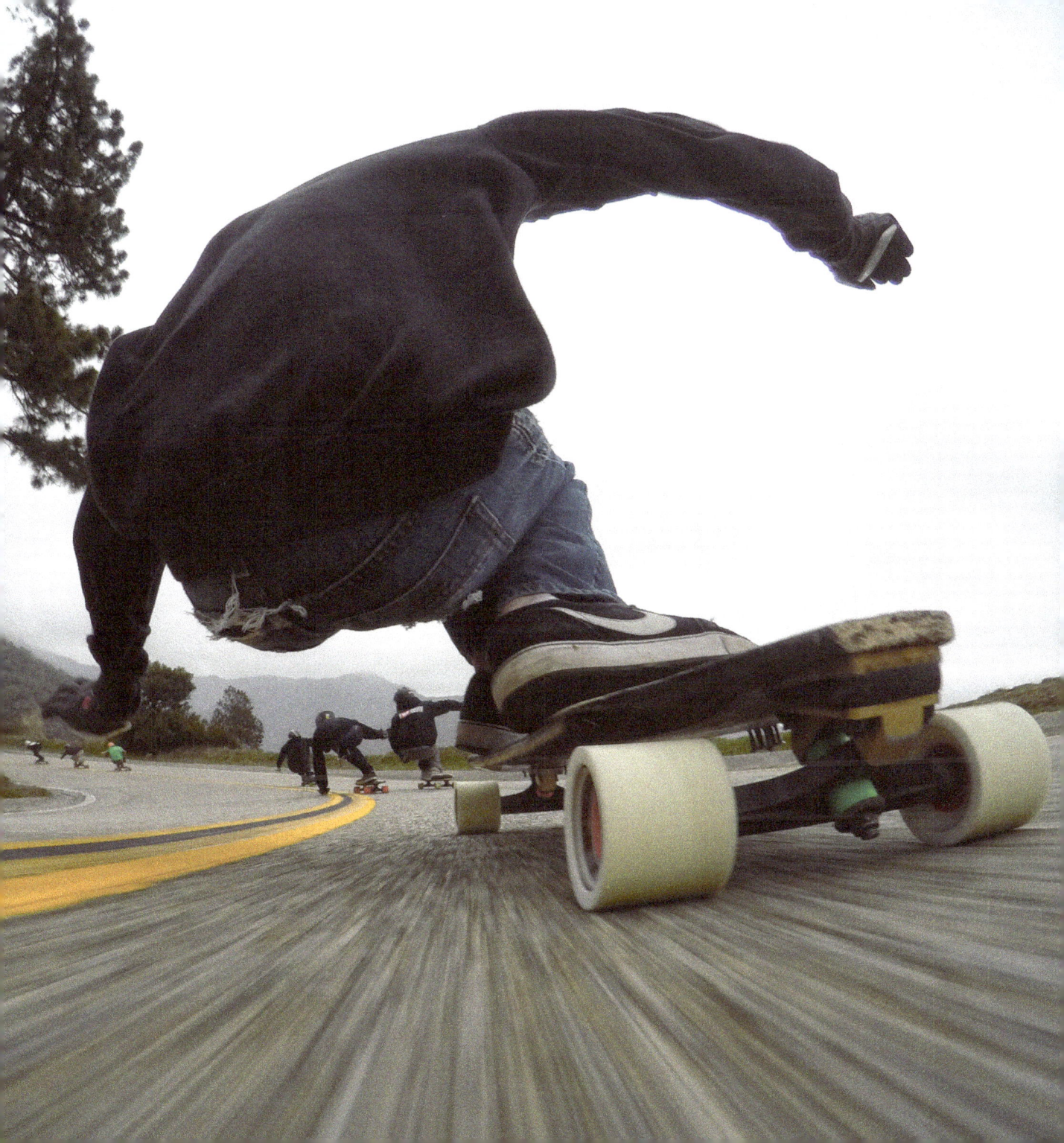

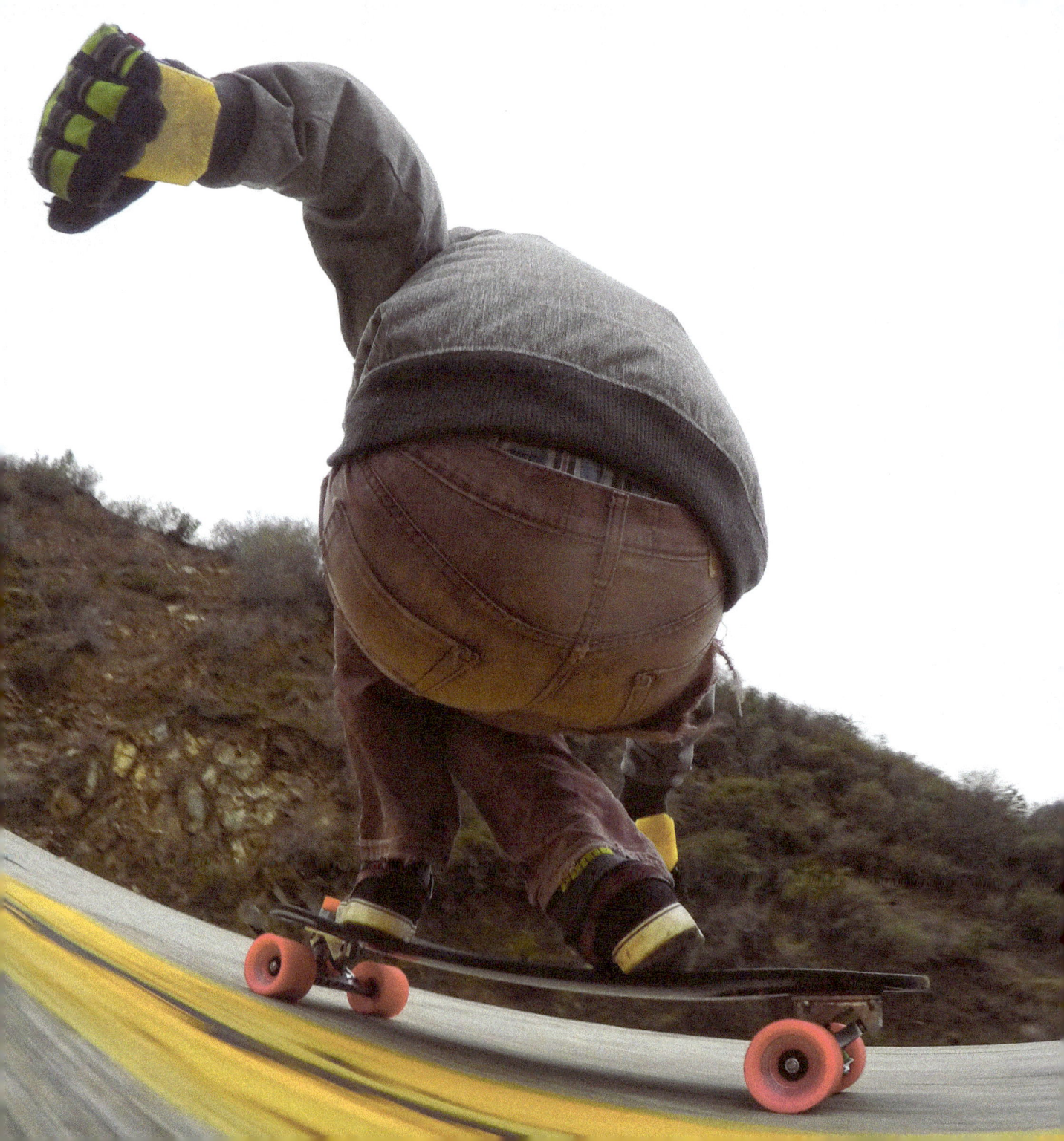

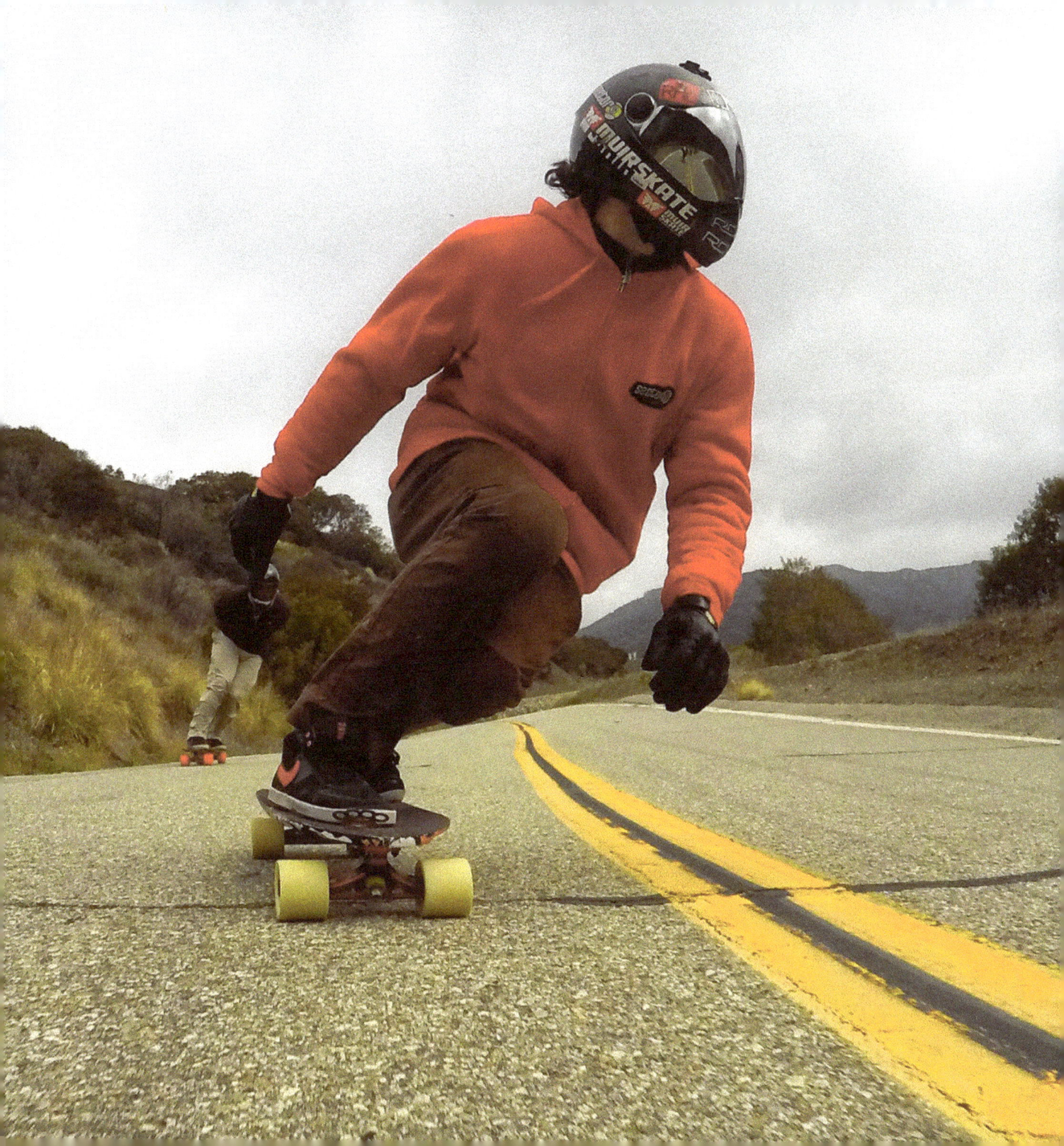

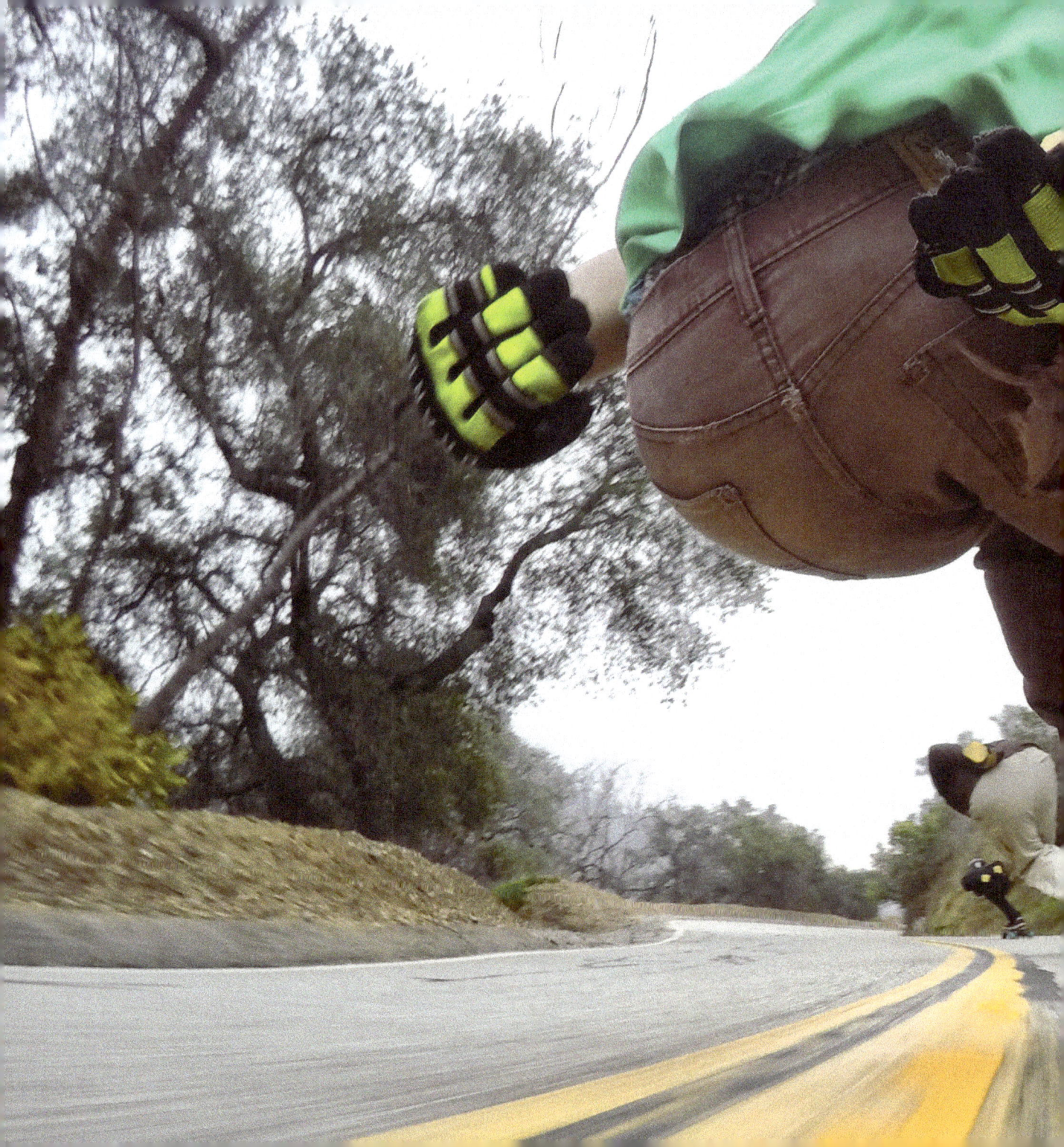

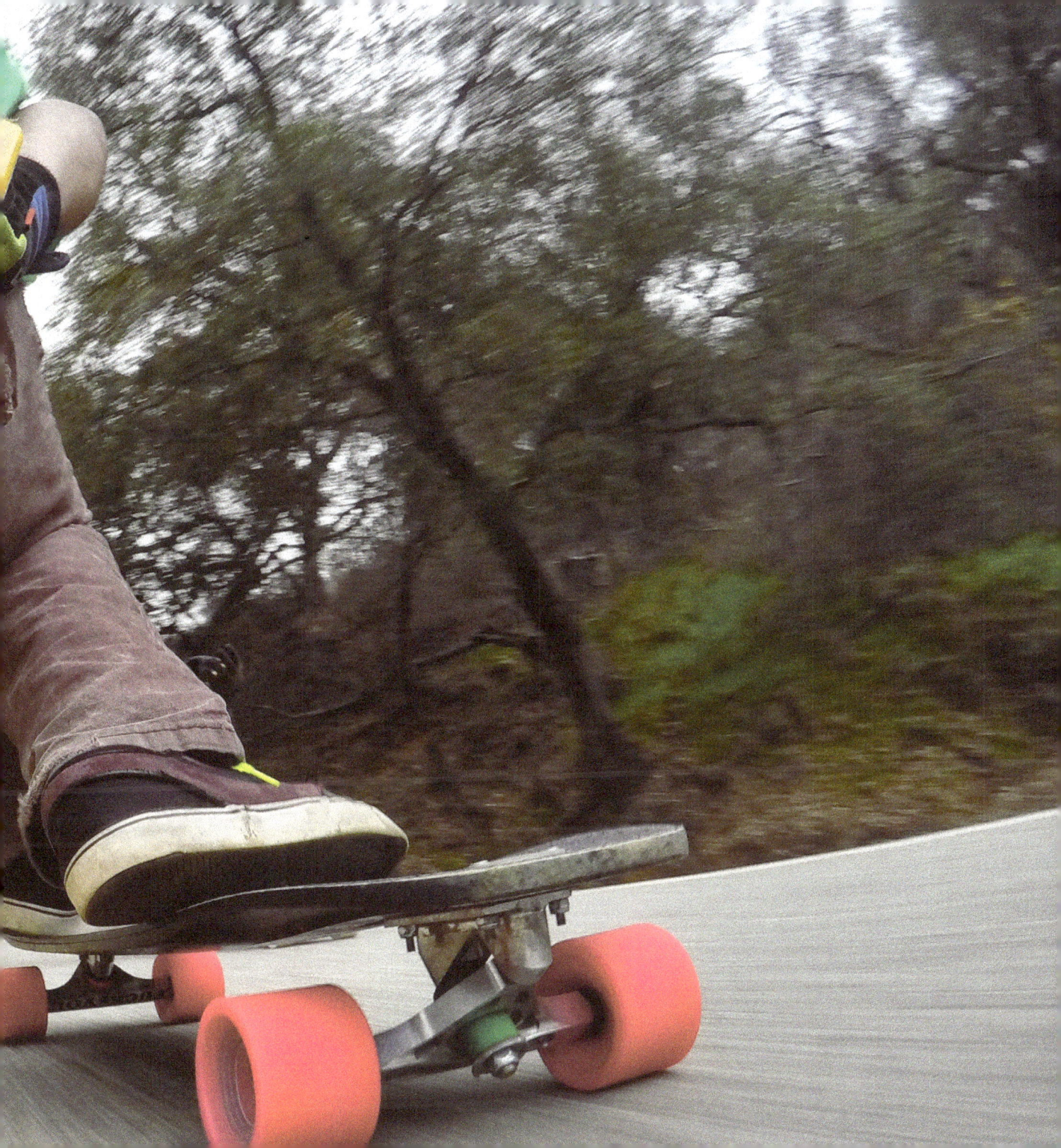

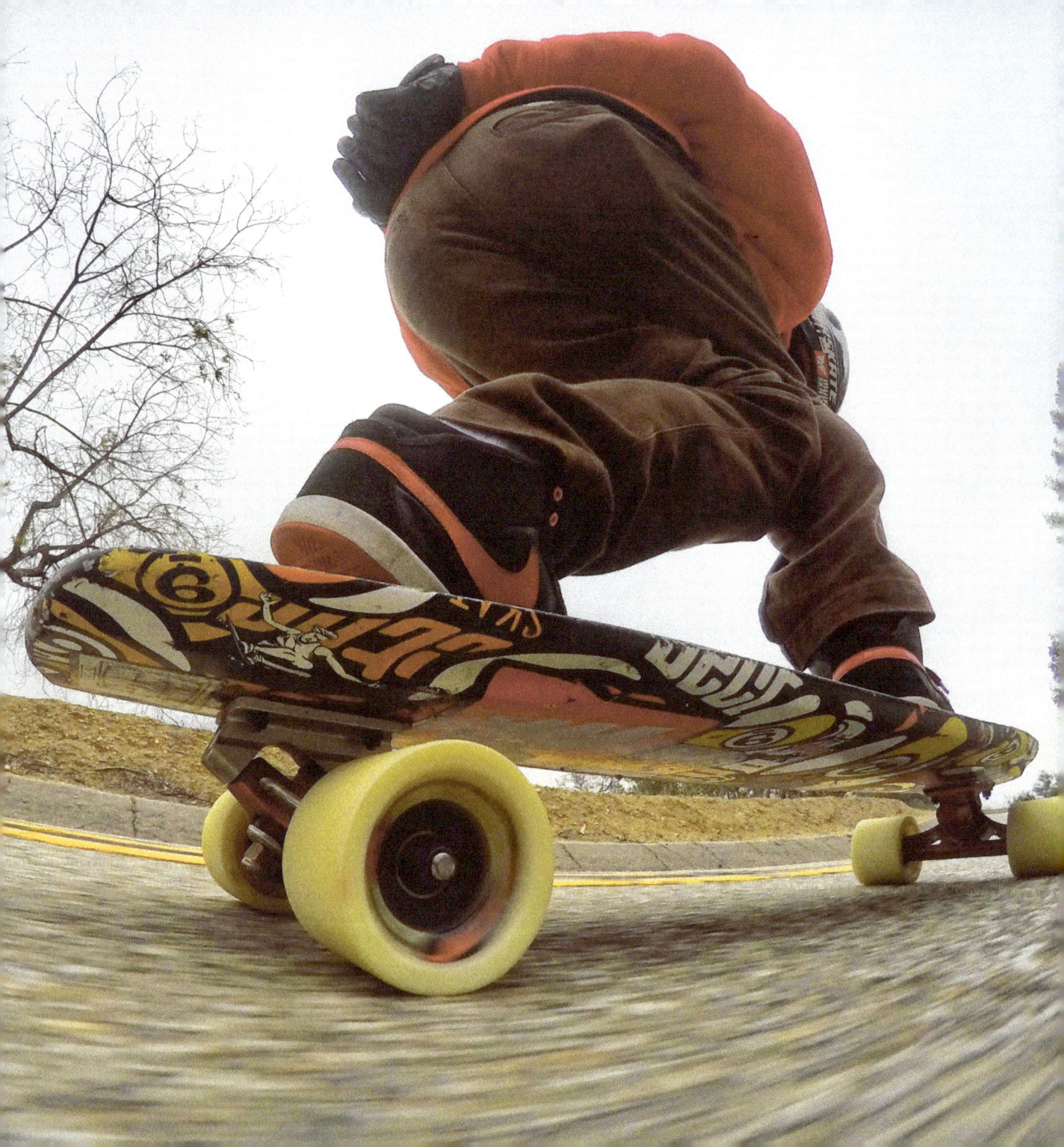

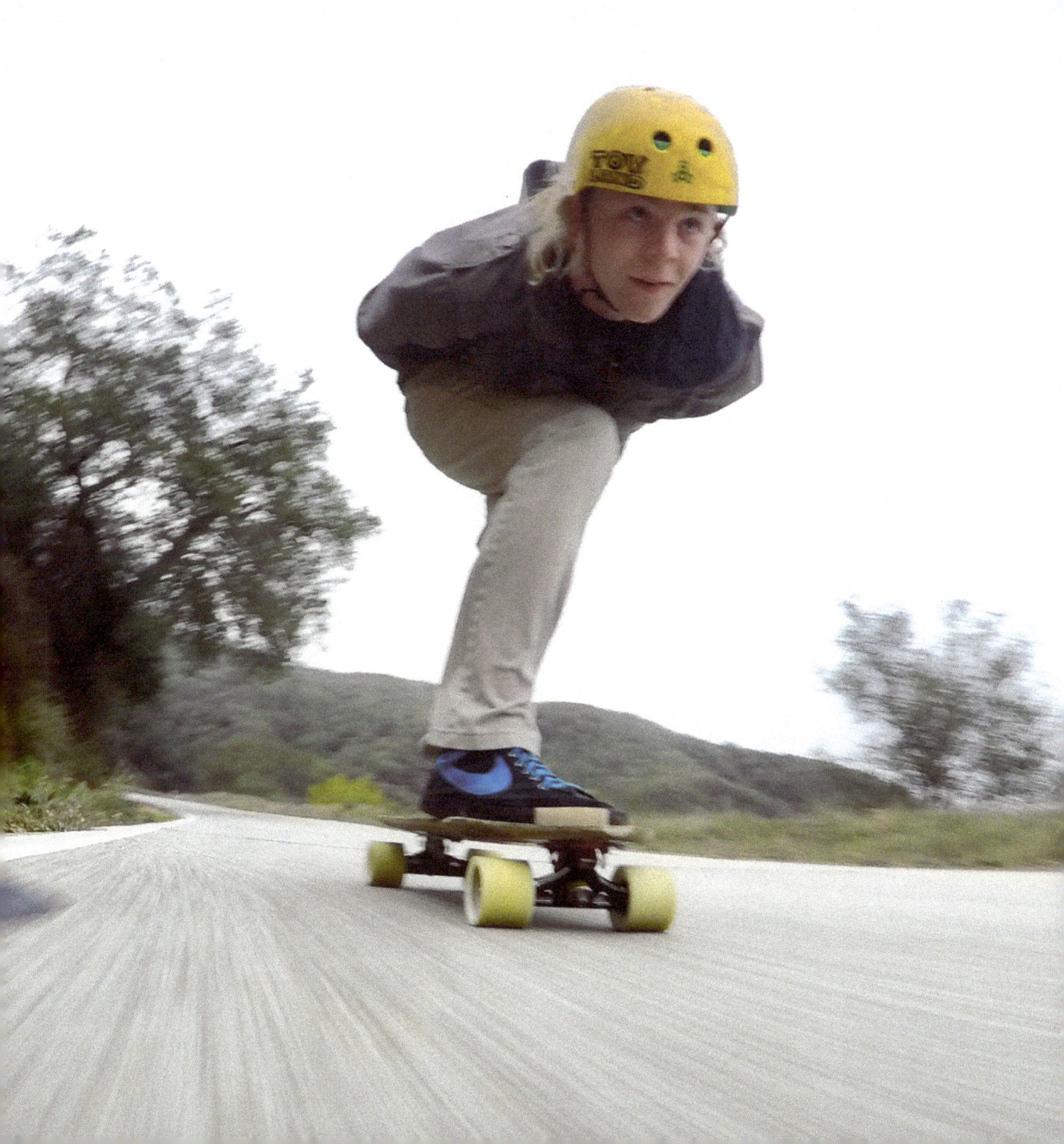

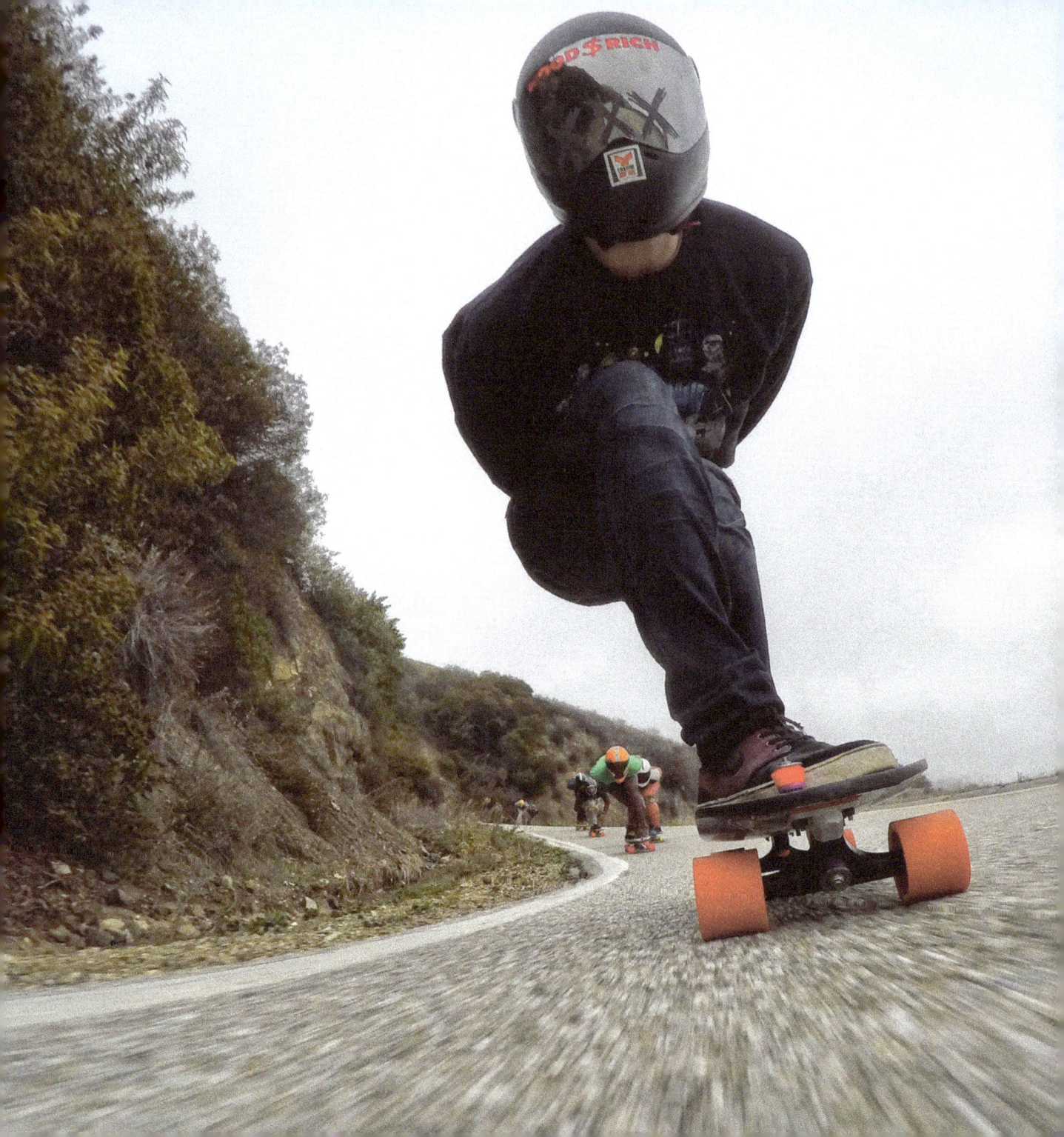

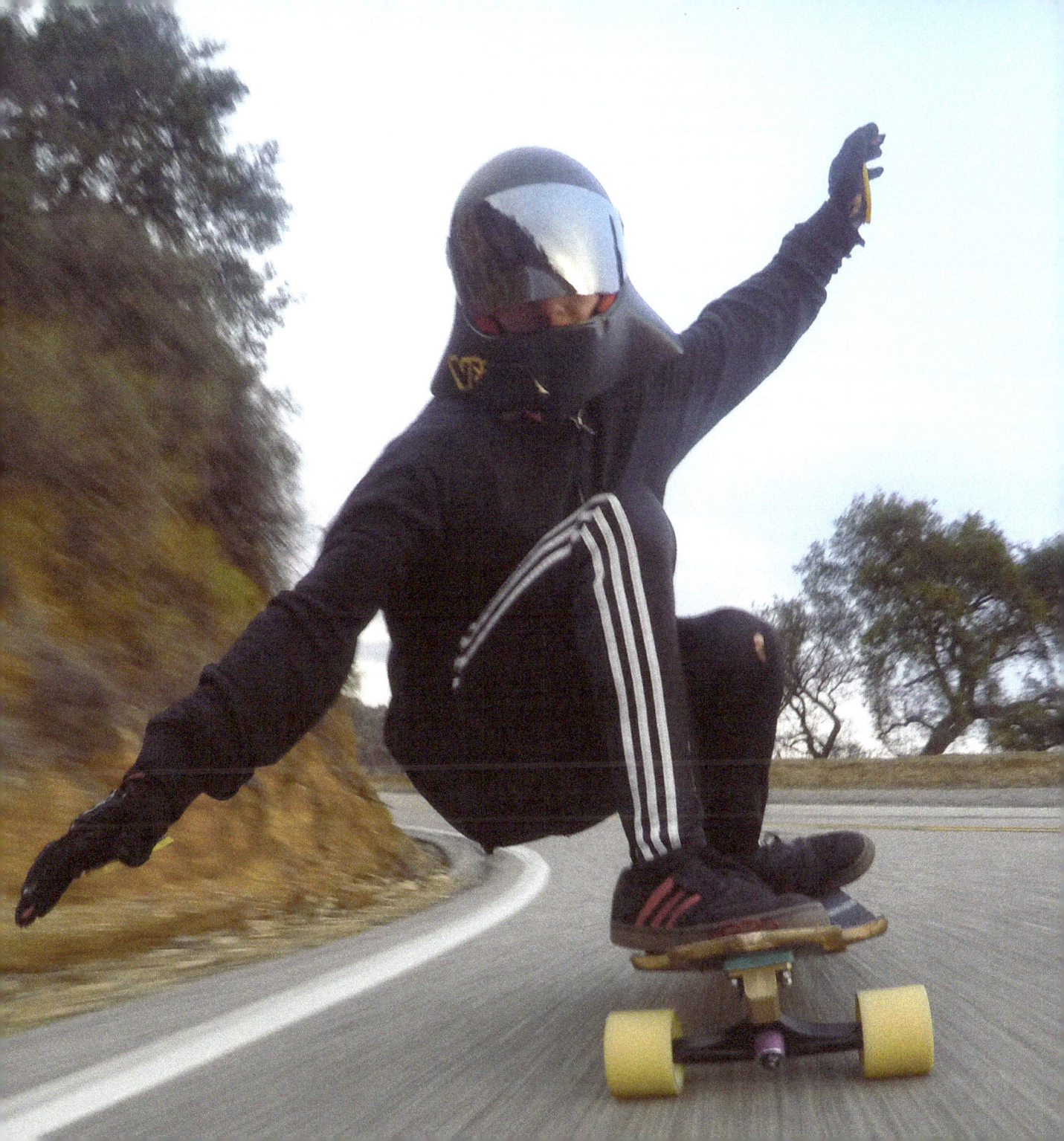

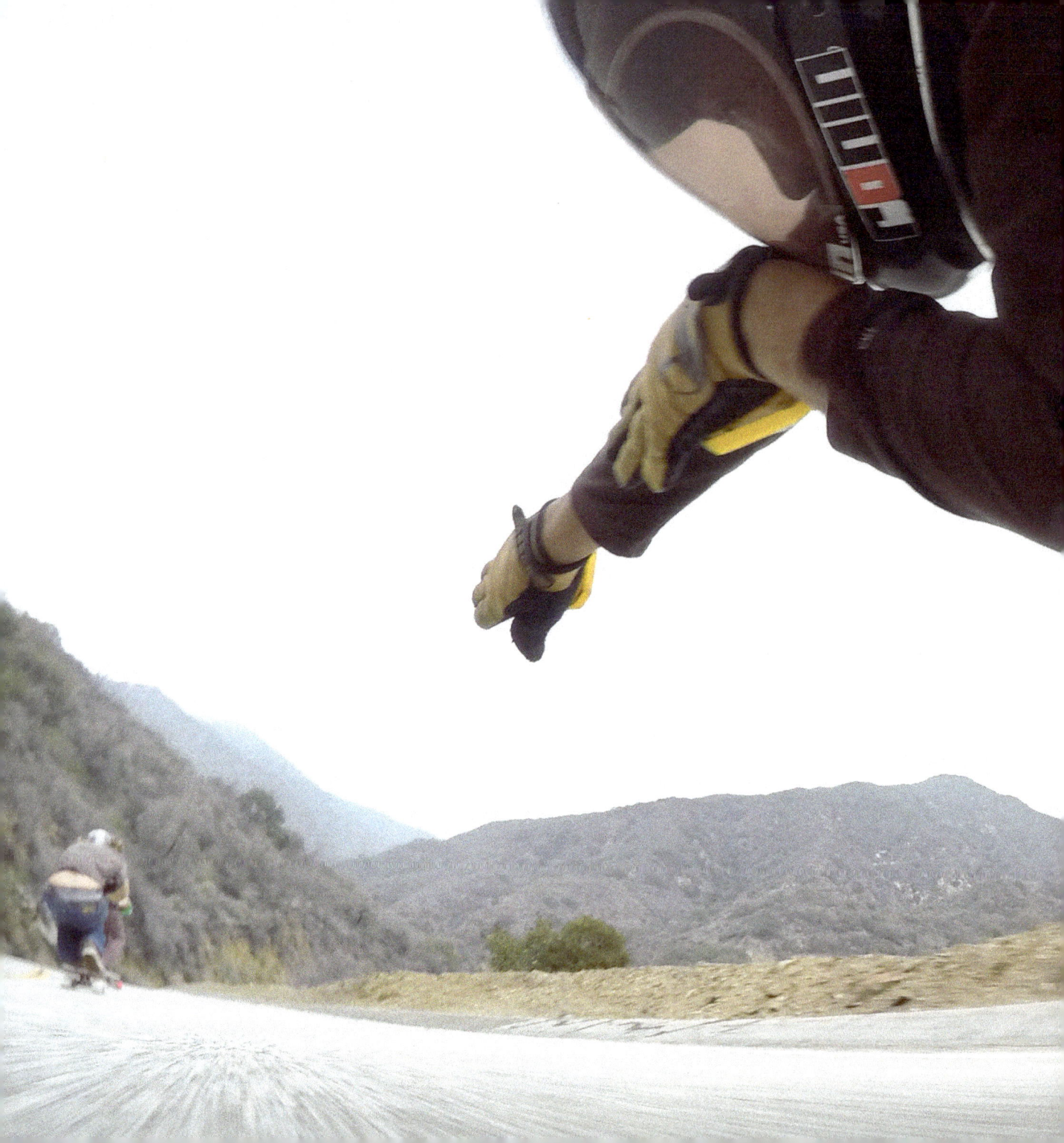

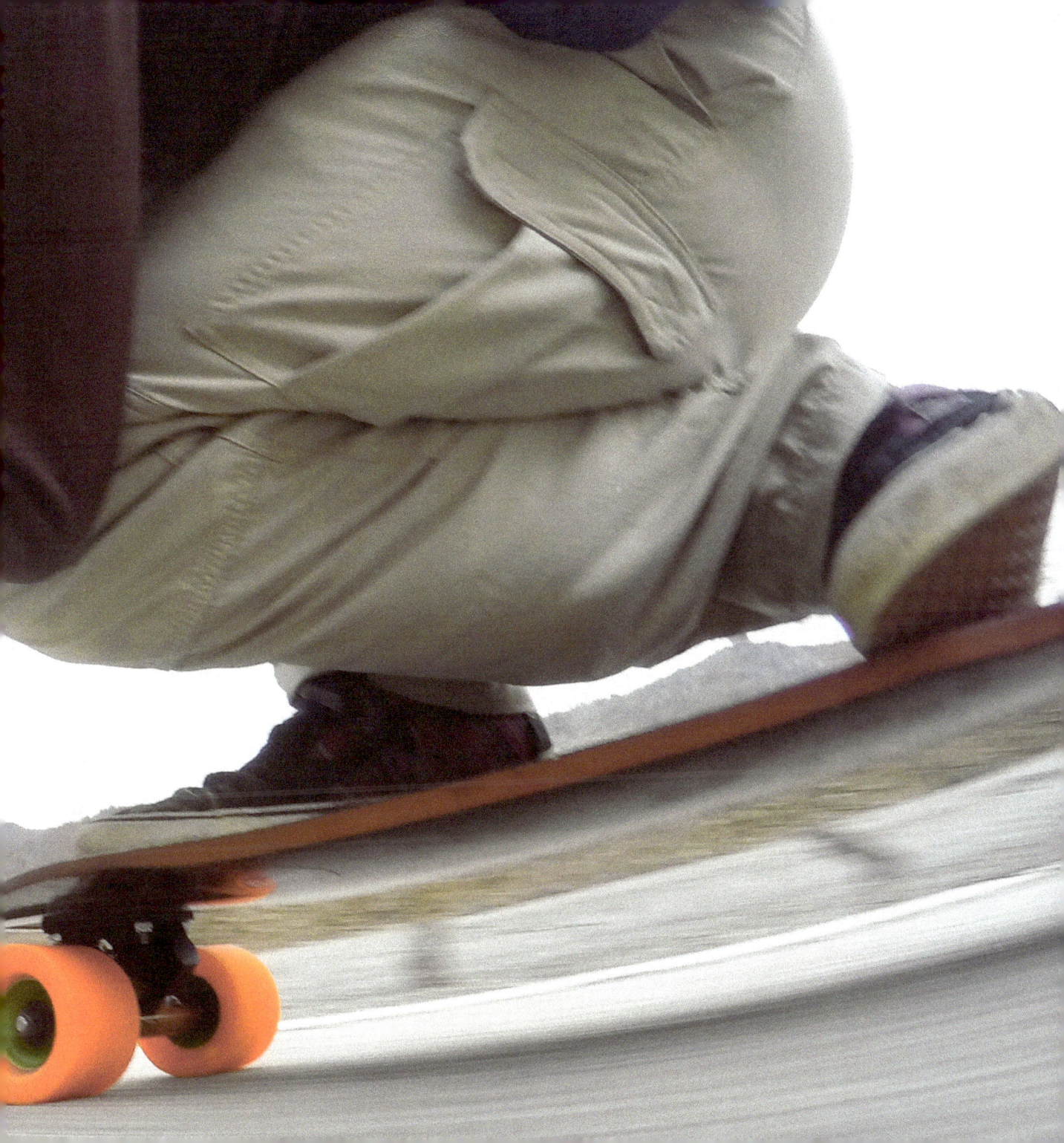

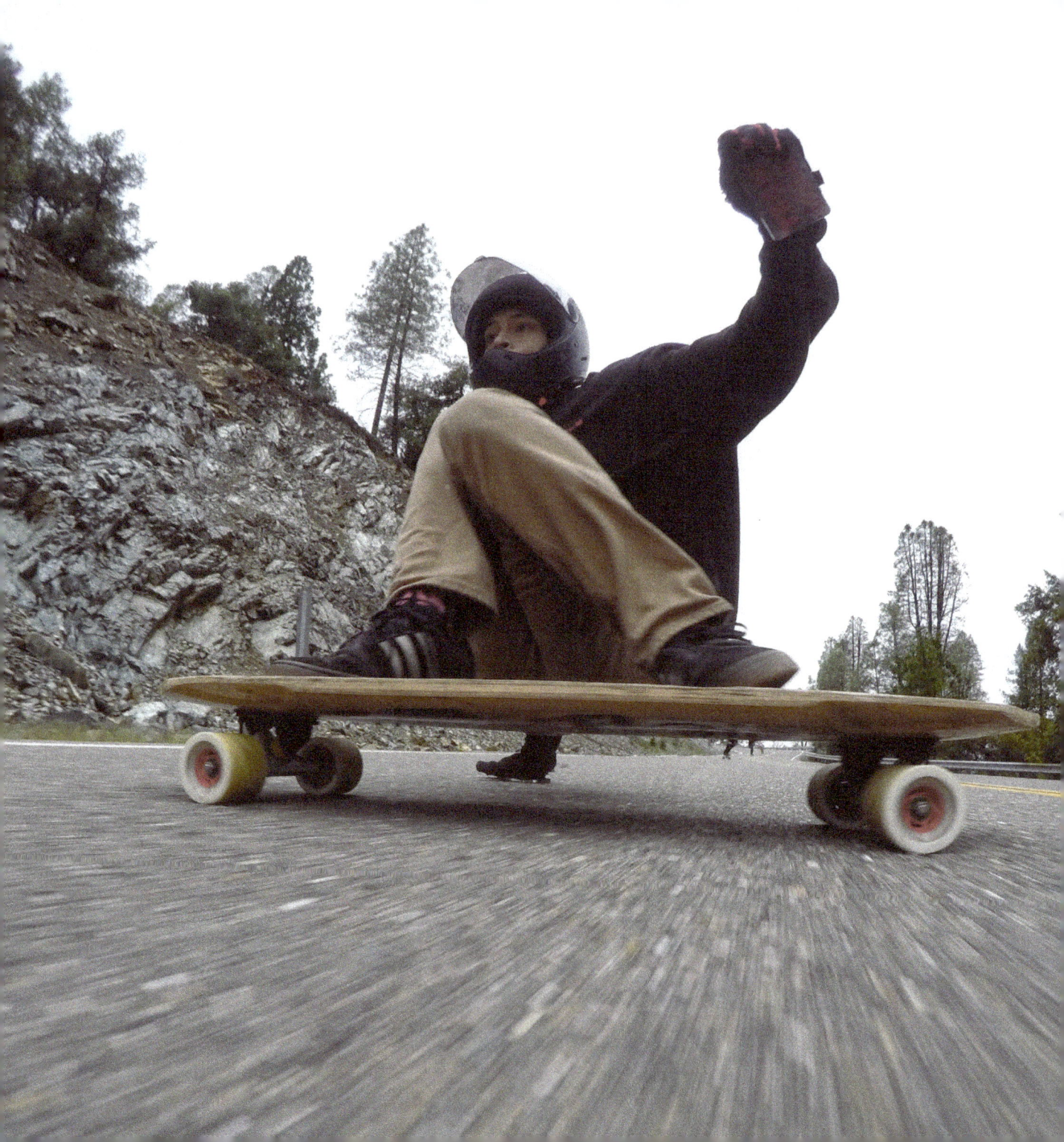

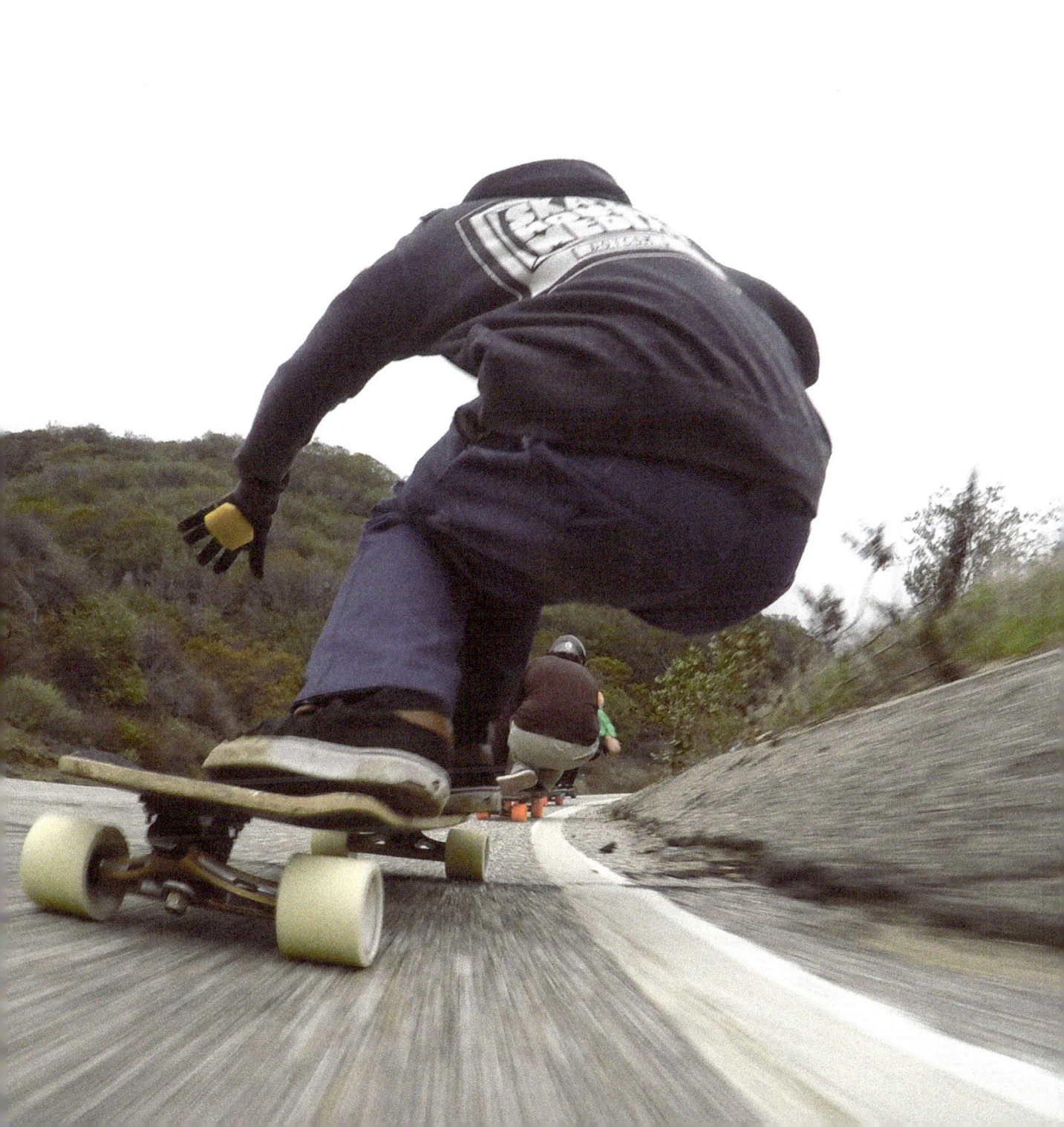

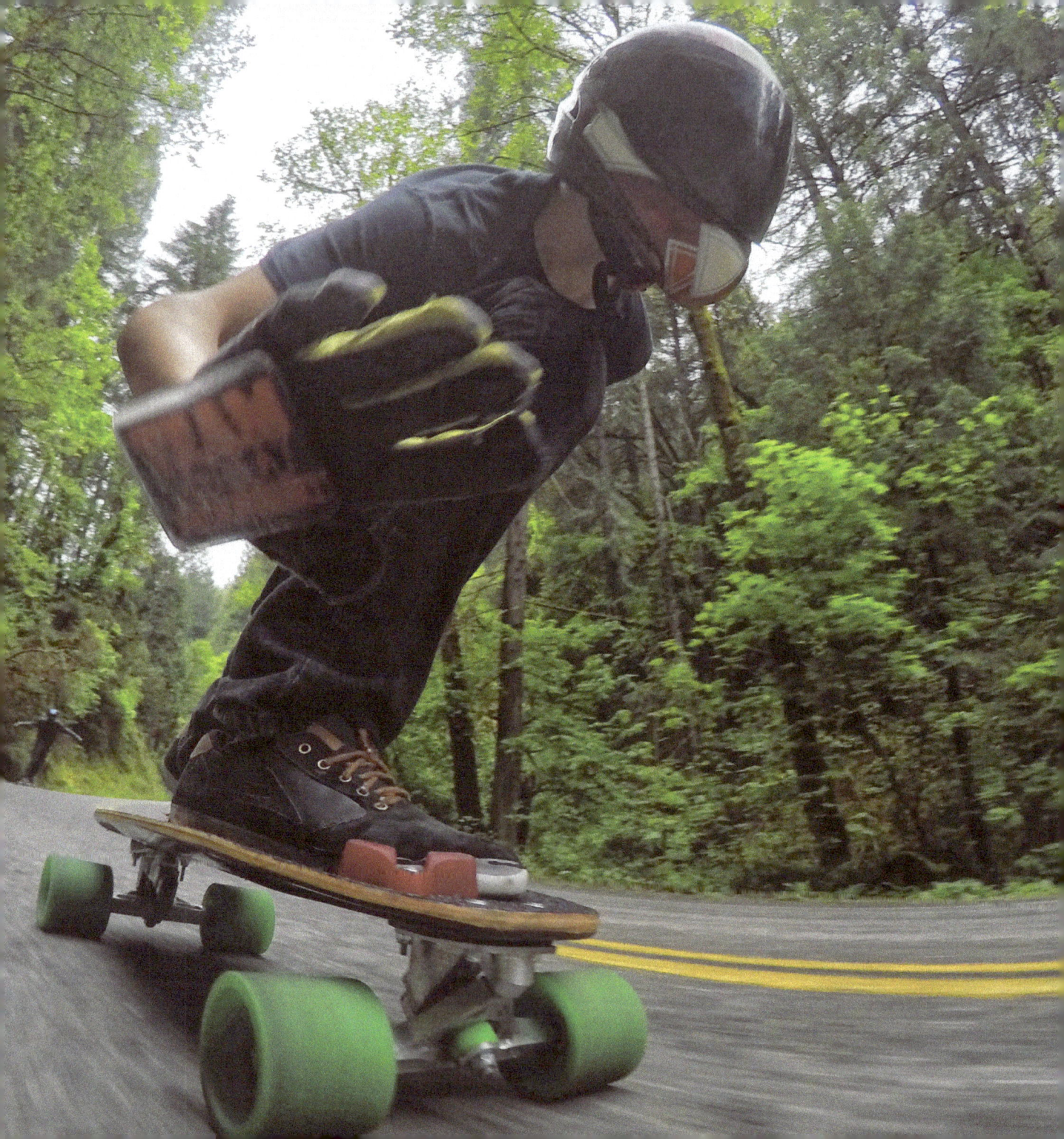

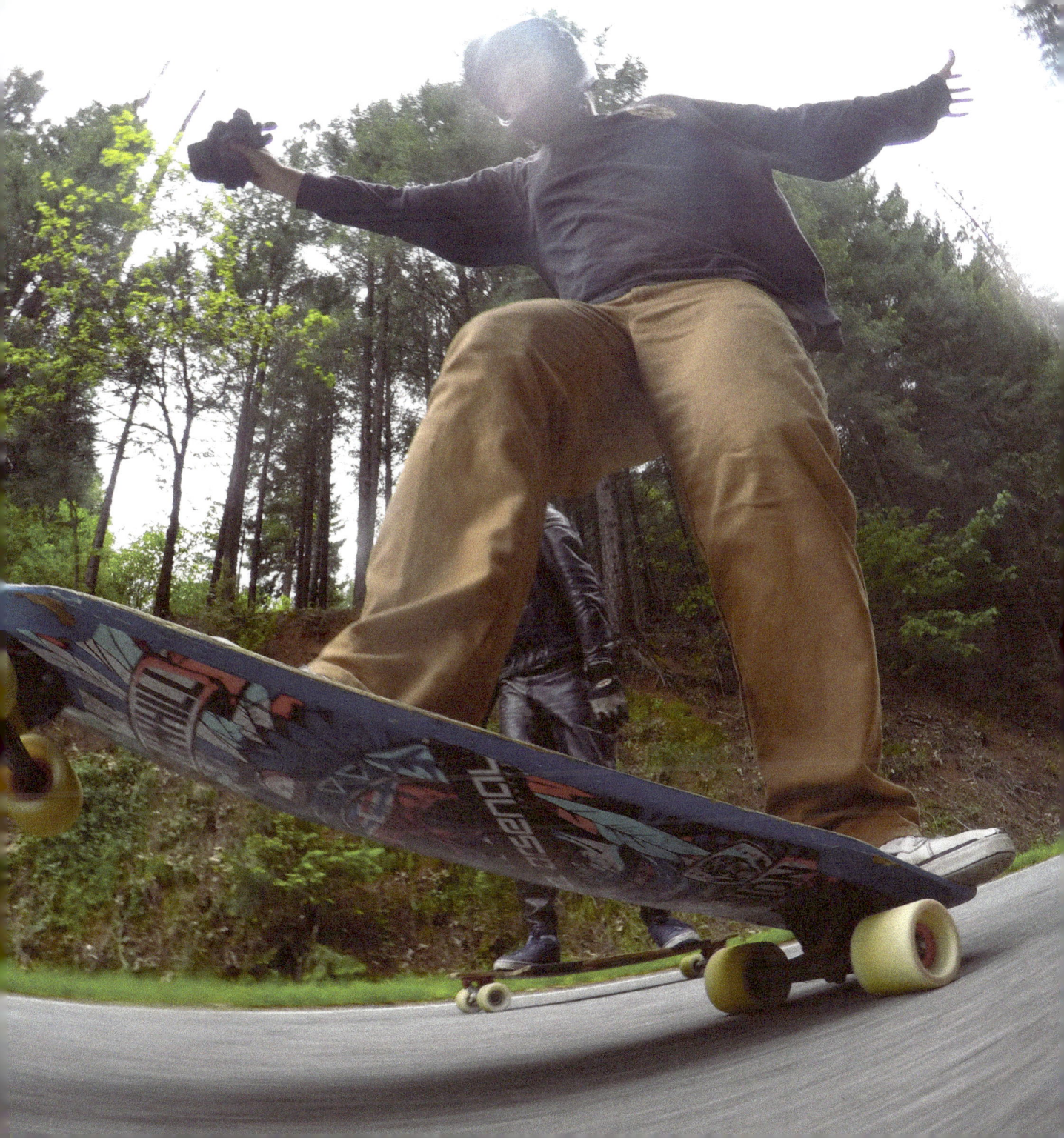

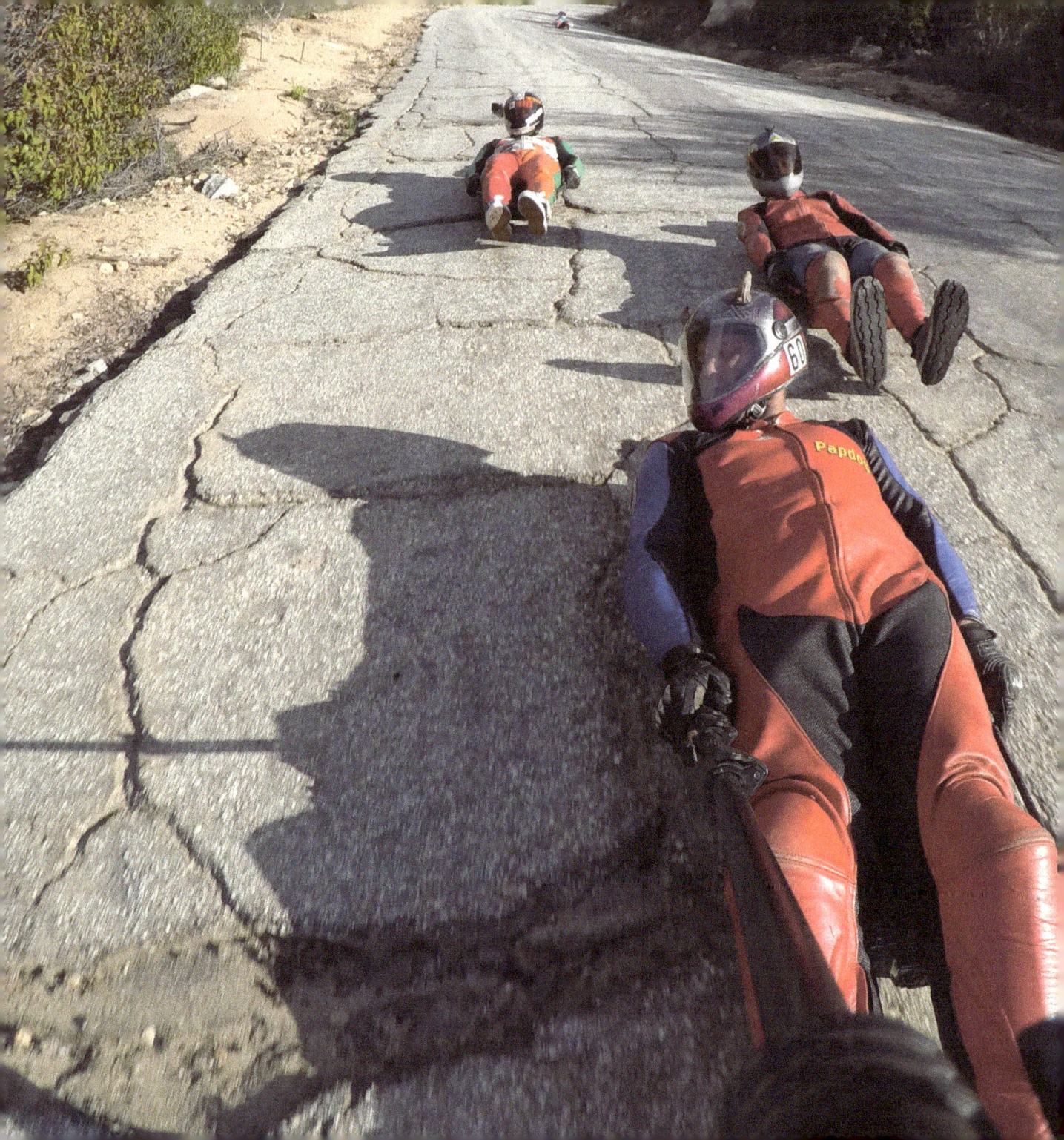

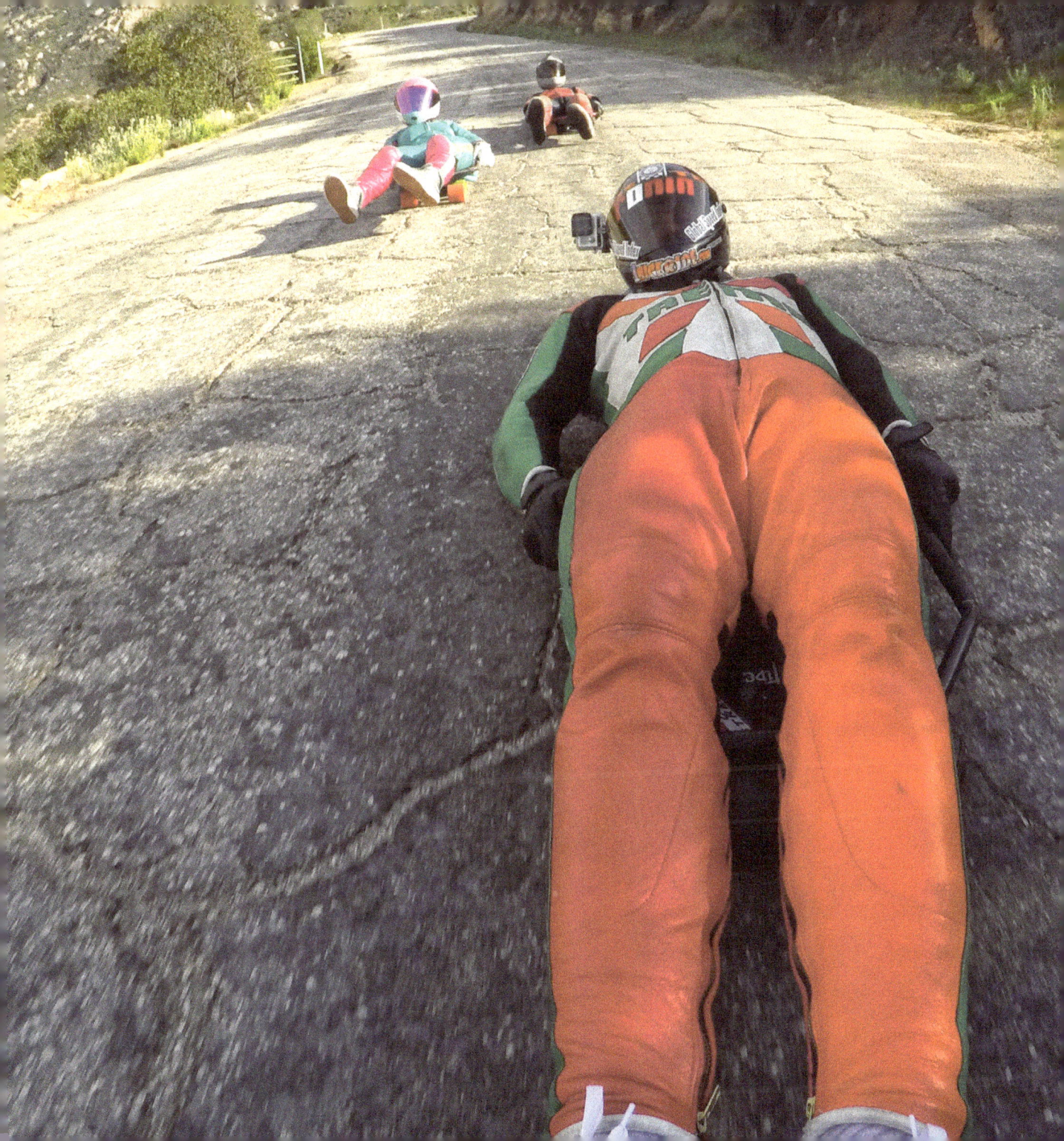

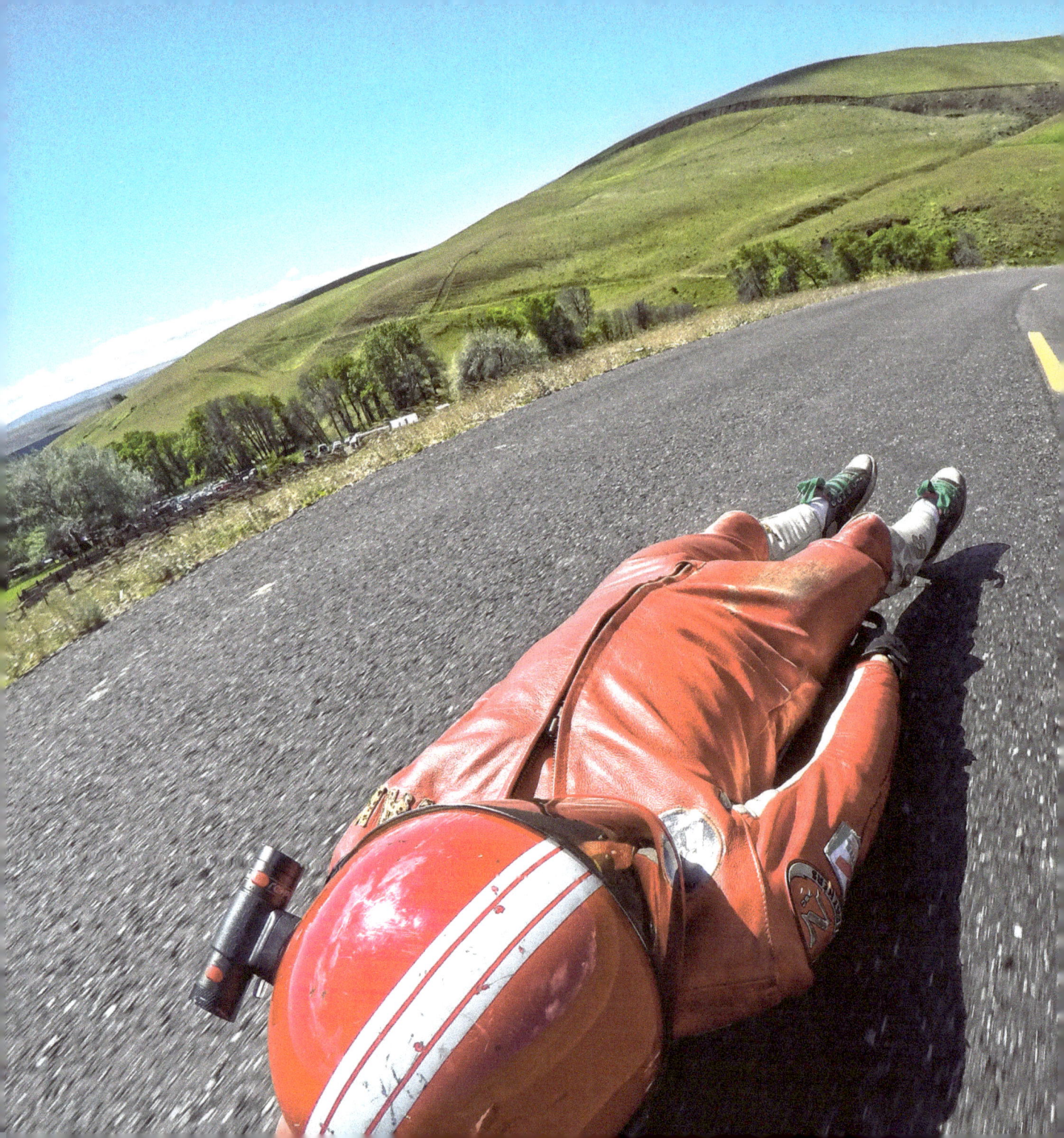

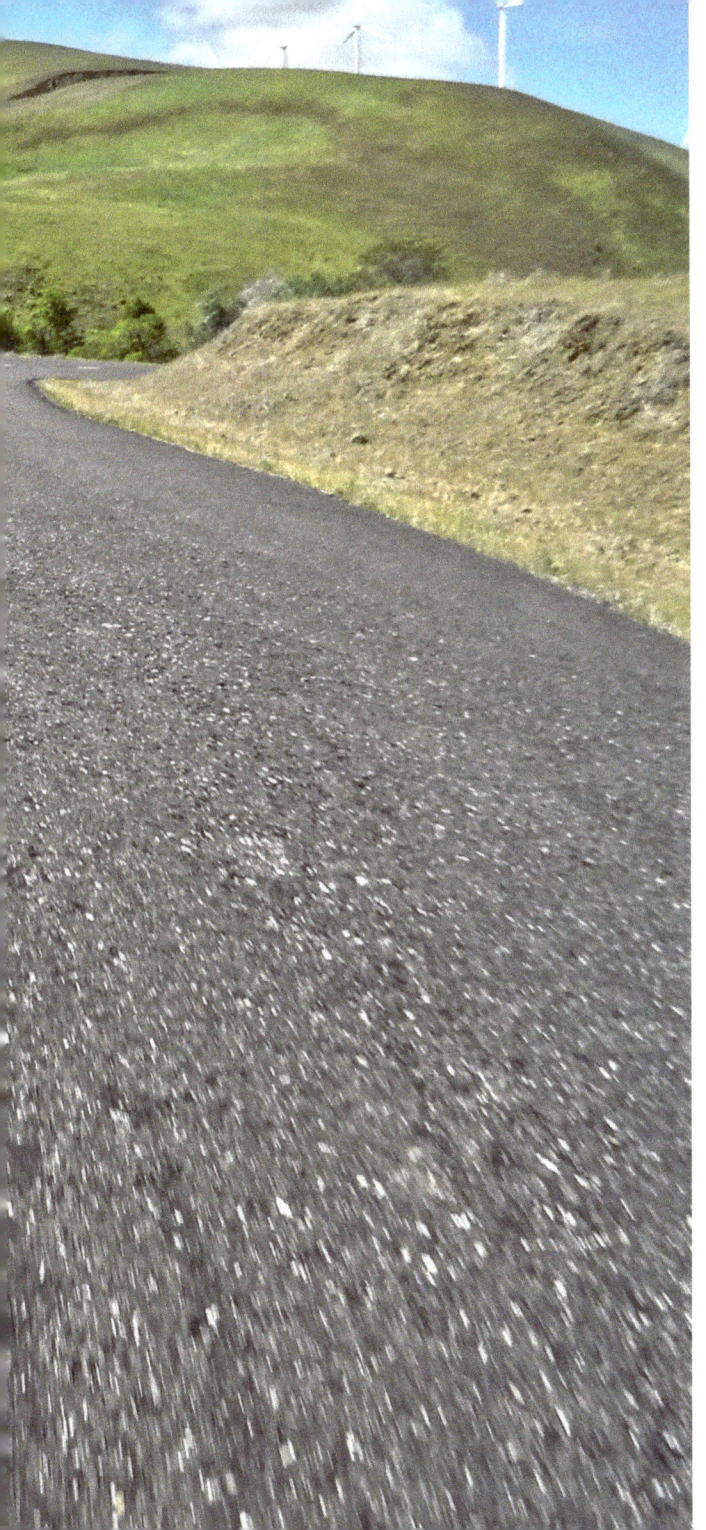

#Maryhillandchill

It just kind of happens. You go to Maryhill and she becomes a part of you. When people say, "I never want to miss a Maryhill Ratz event because it's like you're going to see your family…" they aren't kidding. That hill has given me much more than words can say, so I hope the following images pay her the respect she deserves.

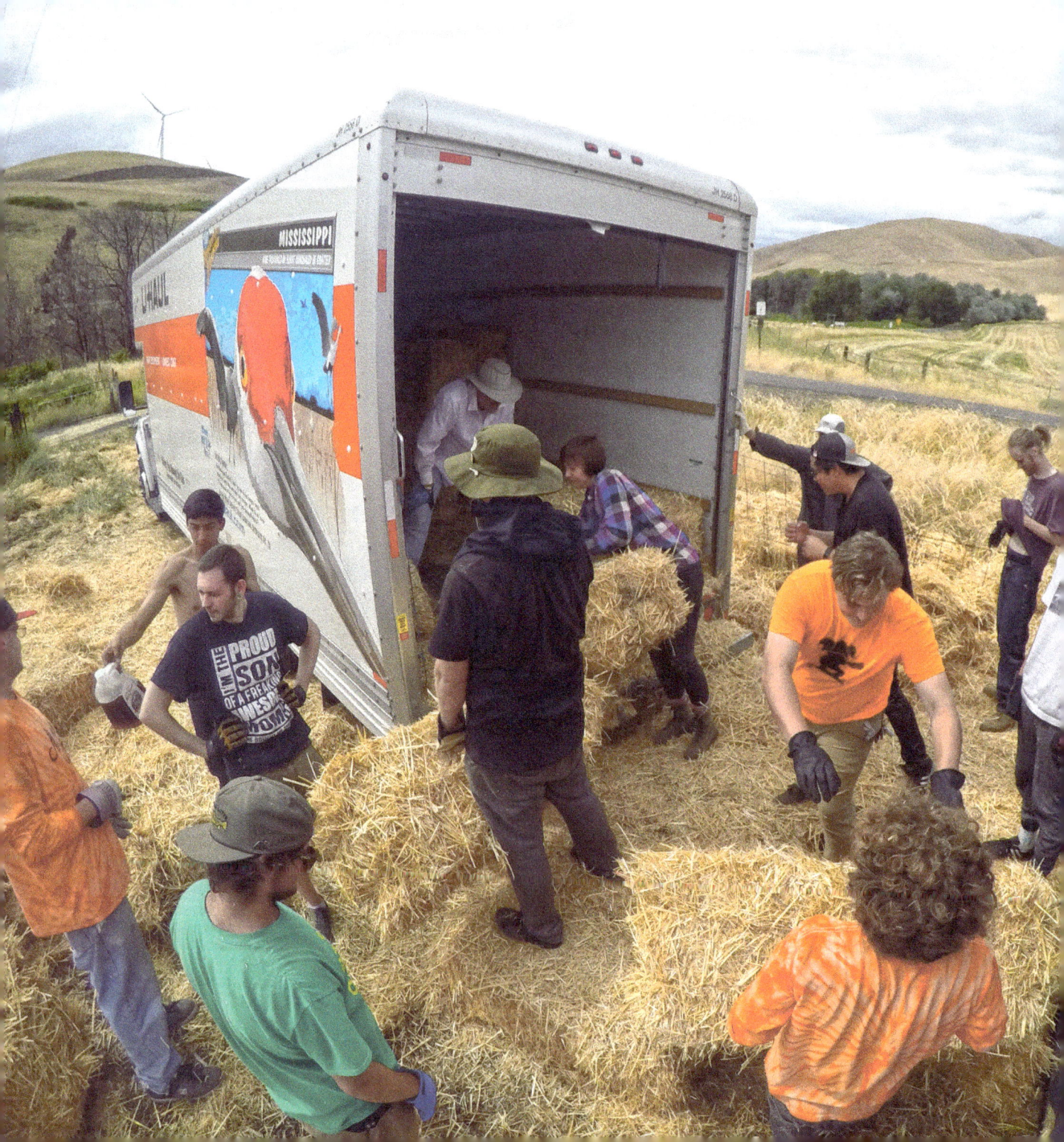

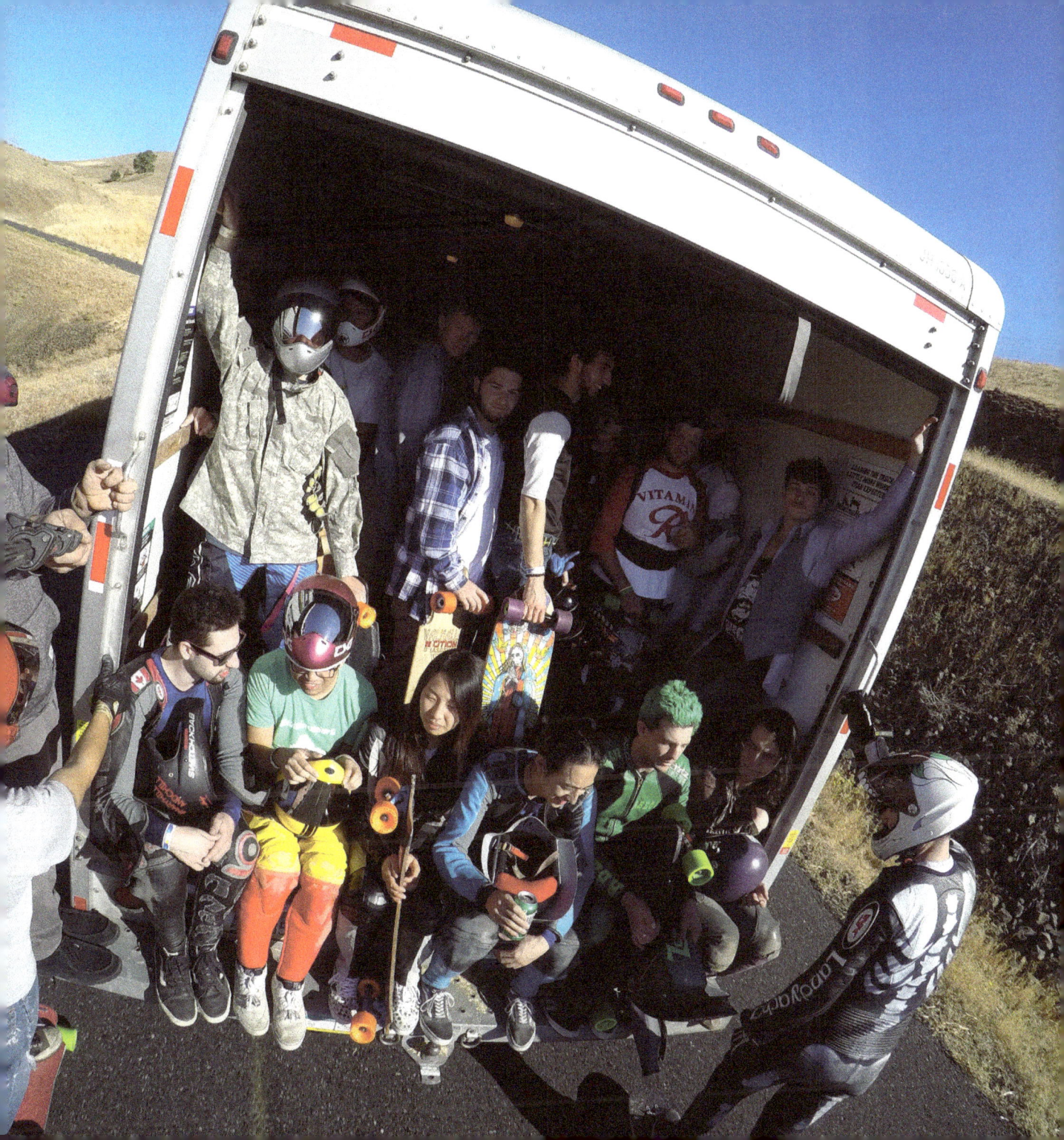

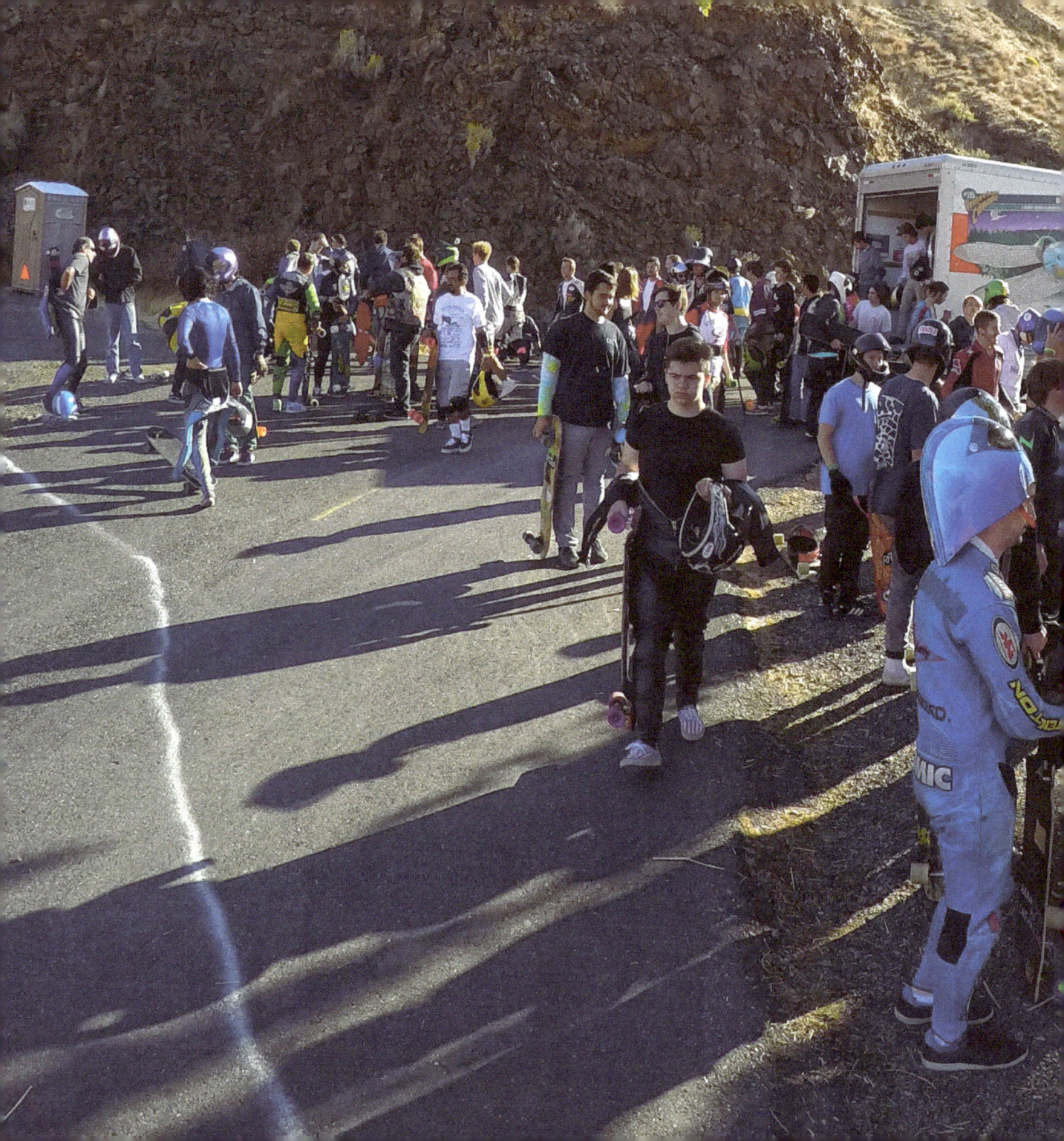

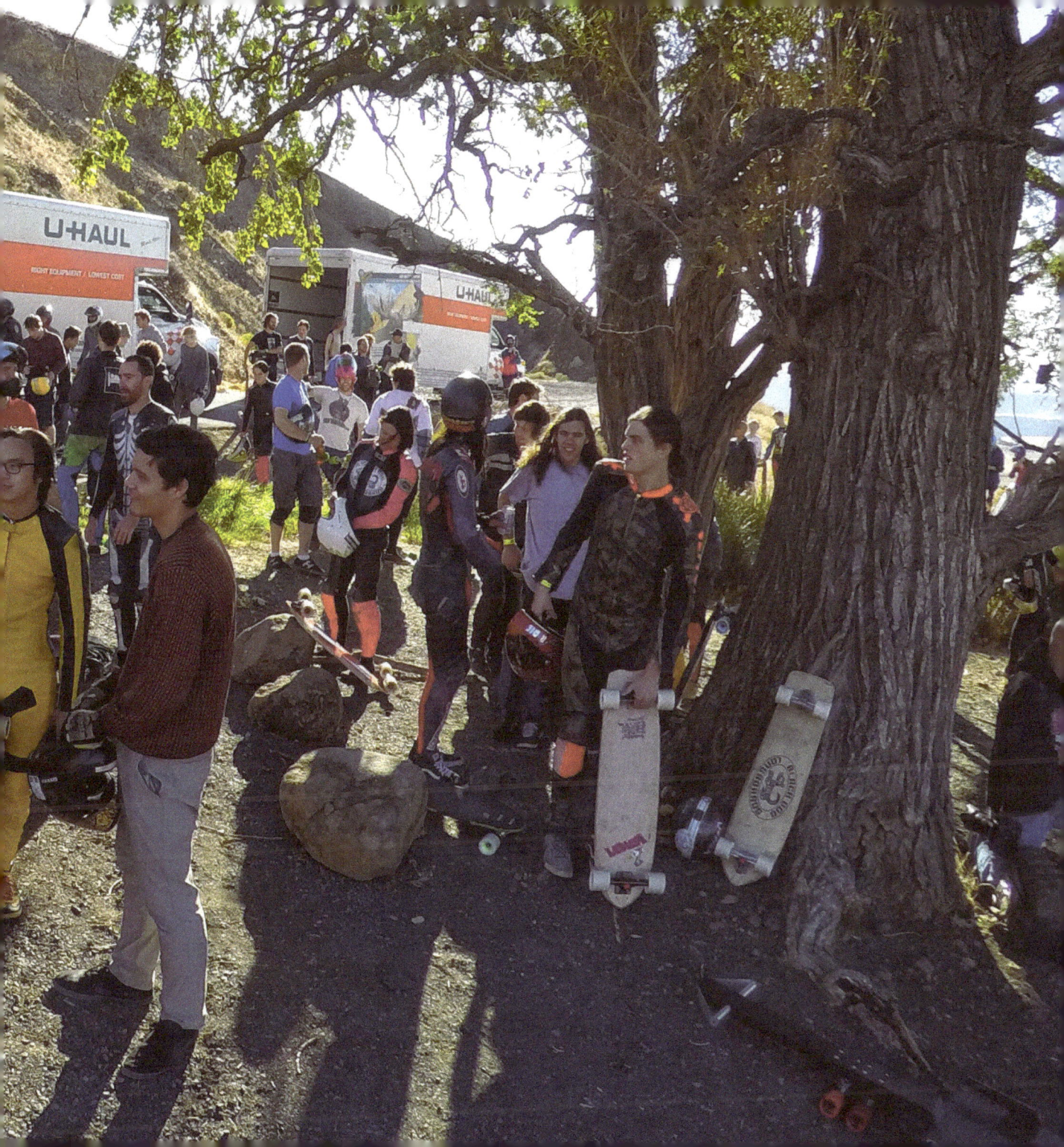

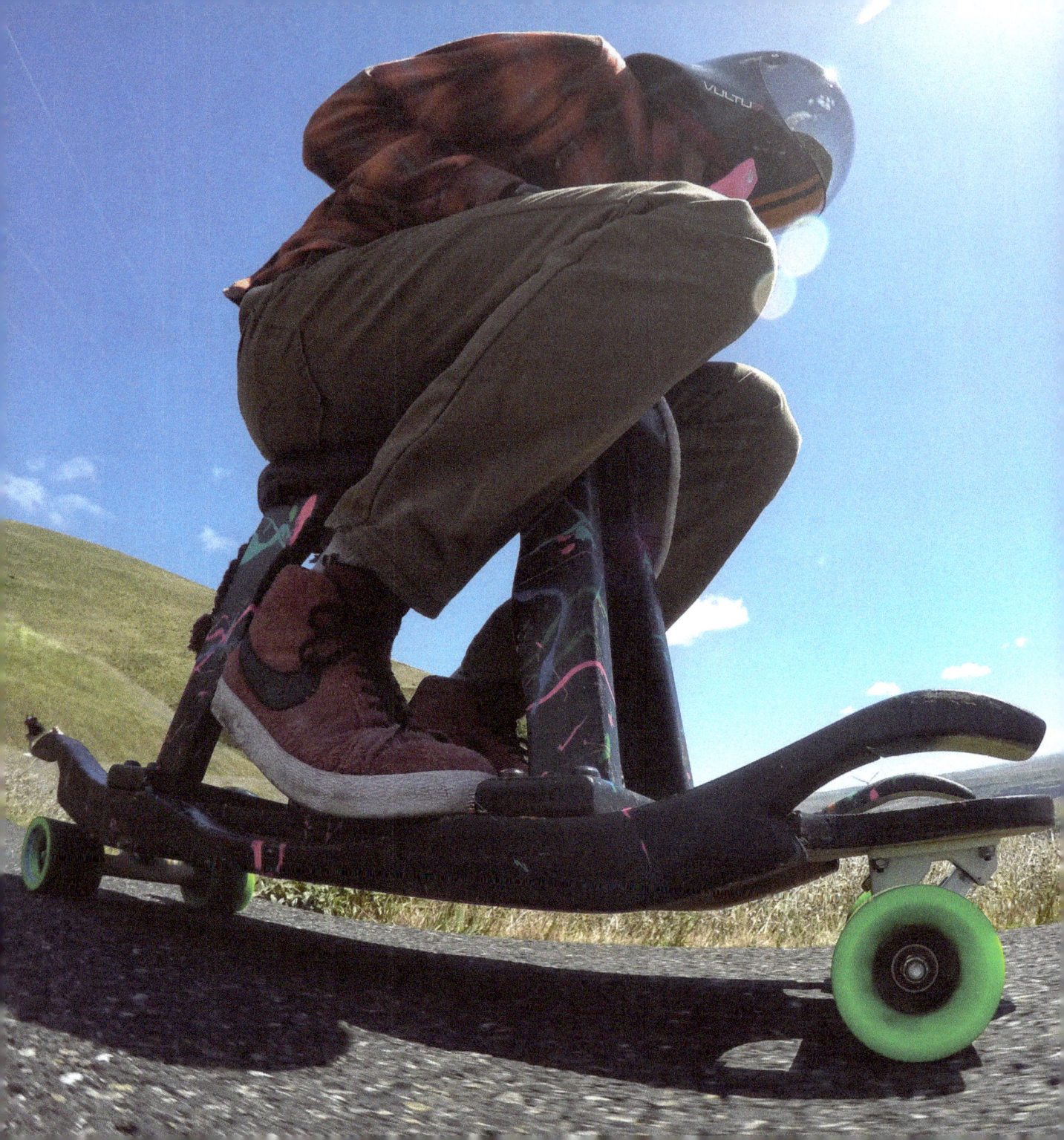

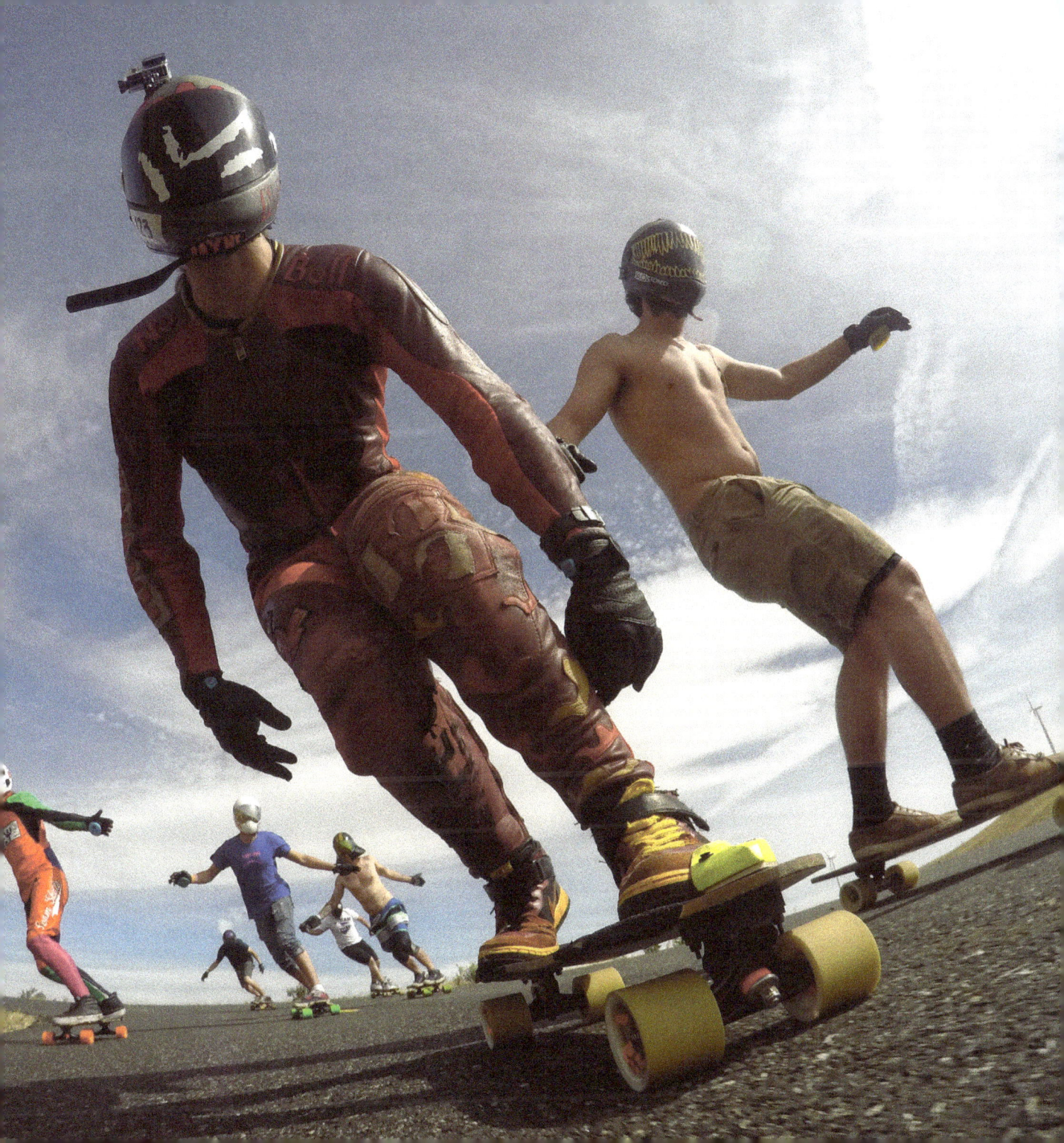

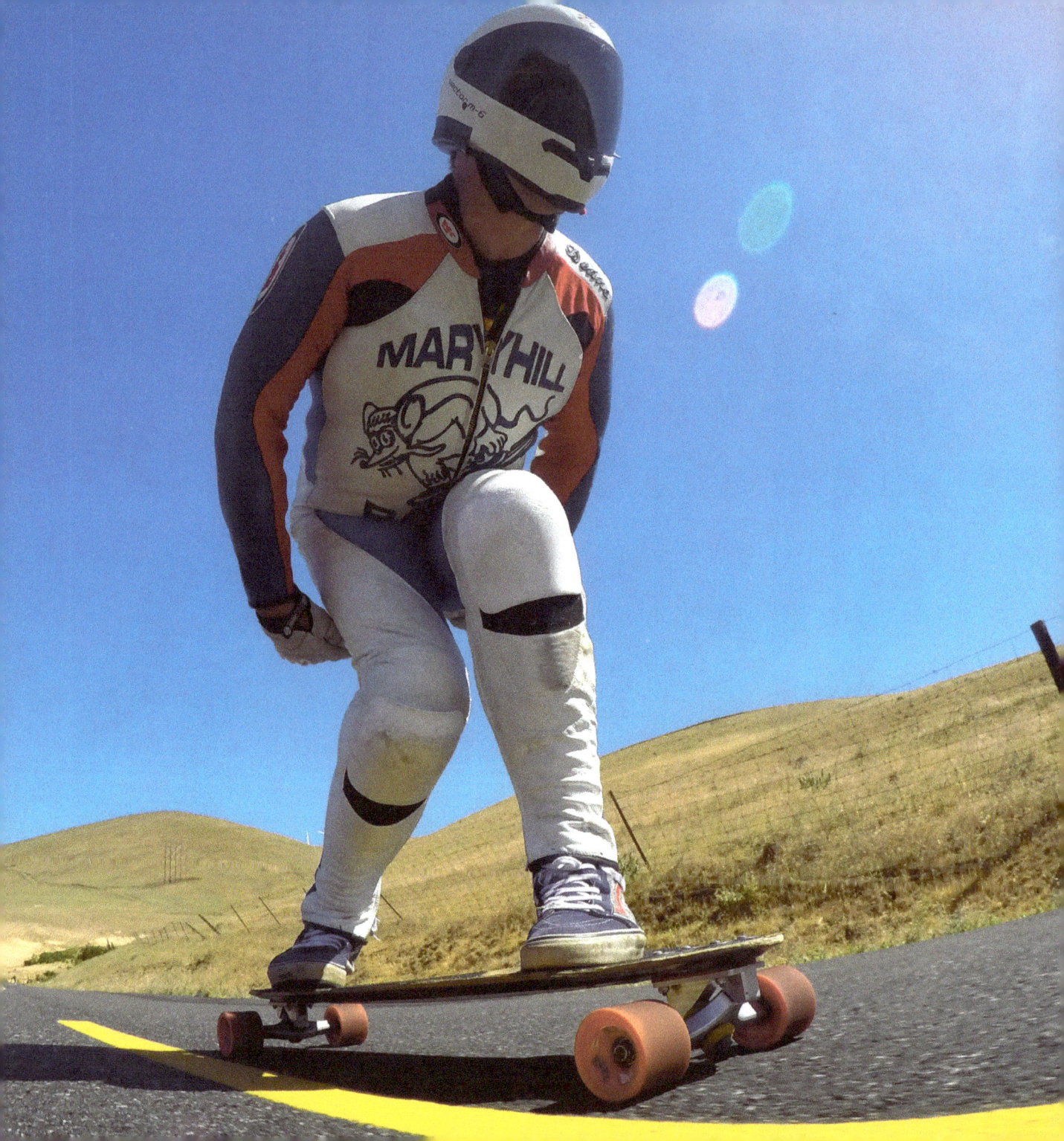

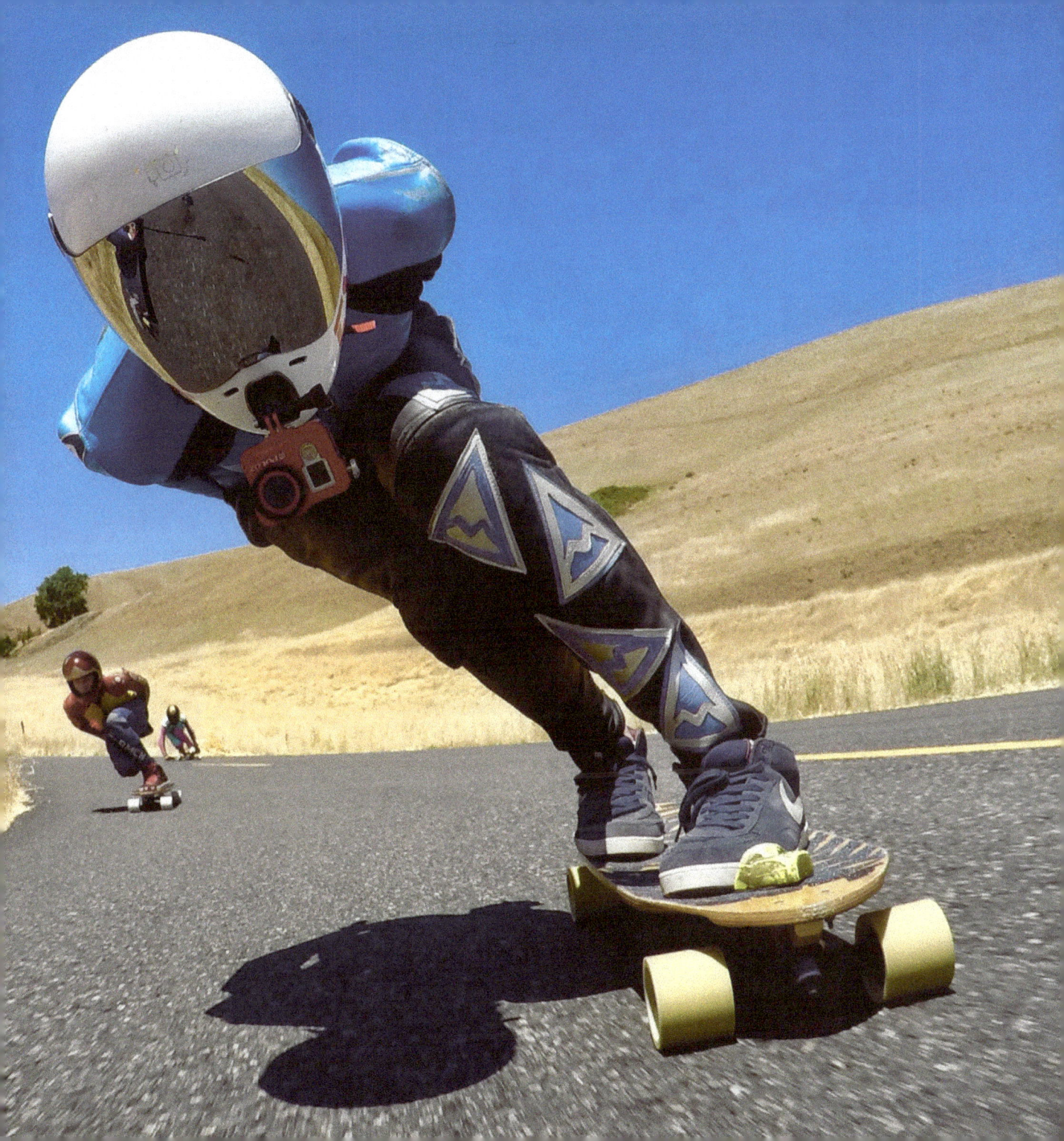

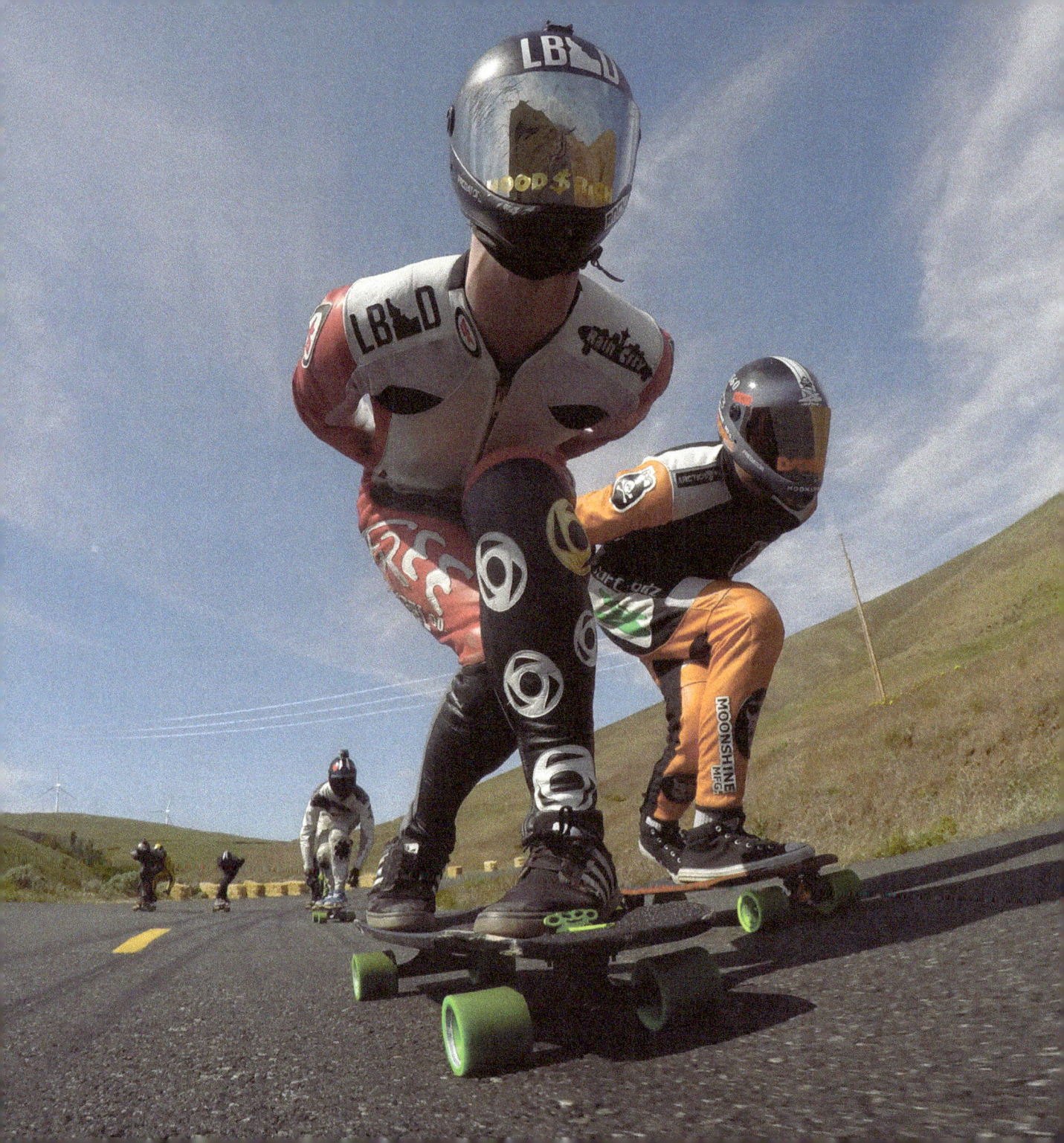

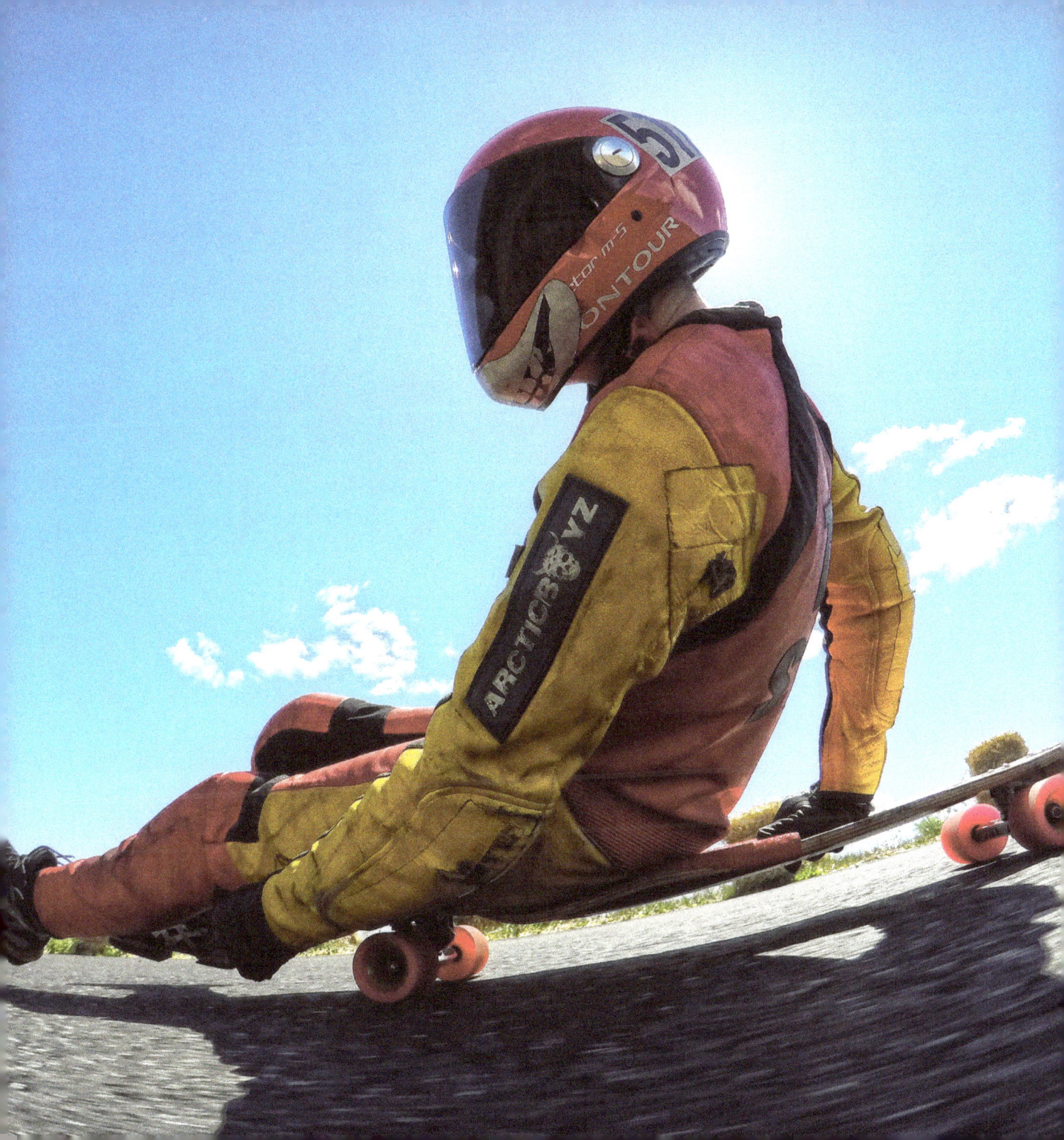

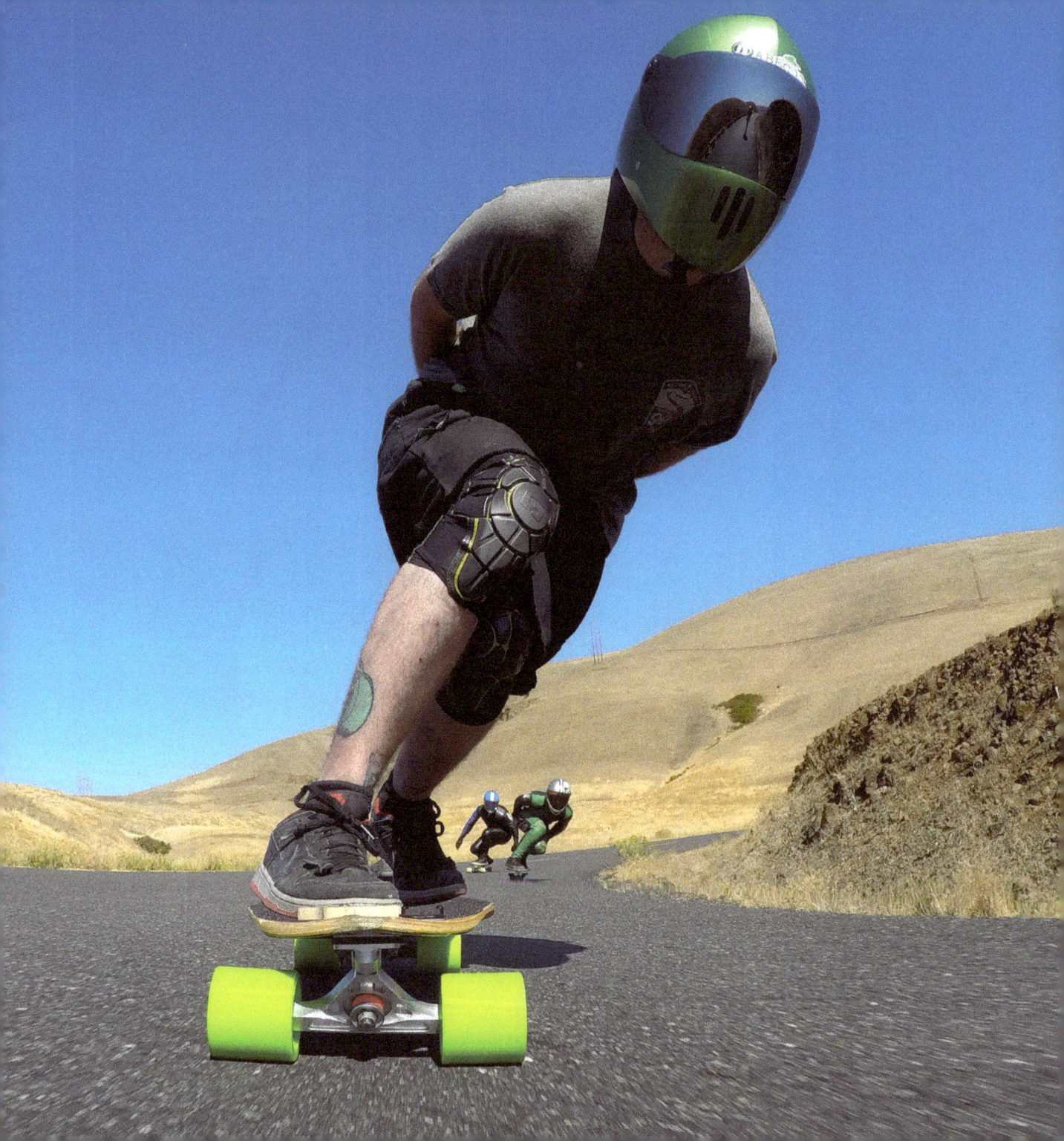

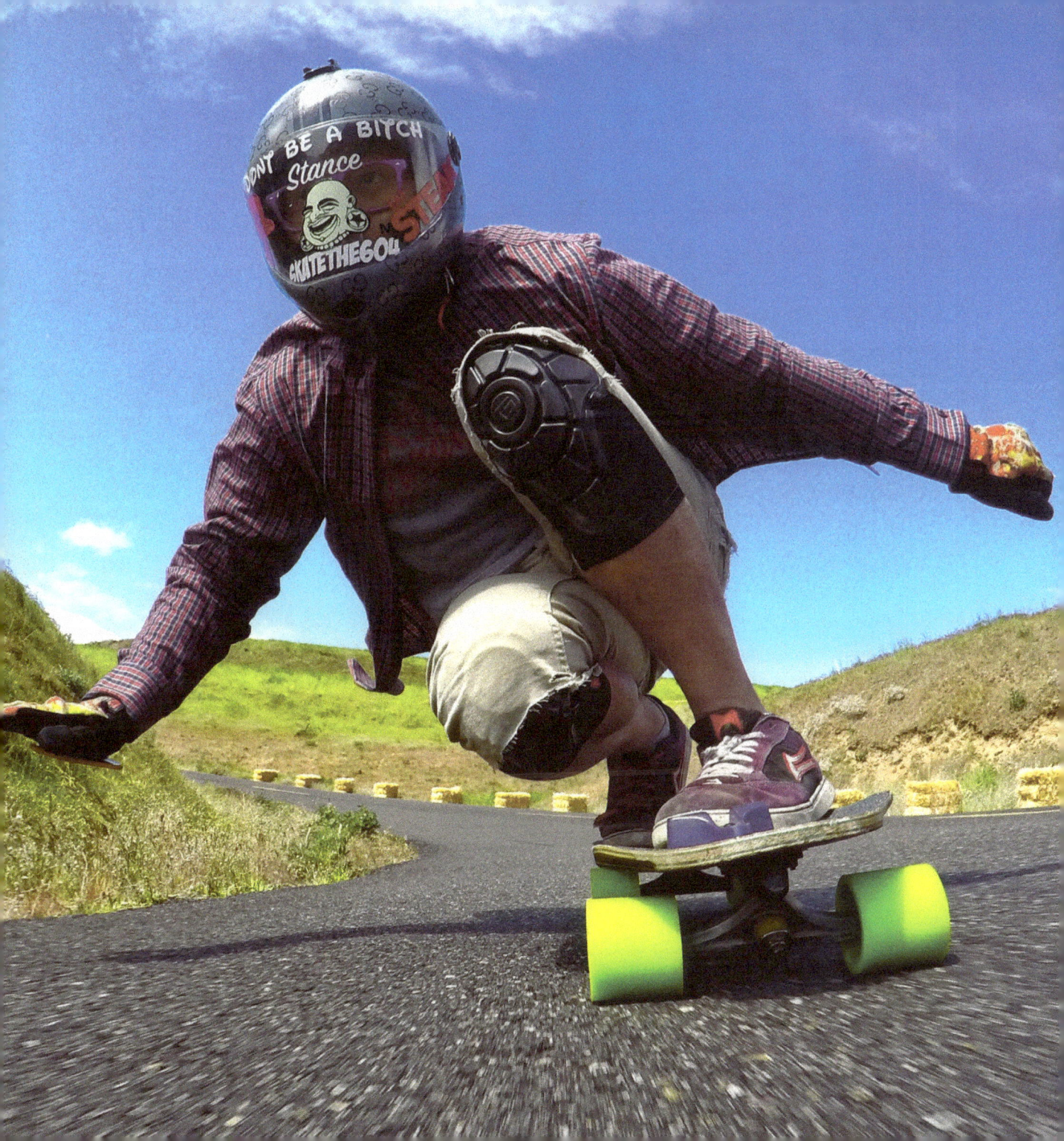

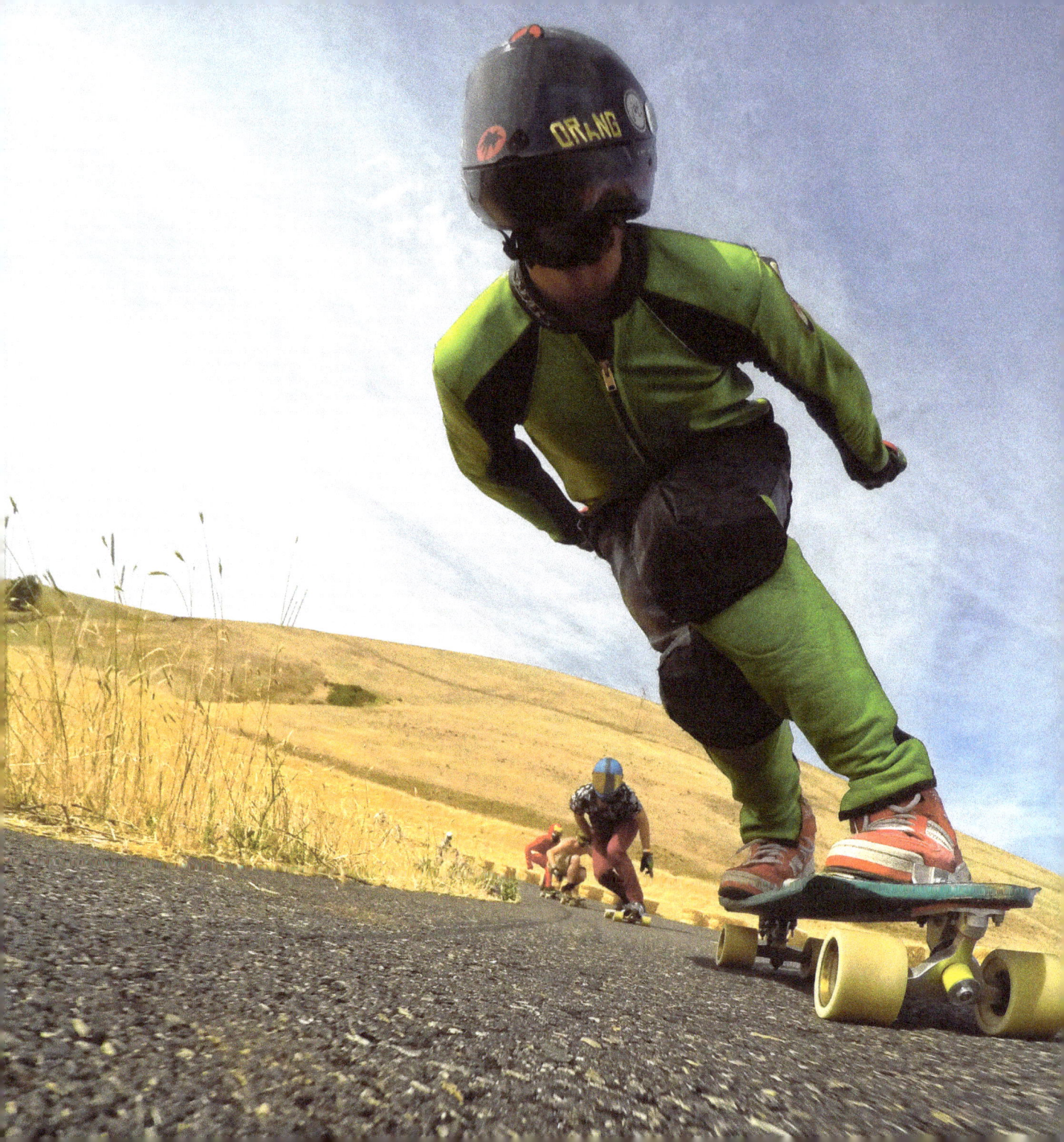

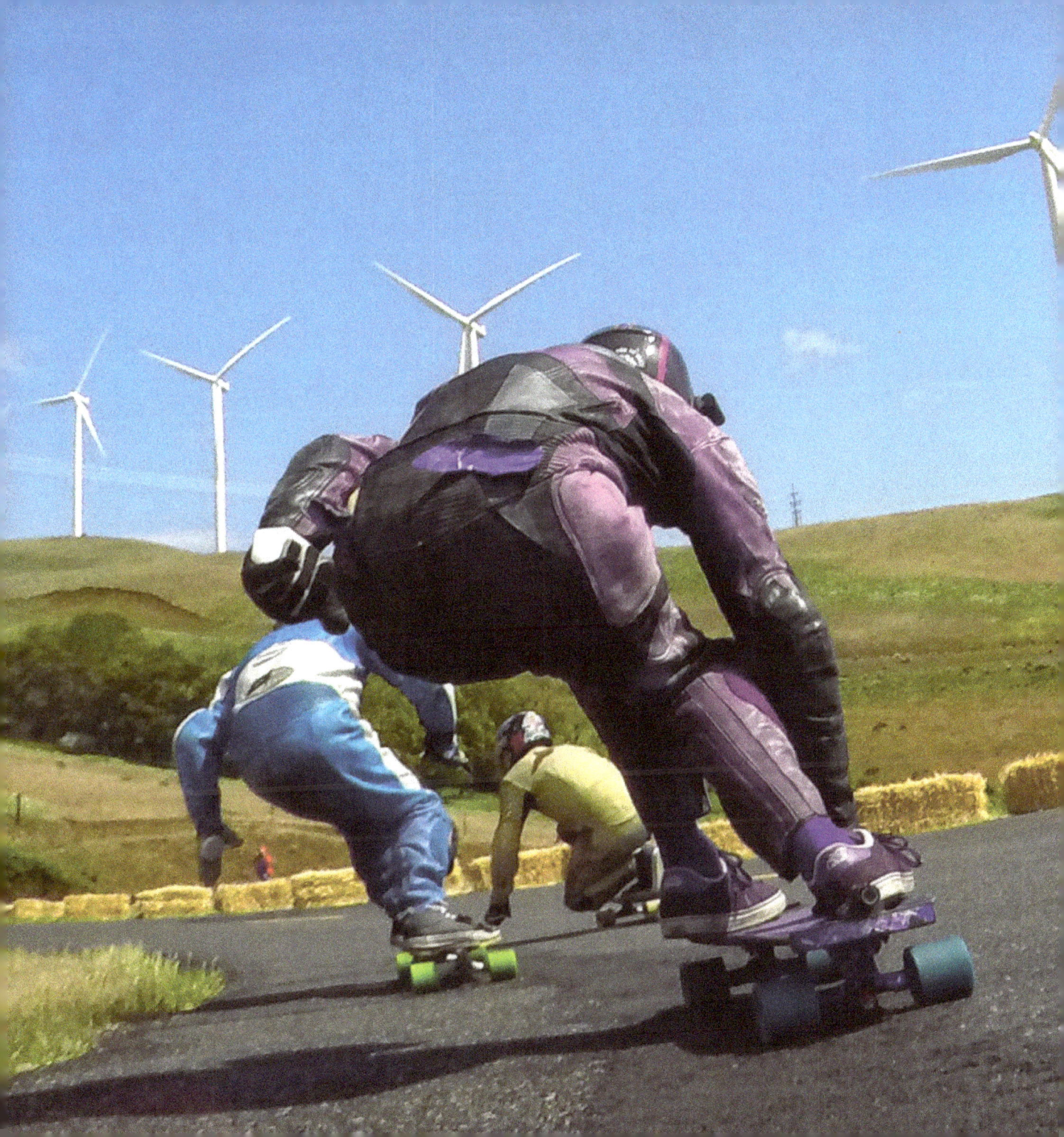

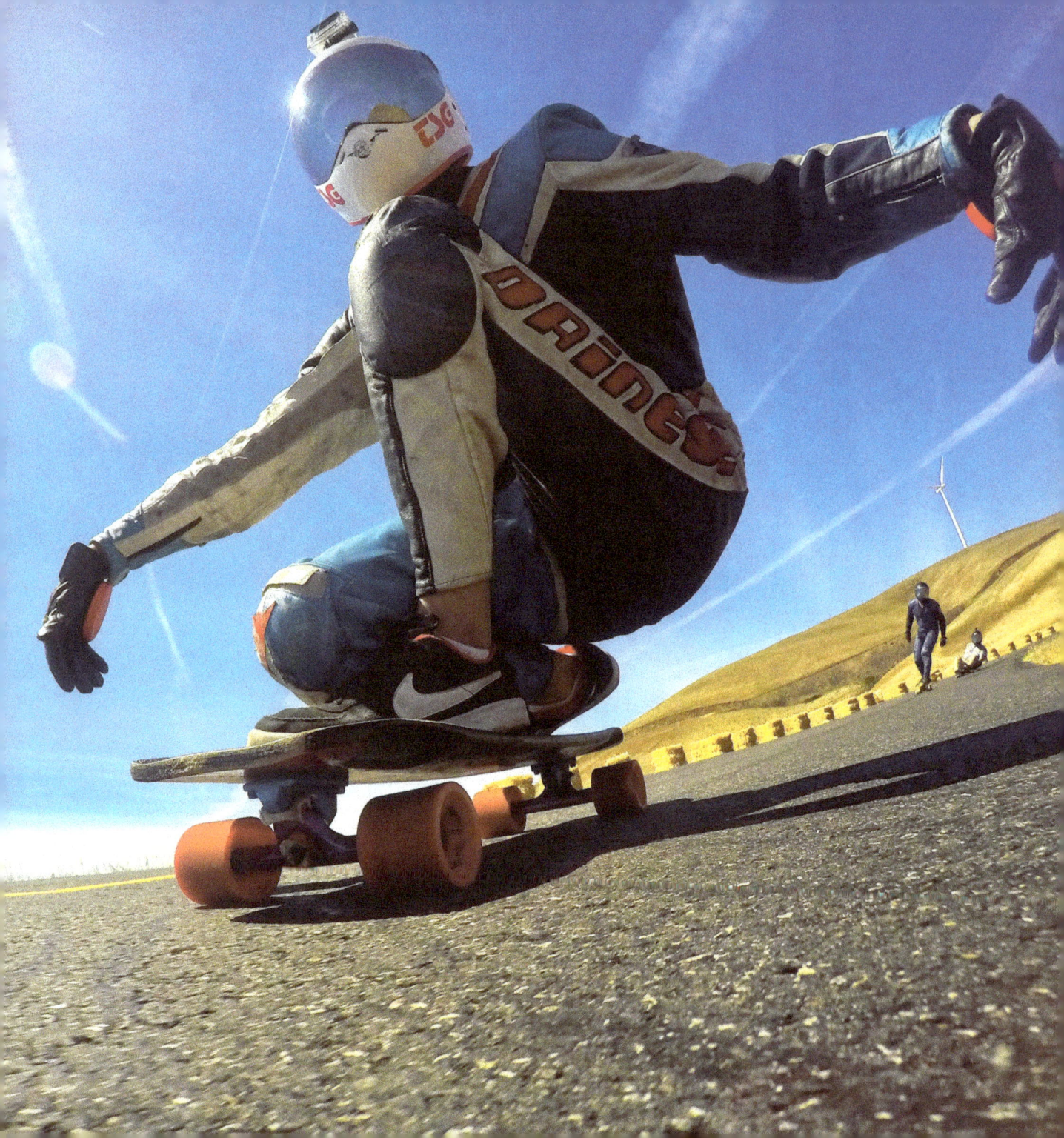

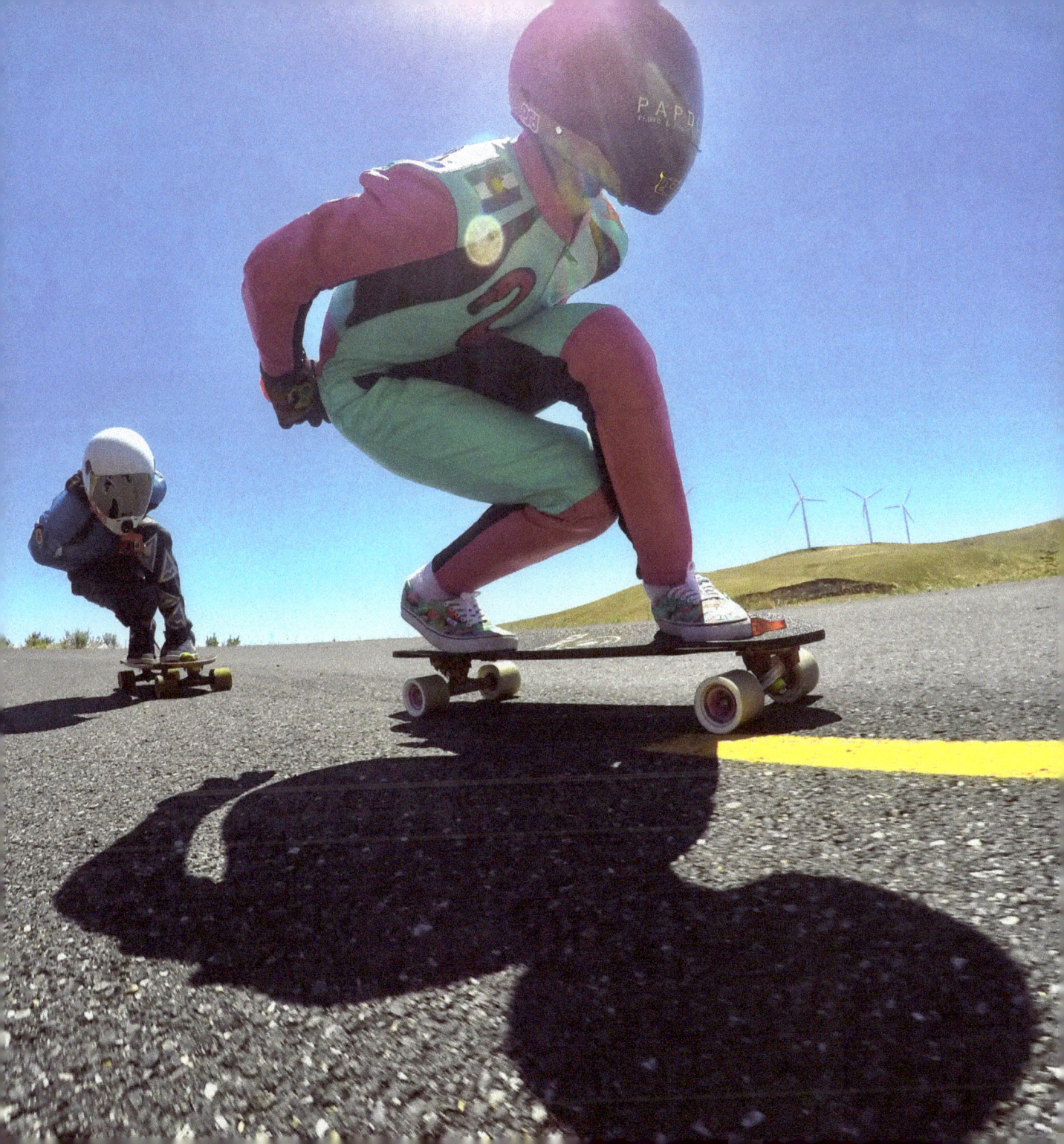

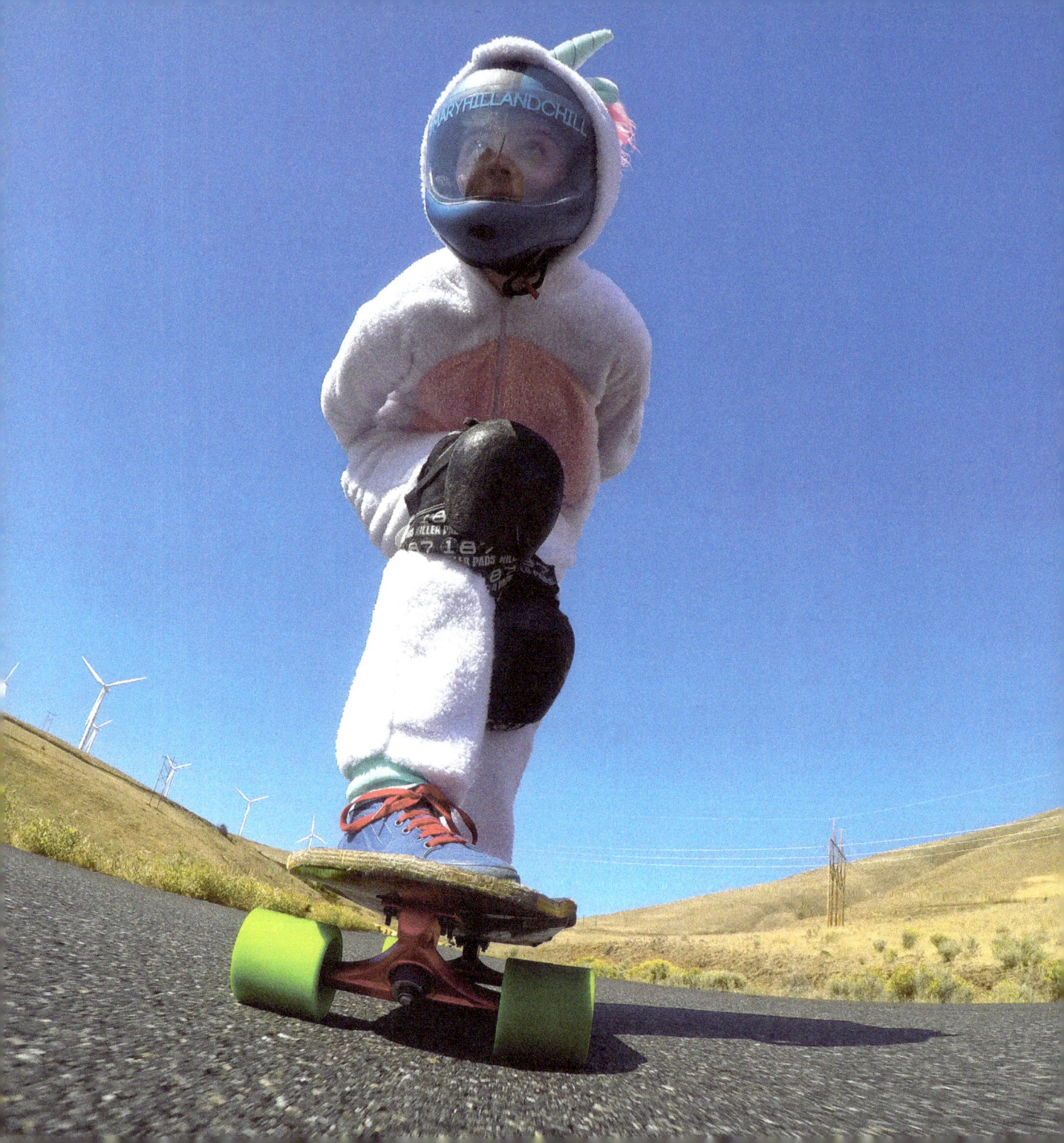

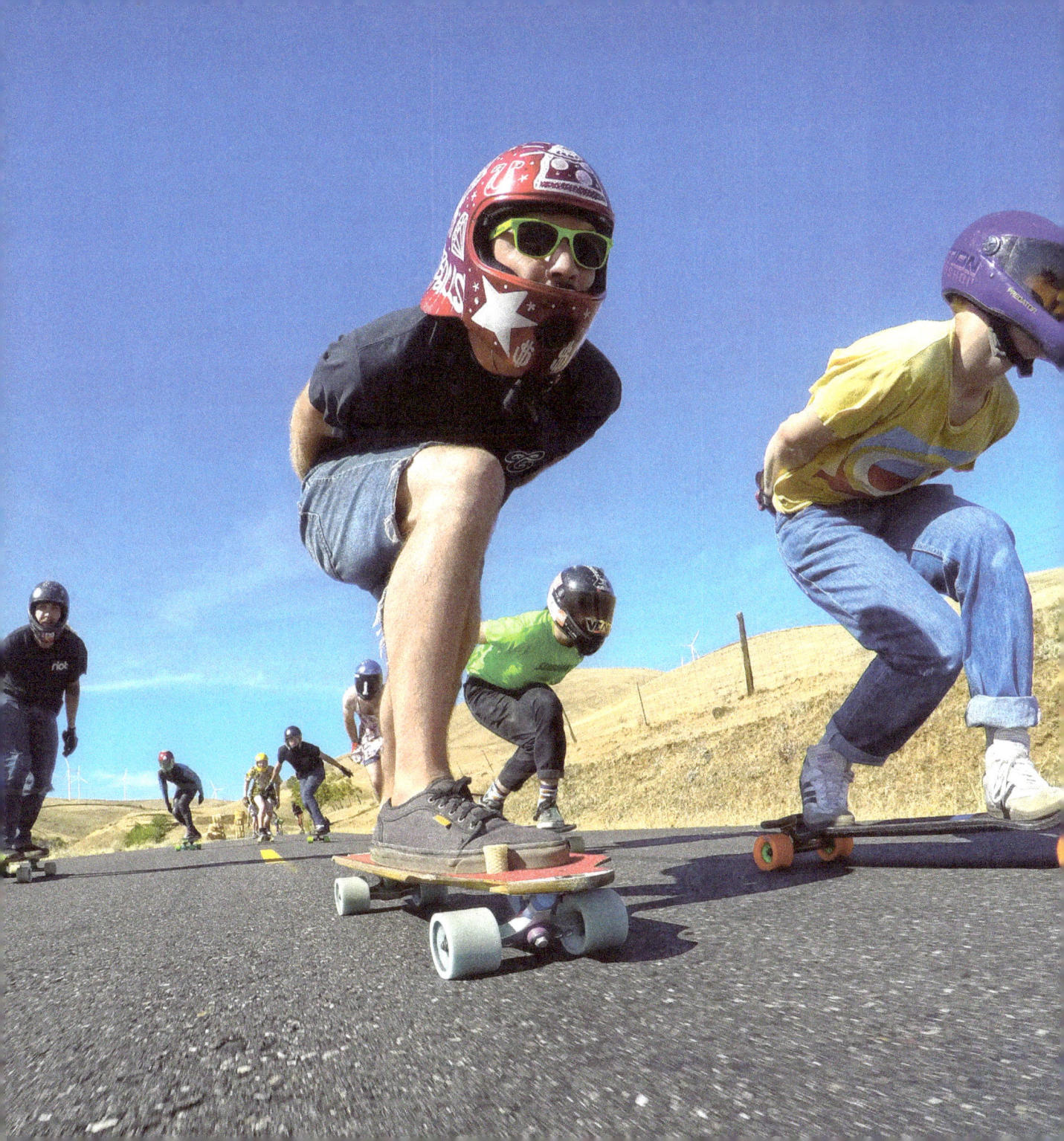

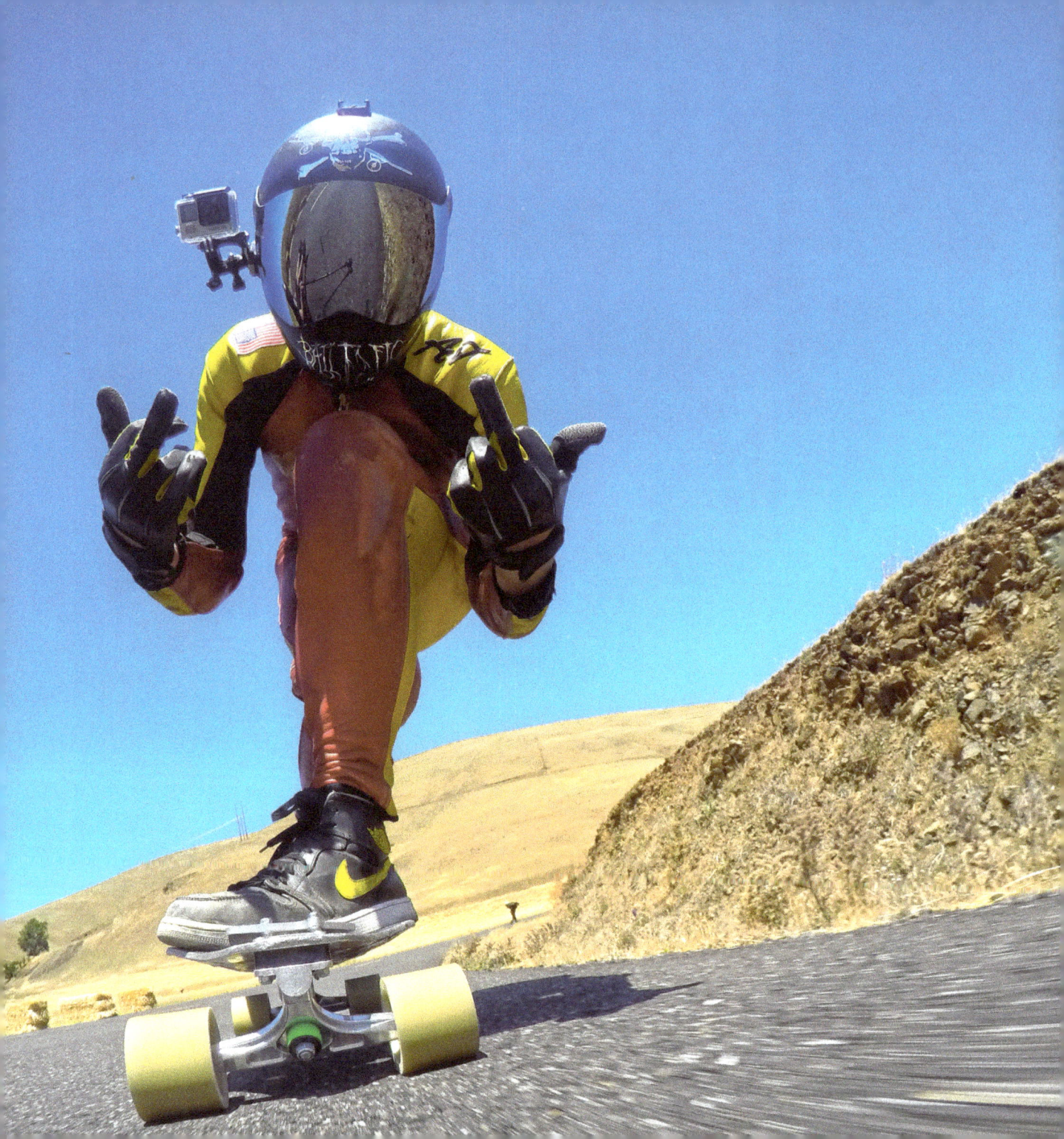

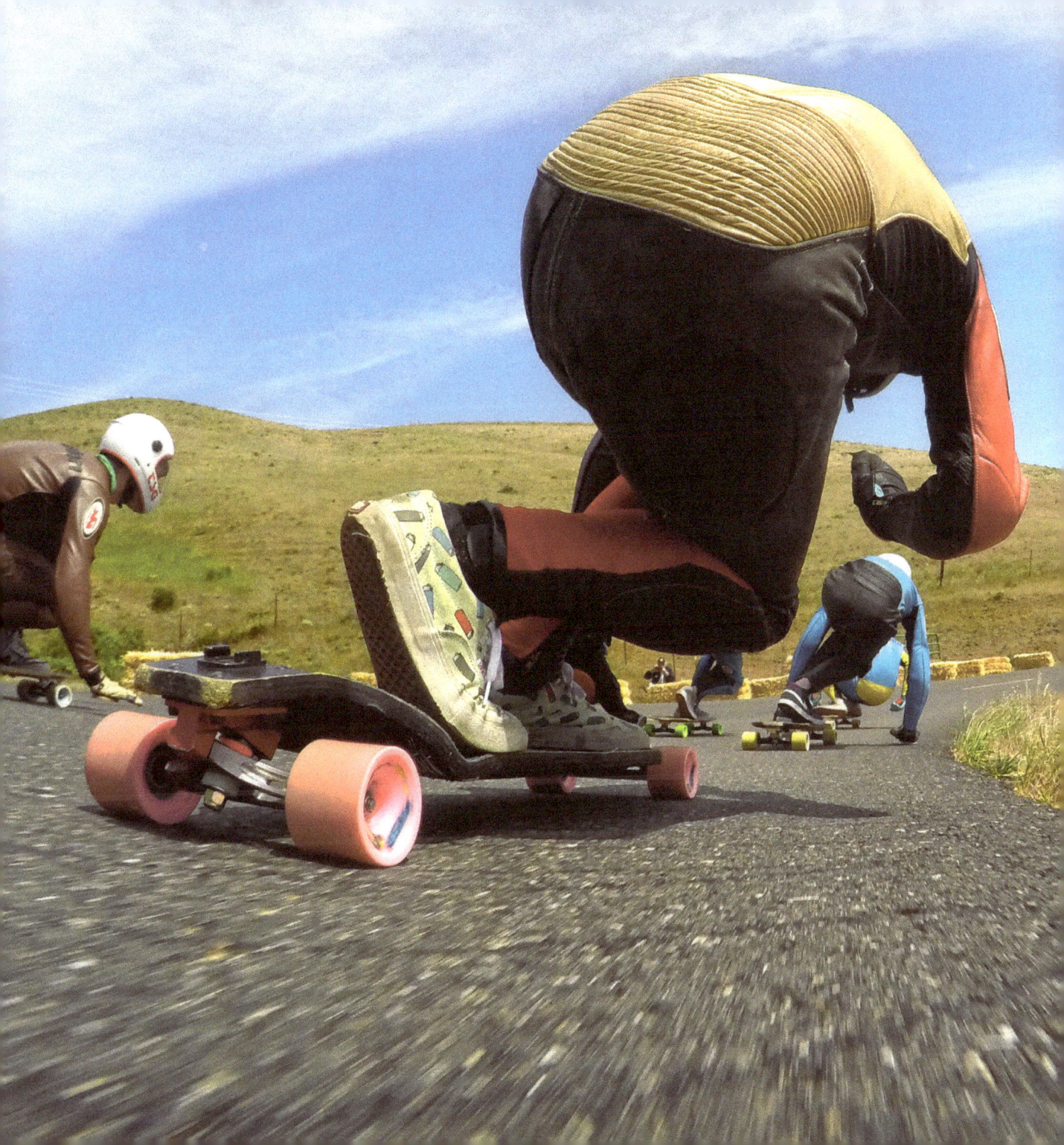

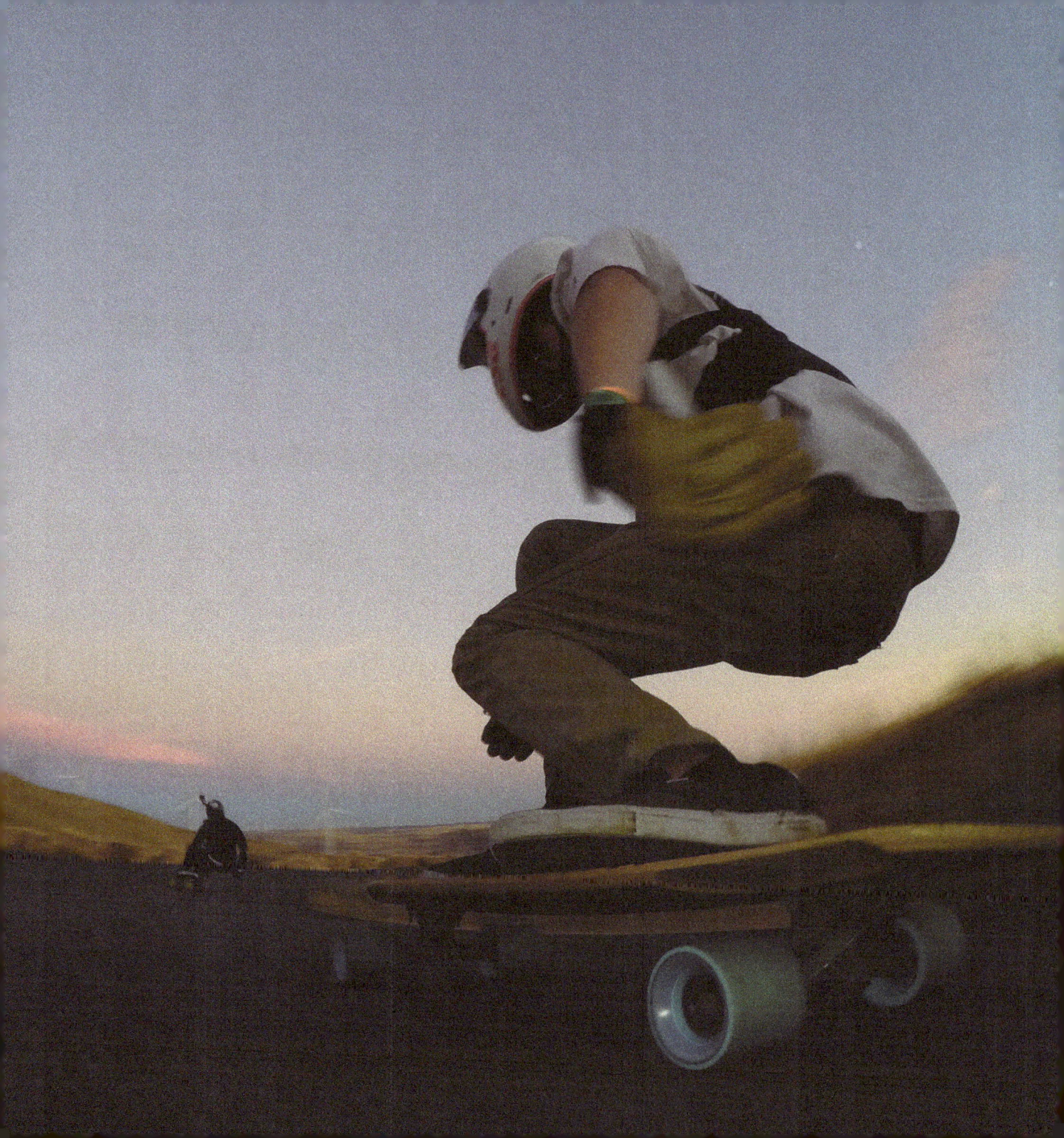

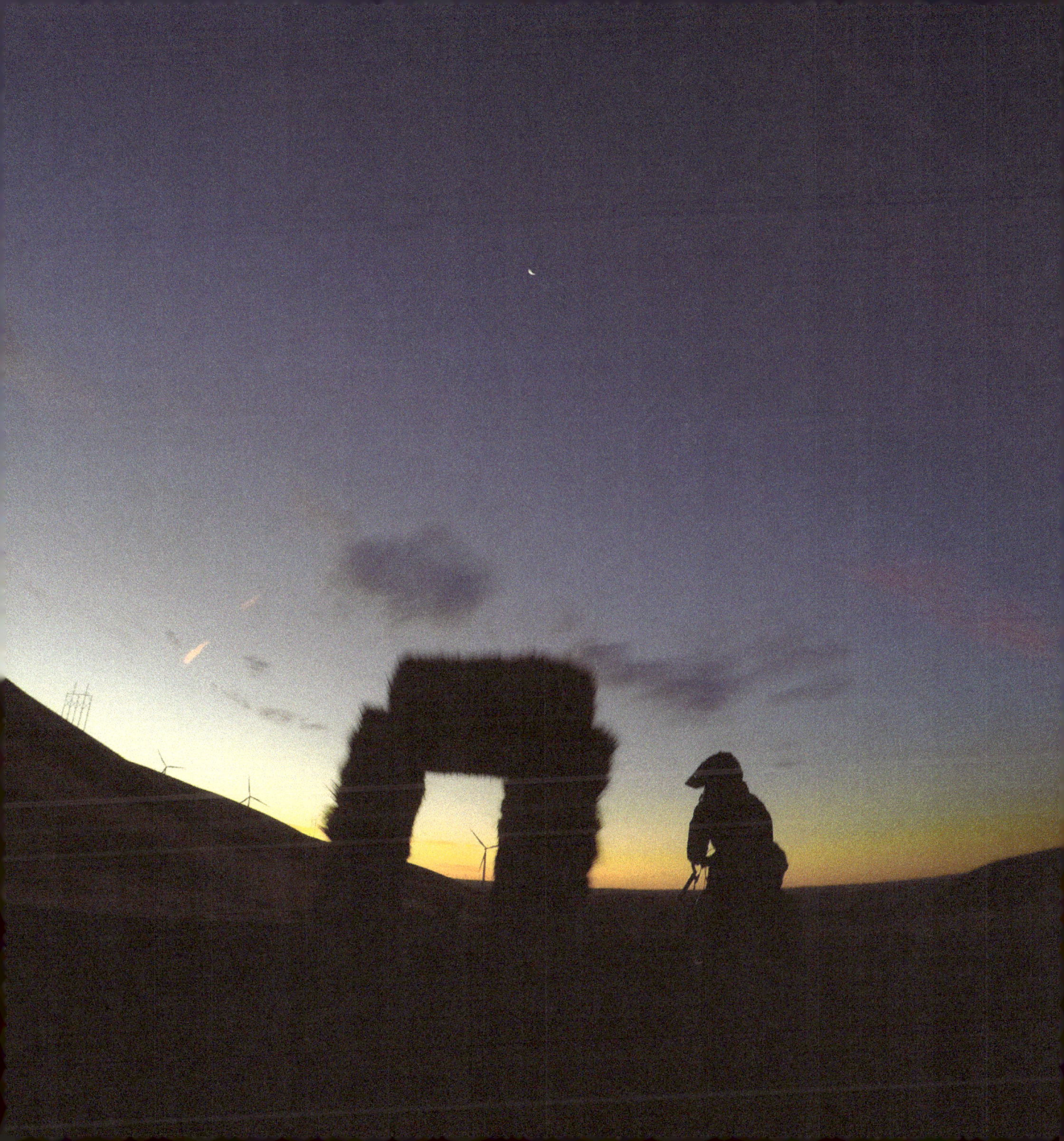

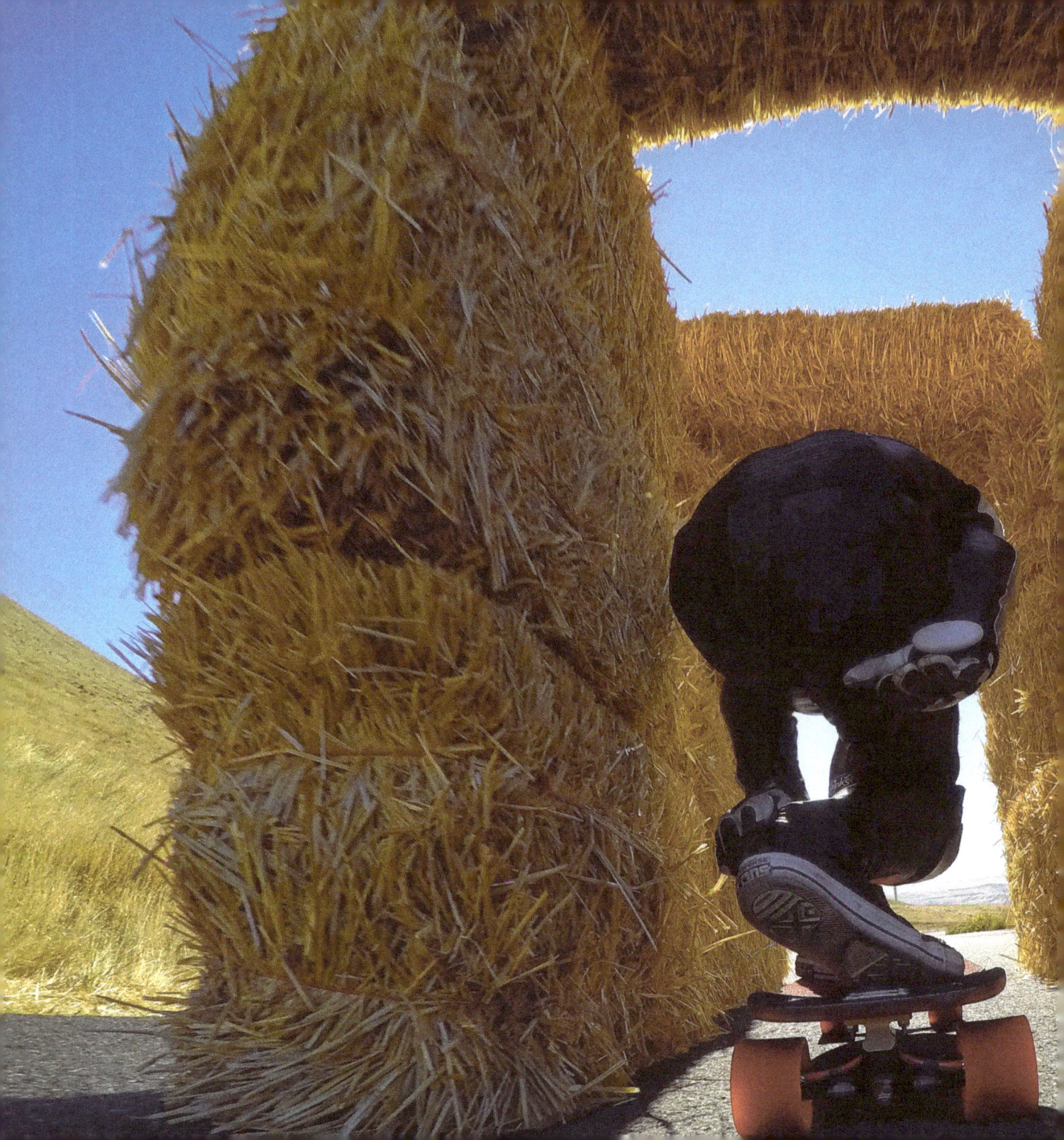

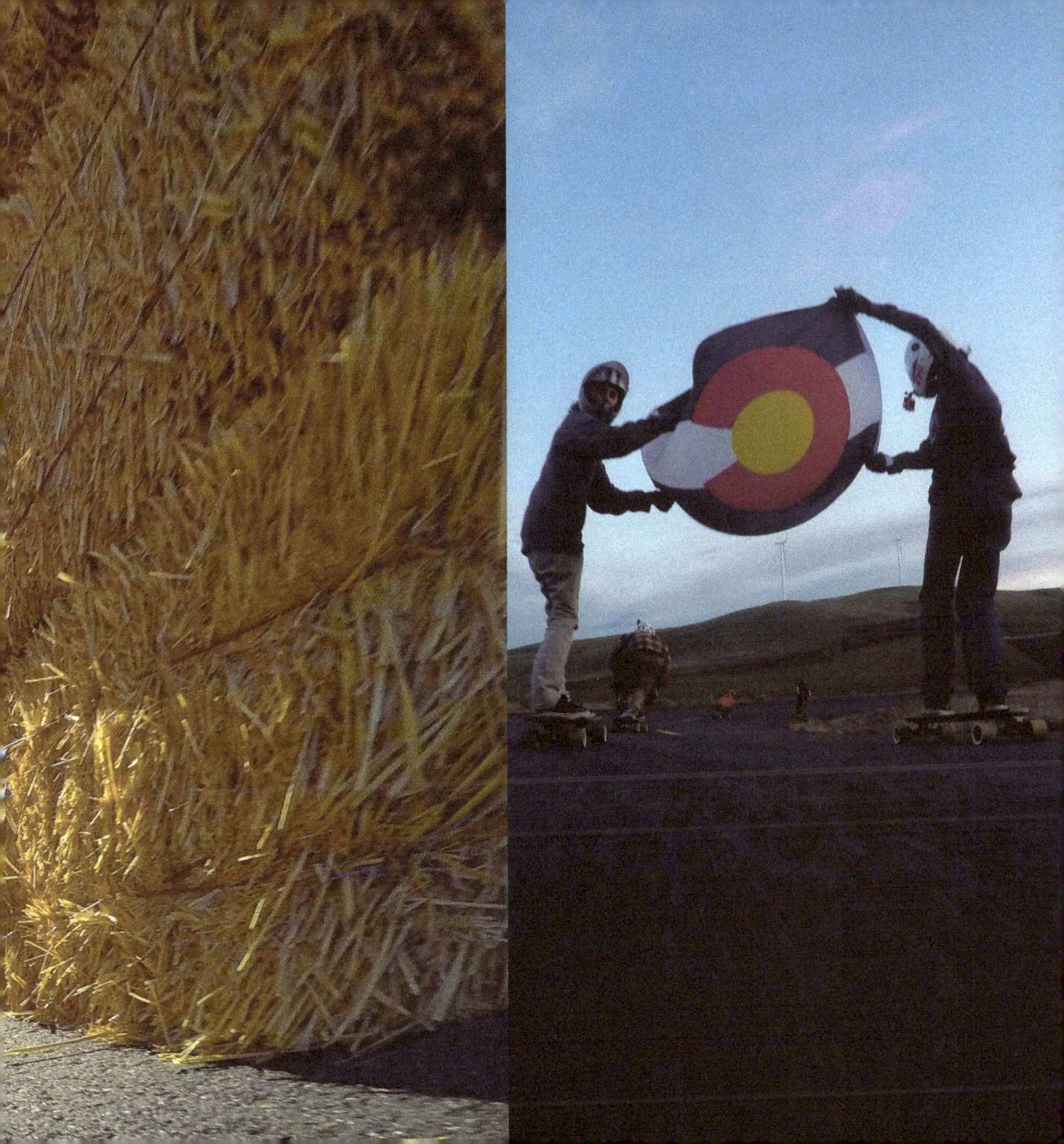

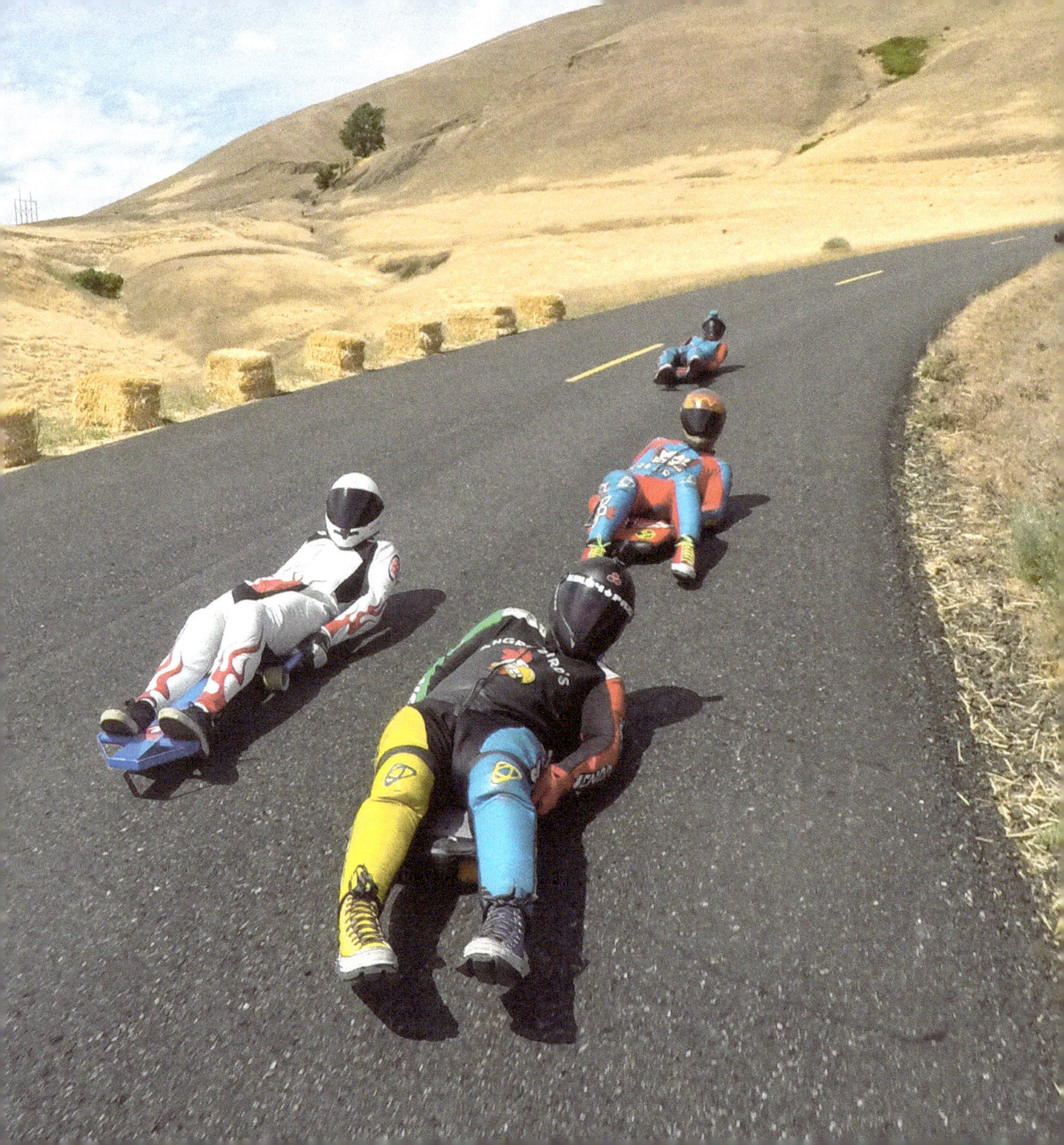

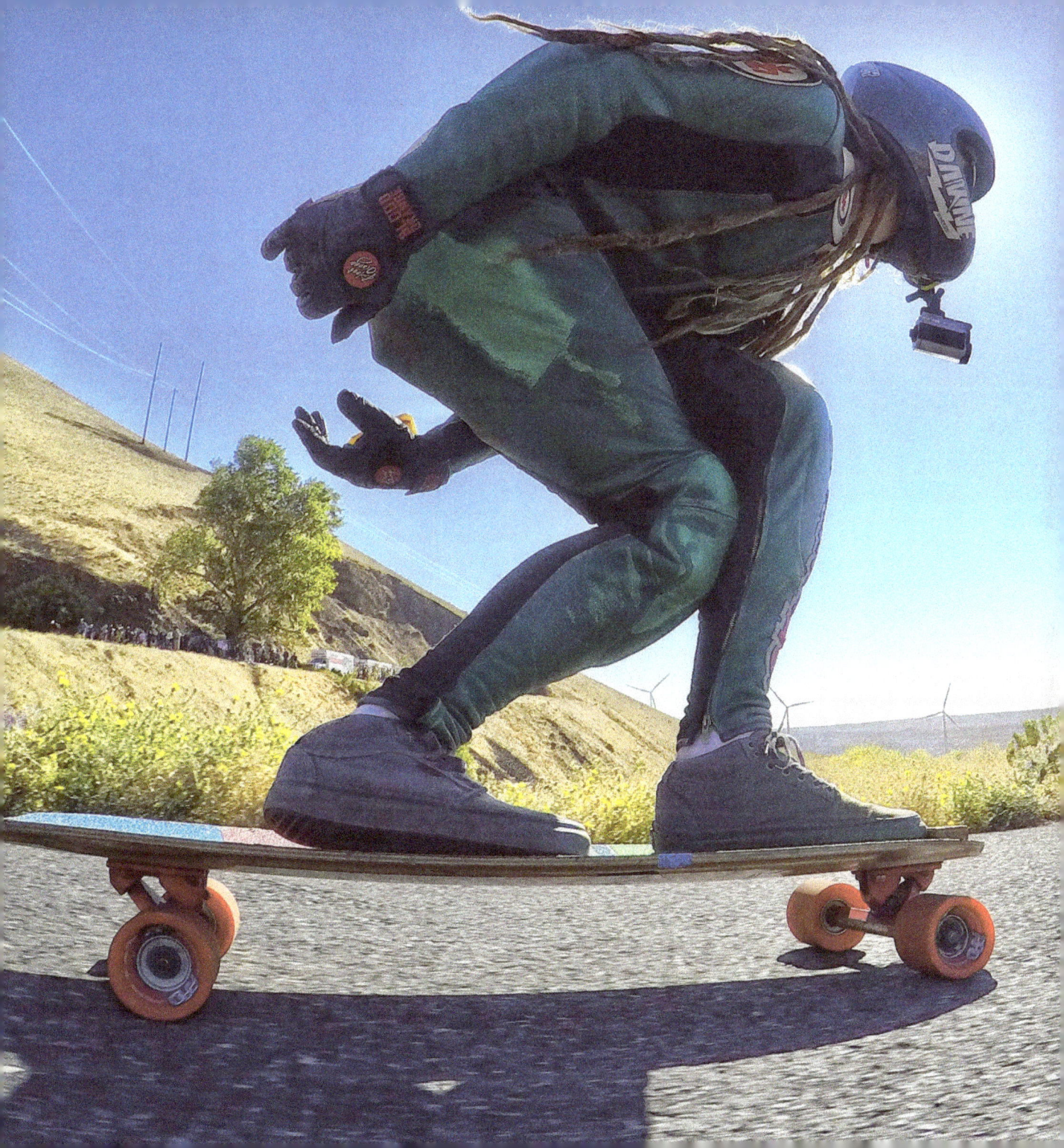

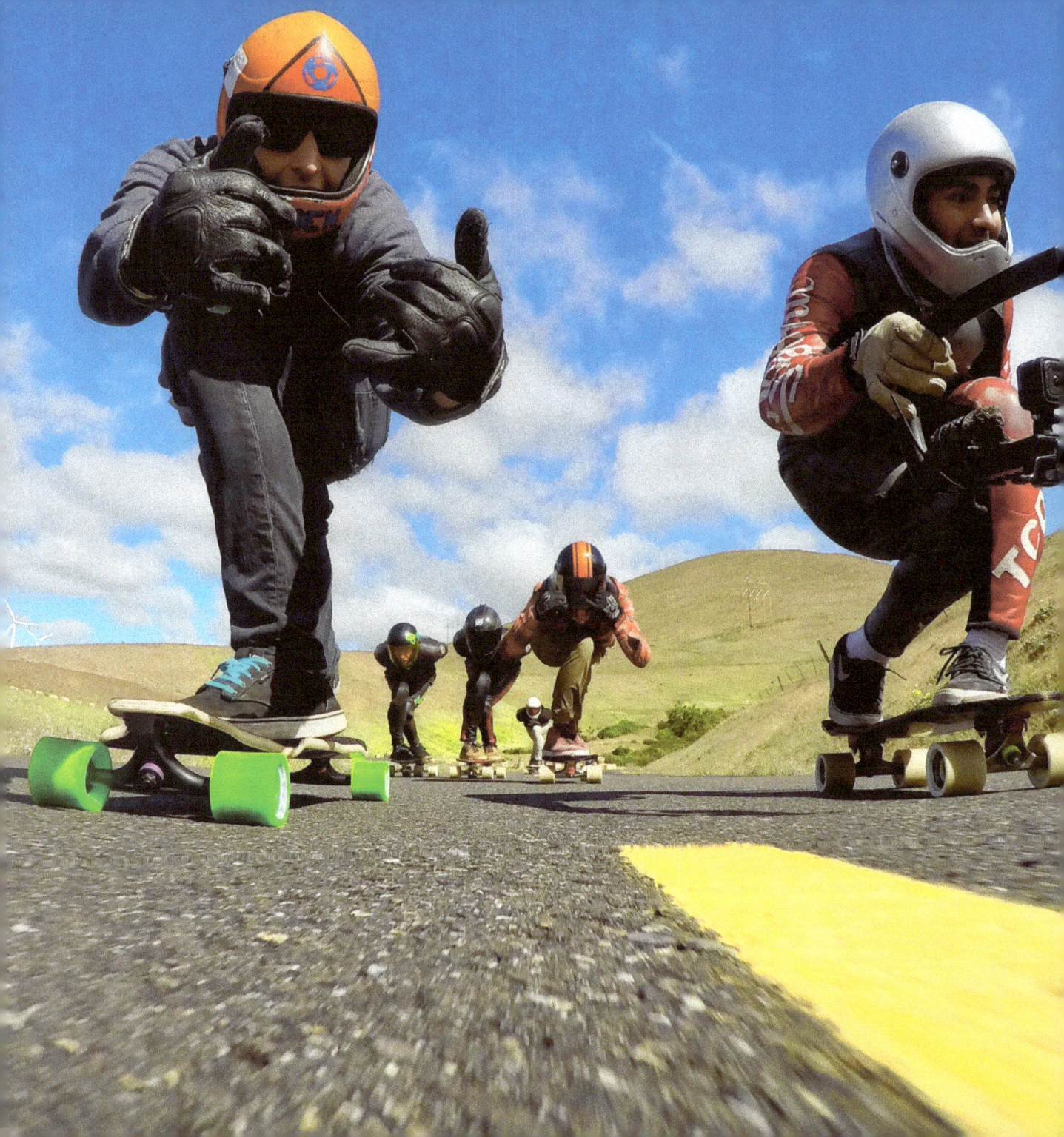

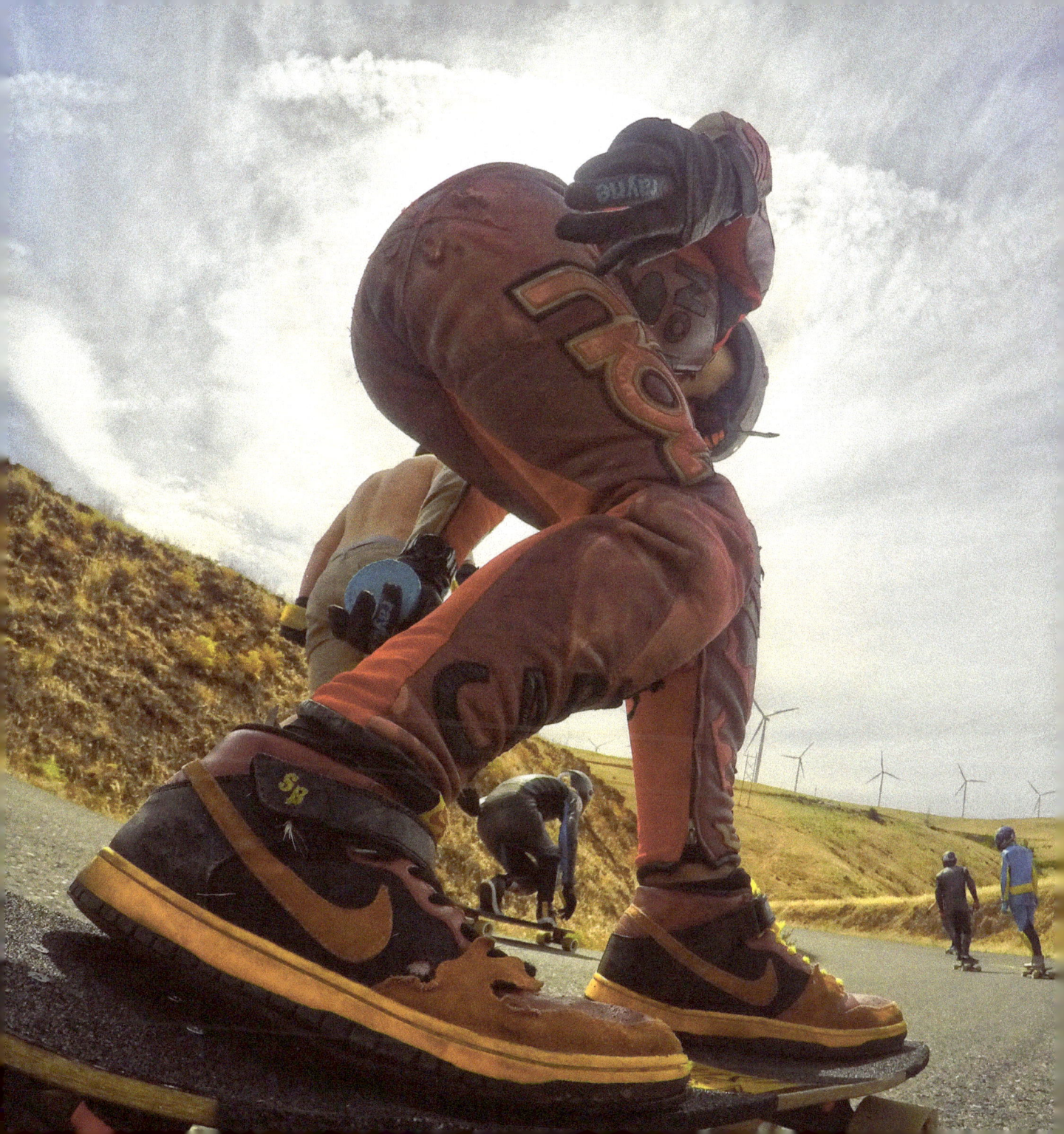

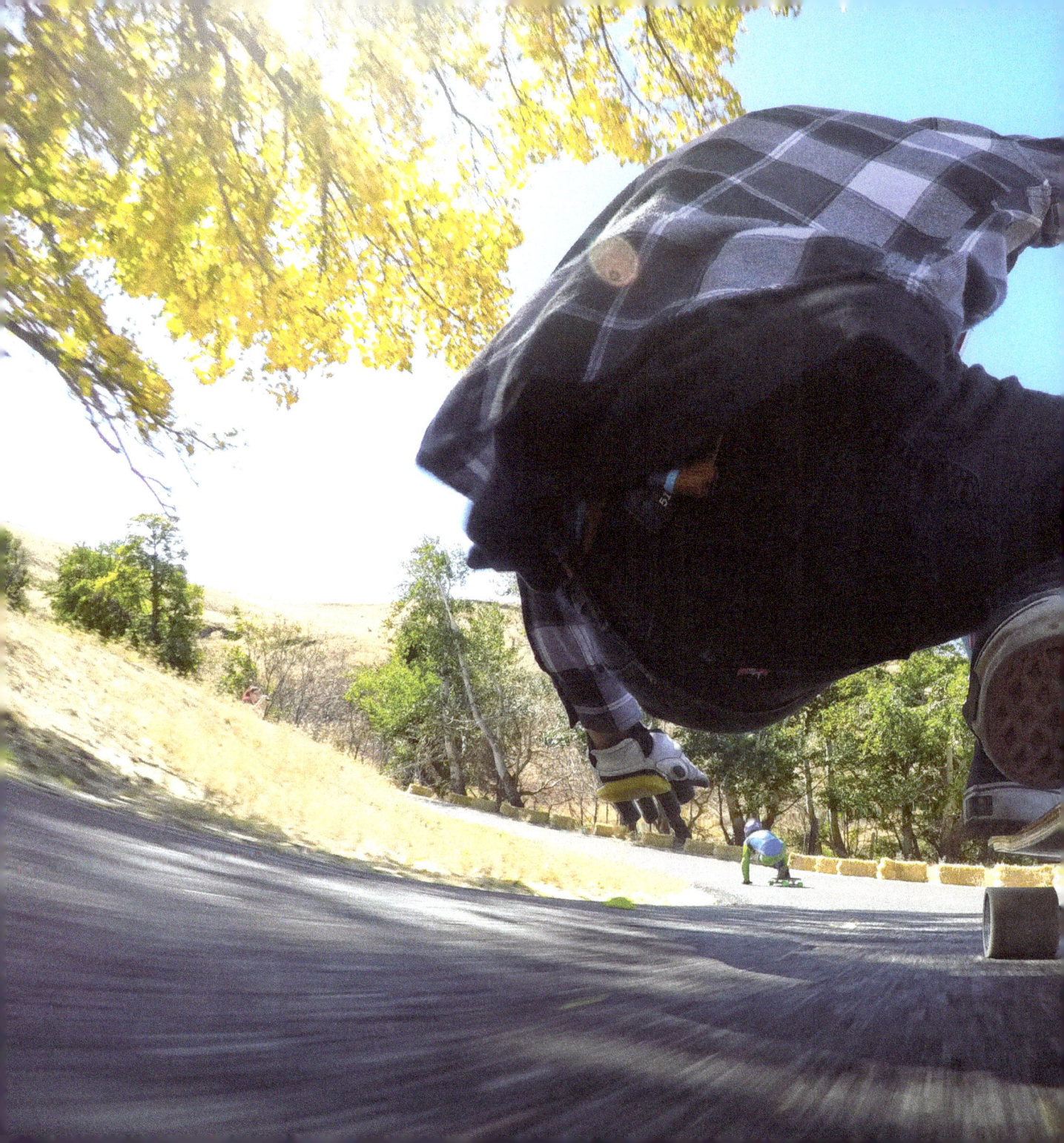

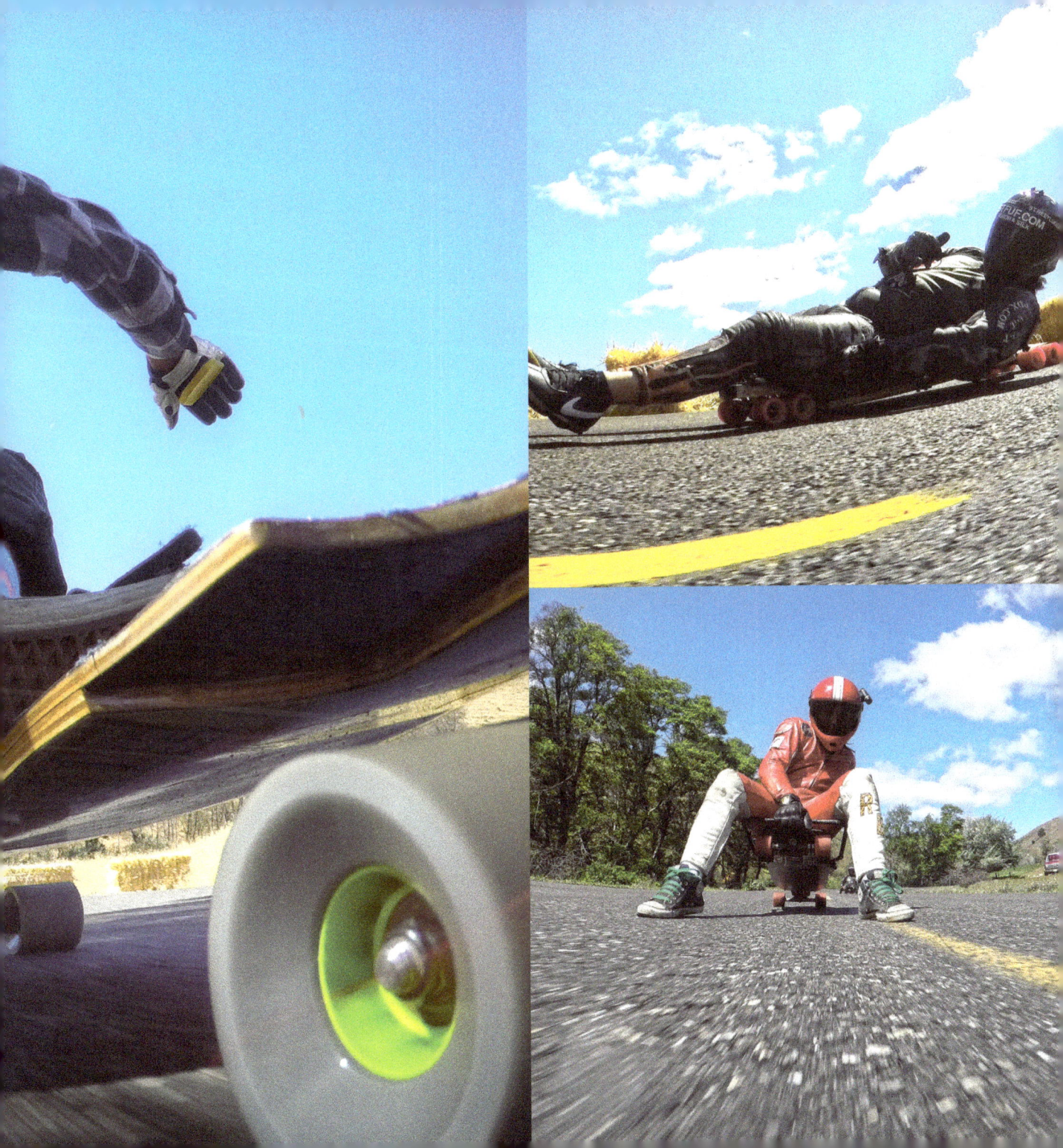

#Sweetpotato

Nothing breaks up the pilgrimage to Maryhill better than the welcoming curves of our beloved Sweet Potato. Pulling up to this special spot reminds us that we're almost to our mecca, and the locals always show us an amazing time. The crew and I could never get down with its Bogus name, so Sweet Potato it is...to us.

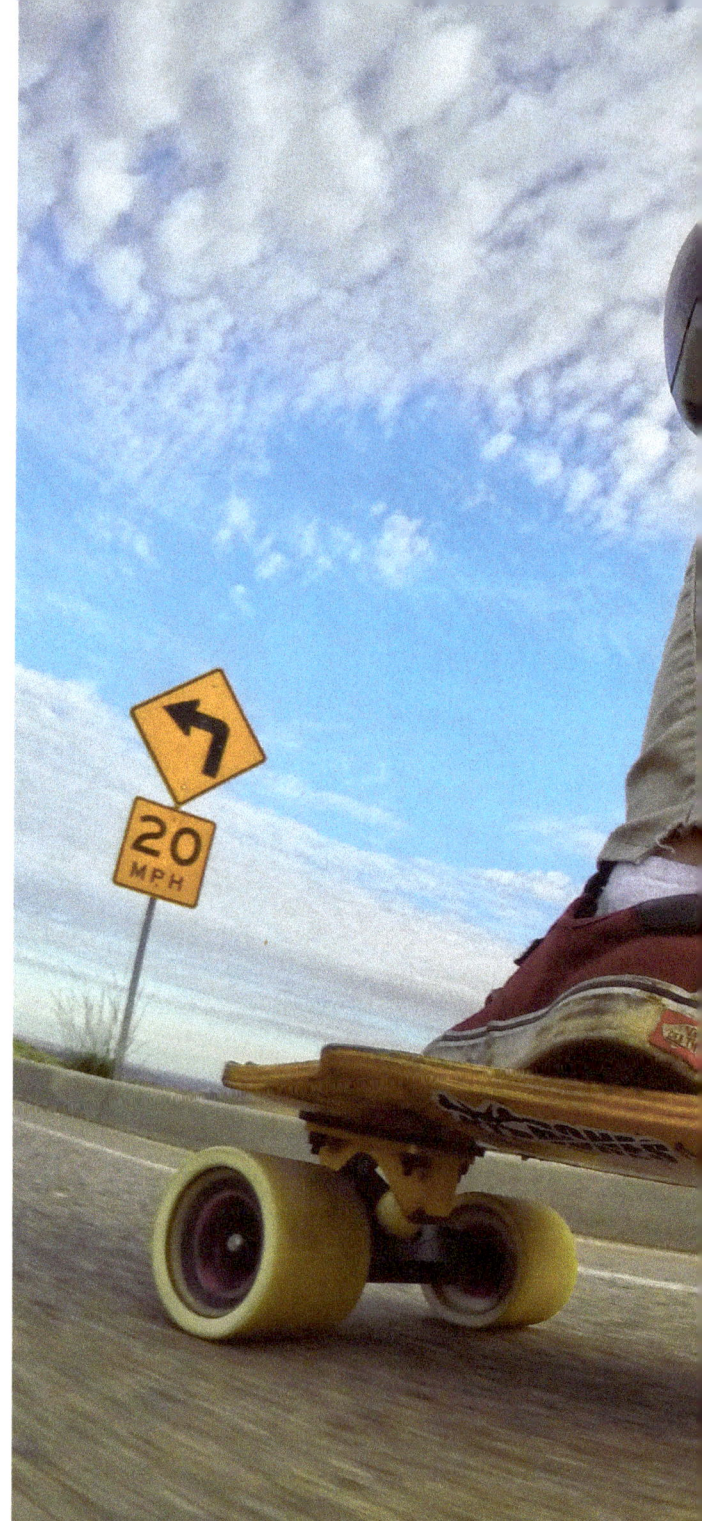

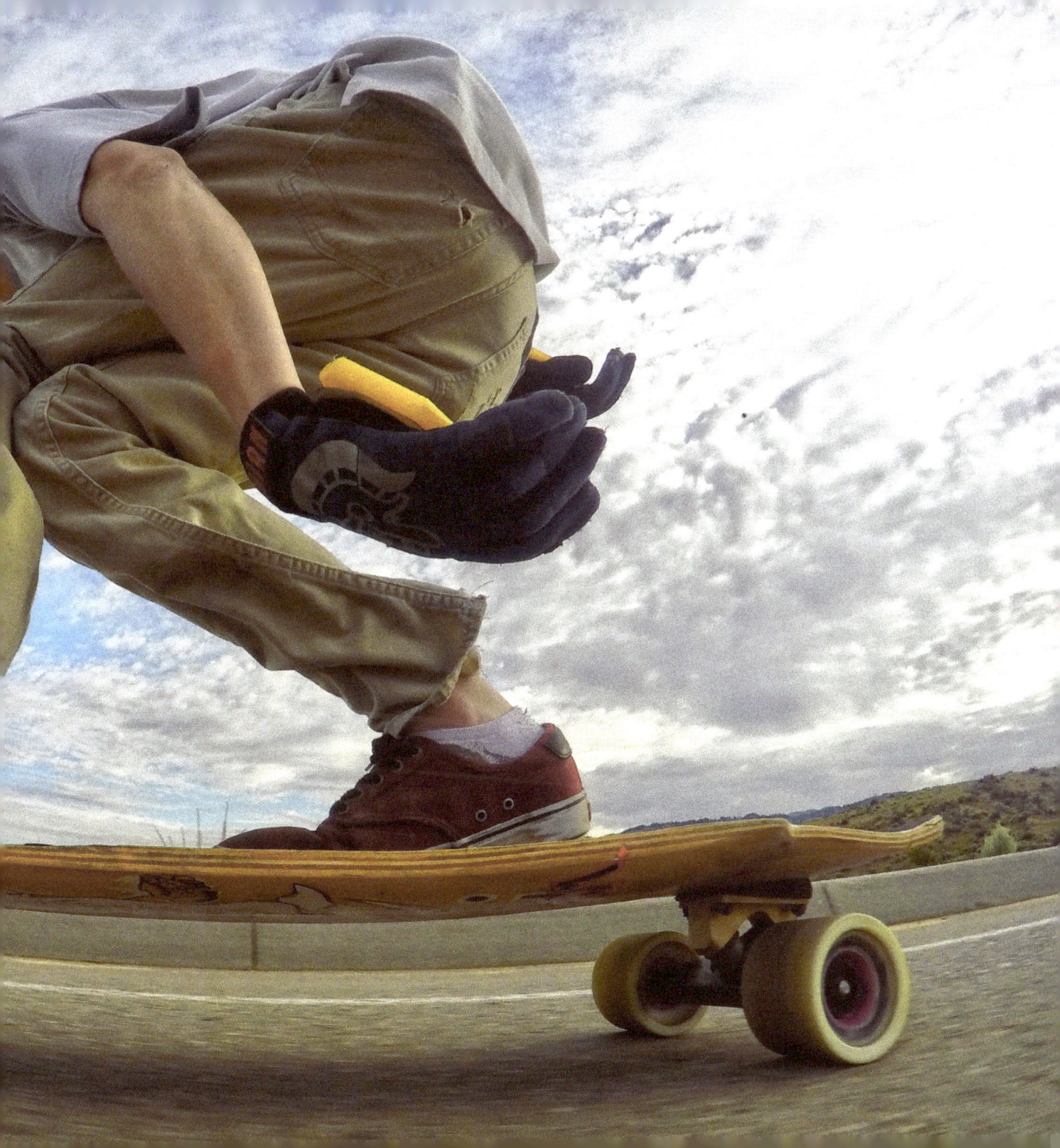

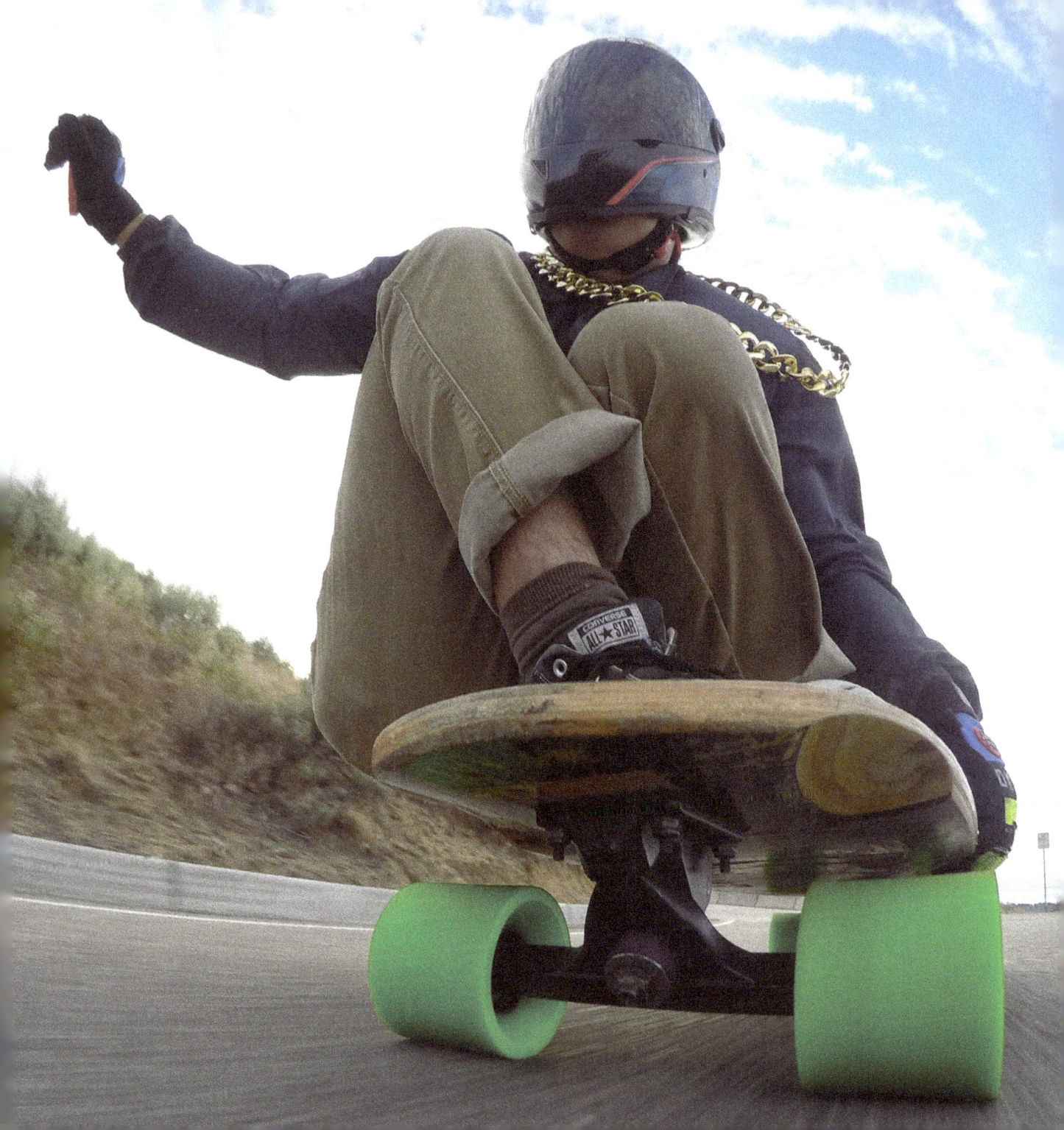

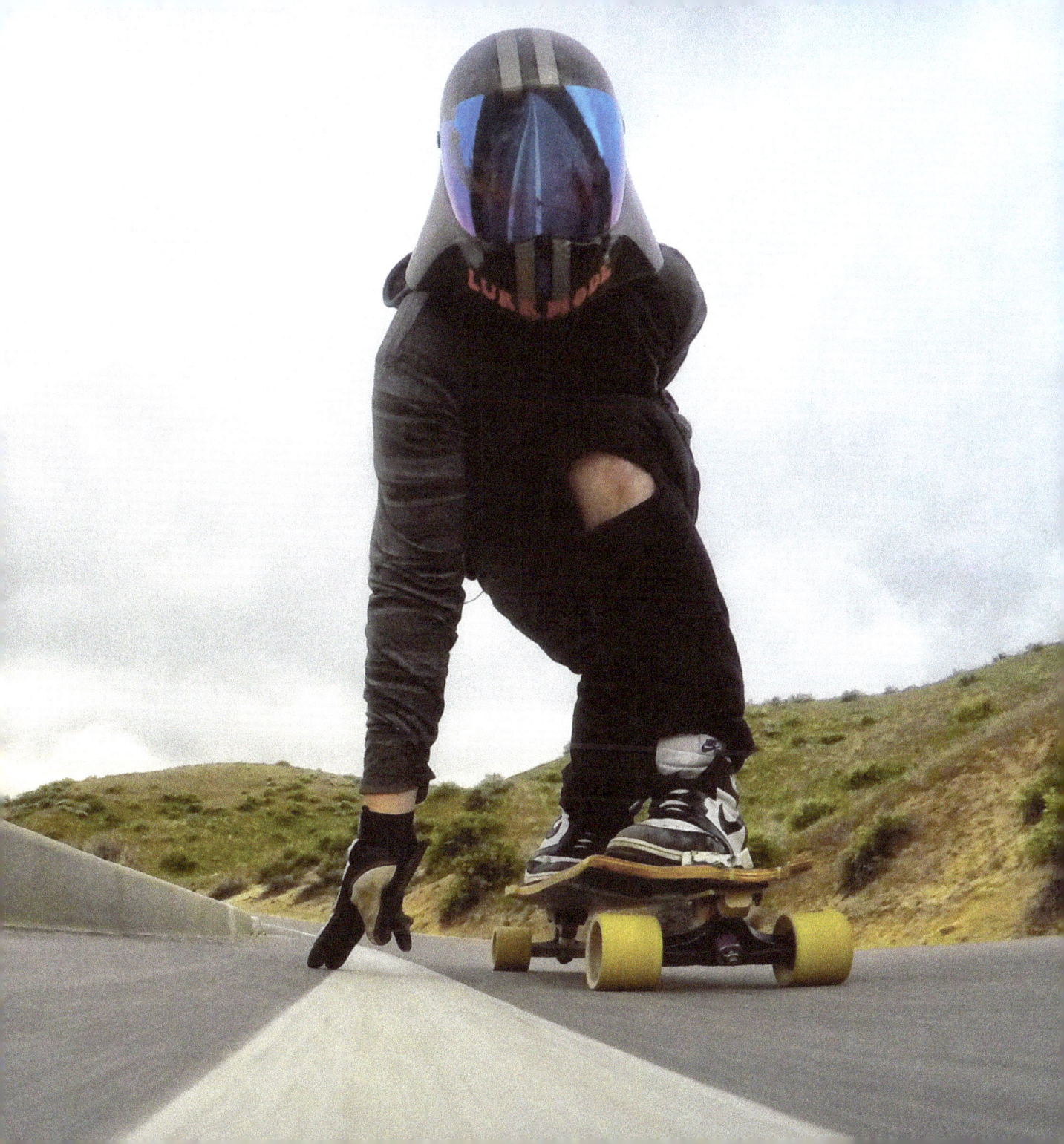

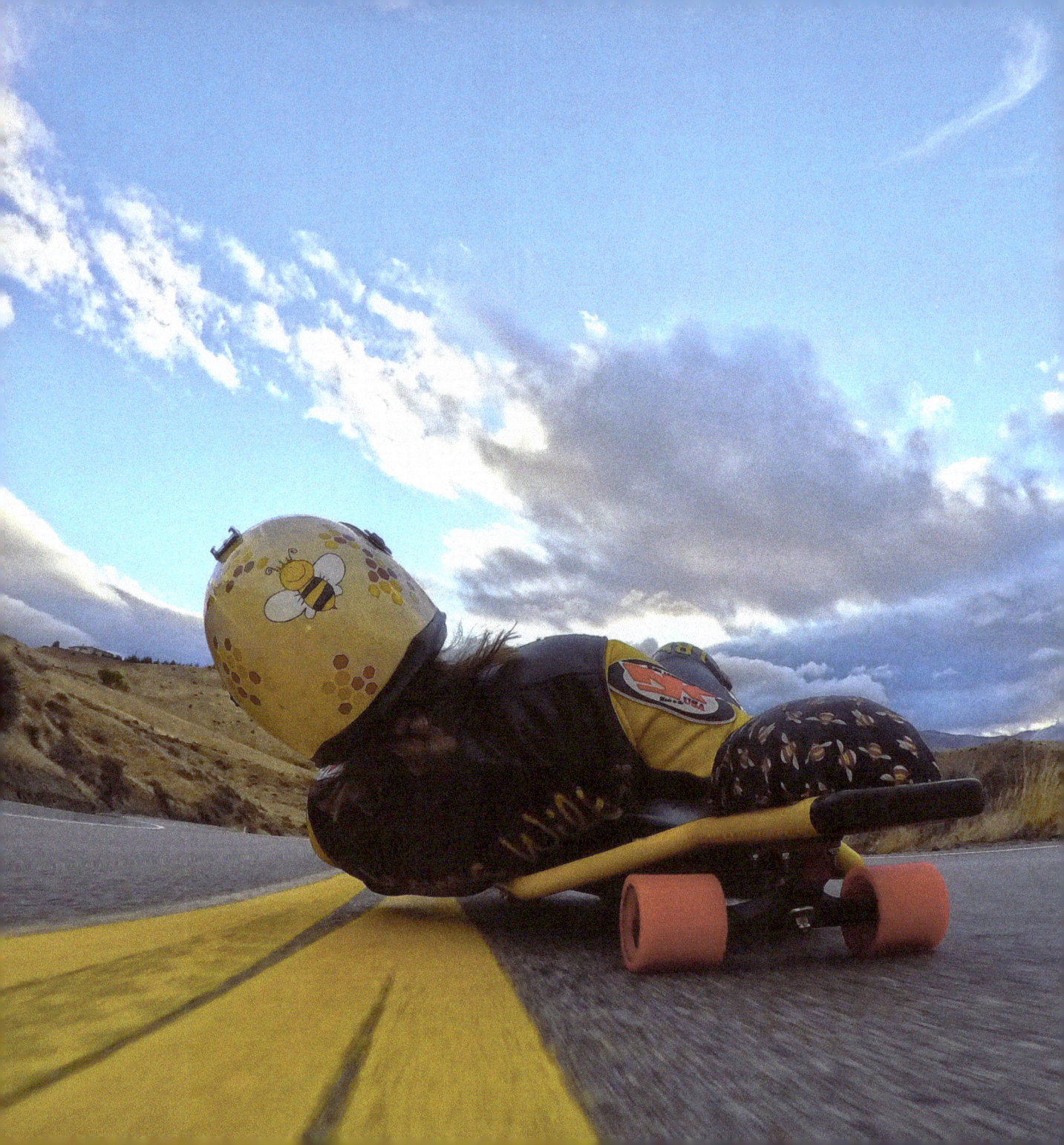

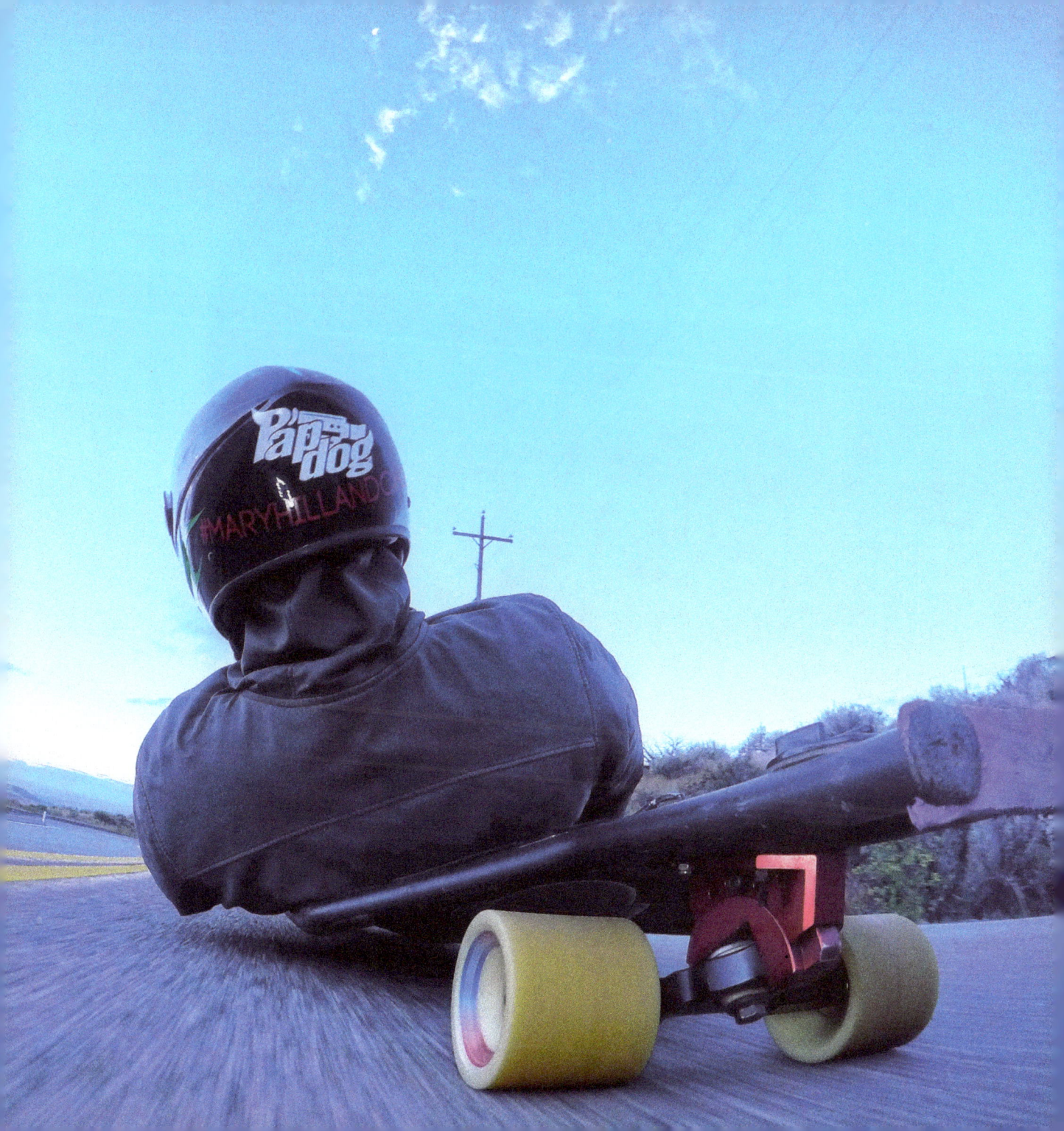

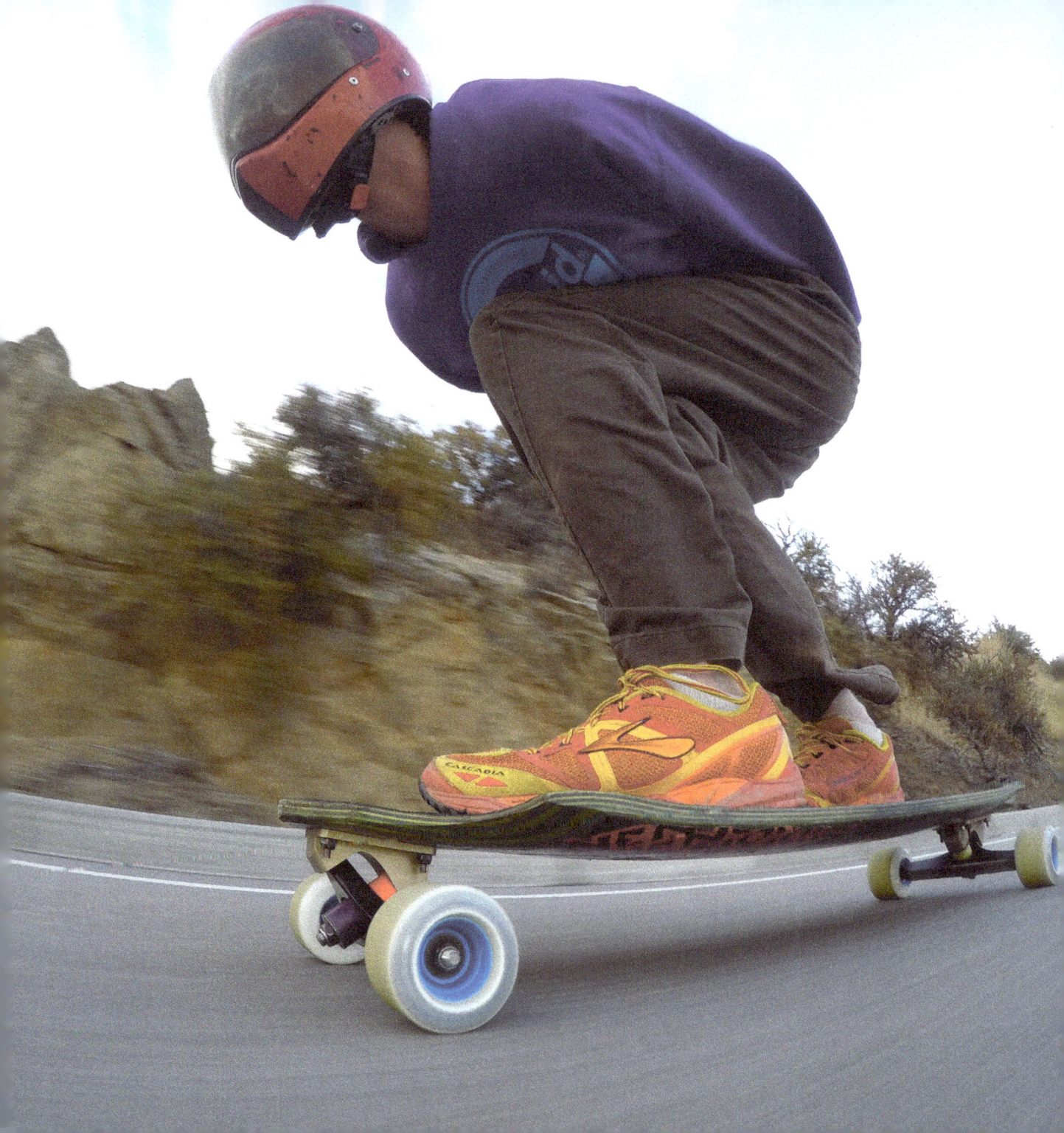

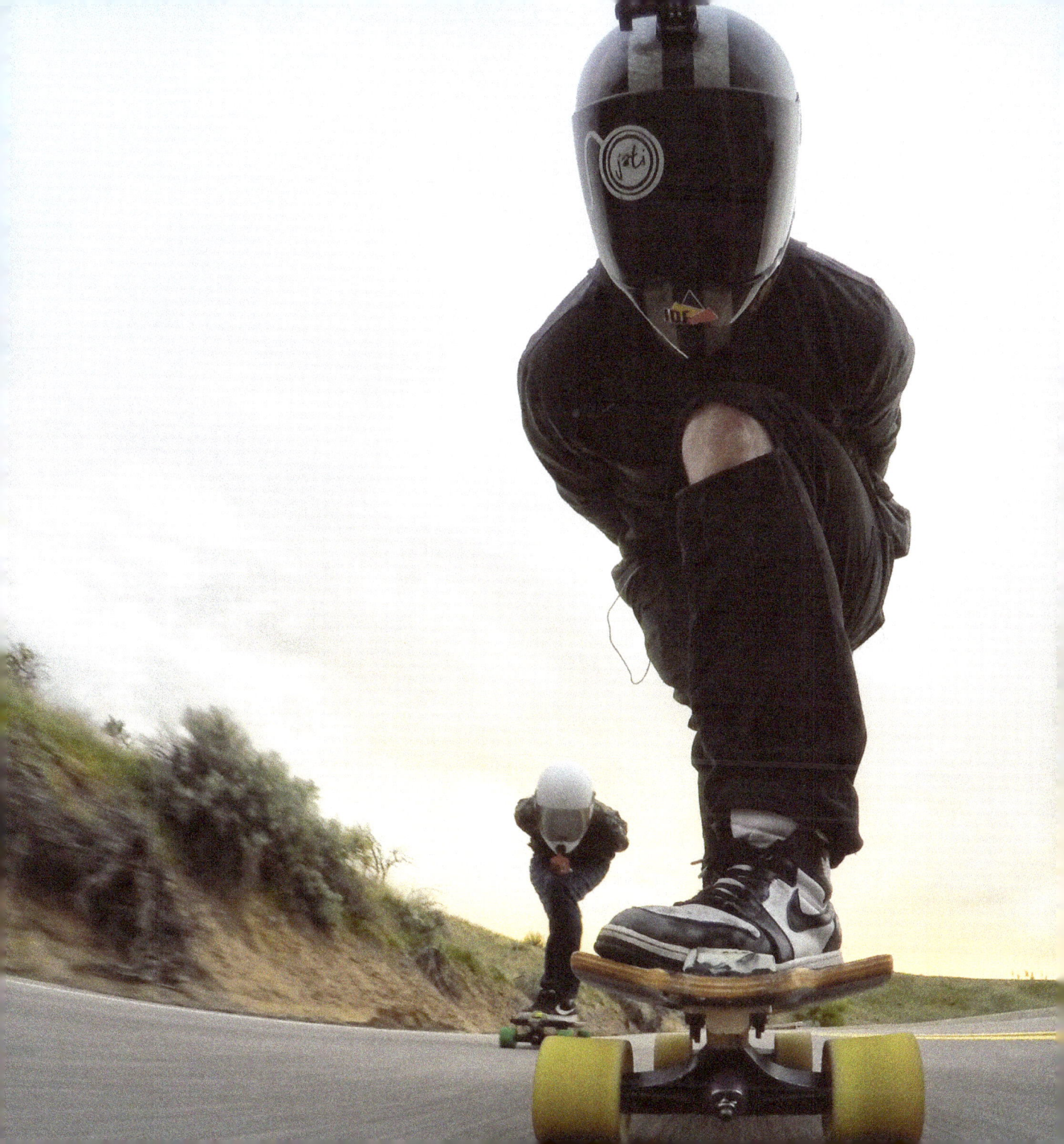

#Instabanger

The best part of this extreme hobby of mine is the sharing…nothing feels better than spreading the stoke so publicly, recognizing amazing talent interacting with Mother Nature so seamlessly. These shots are some of my most-liked on Instagram from 2016. Thank you for all the insta-love and support!

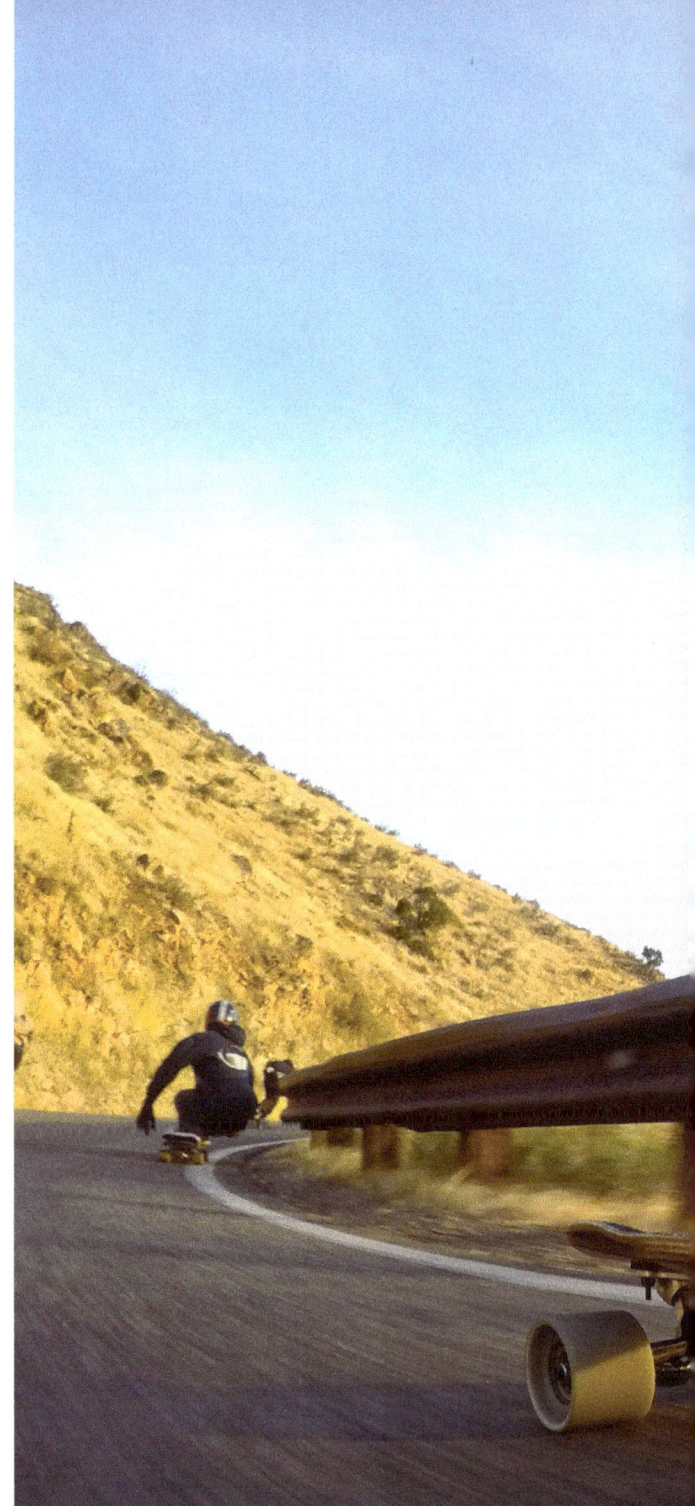

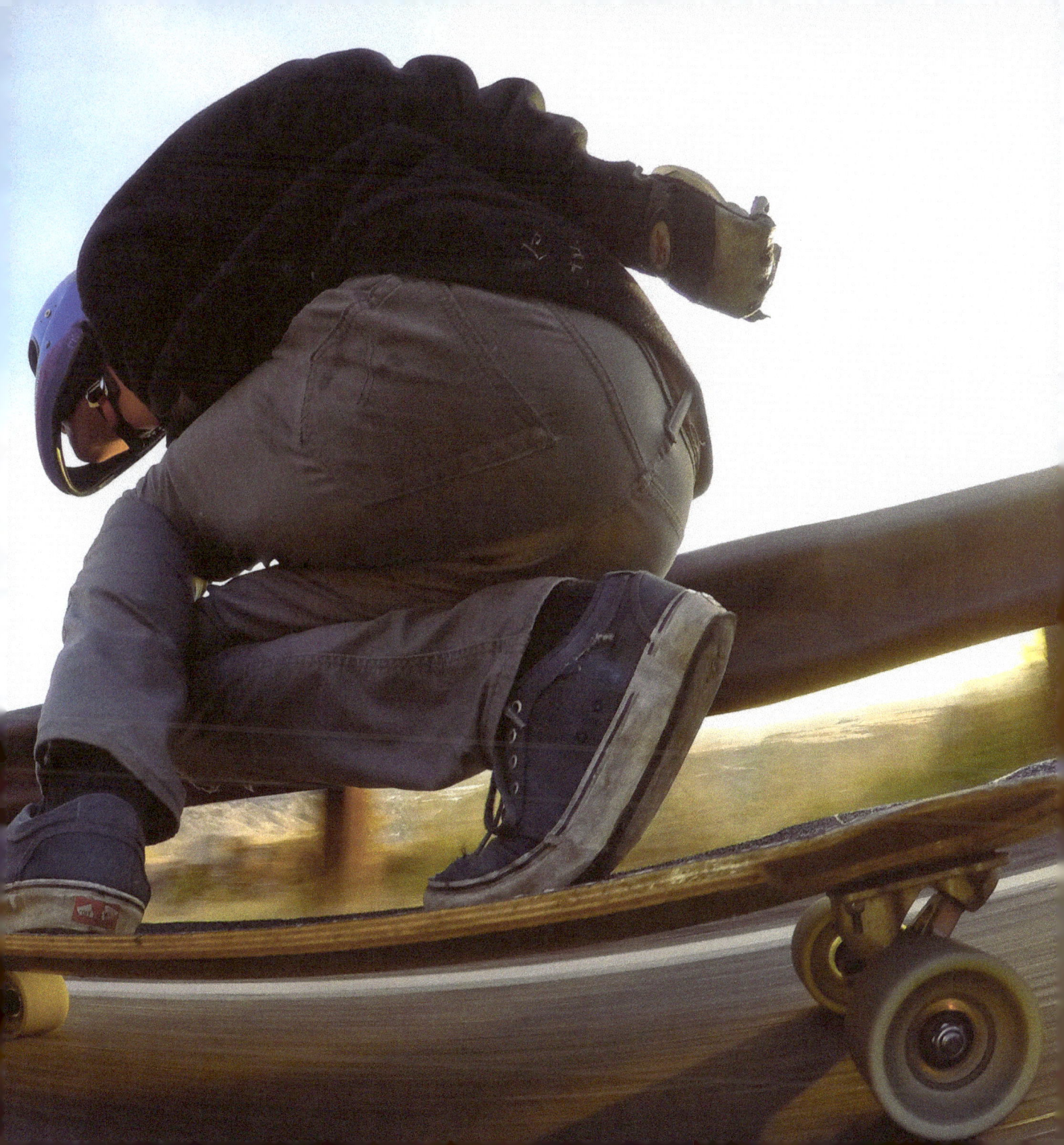

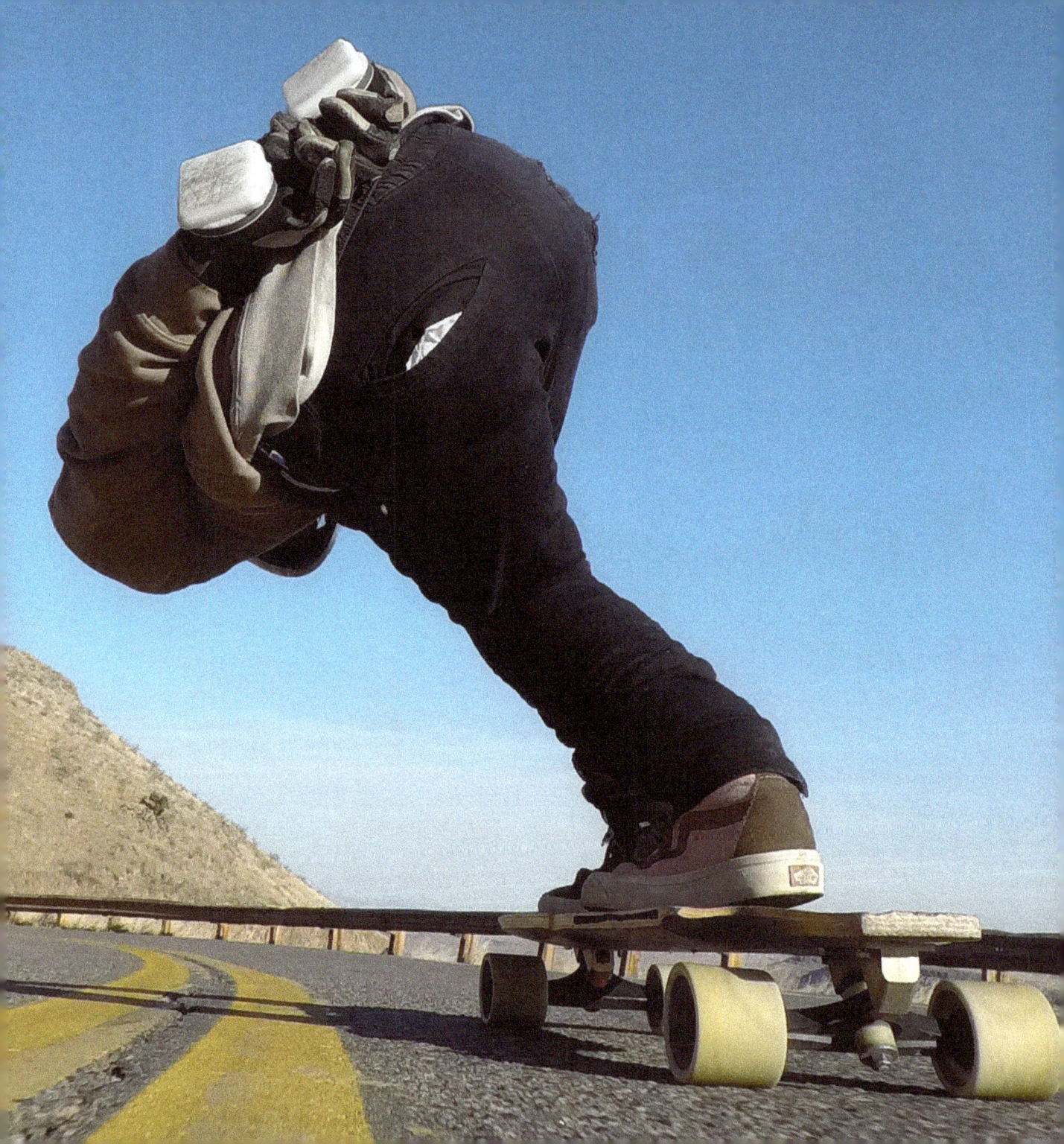

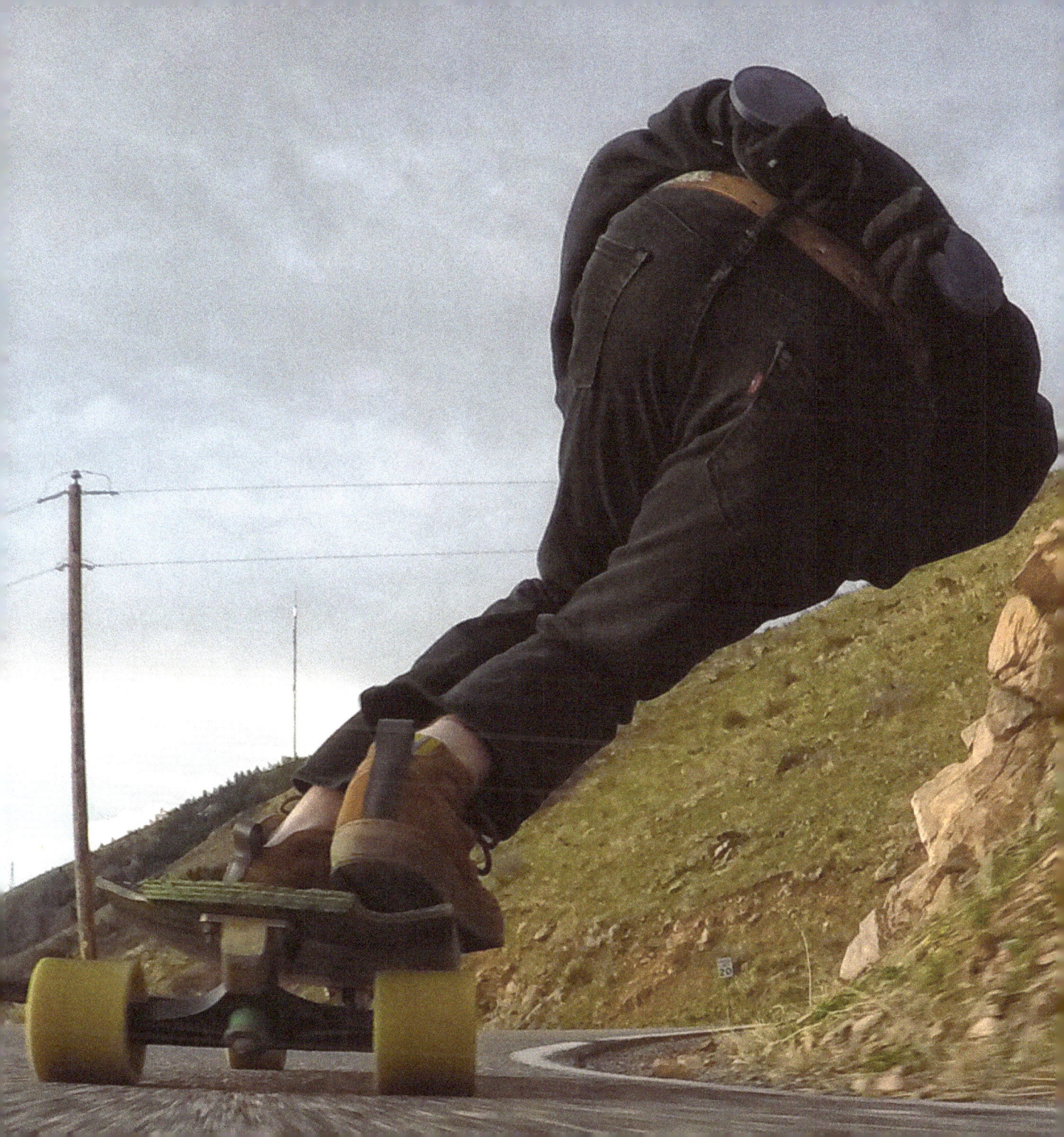

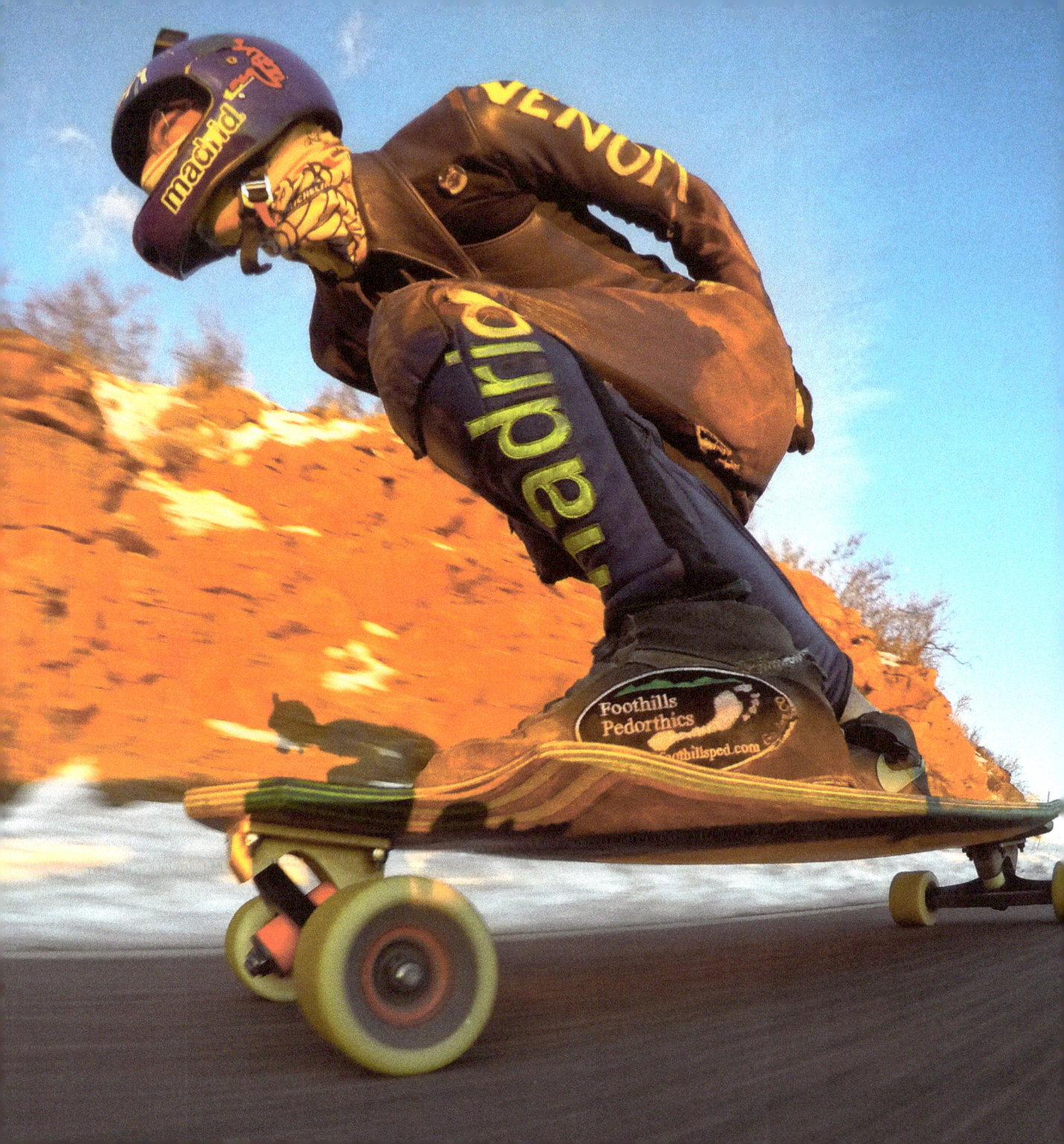

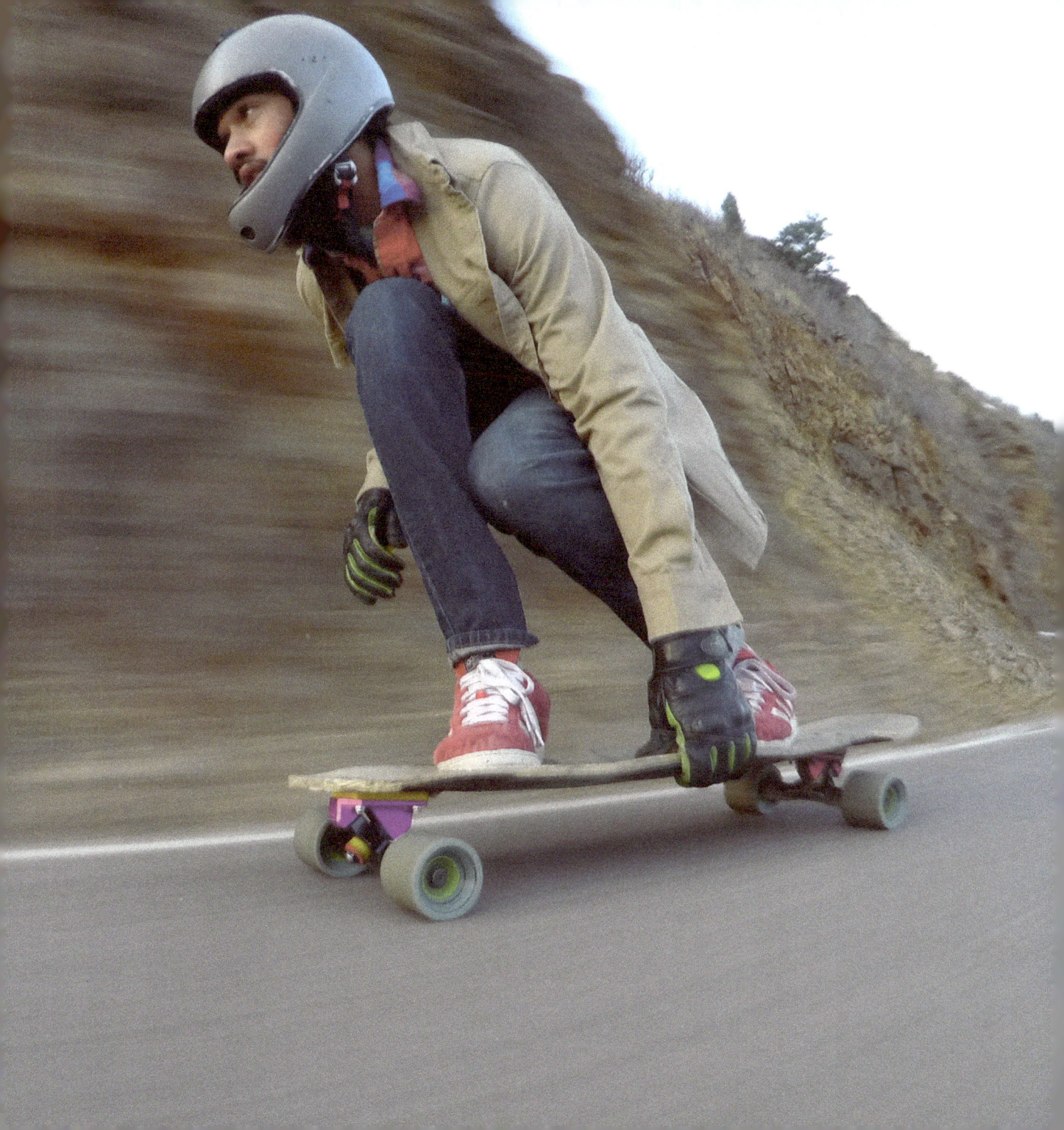

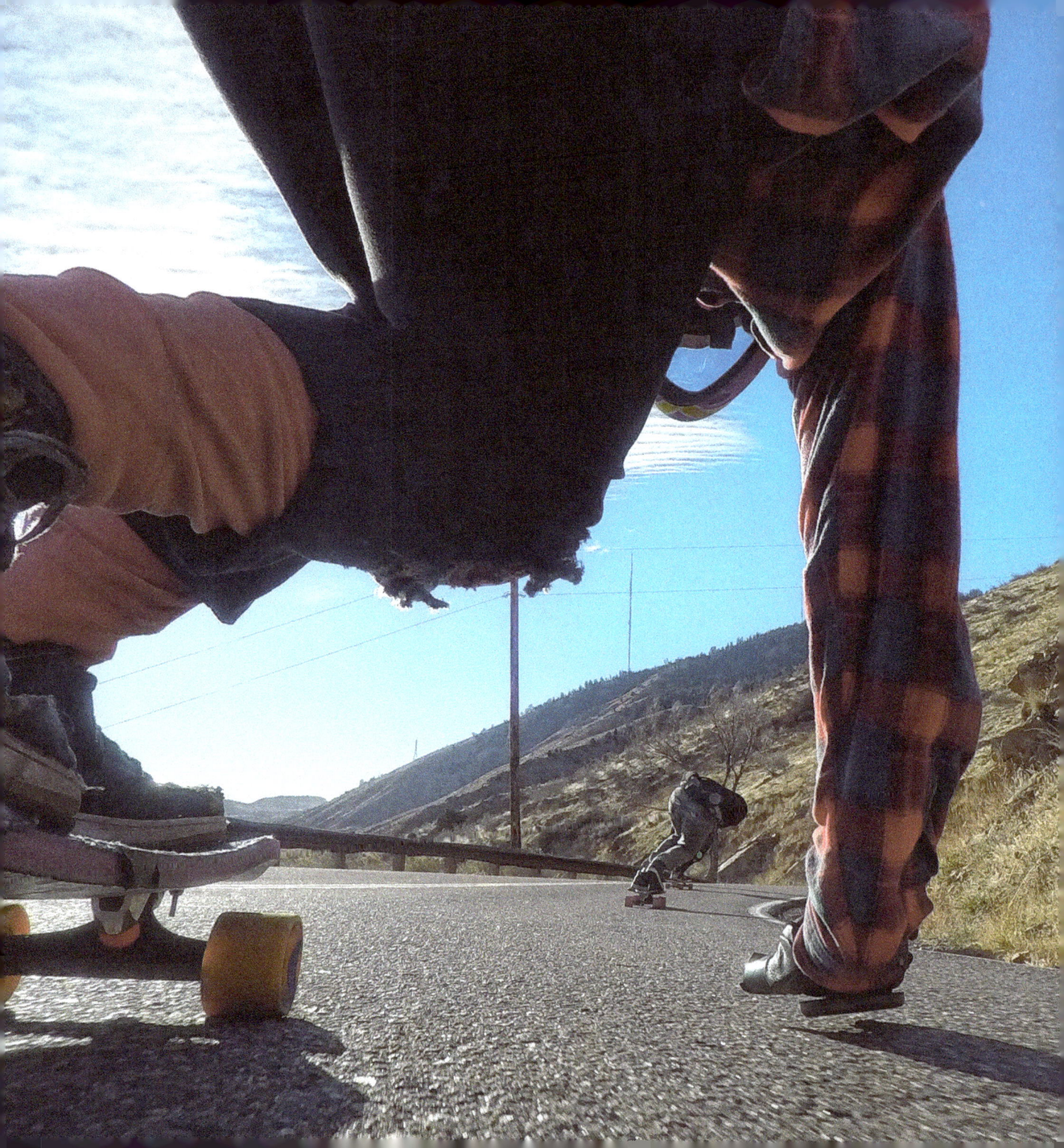

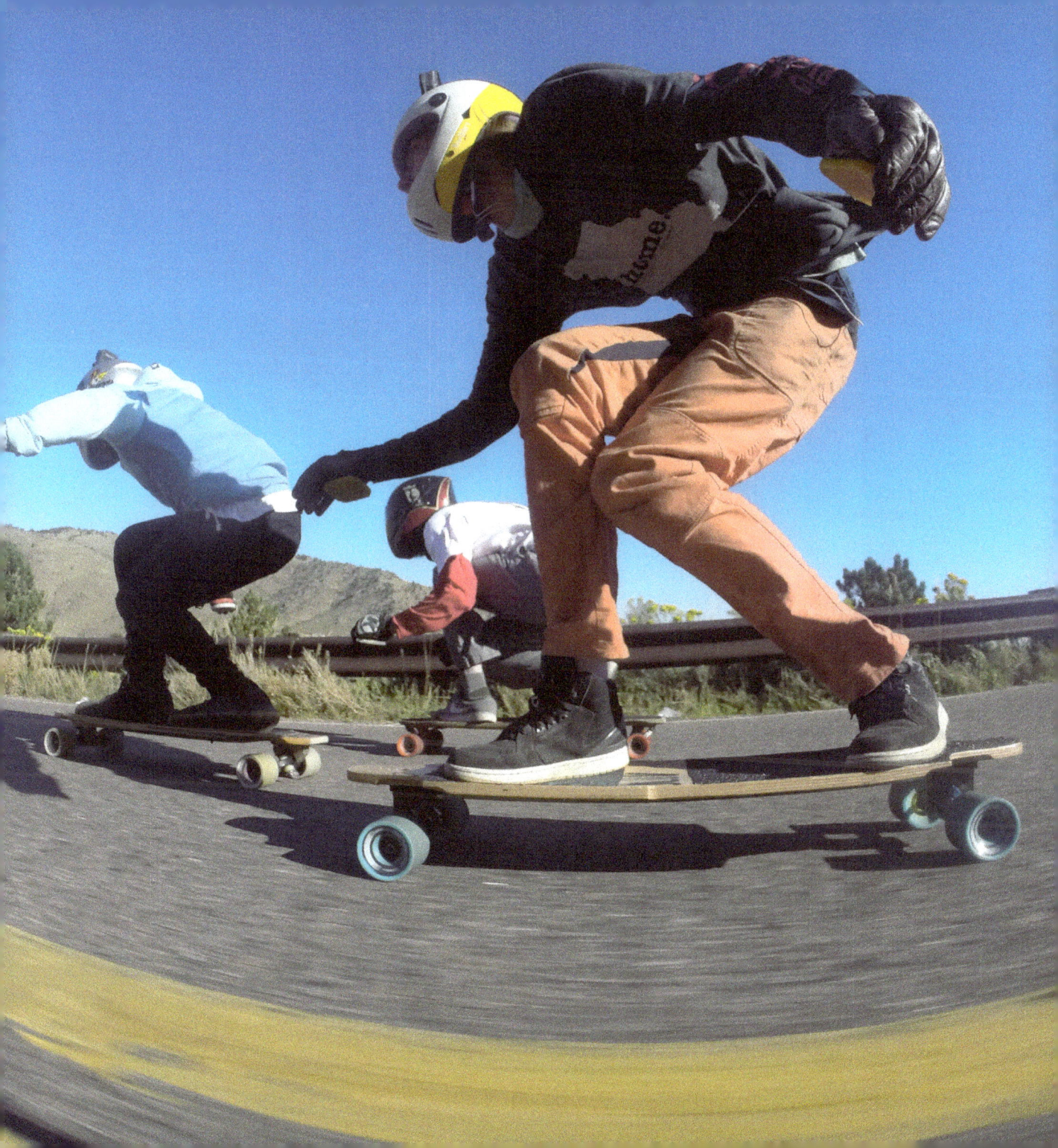

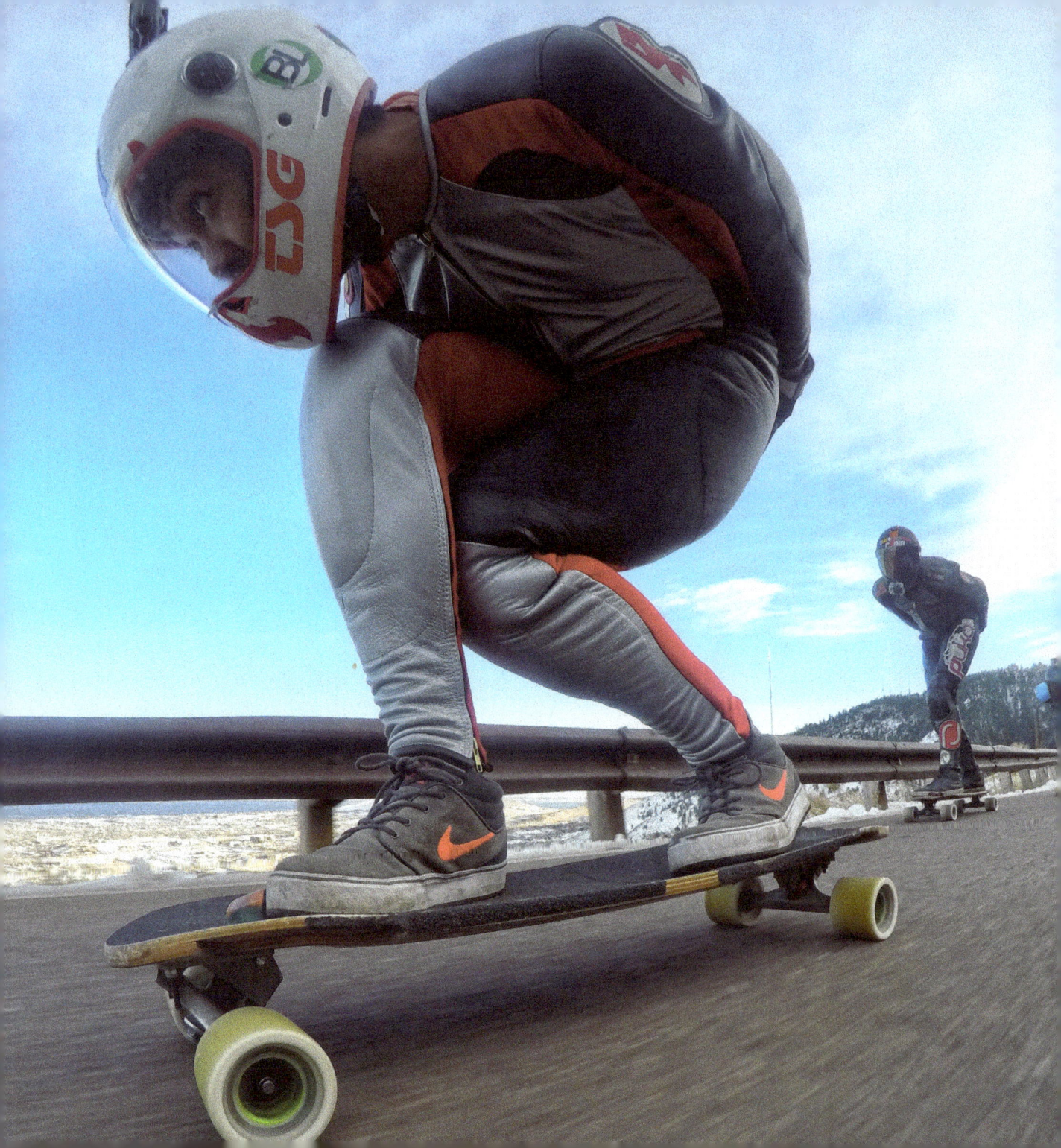

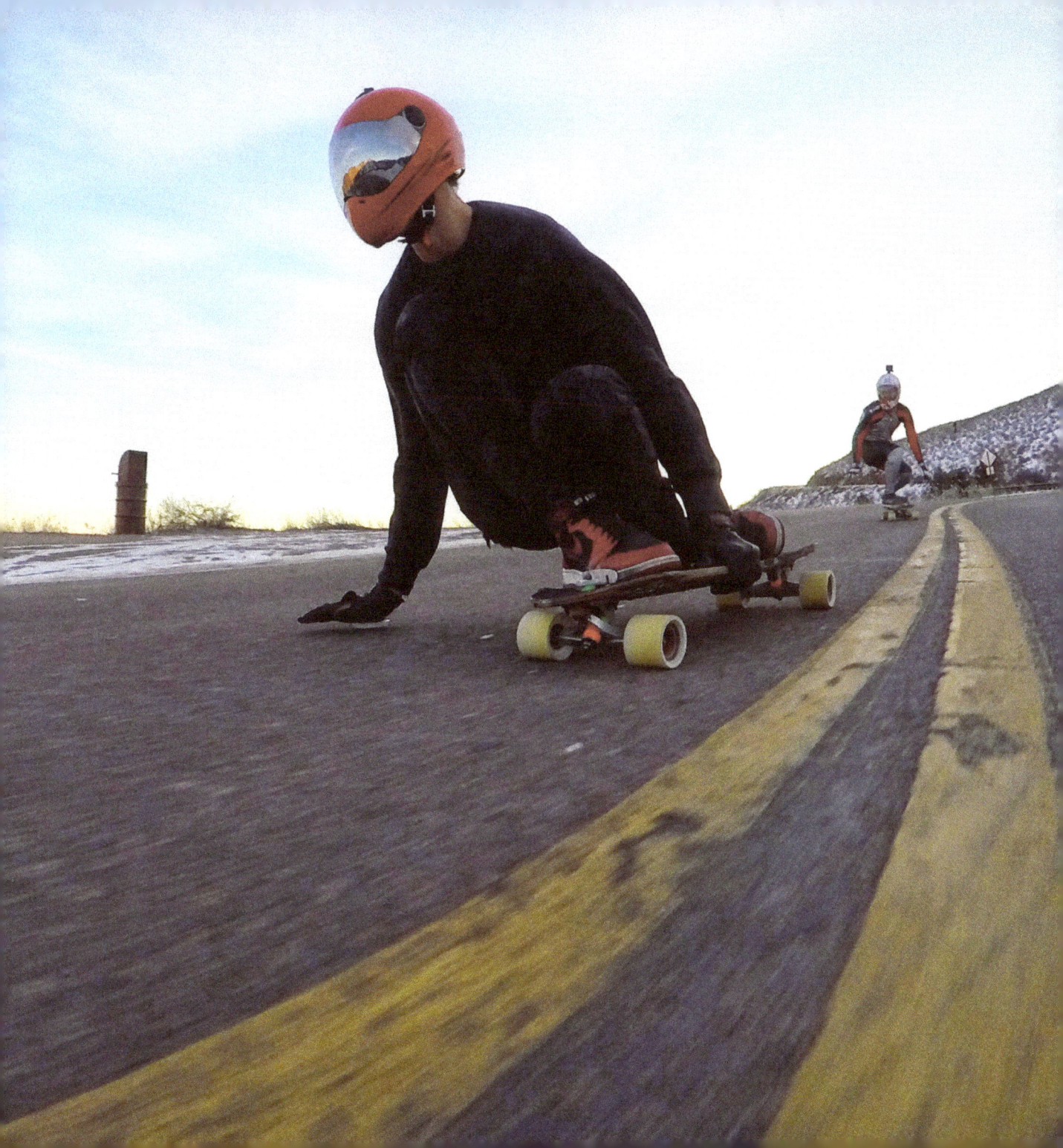

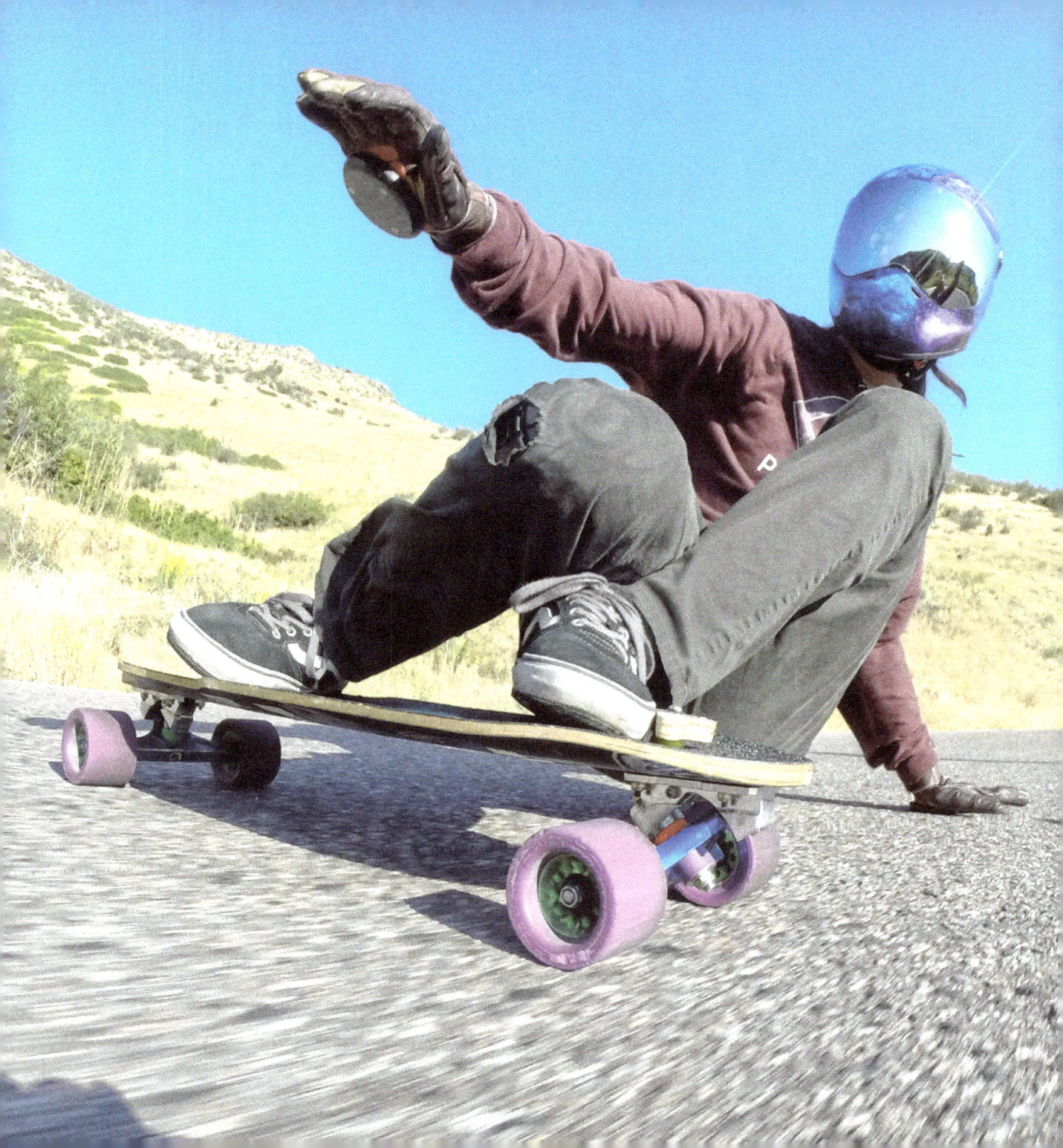

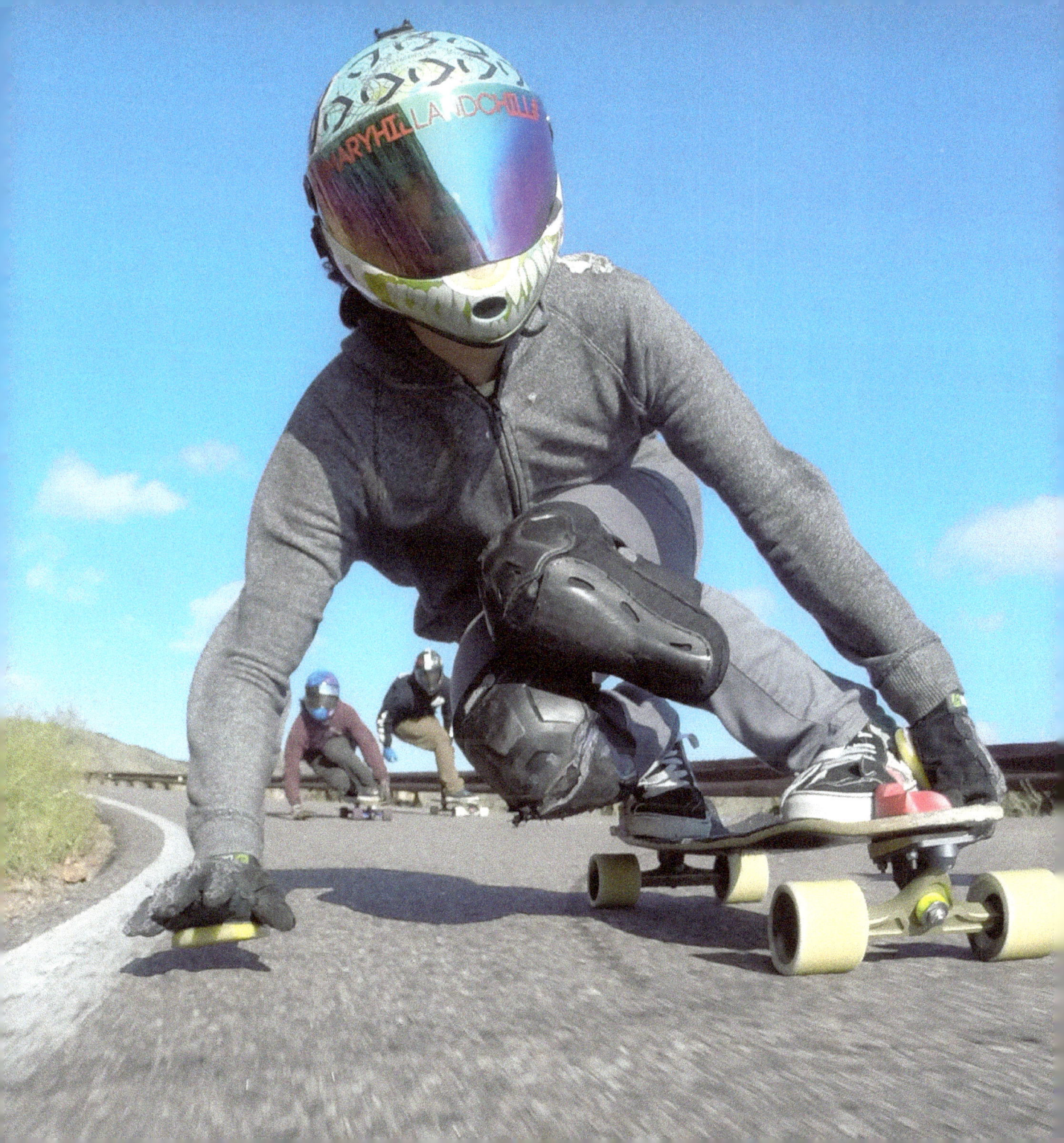

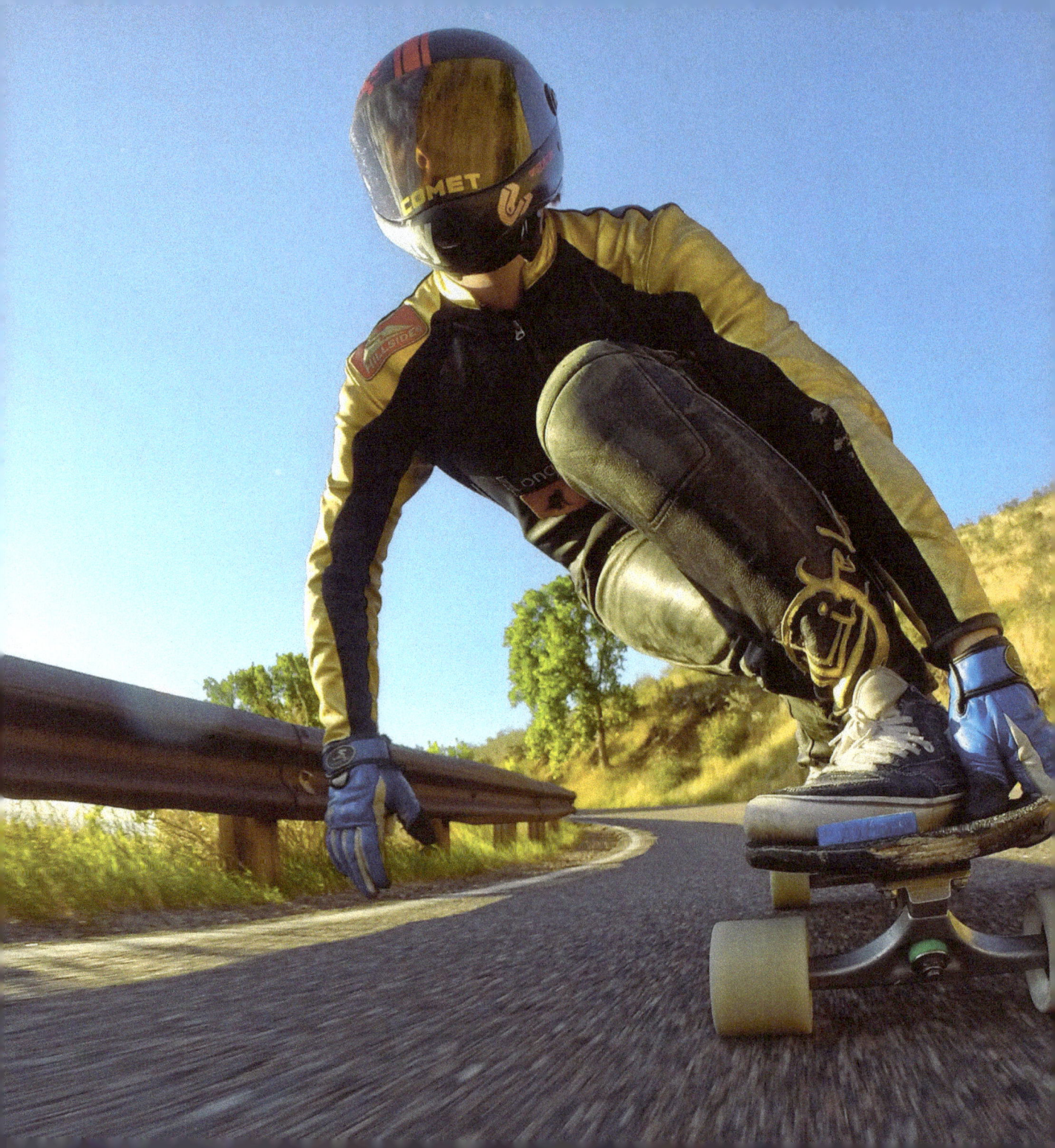

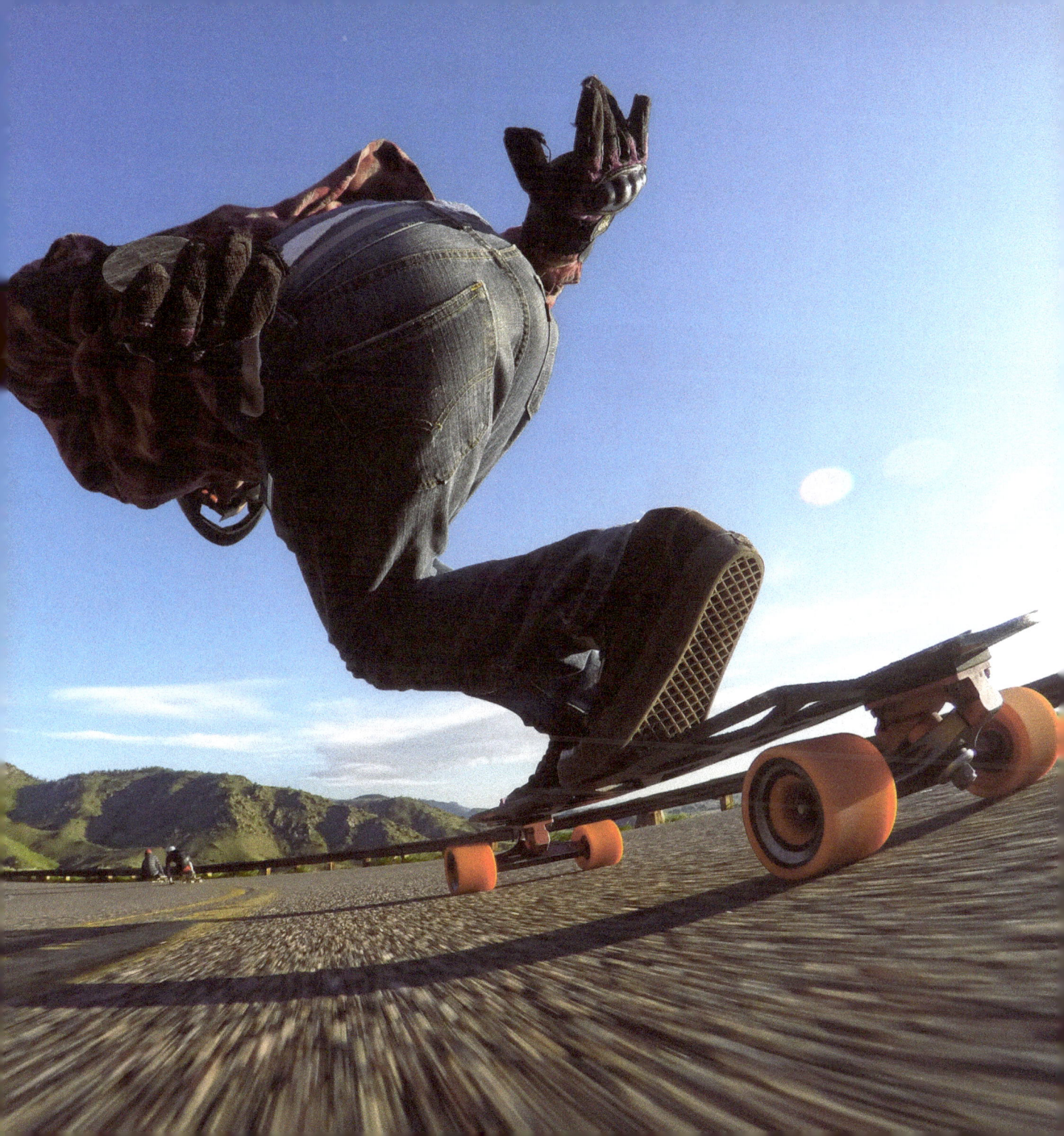

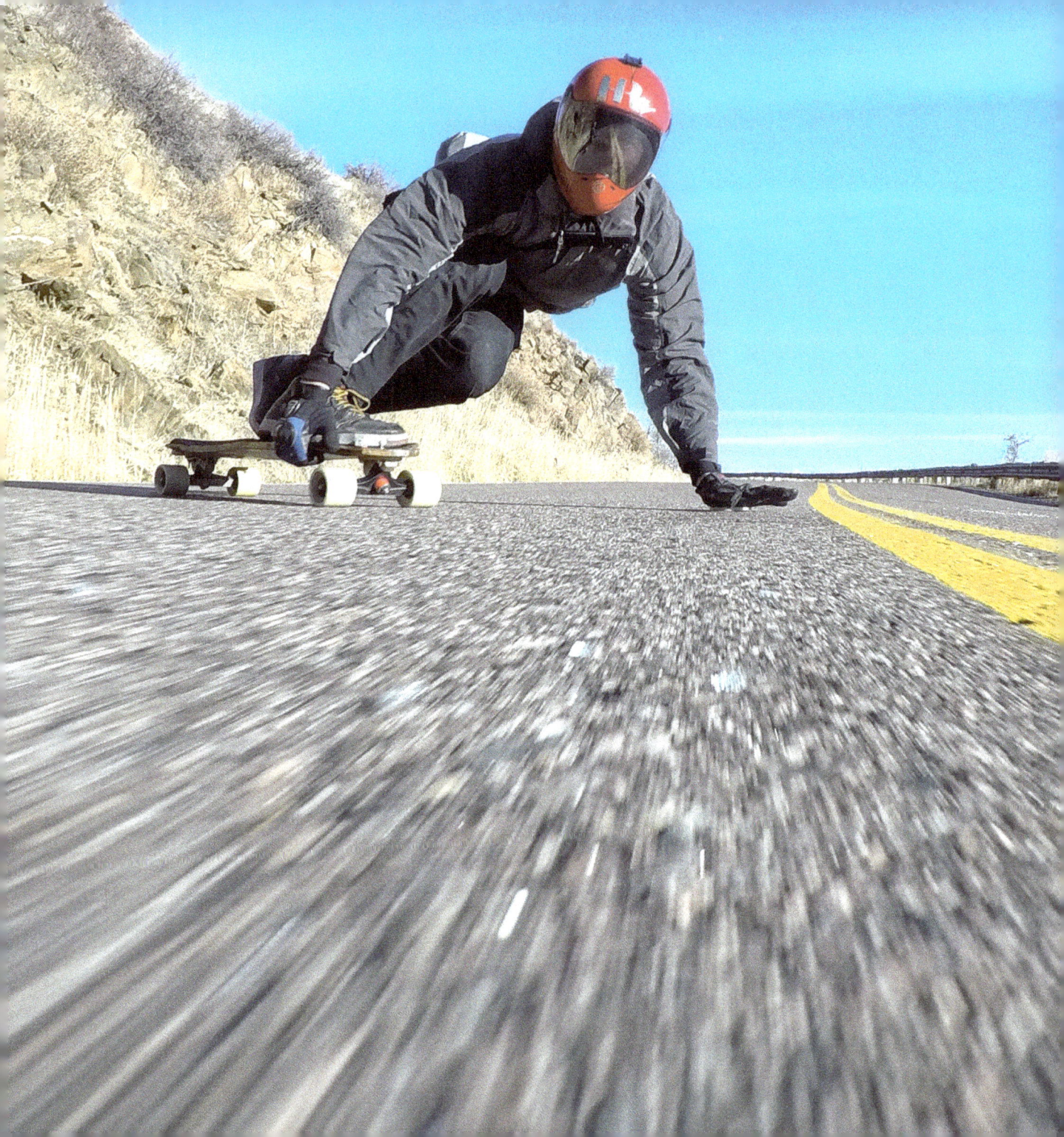

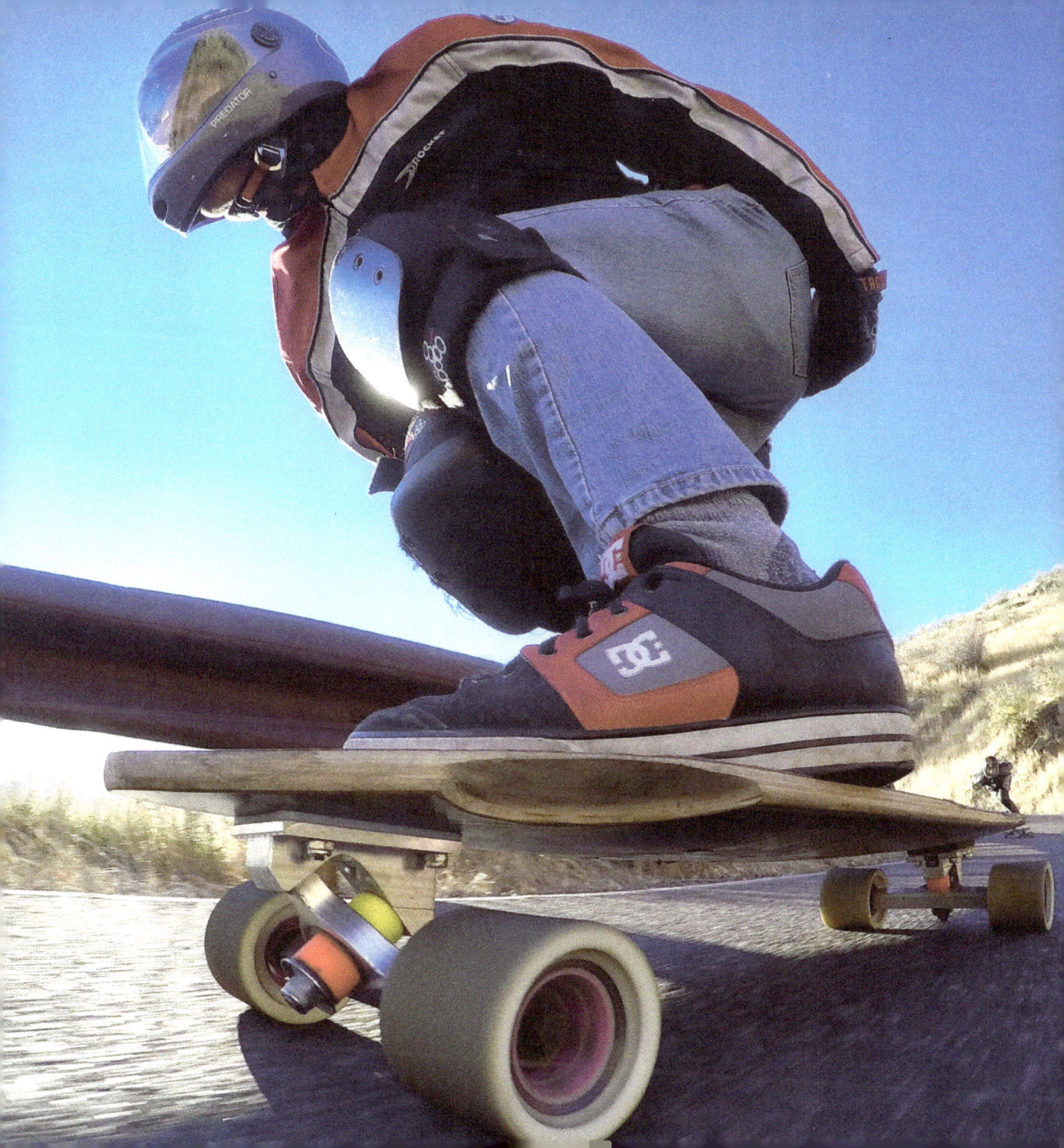

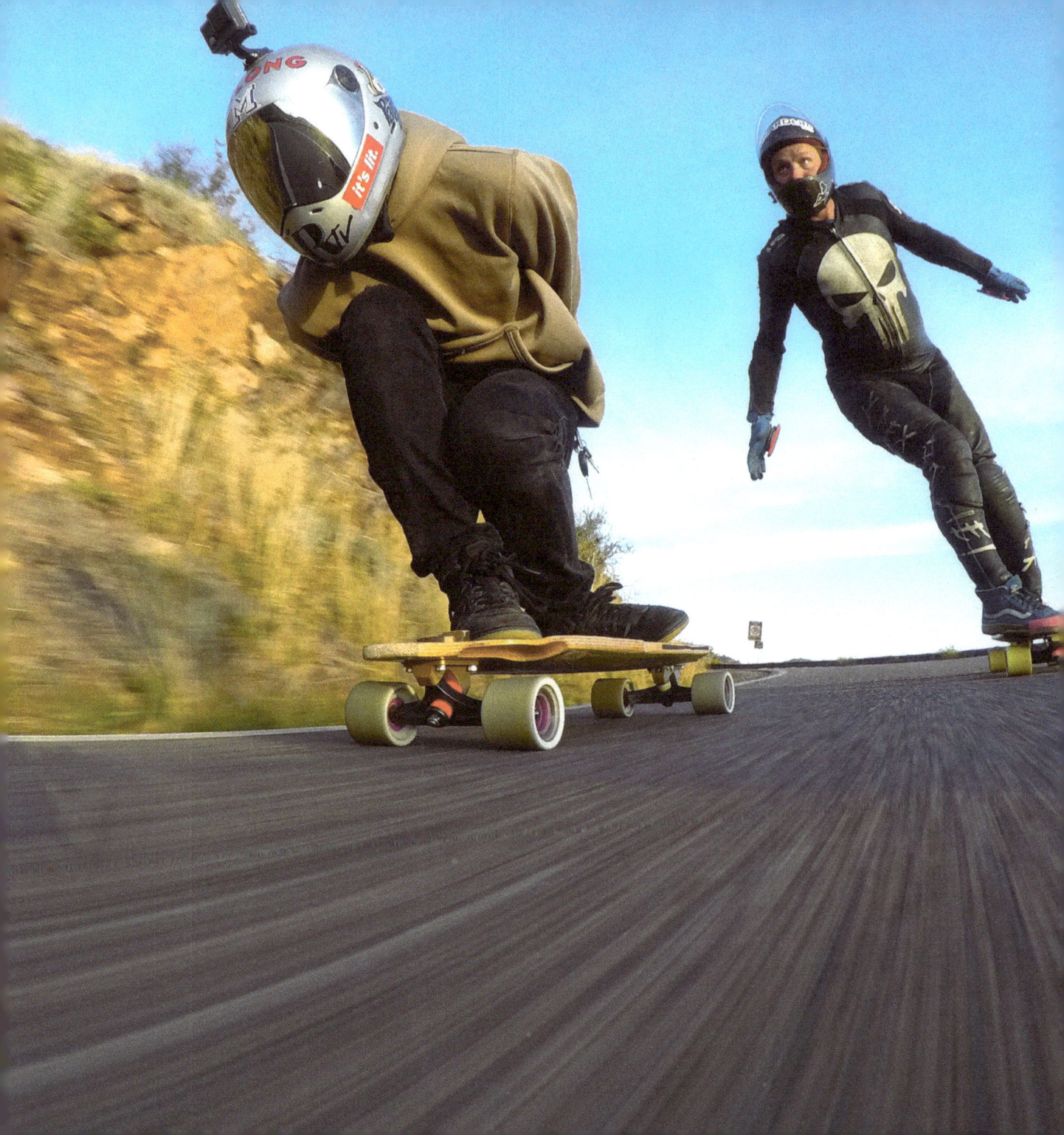

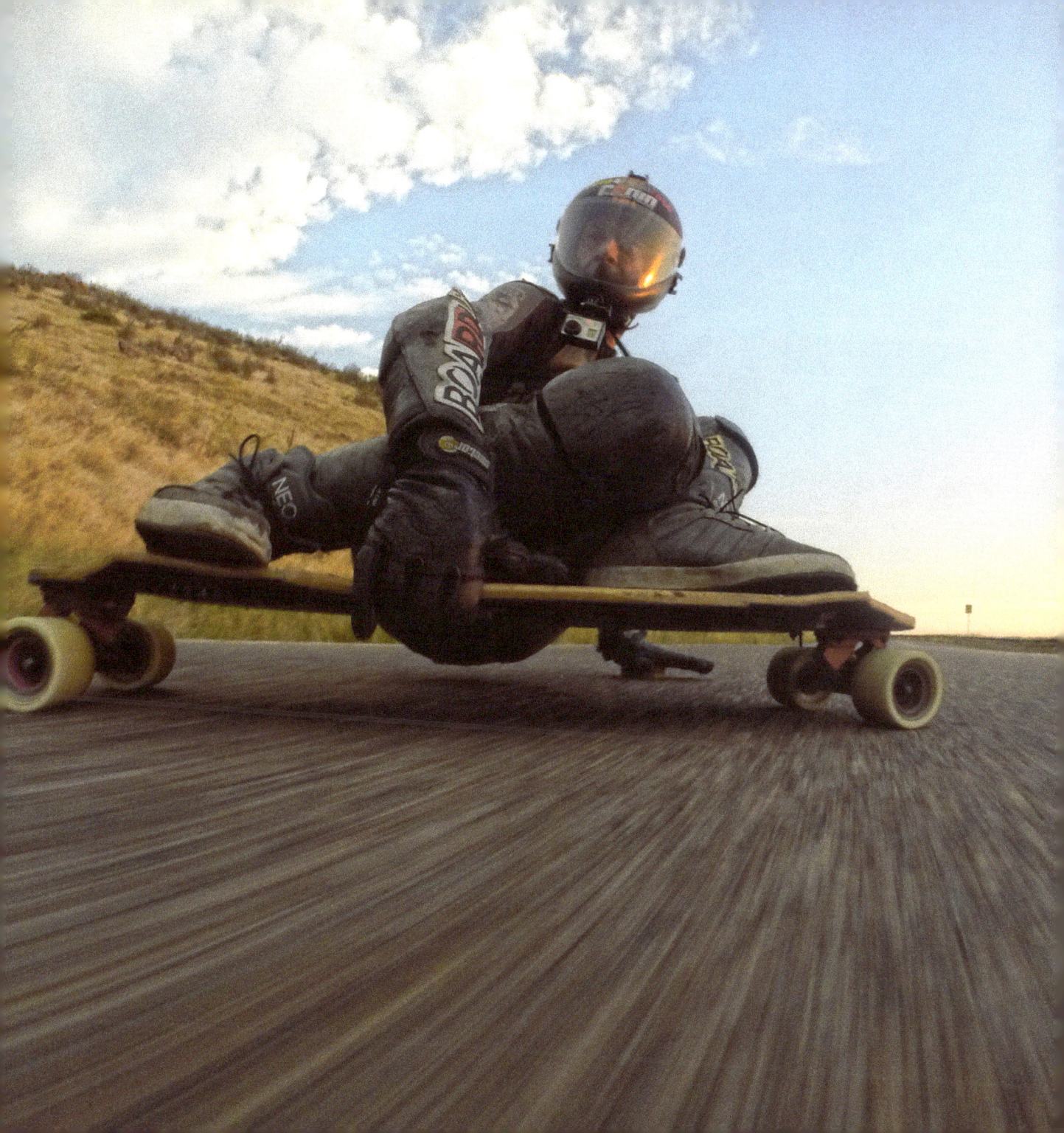

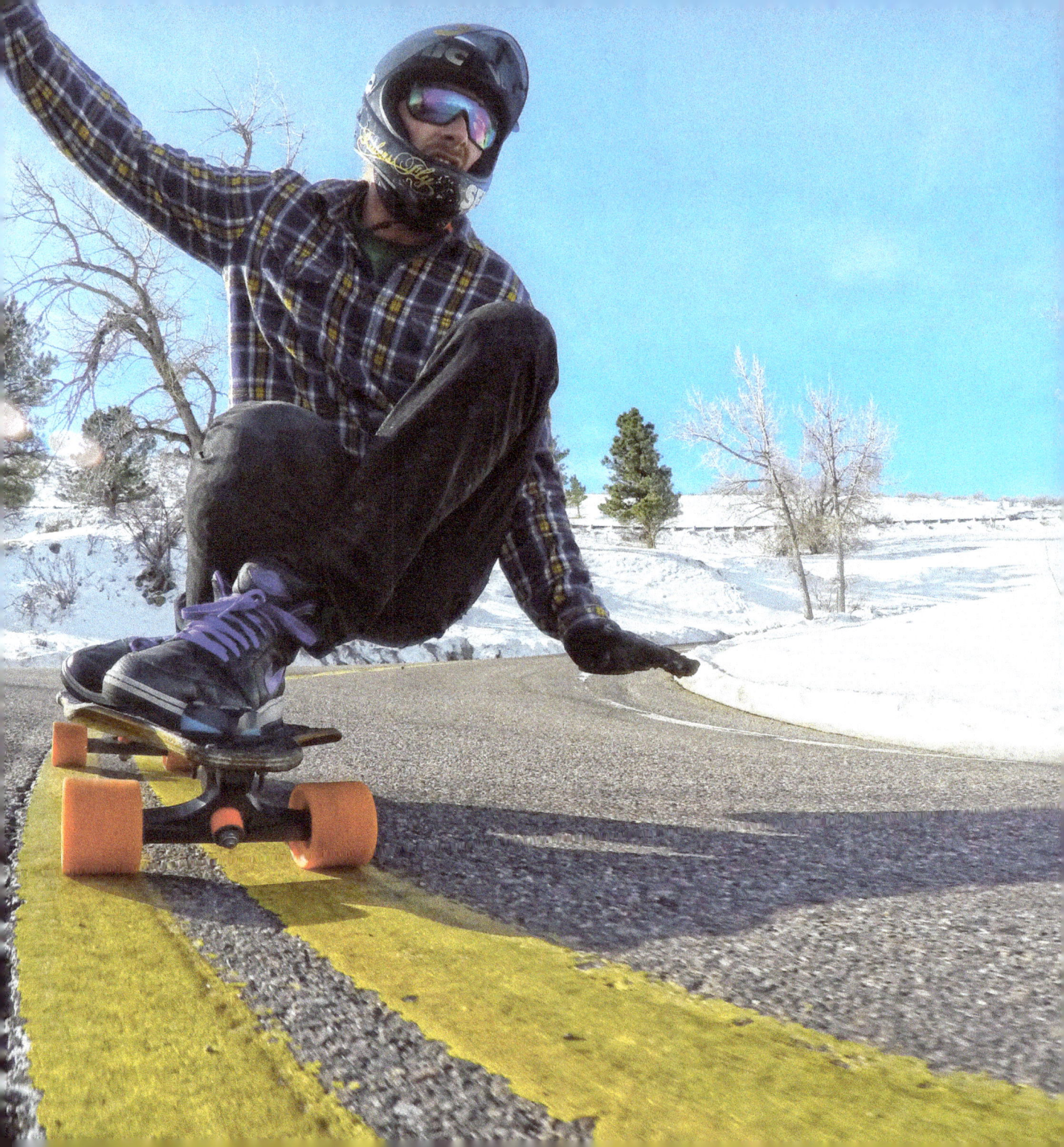

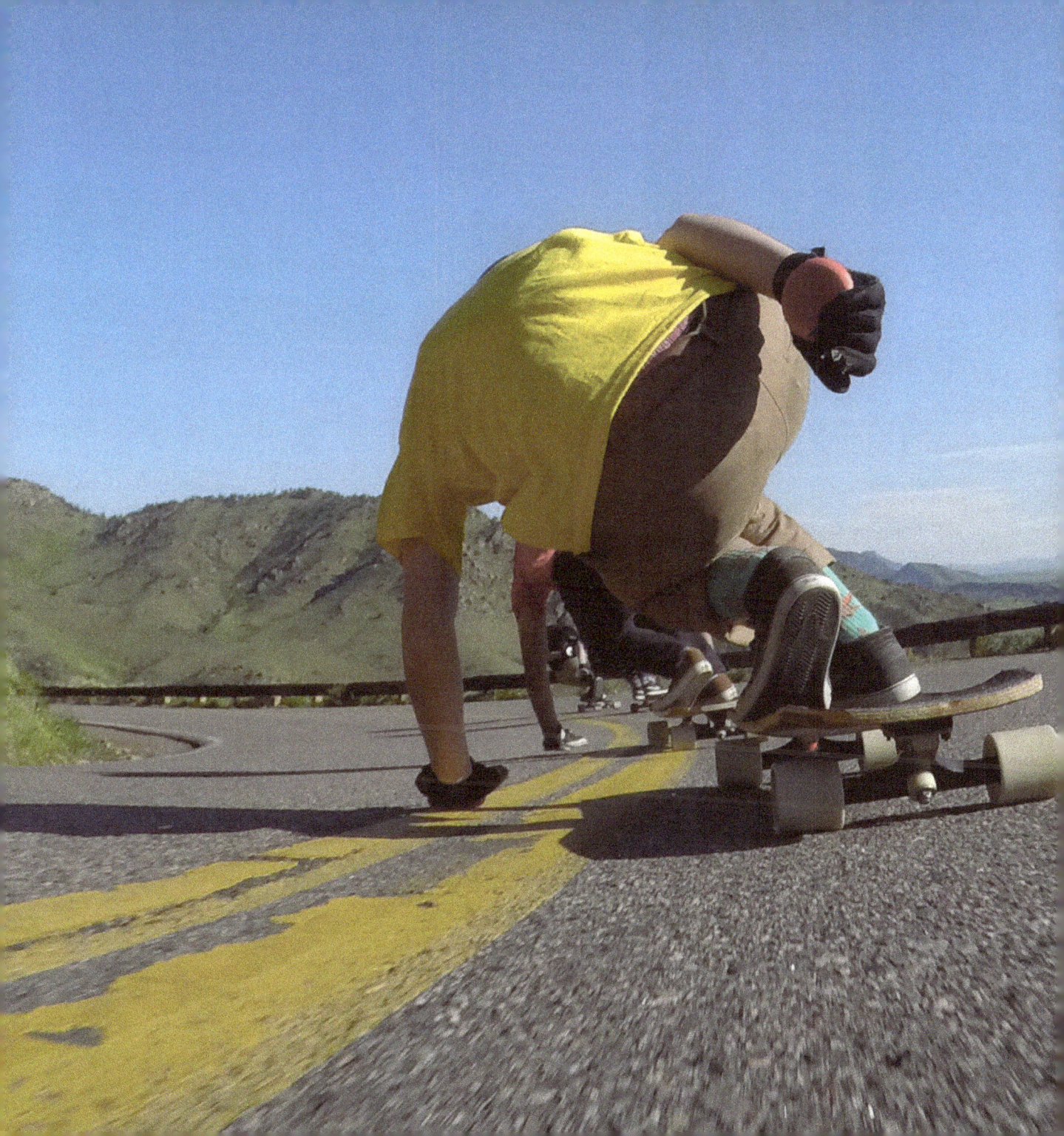

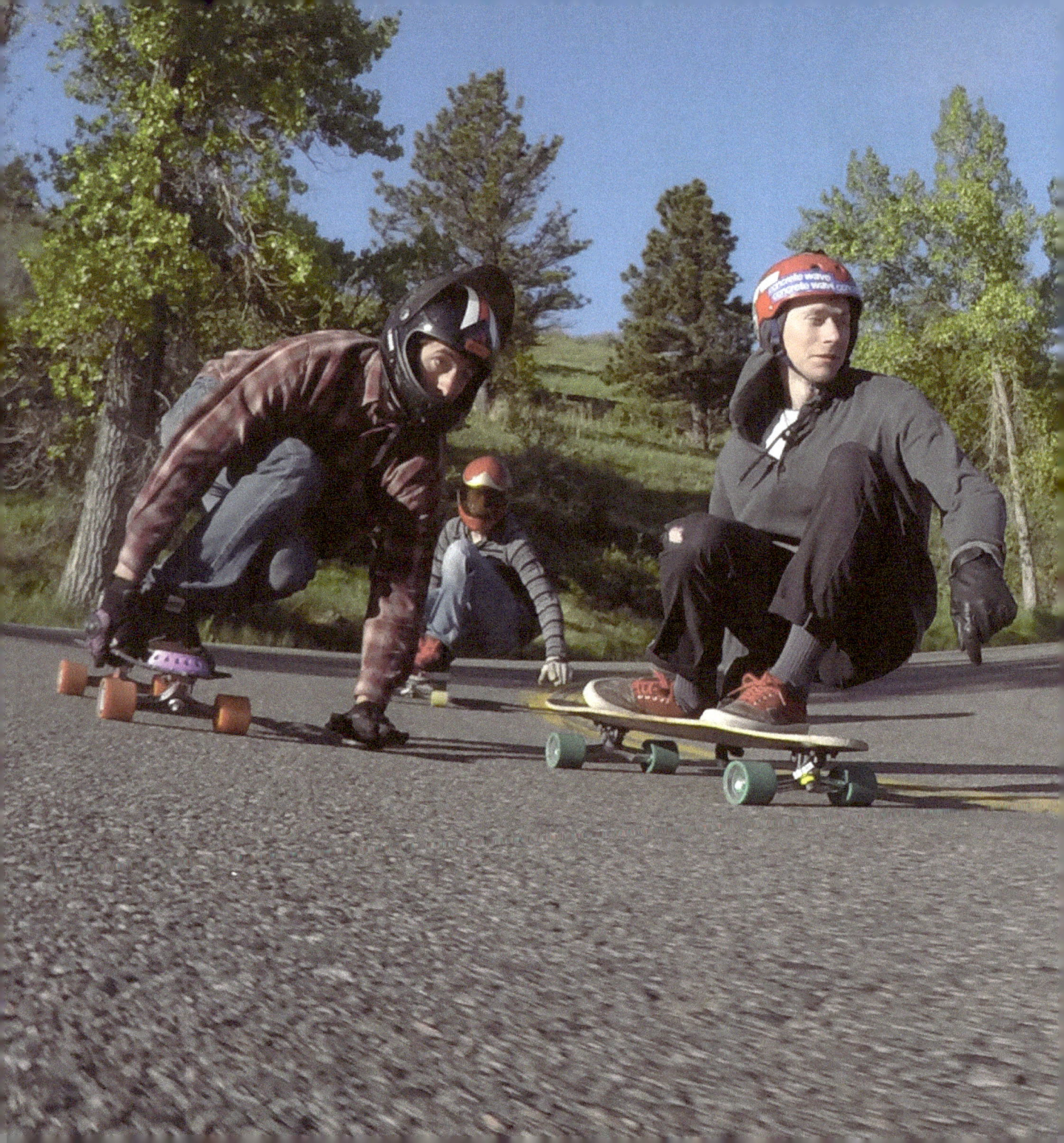

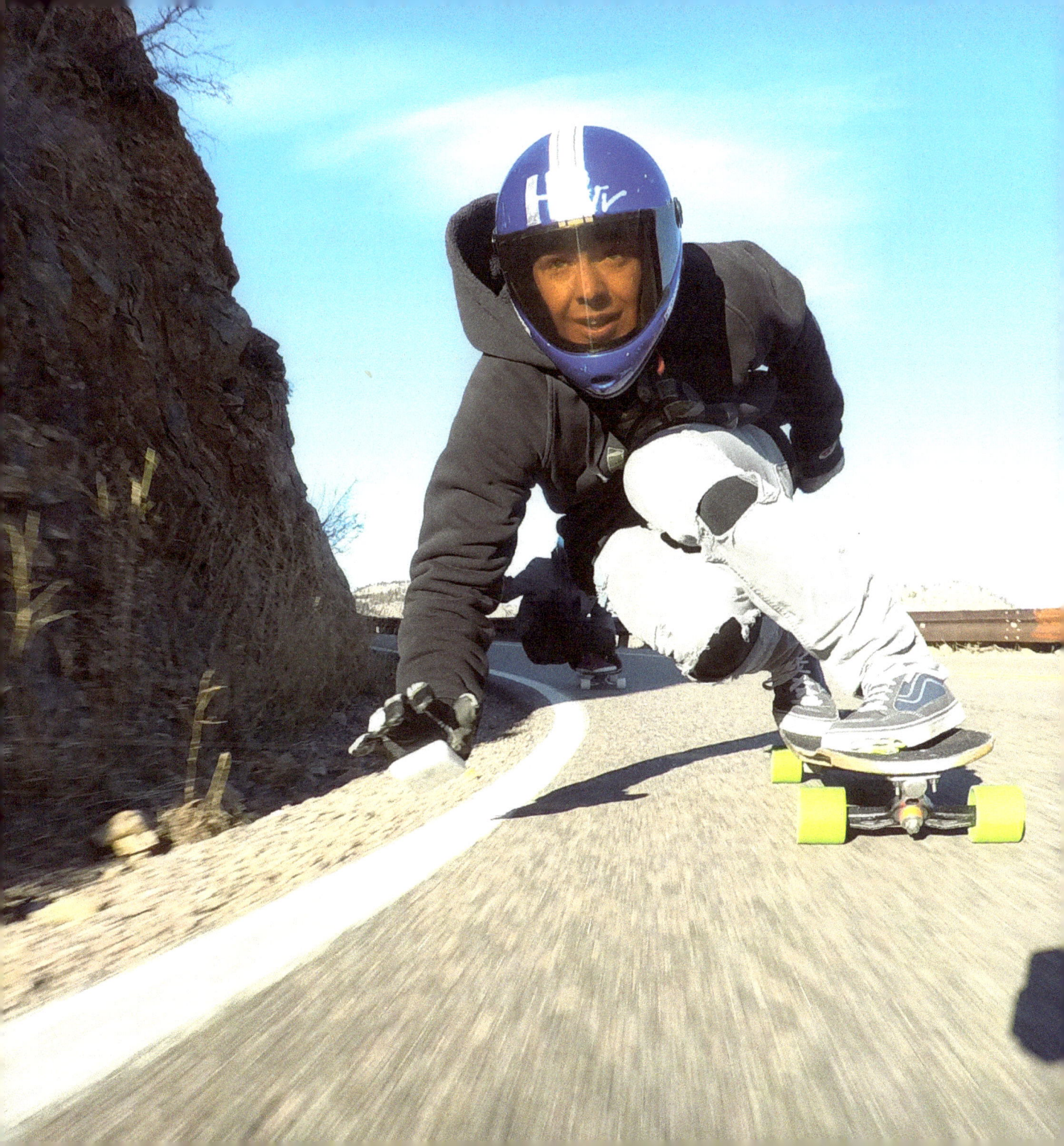

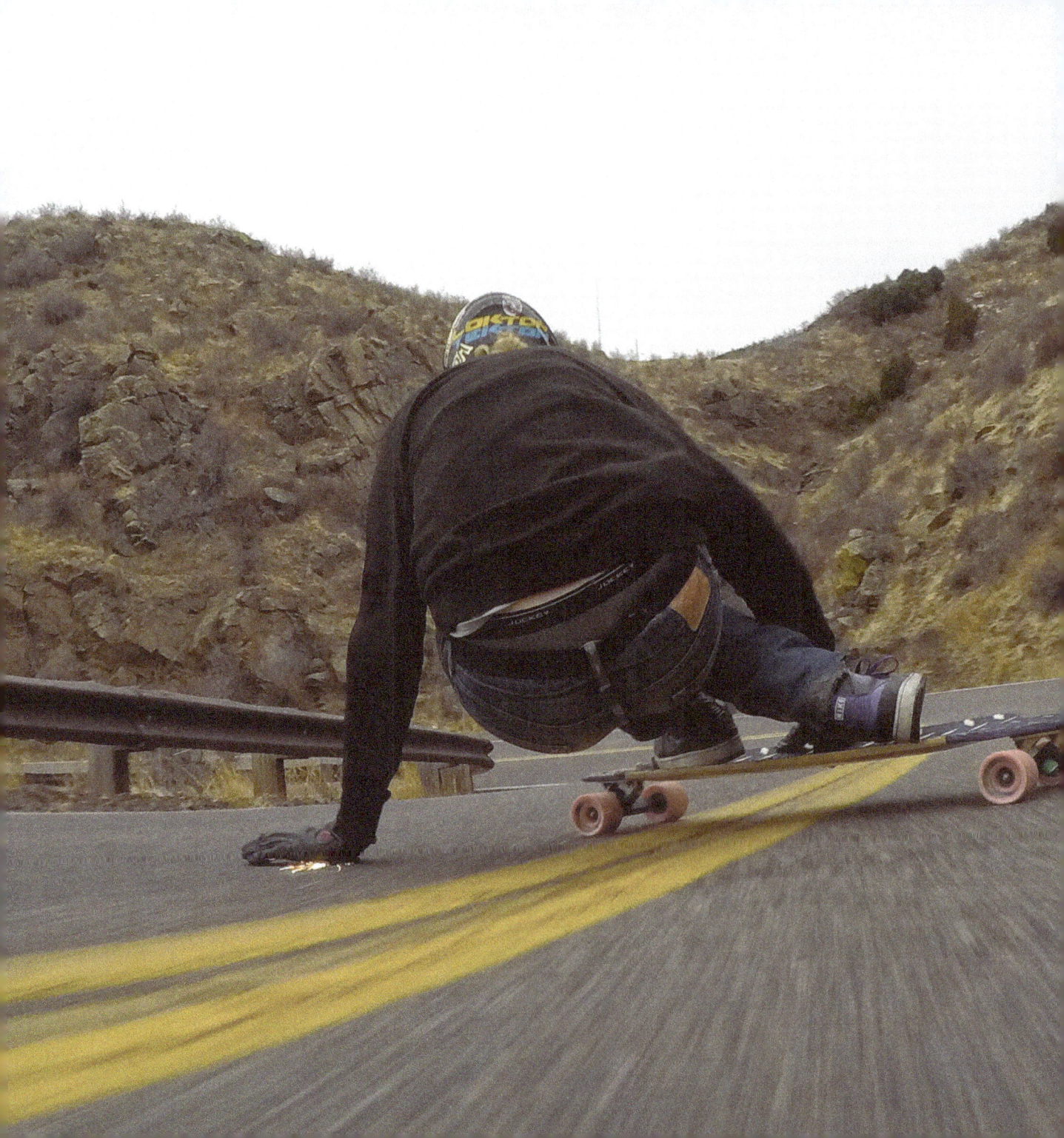

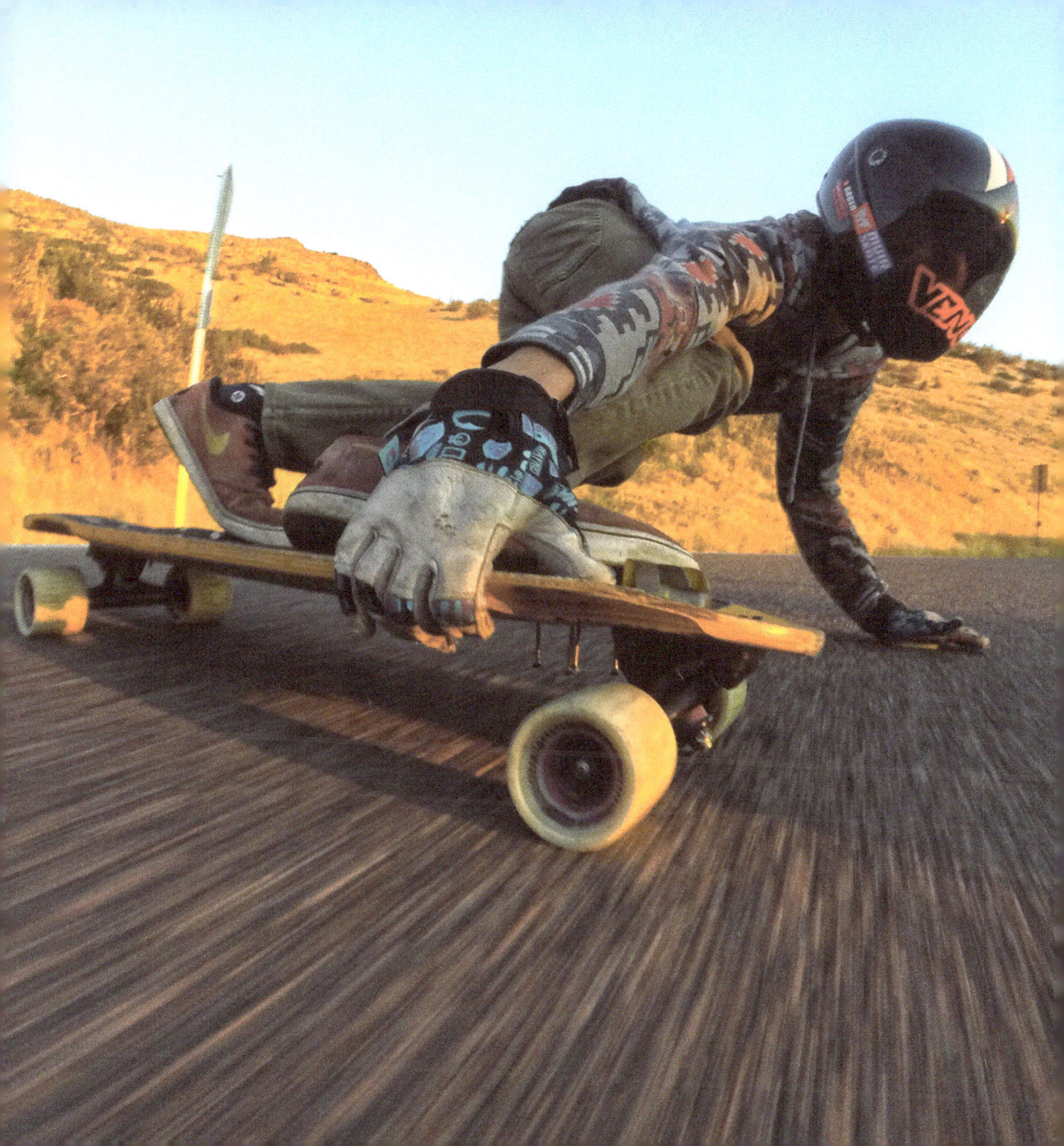

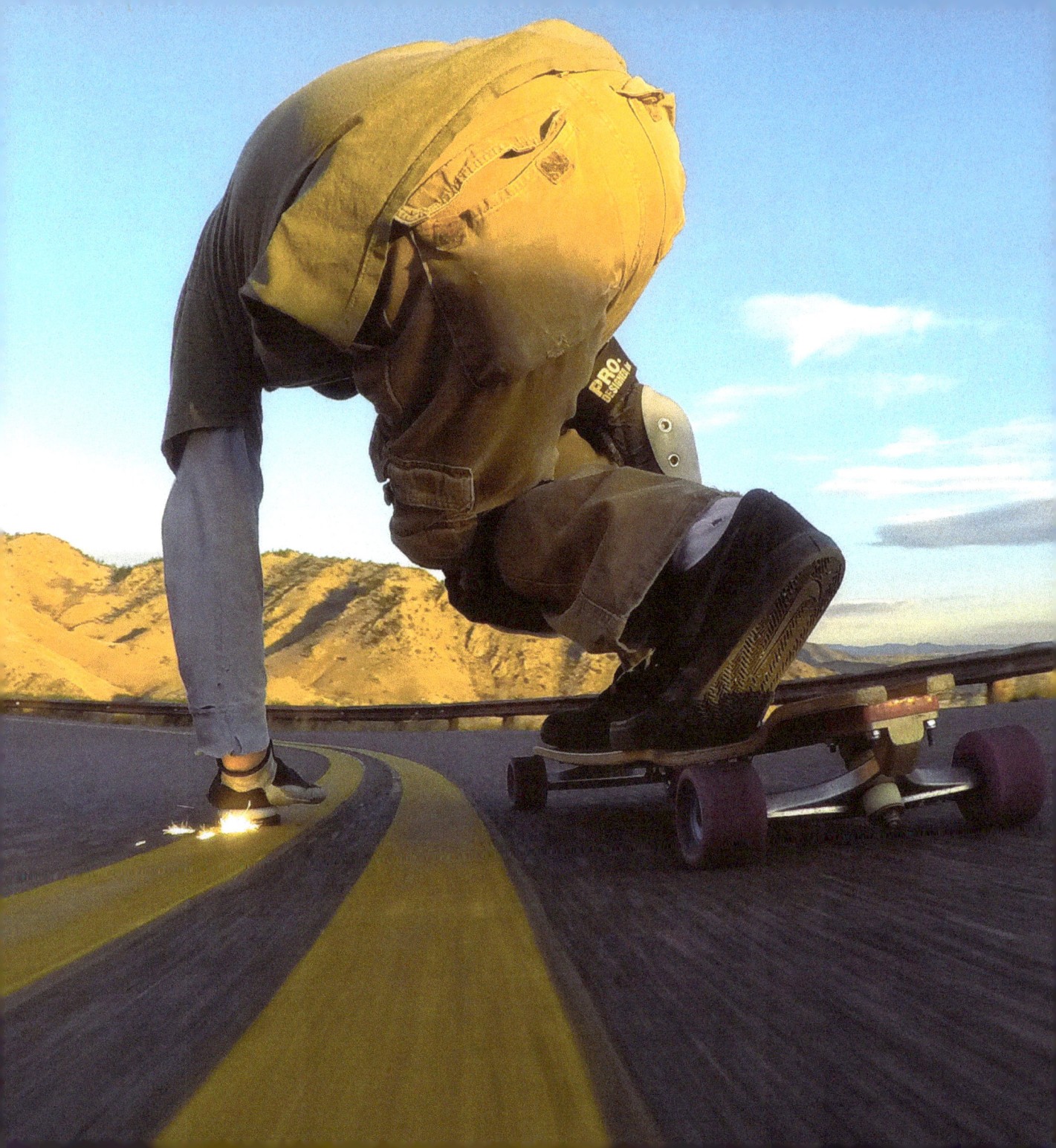

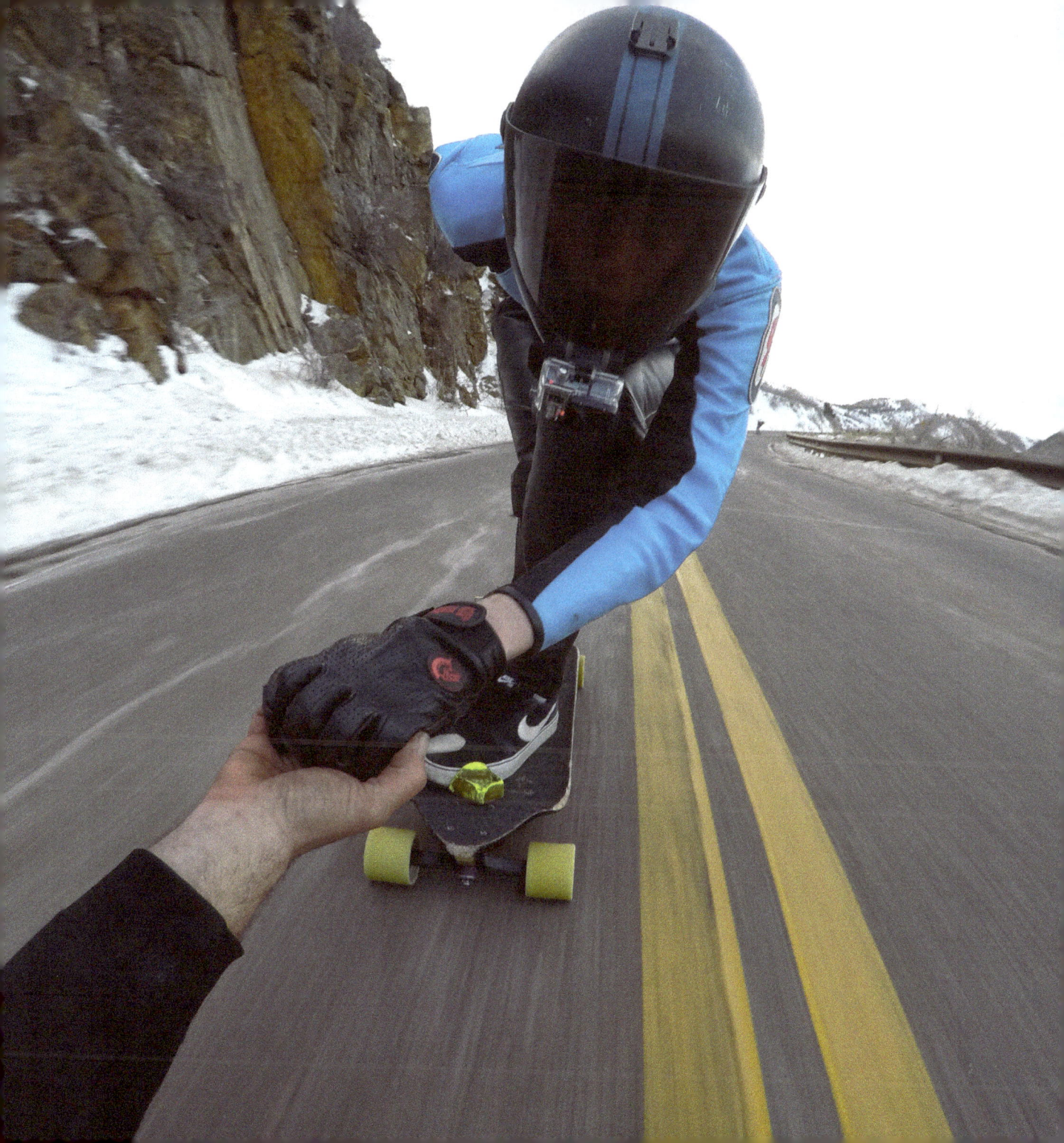

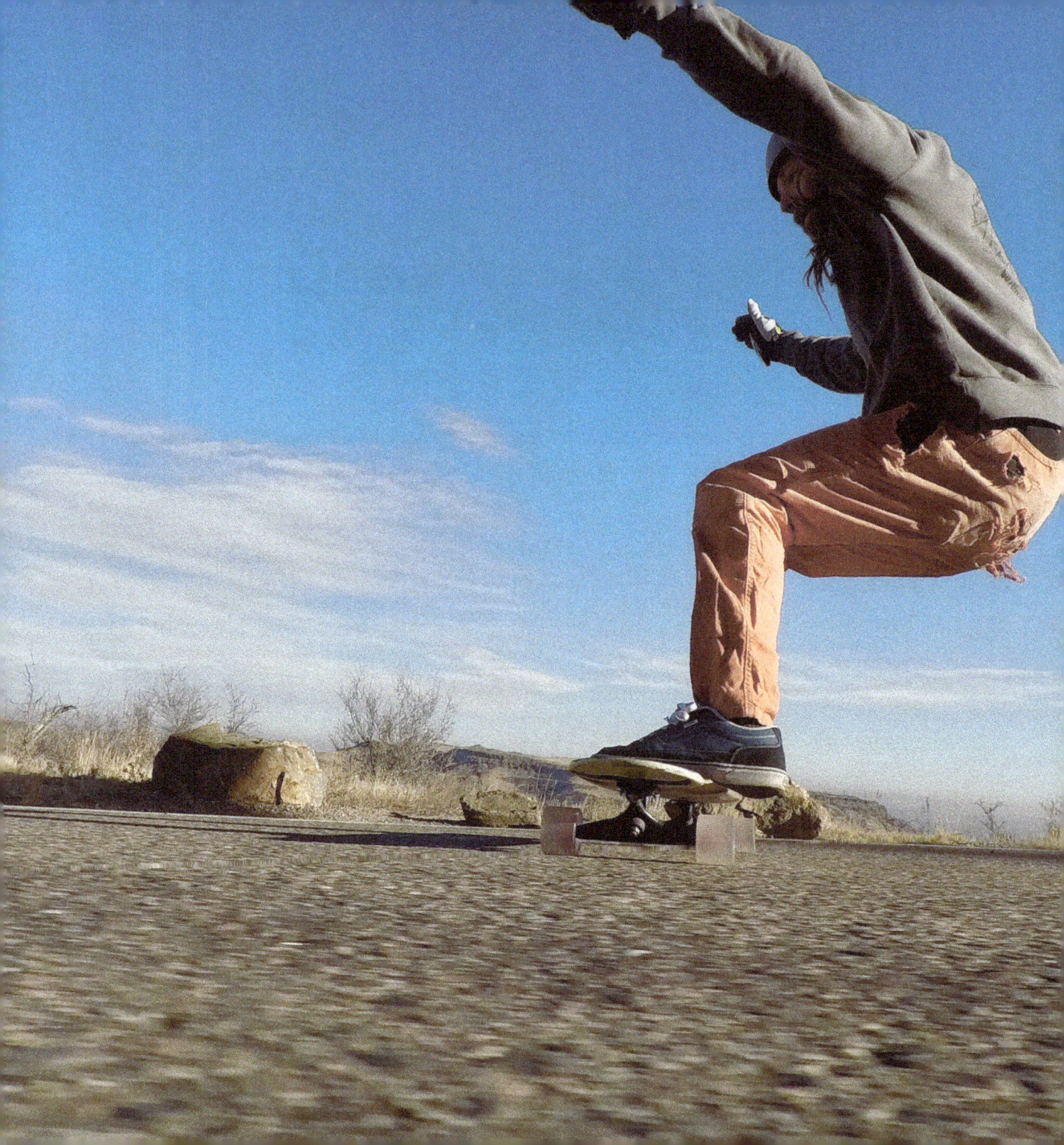

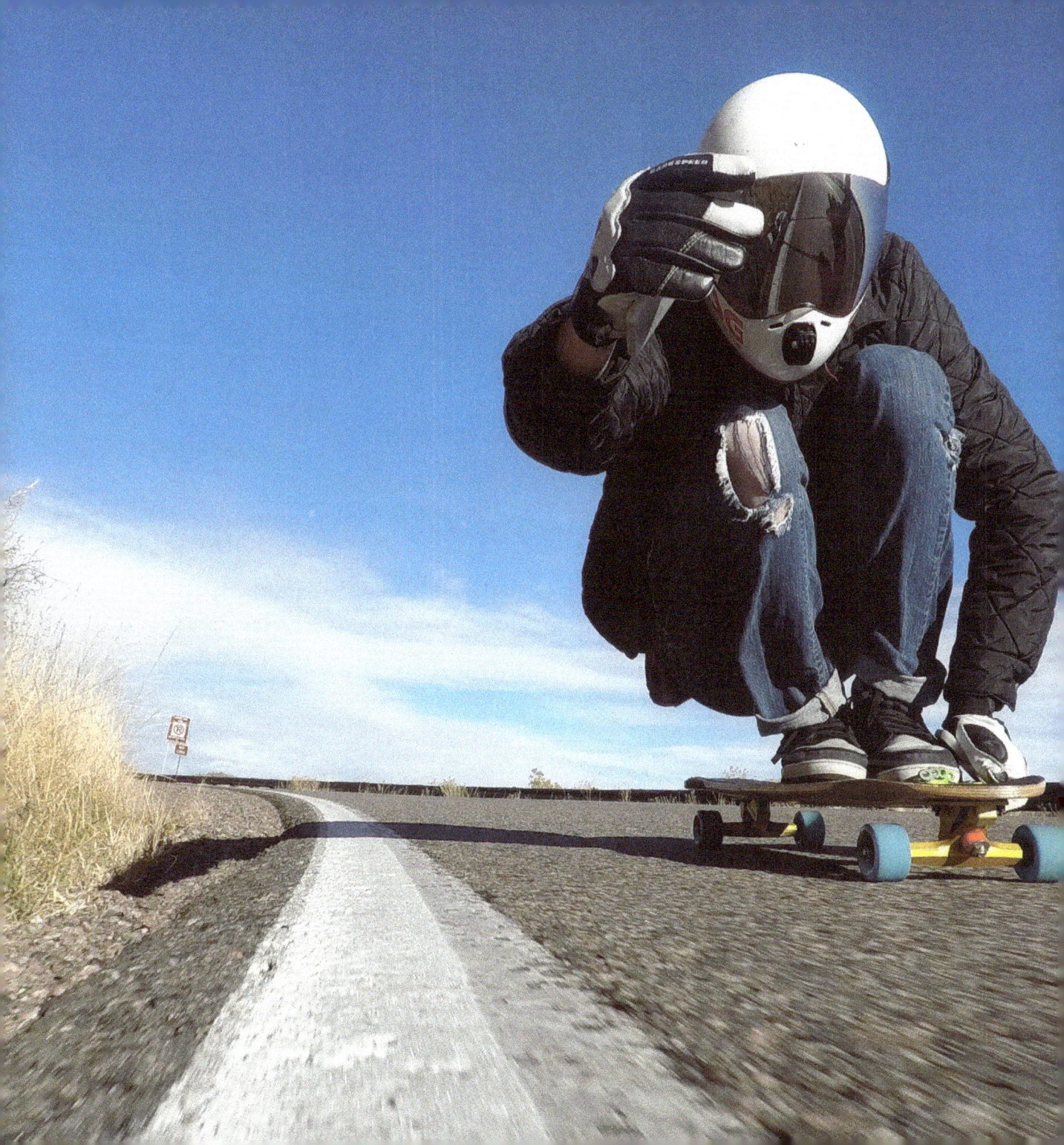

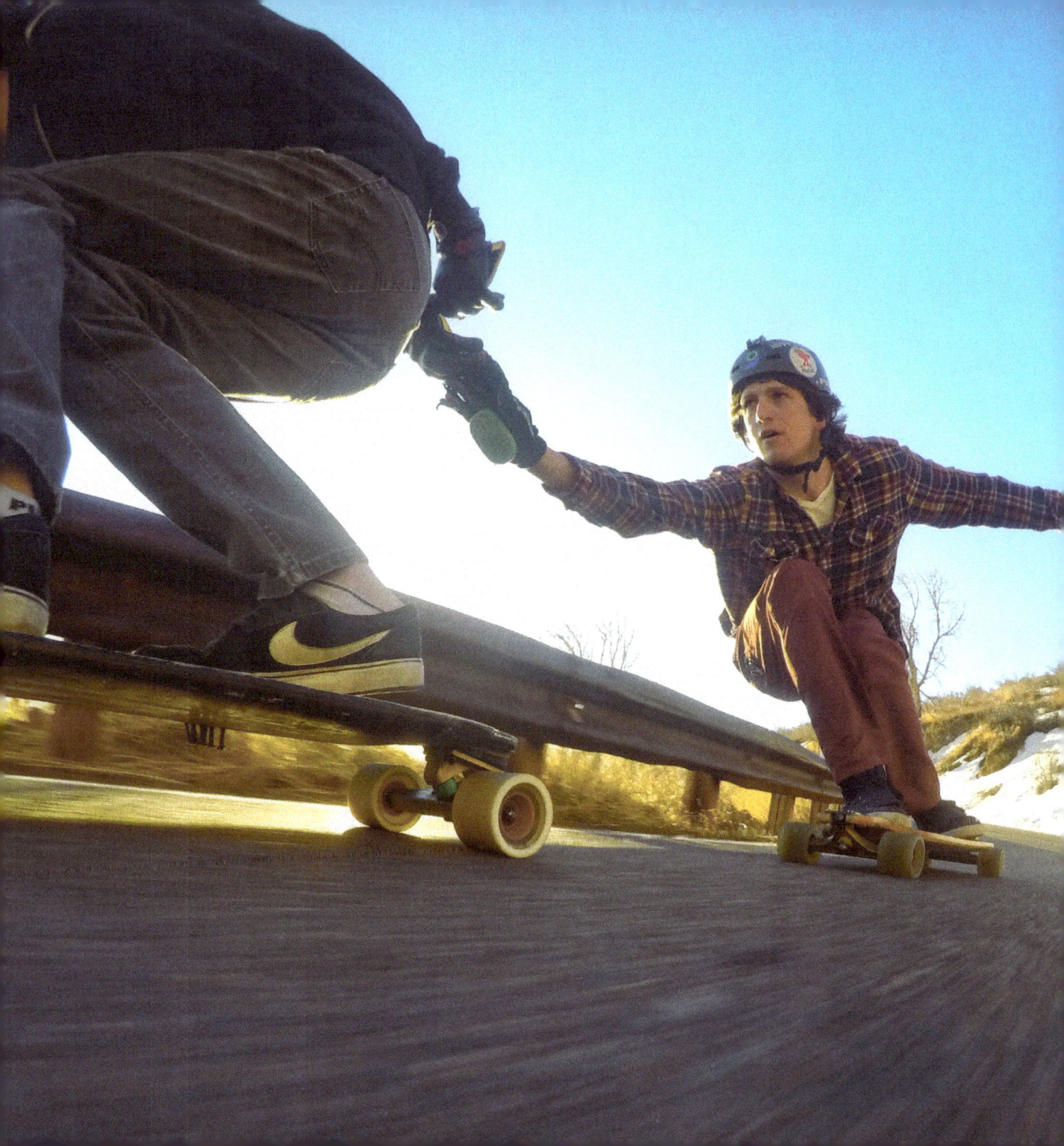

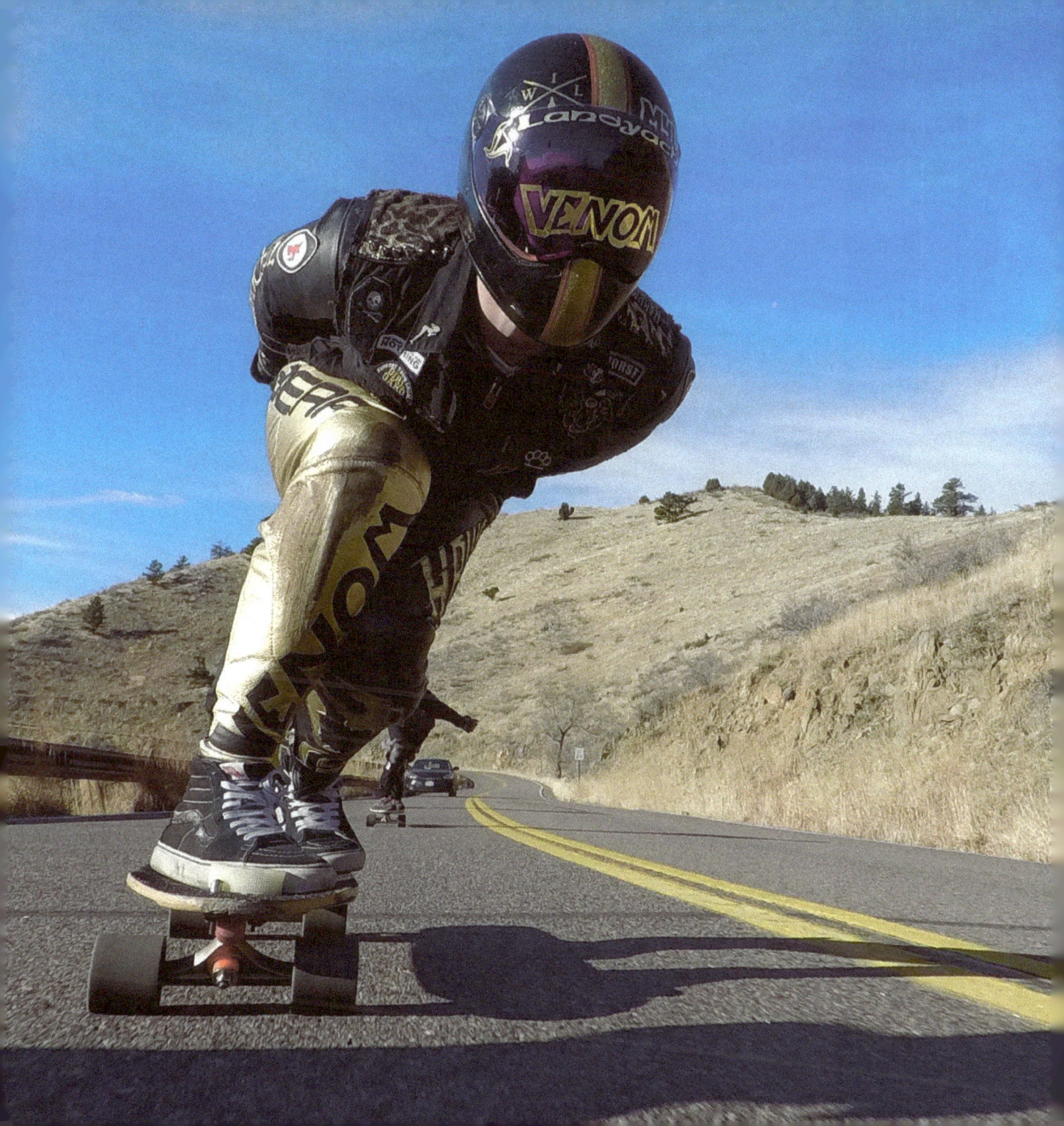

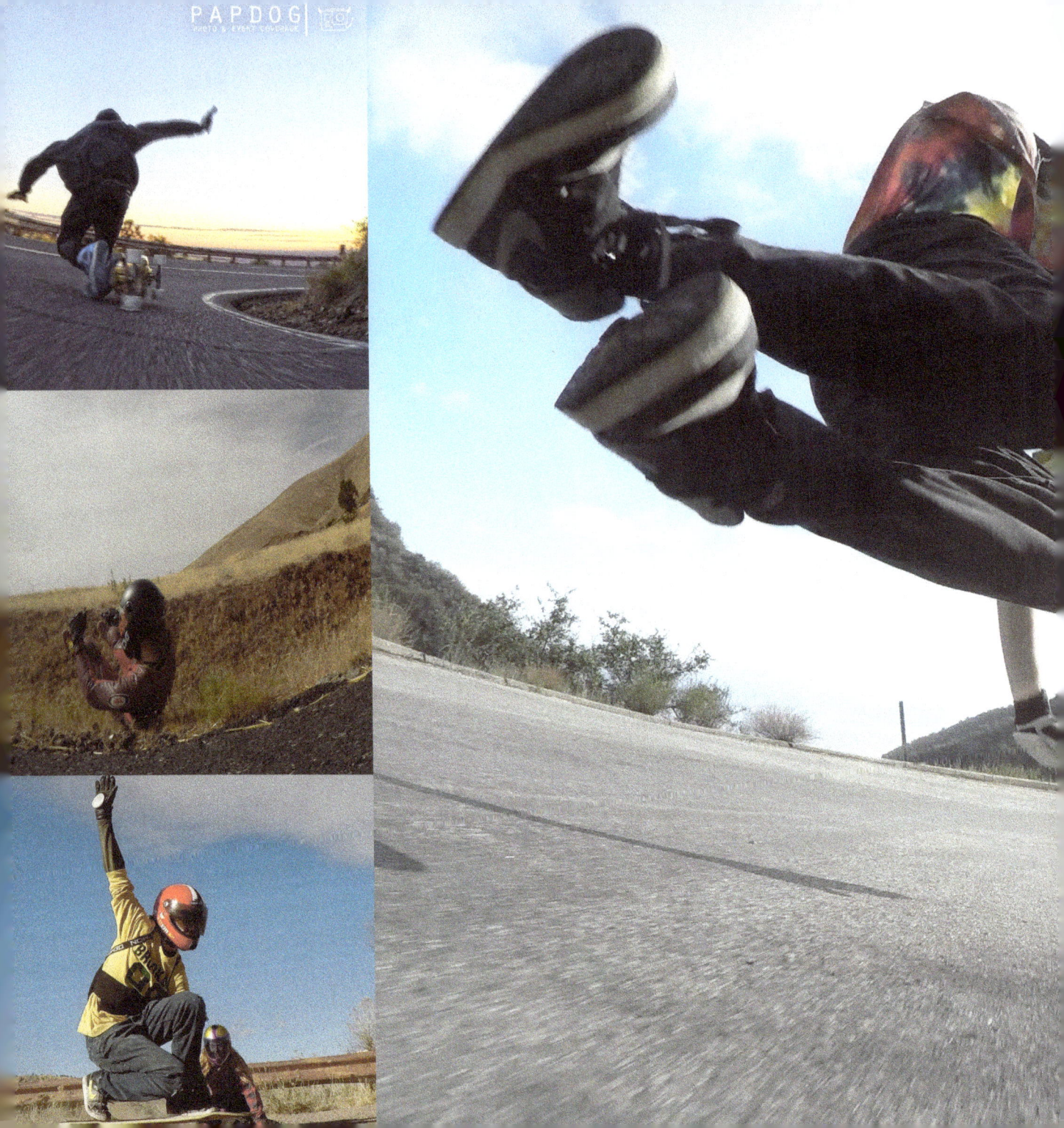

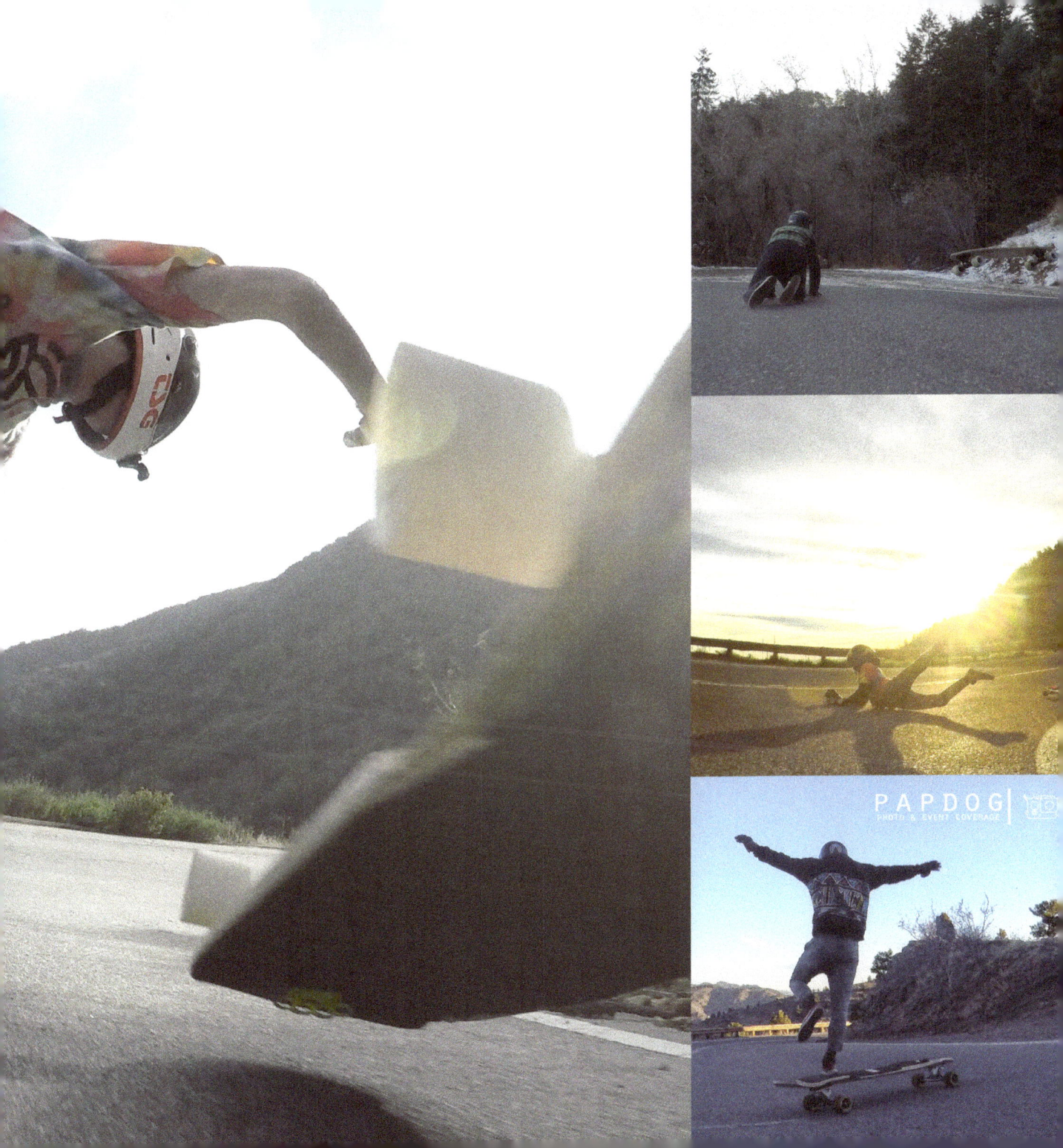

Michael Ambrey	147	Ben Cohen	51,213
Nick Aragon	220	Kyle Connelly	2,3,10,11,18,20 30,33,64,87,90 190,191,211
Austin Arthur	155		
Daina Banks	66	James Contreras	98
Julia Barklow	119	James Cook	152
Swervo Betten	165	Sean Cook	152
Joanna Bleedover	126,152	Aaron Cordero	26
Daryl Boehlig	157	Garrett Creamer	45,54
Billy Bones	153	Don Cudney	15,104,198,207
Cam Brick	156	Nickolas Curtright	171
Rachel Bruskoff	121	Adrin Da Kine	89,177
Mitch Buchite	134,136,137 140	Lee Dansie	97,106,107,176
		Tim DeCamp	27
Joey Carrasco	61	AJ Dill	170
James D. Carter	152	Tuan Dinh	163
Brian Choi	153		
Zack Ciranni	78		

Key Dougherty	82	Dylan Greer	23,83,175,182,183
Tad Drysdale	80,109	Alex Gradillas	39,132,136,137,140,142,143,145
Stephen Dumaine	157,179,220		
Candy Dungan	127,196,220	Joe Gutkowski	137,145
Mikel Echegaray	95,103,110,111,176	Aaron Hampshire	44,46,66,196,208,212
Rylan Raggie English	162	Lyle Hansberger	12,19,32,56,214
Darius Escandar	97,108		
Matt Ewalt	74,197	Mike Hartman	52,220
Ryan Farmer	100,105,150,153,181	Andie Herzog	130,131
		Chase Hiller	21,197
Torre Flagor	152	Eric Hoang	152
Kent Fletcher	8,14,16,87,88	Sam Hoffman	165
C. J. Garner	166	Christina Holmes	155
Johnny BE Goode	157	Shelby Holmes	113
Seth Gouker	77,209	Ronnie Iverson	99,149

Andrew Karnowka	68,203,210	Damond Mastin	37,42,210
Nick Kasch	154	Zack Maytum	79
Andy Kim	53	Chris McBride	108
Jay Knudsen	146	Bryce McGarity	89
Lynn Kramer	116	Austin Meadors	38,47
Gaven Lagrange	75,221	Chandler Melo	140
Kevin Langi	13,18,38,62,77 81,86,90,192 197,198,199 206	Gabe Messa	41,49,83,85 159,210,221
		Larry Mighell	29,76
Scott Lembach	31	Gordon Miller	160
Lexi Loch	118	Michael Millet	152
Tim Locke	180	Louis Mok	155
Miles Long	152	Tanner Morelock	24,25,45,65,81 83,86,92,199 204
Jude Lopez	141		
Marcus Manera	41,50,83	Gunnar Morin	72
Nora Manger	117,168	Peter Morin	205

Jacob Moss	67	Kyle Peel	58,87
Elliot Newey	59	Alex Perkins	172
Benji Nilson	184	Andrew Perkins	152
Dre Nubine	34,71,210	Noel Perkins	173
Marissa Olivia	123	Connor Posey	3,36
Peter Oni	105	Dan Preiner	221
Dean V. Ozuna	80,158	Austin Priester	83
Greg Paproski	3,4,5,10,11,18 28,38,63,82,85 133,158,167 171,175,198 215,217,218	Johnny Raneri	169
		Devin Reese	70
		Lui Reyes	96,148,149
Mike "Papdog" Paproski	6,7,25,38,96 148,153	Sabina Riffenburgh	102,128,149
		Jimmy Riha	132,135,138
Kolby Parks	94,95,108,176	Axel Rock	101,164
Levi Parks	169	Justin Rolo	61
Erin Paul	10,57,84	William Royce	216

Tracy Rudhe	129	Mark Staub	165
Raul Sanchez	35	Evan Steele	43
Parker Schmidt	152,160	Jan Tarradas	93,100,108,176
Blake Schram	48,159,167	Blake Thompson	40
Navin Vinay Sharma	195	Rob Tolette	87,202
Mike Shaughnessy	174	David Townsend	139
Amy Shepard	122	Andrew Tucker	140
Gabriel Shin	200	Jack Tyson	144
Mason Shin	201	Ryan Villa	178
Dylan Shrimpton	156	Katrina Vogel	120
Dan Sielaff	60	Jay Vonesh	96,112,187
Scott Smith	153	Jeff Vyain	218
Jacoby Snook	91	Victoria Waddington	125
Aria Sonallah	88	Taber Waite	91
Ryan Star	100	Moe Wallace	169
Calvin Staub	17,188,193,194		

CJ Hollingsworth Wilkinson	114,115,186
Patrick Wilkinson	185,188
Frank Williams	108,179
Blake Wilson	69
Roy Wolf	9,60,92,206
Tobi Wynne	180,181
Ben Zehner	161
Cya Zoe	124

www.ingramcontent.com/pod-product-compliance
Lightning Source LLC
Chambersburg PA
CBHW040545220526
45473CB00017B/3033